Social History of Africa

"GOD ALONE IS KING": ISLAM AND EMANCIPATION IN SENEGAL

**Recent Titles in
Social History of Africa Series**
Series Editors: Allen Isaacman and Jean Allman

"GOD ALONE IS KING": ISLAM AND EMANCIPATION IN SENEGAL

THE WOLOF KINGDOMS OF KAJOOR AND BAWOL, 1859–1914

James F. Searing

HEINEMANN   JAMES CURREY   DAVID PHILIP
Portsmouth, NH   Oxford   Cape Town

#46976445

Heinemann
A division of Reed Elsevier Inc.
361 Hanover Street
Portsmouth, NH 03801–3912
USA
www.heinemann.com

James Currey Ltd.
73 Botley Road
Oxford OX2 0BS
United Kingdom

David Philip Publishers (Pty) Ltd.
208 Werdmuller Centre
Claremont 7708
Cape Town, South Africa

Offices and agents throughout the world

ISBN 0–325–07074–1 (Heinemann cloth)
ISBN 0–325–07073–3 (Heinemann paper)
ISBN 0–85255–697–7 (James Currey cloth)
ISBN 0–85255–647–0 (James Currey paper)

British Library Cataloguing in Publication Data

Searing, James F.
    "God alone is king" : Islam and emancipation in Senegal :
    the Wolof kingdoms of Kajoor and Bawol, 1859–1914.—
    (Social history of Africa)
    1. Islam and state—Senegal   2. Islam and politics—Senegal
    3. Wolof (African people)—History   4. Senegal—History—To
    1960
    I. Title
    966.3
    ISBN 0–85255–647–0 (James Currey paper)
    ISBN 0–85255–697–7 (James Currey cloth)

Library of Congress Cataloging-in-Publication Data

Searing, James F.
    "God alone is king" : Islam and emancipation in Senegal : the Wolof kingdoms of Kajoor and Bawol, 1859–1914 / James F. Searing.
        p. cm.—(Social history of Africa, ISSN 1099–8098)
    Includes bibliographical references and index.
    ISBN 0–325–07074–1 (alk. paper)—ISBN 0–325–07073–3 (pbk. : alk. paper)
    1. Senegal—History—To 1960.   2. Islam and state—Senegal—History.   3. Islam and politics—Senegal—History.   4. Wolof (African people)—History.   I. Series.
    DT549.7.S43 2002
    966'.3—dc21   2001026389

Paperback cover photo: "Massacre of the French." Copyright Africa Museum, Tervuren, Belgium. Photo by Jean-Marc Vandyck.

Printed in the United States of America on acid-free paper.

06 05 04 03 02 SB 1 2 3 4 5 6 7 8 9

Copyright Acknowledgments

For two mothers

Marie F. Searing

Ruth E. Hickling

CONTENTS

ILLUSTRATIONS

MAPS

FIGURES

TABLES

PREFACE

This book has a long history, beginning with my dissertation, "Accommodation and Resistance: Chiefs, Muslim Leaders and Politicians in Colonial Senegal, 1890–1934" (1985). I wanted to write a social history of the Wolof under colonial rule. After consulting the archives, I realized that the most detailed sources dealt with Wolof notables or elites. After a year of archival research I wrote a study of the dominant social groups of Wolof society from 1890 to 1934. I studied the aristocracy, the Muslim leaders, and the urban politicians.

Research for the dissertation was carried out in the Senegalese National Archives in July–August 1981 and from September 1982 to August 1983. The History Department at Princeton University provided a grant that allowed me to explore the archives in the summer of 1981. The dissertation could not have been completed without the support of a Fulbright dissertation research grant in 1982–1983. I thank my adviser, Robert L. Tignor, who provided support and advice throughout the first stage of this project. I would also like to thank Stanley Stein, John Waterbury, Arno Mayer, and Martin Klein, who served as readers and members of my dissertation committee, and Antonio Gaztambide and Alice Conklin for their comments and interest in my project. In Dakar I met a number of researchers whose comments and friendship were important, particularly Joe Lunn and Christopher Harrison. My thanks go to the staff of the Senegalese National Archives, especially Salilou Mbaye and Mamadou Ndiaye.

When I finished the dissertation, I was aware that each group I had studied claimed to represent "Wolof society" as a whole. Each was at the center of networks of power and dependency that reached deeply into society. Each articulated a vision that legitimated its wealth and authority.

In my dissertation, the competition for power and authority between Wolof rivals was subordinated to an examination of their relations with French colonial authorities. There were also problems with the quality and quantity of archival source materials for the three groups I studied. The colonial archives gave much richer and detailed accounts of Wolof aristocrats, who served as colonial chiefs, and urban politicians, who worked within the French system, than of Muslim leaders, who by comparison were outsiders.

Martin Klein, who was the outside reader on my committee, influenced my subsequent research. He raised a number of questions about slavery and the end of slavery, which I had discussed briefly. He argued that I had taken for granted the emergence of a peasant economy, without linking that development to my treatment of the dominant Wolof social groups under colonial rule.

Was the history of slave emancipation, or of peasant cash cropping, a "colonial" history? How did it relate to the internal struggles between competing elites? Or to the actions of peasants and slaves? I researched land tenure, slavery, and the peasant household economy. This research led to the publication of an article in 1988: "Aristocrats, Slaves, and Peasants: Power and Dependency in the Wolof States, 1700–1850," *International Journal of African Historical Studies* 21, no. 3 (1988): 475–503. The article began a detour that took me backward in time.

In 1988 I returned to Senegal as a Fulbright Lecturer and taught for two years at the Université Cheikh Anta Diop in Dakar. I had spent the summer in France, reading through eighteenth-century archival sources on the history of the slave trade. My exploration of the nineteenth century transition from the slave trade to export agriculture led to the publication of a book, *West African Slavery and Atlantic Commerce: The Senegal River Valley, 1700–1860* (1993). Historians of slavery in Africa argued that slavery expanded in the nineteenth century in response to the decline of the Atlantic slave trade and the expansion of commodity exports ("legitimate commerce"). In the Wolof kingdoms, many changes in the eighteenth century already prefigured these trends. The grain trade was vital for the Atlantic slave trade, leading to a commercialization of grain production in parts of the Senegal River valley. Grain production fed slaves in transit and sustained the urbanization of parts of the Atlantic coast. In the island ports, slaves accounted for a large majority of the population. Slaves worked as sailors and artisans for merchants who purchased slaves in the interior Senegal River valley. Women slaves prepared food for slaves in transit and provided domestic labor for French merchants and African households. Although commercialization was localized in the eighteenth century, it occurred precisely in those regions that pioneered the rapid expansion of peanut exports in the nineteenth century. In short, the imagined divide between the economy of the slave trade and the economy of "legitimate commerce" tended to blur upon closer examination.

My first book traced the history of the dominant groups in Wolof society back into the eighteenth century and the historical context of the Atlantic slave trade. The urban politicians of the colonial period were the successors of the slave-owning merchants of eighteenth-century Saint-Louis. The Four Communes represented a Wolof urban culture that first emerged in eighteenth century Atlantic ports, where a majority of slaves labored alongside a smaller minority of free migrants. Wolof monarchy also based its power on slavery, as royal slaves were the backbone of the army and government. By contrast, Muslim leaders (*sëriñ*) represented village communities. At best they achieved limited self-rule for Muslim villages and provinces. Muslim leaders were the most outspoken critics of aristocratic rule, leading rebellions and movements of secession that prefigured the conflicts of the nineteenth century.

This book completes the story, linking the history of colonial Africa to the history of the Atlantic slave trade. Debates about the impact of the Atlantic slave trade have focused narrowly on quantitative measures of slave exports and their links to the problem of slavery in Africa. Arguments about the impact of the slave trade are inconclusive when conceived in quantitative terms. The extent of disagreement among historians has led to skepticism about any consensus. For the Wolof, I try to measure the impact in qualitative rather than in quantitative terms. The impact of the slave trade is inscribed in the social history of Wolof society.

While I was in Senegal in 1988–1990, I began studying Wolof with a tutor. In retrospect this was a turning point. I owe a special debt to my tutor, Ibou Sarr, who also served as a research assistant in the summer of 1995. He was there to come to my aid when my Wolof failed me. He also asked important questions of his own. My teaching experience in Senegal in 1988–1990 was important, because I was in close contact with members of the History Department and other scholars in Dakar. I shared an office with Mamadou Diouf and Mohamed Mbodj. Our conversations were a great pleasure and an important influence. I also thank Ibnou Diagne, chairman of the department, Mamadou Fall, the late Moustapha Kane, and Boubacar Barry. Old friends played an important role, especially Ismaila Thiam (Billy Congoman), now deceased, and Moctar Niang. The staff of USIS-Dakar and of the American Cultural Center, who administer the Fulbright program, were very helpful. I would like to thank Helen Picard, Jerome Faye, and El-Hadj Sarr in particular.

In the summer of 1995 I returned to Senegal to do fieldwork, supported by an African Area Senior Scholars grant from the Social Science Research Council. My interviews focused on the history of the Murid order, the Sereer Safèn minority in Bawol, and the experience of the peasantry under colonial rule. I divided my time between the Sereer-Safèn village of Bandia, where I had begun fieldwork in 1989, and the Murid town of Darou-Mousty in Kajoor (Cayor). I would like to thank the Social Science Research Council for the support they gave to my research.

My fieldwork in Bandia began with my acquaintance with Babakar Faye. He was the "gardener-guardian" of the Fulbright house where I lived for two years. I learned that he belonged to a small Sereer subgroup, the Safèn, who had struggled to maintain their independence from the Wolof. After visiting his village several times in 1988, I sought permission to conduct field research there. That research began in 1989 and was continued in 1995. My thanks go to the village chief of Bandia, M. Seck, who helped introduce me to the village and its elders. He often guided me on the pathways between "quarters" of the village to make sure I did not lose my way. My thanks also go to the late Farba Cisse, who was considered the "village historian" in 1989, because of his command of oral traditions. I owe a debt of gratitude to the imam of Bandia, Babacar N'Dione, who was very helpful both as an informant and as an advocate for recording the history of the village. I also thank all the elders who participated in interviews.

When I arrived in Darou-Mousty in July 1995, I came unannounced, with no local contacts. I was welcomed and housed by Moustapha Apsa Mbacké, whose guest-house was my base of operations throughout my stay in the village. I also thank Serigne Abdou-Khoudousse Mbacké, the current head of the town, who gave his blessing to my research and therefore opened many doors for me. The historians of Darou-Mousty, Serigne Bassirou Anta Niang Mbacké and Serigne M'Baye Guèye Sylla, were extremely generous with their time. Their expertise became an essential component of my understanding of Murid history. My thanks also go to Pathé Dieng of Darou-Marnane and to members of the extended household of Moustapha Apsa Mbacké. The informal conversations in the courtyard and house of my host became an important source of information for my research. My courtesy visits to my host were often the occasion for his disciples to ask questions about my research and to express opinions about Murid history.

I wrote most of the final version of this work while enjoying a year of leave as a fellow at the Institute for the Humanities at the University of Illinois at Chicago in 1997–1998. Without the time and freedom provided by the Institute for the Humanities I could not have finished this project. My thanks to Mary Beth Rose, the director, and Linda Vavra, for making the year at the institute pleasant and productive.

Over the years I have called upon colleagues in African history to support me in various ways. I thank Martin Klein, Paul Lovejoy, Richard Rathbone, Mamadou Diouf, and Mohamed Mbodj.

Finally, my greatest debt is to my wife, Trish Hickling. In addition to enduring frequent moves while caring for our children, she listened to innumerable conversations about Wolof history. Her comments were always insightful and supportive, even when she would have gladly changed the subject. At crucial moments she encouraged me to pursue my exploration of Wolof culture, even though she knew it would delay the completion of this book. She is the only one who knows the full history of this project, from beginning to end. She became a partner in the project and deserves much of the credit for its final form.

NOTE ON WOLOF

I have used the official system now in use in Senegal for transcribing all Wolof words. For readers unfamiliar with this system, doubled vowels represent elongated pronunciation. Most vowel sounds are pronounced as in European languages. The consonant "c" is pronounced like "ch" in English, while the "c" sound (as in "coal" in English) is represented by the letter "k." The letter "x" is pronounced like the "ch" sound in German, or the Spanish "j." The consonant "ñ" is pronounced like "ny."

Proper names present some difficulties. For persons, I have used the official system of transcription for individuals who didn't write their names in French. As a rule of thumb, people from the precolonial period have their names spelled this way. This results in Lat Joor Joob rather than Lat Dior Diop, for example. For people who regularly wrote their names in French, I have followed their own spellings: Demba War Sall, rather than Demba Waar Sal. For place names I have favored accurate transcriptions rather than the ones used by colonial officials. I prefer "Kajoor" to "Cayor," except in a few cases (direct quotes, official titles), especially when I am referring to the territory of the precolonial kingdom as a whole. For the sake of consistency, I have changed colonial transcriptions of important terms (*ceddo*, *sëriñ*), even in quotations.

INTRODUCTION

It is simple enough to state the main theme of this book, which examines the transformation of Wolof society in the kingdoms of Kajoor and Bawol between 1859 and 1914. Slavery and aristocratic power declined as Islam became the dominant force in Wolof society, with a free Muslim peasantry as its social base. Stating the thesis of the book in this way raises a number of questions. Why did slavery decline and when? How was the rise of Islam connected with the end of slavery? What role did slaves play in this history? And what did all of this have to do with French colonial rule, which began in the 1880s? The period studied in this book is defined by the rapid growth of a cash-crop economy and French colonial rule. Nevertheless, my emphasis is on the internal dynamics of Wolof society, rather than colonialism.

Kajoor and Bawol were the most important Wolof kingdoms in the nineteenth century, based on their power and the size of their populations. The kingdom of Waalo, located to the north of Kajoor, had been in decline since the mid-eighteenth century, due to ecological crisis and the loss of territory. It was absorbed into the French colony of Senegal in 1855. Jolof controlled only a small territory suitable for settled agriculture, with a population base equivalent to one of Kajoor's provinces. Kajoor and Bawol thus formed the core of Wolof society in the nineteenth century and their history is crucial to the understanding of contemporary Wolof society. The Wolof today make up about 40 percent of the Senegalese population, and their language and culture plays a dominant role in contemporary Senegal.

The architecture of the narrative emphasizes conflict and change in Wolof history, rather than French colonial rule. Conceptually, the book is divided into two parts. The first four chapters focus on the conflict between Islam and monarchy that erupted into open warfare in 1859 and continued to shape Wolof responses to French colonial rule in the early colonial period. From a Wolof perspective, the colonial conquest coincided with a civil war between the partisans of monarchy and Islam in Kajoor from 1859 to 1886. During the peace that followed, the French began constructing a colonial state. Nevertheless, the conflicts of the civil war continued in new guises and shaped the history of colonialism more than French policy did. The emergence of a dissident Muslim movement in Bawol in the 1890s, with the birth of the Murid Sufi order, founded by Amadu Bamba, is used as the centerpiece in the discussion of the triumph of Islam in chapters 3 and 4. The second part of the book (chapters 5 through 7) examines social change at the grass roots of society during the long period of peace that followed the colonial conquest (1890–1914). Chapter 5 focuses on slavery and emancipation. Chapters 6 and 7 examine the birth of the new peasant economy that emerged as slavery declined, aristocratic power waned, and Islam made rapid progress. This social history is closely linked to the struggle between Islam and the monarchy.

The book is ethnographic, focusing on the Wolof people and their history. It is also ethnographic in its effort to perceive this period of change through Wolof cultural categories. Most studies of Wolof history have dealt with one aspect of society: Islam, slavery, urban politics, or economic change. Because I locate the dynamics of change in the internal conflicts within Wolof society, I have written a history that treats all of these questions and attempts to delineate the links between political conflict and social change, between Islamic renewal, slave emancipation, and the emergence of a peasant society. To do this, the topics have to be disentangled from narratives of colonialism, which have dominated the historiography of the period.

SOURCES AND METHODOLOGY

Wolof sources play a crucial role in this work, often guiding my reading of French sources. Some of the Wolof sources I use are written, some are oral performances that draw on written sources, others are oral performances of dynastic epics by royal bards. In Wolof society, shared historical memories were created through acts of "commemorative vigilance," through performances which reenacted memory as history. Intellectuals working within well-defined traditions created the performances of this publicly shared history.[1] This archive of "memory" has played an important role in my efforts to decolonize the narrative of this book.

The period from 1860 to 1886 forms a reference point in contemporary consciousness about the past. This is reflected in the major streams of Wolof memory and is not simply a by-product of academic interest in this period. In Wolof society, specialized intellectuals produced and staged public performances about the past. These memories can be interpreted by examining the intellectuals who produced them. In the nineteenth century, two different intellectual traditions competed. One was based in the court and is symbolized by the figure of the Wolof *géwél* or bard, the official intellectual of the old regime. Royal bards staged performances of dynastic history and defended the values embodied in the aristocratic code of honor. The second tradition was based on Islam.

Aristocratic views of history were recorded in French as well as in Wolof. Wolof aristocrats, who were trained as literate chiefs, wrote important memoirs. Their accounts can be compared with more recent performances by Wolof bards. Together, these sources open a window for understanding Wolof historical memories based on the traditions of the monarchy.

Islam provided the basis for a competing tradition based in Muslim schools and in territories where Muslims had been granted powers of local government. Muslim memories of the past concentrate on the lives of major teachers, scholars, and mystics. Murid sources, which focus on the life of Amadu Bamba, provide the most important counterpoint to the narratives and memories of the court. Amadu Bamba's life was linked to the life of Lat Joor, the last Wolof king, through a shared history that began with the jihad of Màbba. Amadu Bamba's father served at the court of Màbba as a teacher and judge. He would later serve as Lat Joor's spiritual guide and as a judge in Kajoor. Based on this shared history and on later conflicts between Lat Joor and Amadu Bamba, Murid sources reply to the narratives of the court. Murid Islam is treated in more detail than other forms of Islam because of this connection. Murid Islam began as a dissident movement, which contested the power of the court. For the same reason, Murid sources often reply directly to royal narratives.

The fieldwork carried out while researching this book was designed to fill in some of the major gaps in the written sources. This involved two different problems. In the case of the Murid order there was an abundance of archival material, but the source material was biased by French preconceptions about the order. My fieldwork in Darou-Mousty in 1995 was designed to address this problem. The second case centered on the independent Sereer communities which were conquered by the Wolof with French aid in the 1890s. There were no archival sources that reflected the Sereer experience. My research on the Sereer minorities was an examination of the margins and borders of Wolof society, "the enemy within," the Wolof "other." This research helped me conceptualize the relationship between Islam and the monarchy in the nineteenth century. I carried out fieldwork in the Sereer-Safèn village of Bandia in 1989 and in 1995.

I have emphasized the importance of Wolof sources and of my fieldwork because of their importance in shaping my interpretation of Wolof history. While writing the final draft of this book, I came across the recent work of Pierre Nora in French history. Nora's conception of "sites of memory" blurred the distinction between "oral traditions" and "history," even though Nora clung to the distinction by opposing "memory and history."[2] Nora's conception expanded the scope of historical evidence by calling for a systematic examination of what he called *lieux de mémoire*, "sites of memory": these were buildings, monuments, cemeteries, festivals, anniversaries, medals, relics, and battlefields. Nora described them as "the rituals of a ritual-less society, fleeting incursions of the sacred into a disenchanted world."[3] Nora argued that *lieux de mémoire* arose in societies where real or spontaneous memory was dead: "hence we must create archives, mark anniversaries, organize celebrations, pronounce eulogies."[4] These acts of "commemorative vigilance" were necessary to preserve things that history otherwise would sweep away. Nora also argued that "sites of memory" were created by subgroups and subcultures in modern societies as a way of countering the master narrative of national history. The "sites of memory" created by colonized peoples can be used to criticize the master narrative of colonial domination.

While I have avoided taking my interpretation and narrative from the colonial archives, the colonial sources provide crucial documentation for this work. I worked in the National Archives of Senegal in Dakar in 1982 to 1983, the French National Archives in 1988, and the Senegalese archives again from 1988 to 1990. I read the archives from the "bottom up" as much as possible. I concentrated on the records of government at the district (*cercle*) level, where the colonial state intersected with Wolof society. It was in these district archives that Wolof voices were heard most frequently, while documents from Saint-Louis and Dakar frequently reflected only colonial concerns.

OUTLINE

This book begins where my first book ends, in 1859, at the beginning of a long period of conflict. It builds upon my study of slavery

and the slave trade in the Lower Senegal and situates the colonial period in a long-term view of Wolof history.[5] The differences between
my work and that of other scholars can best be seen by addressing the
larger themes discussed in the book. My analysis of the conquest focuses on the struggle between monarchy and Islam rather than on
French colonial policy. The best recent study of the conquest is
Mamadou Diouf's study of nineteenth-century Kajoor.[6] His account
pays more attention to French colonial policy and the larger
Senegambian canvas, while I focus more on domestic politics in Kajoor
and civil war. Because his book ends with the conquest, it does not try
to link the struggles of the conquest to later developments.

The French conquered the Wolof by participating in a civil war already in progress. They used their military forces and those of their
Wolof allies, recruited in the coastal cities and districts under French
control. Governor Faidherbe created a coalition of pro-French Wolof
forces strong enough to tip the balance of power. This "French" party
contained a "Senegalese" party within it, representing the interests of
Africans and *métis*, who as "sons of the soil" shared some interests.
Both groups supported the French, but shared fears about the consequences of colonial rule.

The French intervened at crucial moments and on various sides until a
final settlement was reached. Even when the French imposed solutions
through military force, they made calculations about which Wolof party
would be most useful in the construction of a new colonial order. French
policies during the conquest were largely opportunistic, leading to the
alienation of most of their Wolof "allies." Although the French began by
expressing sympathy for the Muslim party, by 1883 their most important
allies were the royal slaves of Kajoor. The royal slaves formed the core of
the monarchy's military power and they became the main agents of French
rule in Kajoor. After 1886, Kajoor became a base for further expansion
and a model for the conquest of Bawol and Jolof in 1890. By allying
themselves with the Wolof aristocracy at the beginning of the colonial
period, the French set the stage for conflicts with Islam and with the populations of the coastal cities. French policies therefore contributed indirectly
to the triumph of Islam over civil society in less than two decades. During
the conquest, tensions also increased between the French and their
Senegalese "allies," who were transformed from French subjects to French
"citizens" by reforms enacted under the Third Republic. By the turn of the
century these African "citizens" were known as *originaires* and they were
deeply alienated by colonial rule.

While chapter 2 focuses on Kajoor, chapter 3 explores the conflict between monarchy and Islam that played itself out in Bawol in the aftermath

of the colonial conquest. I discuss the emergence of Sufi Islam, as embodied in the "dissident" Murid order. I show how France's Wolof allies in Kajoor used their influence to get the French to arrest Amadu Bamba in 1895. Most previous discussions of this period have taken their "narrative" from the archives. Whether intentionally or by default, "colonialism" becomes the explanation for what happened. One important example is the "French decision" to arrest Amadu Bamba in 1895, as interpreted by Donal B. Cruise O'Brien or David Robinson.[7] I argue that historians who have situated this event in a colonial narrative of French policy toward Islam have taken the event out of its historic context, which was a settling of accounts in the aftermath of civil war. By anchoring the narrative in Wolof history, I have tried to avoid creating a hiatus between precolonial and colonial history.

My analysis revises standard accounts of the emergence of the Murid order by using Murid sources to critique French archival sources. Intellectuals whose most conspicuous characteristic is literacy in Arabic and Wolof (written in Arabic script) produced the Murid sources used in this book. The sources include the Arabic poetry of the founder, a biography of the founder written by one of his sons, and biographies of the founder by prominent disciples. I read these works, but I also interviewed prominent contemporary Murid scholars in Darou-Mousty to gain an understanding of this tradition. In addition to consulting scholars, I utilized sources that came from a developing performance tradition within the Murid order. Popular preachers, many of them converted bards, address the faithful with commentaries on Amadu Bamba's poetry that give a Murid perspective on the life of the founder. These sources are particularly important to the reinterpretation of Murid history given in chapter 3.

Part II focuses on the history of slavery and emancipation in the early colonial period. My interpretation of slave emancipation differs from that presented by Martin A. Klein in his recent book, *Slavery and Colonial Rule in French West Africa* (1998). In Klein's narrative of slavery and emancipation there are two lines of analysis. One focuses on French policies toward slavery and gives a detailed account of the encounters between French officials, slaves, and slave owners throughout French West Africa. The second line of argument deals with the story of the slaves, as documented by the French, and as remembered by slaves, slave owners, and their descendants. Emancipation emerged from the dynamic interaction between colonial rule and the actions taken by slaves. In my account of emancipation, I give much greater weight to cash crops, religion, and migration than to French policy. My analysis of emancipation centers on the opportunities that emerged with the dramatic growth of peasant cash cropping, especially in the period after the conquest.

The history of peanut exports is interwoven with the history of slave emancipation and the rise of a free Muslim peasantry. The Wolof region of Senegal is often simply identified as the "peanut basin," because of the crucial role it played in the history of export agriculture. Peanut exports began in the 1840s, well before the beginning of colonial rule, and expanded rapidly thereafter, even during the period of civil war. The Wolof were one of the first peoples in West Africa to devote considerable time and energy to the cultivation of cash crops for export. Historians talk about this period of the nineteenth century in terms of a transition from the "slave trade" to "legitimate" commerce. Viewed in this way, the transition appears to have been exceptionally rapid and successful in Senegal. Peanuts were a cultivated crop, unlike early exports from other regions in West Africa, such as palm oil. Production expanded as more land and labor were devoted to peanuts. For producers, peanuts provided the currency to purchase cloth, manufactured goods, rice, tea, and sugar, and the money to pay taxes. Peanuts became crucial for peasants who attempted to accumulate wealth for marriage and other investments in the peasant economy. In short, peanuts provided a welcome connection to the world market.

Wolof enthusiasm for peanut exports must be seen in the light of Wolof history. The cash crop economy opened new opportunities for many groups in Wolof society, including peasants and slaves. I have focused on the social history of cash cropping, rather than on macroeconomic narratives which treat cash-crop agriculture as part of a larger story about colonial development or underdevelopment and the subordinate position of Africa in the world economy. My object is not to contest those narratives, but to explore the links between cash cropping and the emergence of a Muslim peasant society in the Wolof countryside.

The goal of the book is to create as seamless a narrative as possible between Wolof history and Senegalese history, with World War I as the transition between the two. I have discussed French colonial policies and actions only when they were relevant to my purposes, but not as an end in themselves. My approach has required a search for new Wolof sources and a systematic effort to use and reinterpret the colonial archive.

MAJOR THEMES

My analysis of Wolof history addresses larger issues about the history of the colonial period, which can be addressed by summarizing some of the main arguments of the book and situating them in the broader context

of African social history. Three themes will be used to illustrate my conclusions: the history of Sufi Islam, the abolition of slavery, and peasant
cash cropping.

Sufi Islam influenced the course of Wolof history by undermining
the authority of the old regime and providing alternatives to peasants
and slaves. I argue that the history of slavery and emancipation cannot
be separated from the larger context of Wolof history in a dramatic
period of conflict and change. During periods of civil war and colonial
conquest, slaves could and did flee from their aristocratic masters, often to join Muslim communities or to disappear into the expanding
peasant society that prospered as the monarchy and slavery declined.
These changes occurred rapidly in Wolof society, for reasons specific
to its history. Islam was a powerful counterforce to the monarchy,
rooted in peasant villages that had achieved a kind of self-rule in the
eighteenth century. This sector of society, with Muslim scholars in command, was rebellious, had a strong peasant following, and took advantage of every opportunity to attack the monarchy. In Kajoor, Muslims
rebelled in 1859 and took advantage of the conquest to secure the independence of Njambur, the heartland of Muslim power, in a separate
treaty with the French. By the 1890s, two new Sufi orders, based in
Kajoor and Bawol, presented a powerful ideological challenge to the
legitimacy of aristocratic rule. This context made it easier for slaves to
leave their masters. The development of cash cropping had the same
effect because it provided opportunities for slaves to relocate and enter
the expanding peasant economy as migrants.

Recent studies of religious conversion, mission churches, and independent African churches have emphasized the need for a culturally
grounded understanding of the meanings of African Christianity in the
colonial context. Paul Landau's study of the Bangwato Church in colonial Botswana argued for the importance of understanding how Africans appropriated and internalized Christianity in a "realm of the Word"
that can only be understood by paying careful attention to the "language" of belief, in this case Setswana.[8] He also shows how the church
became an instrument of elite diplomacy in dealing with colonial officials and how the church also became a site of struggle where issues
like beer drinking, the role of women, and class identities were debated. My analysis of the Sufi orders in Wolof society is similarly
grounded in the analysis of Wolof language sources that reveal the critical stance of both the Tijani and Murid orders toward the monarchy
and their links to the Muslim rebellions of the nineteenth century. At
the same time, each order adopted a different stance to the colonial
regime created by the French. The Tijani were openly pro-French, see-

ing the French as useful instruments for the destruction of the monarchy. The Murid order tried to create a Muslim rural society by founding new, independent villages under their control, a project that threatened Wolof aristocrats and provoked French intervention.

Karen E. Fields' perceptive study of religious revival and rebellion in Central Africa emphasizes how the system of indirect rule created a structural opposition between grassroots revival and colonial chiefs. The Watchtower slogan, "Pray to God Alone," had sinister overtones for British officials. In 1919 one Watchtower preacher summed up his experience, saying, "God only is to be respected and obeyed, nobody else on earth has any right to it; no more the European than the native chiefs."[9] In practice, colonial chiefs were more frequently criticized than colonial officials. The Nazareth Church founded by Isaiah Shembe in South Africa also emphasized the sovereignty of God with its slogan, "Jehovah alone is Inkosi [King]." Shembe's slogan was linked to his criticism of the historical Zulu monarchy.[10] The Murid order in Senegal also proclaimed the idea that "God Alone Is King," a slogan directed against Wolof chiefs who ruled for the French. These comparisons are a reminder that Murid Islam drew much of its strength from its opposition to the monarchy. Fields' criticisms of the way in which colonial officials and some subsequent scholars have dismissed revivalist movements as "irrational" or as failed "adaptations to modernity" also apply to French colonial stereotypes of Murid "fanaticism." The rebellious stance of the early Murid order has been obscured by studies that focus on its later evolution, when earlier battles over the rights of Wolof peasants and runaway slaves to join the order by migration had come to an end.

The differences between the Tijani and Murid orders, in terms of their social base and attitude toward colonial rule, display striking similarities to the differences between orthodox mission churches, on the one hand, and prophetic churches, on the other. The Tijani order developed a strong social base among the French-educated elite, in the coastal cities, and in the rural regions of Kajoor that had been touched earliest by railroad construction and export agriculture. This pattern resembled that of the the strongholds of mission orthodoxy in colonial Nigeria and South Africa. By contrast, the Murid order developed a following of peasants, rural notables, and runaway slaves in the Wolof hinterland, and was more hostile both to the aristocratic culture of the monarchy and to French education. The cultural stance, religious style, and social base of the Murid order resembled more closely that of the adherents of the Aladura churches of western Nigeria and the independent prophetic churches of South Africa. Like some of the prophetic

churches in South Africa, the Murid order developed an extensive social network of support for its peasant base. Like them, the Murid
order's religious mission combined withdrawal from this world with
material accumulation, while its political stance was an ambiguous
mixture of otherworldliness and resistance.[11]

Recent debates about slave emancipation in West Africa have focused
on the interaction between colonial policy and the actions taken by slaves
themselves, particularly by runaway slaves who fled their masters.[12] The
debate about emancipation has reflected differing interpretations of slavery, as those historians who have emphasized slave runaways have also
stressed the harsh characteristics of slavery. Although this debate has advanced our understanding of emancipation, neither colonial policies nor
slave initiatives, separately or in combination, can account for the marked
variations between the process of emancipation in different regions and
societies. Other, more global, societal explanations account for these variations more satisfactorily. For example, in Northern Nigeria, the ruling
classes of the Sokoto Caliphate had more legitimacy than their Wolof coun-
terparts, based on their role in the jihad that founded the state. While
oppositional forms of Islam existed in Northern Nigeria,[13] most Islamic
authorities supported state power and slavery. Although official British
policy toward slavery resembled French policy, the alliance between the
British and the caliphate authorities was much stronger than the French
alliance with the Wolof chiefs. Finally, the railroad reached Kano only in
1910, with the result that the Nigerian peanut boom occurred twenty-five
years later than it did in in coastal Senegal.[14] All these factors help explain
why slave emancipation occurred much later in Northern Nigeria than in
Wolof society, and why it was more effectively controlled by colonial officials and African elites.

Similar arguments apply to the dramatic exodus of slaves from
Maraka masters in the Middle Niger valley, as studied by Martin Klein
and Richard Roberts.[15] The exodus was large and occurred rapidly between 1904 and 1907. Specific circumstances contributed to the massive exodus. There were many newly enslaved persons who remembered their homelands and tried to return to them. The specific characteristics of Maraka society also played an important role. The Maraka
were a merchant group who specialized in grain and textile production
and long-distance trade. Slaves provided labor, but had few opportunities to improve their status. The Maraka were not a ruling class, and
the system of slavery they developed did not provide opportunities for
slaves to participate in their masters' political power, as was often the
case in aristocratic slave systems. As a result, the conflicts between
Maraka masters and slaves were perceived in strictly economic terms,

and slaves saw few benefits in renegotiating their status with masters intent on profiting from their labor. The factors behind the slave exodus were thus specific to Maraka society.[16]

For these reasons, it is unlikely that any one model or line of argument can account for the course of emancipation in different regions and societies. My approach stresses the need to approach emancipation as part of the larger cultural and social history of Wolof society as a whole. The most important example of this is my effort to show the links between slave emancipation and the expansion of peasant cash cropping in the period between the conquest and 1914. I present evidence to support my argument that the majority of slaves had fled before the French ordered a census of slave populations in 1903–1904. I argue that there is some evidence for large-scale flight in the period from 1883 to 1890, when French intelligence about what was happening on the ground was sparse. The Murid order clearly absorbed some runaways, but not all of them. My argument about where they went is simple. They disappeared into the peasant economy as migrants. Peasant households welcomed thousands of migrants a year, because migrant farmers added to the wealth of the household as well as earning income for themselves. Many migrants were outsiders to the region. Some were free, and others were slaves, as shown by François Manchuelle in his study of Soninke migrants. Migrant farmers, usually young males, sought cash income to take home to their regions of origin. Alongside these migrants, many Wolof peasants relocated, seeking better land, fewer duties to pay to local landlords, or escape from domestic conflicts.[17] Acculturated slaves, with no homeland to return to, possessed the cultural knowledge required to merge into these two streams of migration.

The cash-crop economy became a peasant economy because peasants took advantage of peanuts to pursue their own agendas. My analysis stresses the positive social gains for peasants and slaves from cash cropping in the early colonial period. This approach combines the insights of an early body of research on West Africa, which stressed African initiative,[18] with more recent studies of southern Africa that stress the "peasant option" as a form of resistance to proletarianization, based on preserving the autonomy of a rural landowning household.[19] In southern Africa, many migrants who took jobs in the mining economy didn't think of themselves as workers, but pursued a rural strategy, investing their wages in bride-wealth and cattle in their home area. Their goal was to head a rural household on their return. Although the historic context was very different in southern Africa, the southern African migrants' goals were very similar to those of the

Soninke migrants studied by Manchuelle, whose cash earnings were invested in the rural economy.

Peasant economies in West Africa cannot be taken for granted, as many of them emerged from the ashes of rural societies previously dominated by slavery. Cash-crop income was central to emancipation, because it could be reinvested in ways that enlarged the social base of the peasantry. Cash income accelerated the process of household formation by giving young men the means to marry at an earlier age, and stimulated the internal migrations that led to the formation of many new villages and the opening of new lands to settlement. Migrating peasant households were able to choose new religious and political patrons. Peasant households also hired many migrant farmers, many of whom were former slaves seeking entry into the peasantry. Over time, the cumulative effect of these changes was to strengthen the new Sufi orders, undermine slavery as a viable labor system, and weaken the power of colonial chiefs who represented the remnants of the monarchy.

STRUCTURE

The structure of the book follows from my analysis. The history of slavery and emancipation cannot be studied in isolation, because both slavery and emancipation were intertwined with the larger conflict between monarchy and Islam. Internal factors were more important than colonial policy in determining the outcome of important conflicts. For this reason a Wolof-centered chronology of historical transformation, focusing on Wolof agency, is developed in Part I. The battle between Islam and monarchy is the story of the overlapping transformations in political power, religious belief, and social power that set the stage for social changes emerging from below. The conquest and its aftermath substantially altered the relationships of power and dependency in Wolof society. The first part of the book provides the social and cultural context for understanding slave emancipation and its links to the dynamic growth of peasant cash cropping.

NOTES

1. I agree with the arguments for studying the performance and the performer presented in Leroy Vail and Landeg White, *Power and the Praise Poem: Southern African Voices in History* (Charlottesville, Va., 1991), 1–39.

2. For Nora's distinction between memory and history, see Pierre Nora, ed., *Realms of Memory: Rethinking the French Past. Volume 1: Conflicts and Divisions* (New York, 1996), 2, 3.

3. Ibid., 7.

4. Ibid.

5. James F. Searing, *West African Slavery and Atlantic Commerce: The Senegal River Valley, 1700–1860* (Cambridge, 1993).

6. Mamadou Diouf, *Le Kajoor au XIXe siècle: Pouvoir ceddo et conquête coloniale* (Paris, 1990).

7. The classic study is Donal B. Cruise O'Brien, *The Mourides of Senegal: The Political and Economic Organization of an Islamic Brotherhood* (Oxford, 1971). For David Robinson's more recent contributions, see David Robinson, "The Murids: Surveillance and Collaboration," *Journal of African History* 40 (1999): 193–213, which announces a forthcoming study with the title "Paths to Accommodation: Muslim Communities, Colonial Authorities and Civil Society in Senegal and Mauritania." See also David Robinson, "Beyond Resistance and Collaboration: Amadu Bamba and the Murids of Senegal," *Journal of Religion in Africa* 21 no. 2 (1991): 149–71; David Robinson, "An Emerging Pattern of Cooperation between Colonial Authorities and Muslim Societies in Senegal and Mauritania," in *Le temps des marabouts: Itinéraires et stratégies islamiques en Afrique Occidentale Française v. 1880–1960,* ed. David Robinson and Jean-Louis Triaud (Paris, 1997), 155–80; and David Robinson, "French 'Islamic' Policy and Practice in Late Nineteenth Century Senegal," *Journal of African History* 29 (1988): 415–35.

8. Paul S. Landau, *The Realm of the Word: Language, Gender and Christianity in a Southern African Kingdom* (Portsmouth, N.H. 1995).

9. Karen E. Fields, *Revival and Rebellion in Colonial Central Africa* (Princeton, N.J. 1985), 135–36.

10. Benjamin C. Ray, *African Religions: Symbol, Ritual and Community* (Upper Saddle River, N.J., 2nd edition, 2000), 181.

11. See Ray, *African Religions*, 168–97; Jean Comaroff, *Body of Power, Spirit of Resistance: The Culture and History of a South African People* (Chicago, 1985); and J.D.Y. Peel, *Aladura: A Religious Movement among the Yoruba* (London, 1968).

12. For an overall presentation, see Suzanne Miers and Richard Roberts, eds., *The End of Slavery in Africa* (Madison, 1988). For representative studies that emphasize slave initiatives, see Paul E. Lovejoy and Jan S. Hogendorn, *Slow Death for Slavery: The Course of Abolition in Northern Nigeria, 1897–1936* (Cambridge, 1993); Martin A. Klein, *Slavery and Colonial Rule in French West Africa* (Cambridge, 1998); and Richard Roberts, *Warriors, Merchants, and Slaves: The State and the Economy in the Middle Niger Valley, 1700–1914* (Stanford, Calif., 1987).

13. See Paul E. Lovejoy and Jan S. Hogendorn, "Revolutionary Mahdism and Resistance to Colonial Rule in the Sokoto Caliphate," *Journal of African History* 31 (1990): 217–44.

14. Jan S. Hogendorn, *Nigerian Groundnut Exports: Origins and Early Development* (Zaria, Nigeria, 1978).

15. For the first presentation of this thesis, see Martin A. Klein and Richard Roberts, "The Banamba Slave Exodus of 1905 and the Decline of Slavery in the Western Sudan," *Journal of African History* 21 (1980): 375–94.

16. Richard Roberts, "The End of Slavery in the French Soudan, 1905–14," in *The End of Slavery in Africa,* ed. Suzanne Miers and Richard Roberts (Madison, Wis. 1988). For a contrasting case, where ties of patronage and the desire to maintain

access to land limited slave flight, see François Manchuelle, *Willing Migrants: Soninke Labor Diasporas, 1848–1960* (Athens, Ohio, 1997), 130–45.

17. The classic study of colonial peasantries in Senegal is Paul Pelissier, *Les paysans du Sénégal* (Saint Yrieix, France, 1965), which discusses these migrations.

18. See, for example, Polly Hill, *The Migrant Cocoa Farmers of Southern Ghana: A Study in Rural Capitalism* (Cambridge, 1963); and the literature summarized in Anthony G. Hopkins, *An Economic History of West Africa* (New York, 1973).

19. For a general discussion of the "peasant option," see Terence Ranger, *Peasant Consciousness and Guerrilla War in Zimbabwe: A Comparative Study* (Berkeley, Calif., 1985). For the themes I mention, see Patrick Harries, *Work, Culture and Identity: Migrant Laborers in Mozambique and South Africa, c. 1860–1910* (Portsmouth, N.H., 1994); and T. Dunbar Moodie, with Vivienne Ndatshe, *Going for Gold: Men, Mines, and Migration* (Berkeley, Calif., 1994).

PART I

ISLAM AND MONARCHY

Map 1.1 Kajoor and Bawol in 1860
Source: Map based on projections and information in *Atlas National du Sénégal* (Paris, 1977).

1

KAJOOR AND BAWOL IN THE MID-NINETEENTH CENTURY

The history of Kajoor and Bawol had been linked together since the beginning of the eighteenth century, when the Geej dynasty united both kingdoms under its rule. For most of the next century and a half, the Geej, an aristocratic clan that traced its descent from the mother of the founding king, dominated both kingdoms.

This chapter sets the stage for my interpretation of the colonial conquest by analyzing the growing tensions between the monarchy and Islam. The conflict between the monarchy and Islam eventually erupted into civil war between aristocrats defending their traditional rights and Muslims challenging them. I begin by presenting this conflict in the cultural terms used by the Wolof, who describe the factions as "traditionalists" and "Muslims." The next two sections of the chapter explore the world of the court, and its historic relations with Islam. My goal is to present a more nuanced, historically grounded portrayal of these conflicts than is presented in the existing literature.

The chapter also introduces some of the leading figures of nineteenth-century Wolof society, as portrayed in Wolof sources. They include Lat Joor, who was recognized as king in 1871 and ruled until 1883. His reign was dominated by conflicts over the role of Islam and French power. My analysis emphasizes the conflicts of this period and how they shape Wolof interpretations of the fall of the monarchy in 1886, symbolized by the martyrdom of Lat Joor and the betrayal of Demba War Sall, the royal slave who ruled Kajoor for the French until his death in 1902.

WOLOF SOCIETY IN THE NINETEENTH CENTURY:
"TRADITIONALISTS" AND "MUSLIMS"

Wolof memories depict the nineteenth century as a struggle between *ceddo yi* and *sëriñ si*, between "traditionalists" and "Muslims." The Wolof terms are ambiguous, but they indicate how the Wolof viewed the recurring, violent confrontations between the monarchy and Islam. The outcome of the struggle was inconclusive in 1886, when the monarchy in Kajoor was abolished. Lat Joor, the last independent king, symbolizes the ambiguous end to years of conflict and civil war. He is regarded by some as a Muslim king, while others see him as a political opportunist who defended the monarchy and the privileges of the ruling class.[1] While I will argue that the conflicts in Kajoor can best be understood as a political struggle between the monarchy and Islam, it is important to understand why the Wolof describe them as a battle between "traditionalists" and "Muslims."

One can begin with the word *ceddo*, which has been interpreted diversely. French documents abound with references to *ceddo* (usually spelled *tyeddo*). The term is frequently opposed to "Muslim," as it is in Wolof usage. Governor Faidherbe wrote of two parties in Wolof society. In Faidherbe's discourse, each party is labeled with three characteristic adjectives: one party was made up of "brutal, pillaging, drunken" *ceddo*, the other of "sober, peaceful, hard-working" Muslims.[2] Many French documents use *ceddo* in a narrower sense, to describe the professional warriors of the Wolof court. Historians have frequently followed this last usage, using *ceddo* to describe the warriors of the old regime.

Few Wolof speakers define *ceddo* narrowly, as a synonym for warrior. Lat Joor's grandson comes closest to this meaning, as he defines *ceddo* as someone holding a position of political power, as opposed to a *baadoolo* (peasant), whom he defines as a person without power.[3] In most Wolof usage, *ceddo* has a wider field of meaning, based on its opposition to Islam. In interviews, Murid scholars used the terms *ceddo yi* and *sëriñ si* to describe the division which existed between those in the orbit of the court (the *ceddo*), and those in the orbit of Islam.[4] Yoro Dyâo (Jaw), an aristocrat writing in the early colonial period, defined *ceddo* by evoking the religious beliefs of the Sereer.[5] For the Wolof, the Sereer are a familiar example of "non-Muslims." This usage has led some scholars to translate *ceddo* as "pagan," although "traditionalist" would be better. When asked what *ceddo* means, Wolof speakers describe types of behavior, especially drinking alcohol. Abbé David Boilat,

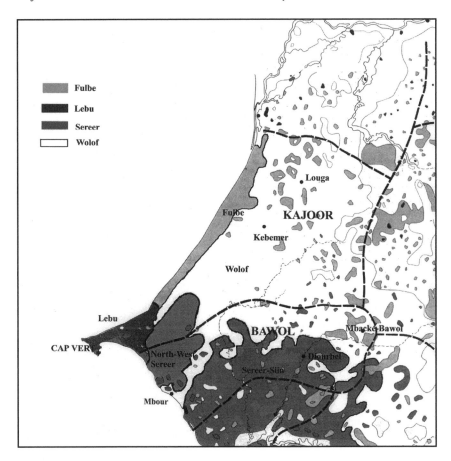

Map 1.2 Linguistic, Ethnic Map of Kajoor and Bawol, c. 1900
Source: Map based on projections and information in *Atlas National du Sénégal* (Paris, 1977).

who was part Wolof and part French, painted a series of portraits in the mid-nineteenth century. His portrait of the *ceddo* emphasized the consumption of alcohol, depicting a seated man, richly dressed, with a bottle of imported liquor prominently displayed. In the text which accompanied his illustration Boilat wrote:

> The word *ceddo* is opposed to cleric; it designates an unbeliever, an impious person, a man without faith or morals. This sort of man forms

the . . . military forces of these countries. Living from theft and pillage, their true vocation is war. [6]

The meanings of *ceddo* range from "warrior" or "courtier" to "drinker of alcohol" and "non-Muslim." This evokes the image of the Wolof aristocracy and its clients. They were a military class that drank alcohol in defiance of Islam, and whose behavior was compared to the non-Muslim neighbors of the Wolof.

Wolof discourse has inspired diverse interpretations. Most research has emphasized the conflicts between Islam and the political order, particularly in the period between 1790 and 1880. Wolof society, it is argued, was divided into an "Islamic" party and a "pagan," "semi-pagan," or "*ceddo*" party: these fought a prolonged battle for power over the course of the nineteenth century. Vincent Monteil followed the logic of Wolof discourse literally, and argued that Lat Joor's "conversion to Islam" was the precipitating factor behind the mass adhesion of the Wolof to Islam.[7] Monteil read *ceddo* as "pagan" and looked for a moment of conversion. But this "reading" reduces complex conflicts to simple caricatures. As Lucie Colvin pointed out in a seminal article, the reports in European sources of conflicts between "Muslim" and "pagans" were based on a literal understanding of the labeling, name-calling, and propaganda that accompanied religious and political conflict.[8] She argues that many sources reflect a Muslim bias, and that the label *ceddo*, which she too interprets as "pagan," cannot be taken literally. She supports her interpretation by documenting the ways in which Wolof kings invoked and used their status as Muslims in their diplomacy with Muslim and non-Muslim neighbors. Lucie Colvin's most important insight is that Wolof descriptions of individuals as *ceddo* or *sëriñ* were judgments about "vocation, political allegiance, and life-style."[9]

Colvin overlooks the fact that the opposition between *ceddo* and *sëriñ* does not appear only in Muslim sources. Wolof bards, who were the official intellectuals of the old regime, use the same terminology. In one epic about Lat Joor, the hero first appears as a youth living in the court. When he falls off his horse during a military exercise, his maternal brother, the reigning king, mocks him and tells him he will never become king. In response, Lat Joor leaves for Kokki, a Muslim village that was the home of his father's family, and he begins studying the Quran. His intent is to become a religious leader. Then Demba War Sall, the military commander of the royal slaves, tries to convince him to become the candidate of the Geej dynasty. The bard describes the encounter between Demba War Sall and Sëriñ-Kokki, the Muslim leader in charge of Lat Joor's education. Demba War asks that Lat Joor be given over to him, because he wants to have him crowned king. Seriñ-Kokki, who wishes to refuse, says:

Lat-Joor sëriñ la
Te yeen ceddo ngeen.

Lat Joor is a Muslim, but you are *ceddo*.[10]

The term *ceddo* was used by Muslims and by "traditionalists" to describe political partisans of the old regime, particularly members of the Wolof court and their military slaves.[11] The *ceddo* party was not a "pagan" party, but the party of the aristocracy.

The word *ceddo* has the connotation of "nonbeliever" or "pagan" in Wolof, but it does not indicate a set of religious beliefs. *Ceddo* evokes attachment to ancestral customs. The "customs" defended by the aristocracy were the traditions of the monarchy. Wolof aristocrats drank alcohol, hunted, feasted on meat, and were entertained by bards with music and dance, in a riot of consumption that scandalized pious Muslims. Wolof dynasties were matrilineal clans, whose members traced their descent through the female line. "Matrilineal" inheritance suggests another meaning of *ceddo* identity. Most Wolof inherited property and land through the paternal line, in accordance with Islam. On the other hand, most Sereer, who identify with "traditional" African religion, emphasized "matrilineal" descent. Put in Wolof, one can say of both the Sereer and the *ceddo*: "According to their customs, the nephew inherits from his maternal uncle," or "In the past the nephew inherited from his maternal uncle."[12] Aristocratic customs appear to preserve "archaic" features of Wolof society that harken back to the period before Islam. Put starkly, Wolof aristocrats behaved like "traditionalists" rather than like Muslims.

Aristocratic traditionalism served political interests, as can be shown through an analysis of matrilineal inheritance and alcohol consumption. Matrilineal inheritance allowed a dynasty to pass on property in slaves and cattle from one king to another, while strict adherence to Islamic law led to the division of property. In the eighteenth and nineteenth centuries matrilineal inheritance became essential to the survival of dynastic power. A Wolof king's most important inherited asset was the loyalty and service of the royal slaves. The slaves of the Geej dynasty symbolized the importance of this. They became the arbiters of royal power and the symbols of the state itself. Alcohol played an important role in Wolof military culture. Warriors gathered for drinking bouts on the eve of battle, to pledge loyalty to one another and to boast about coming acts of bravery. This ceremony, the *xas*, played a key role in defining "honor," because the words spoken in the *xas* could not be taken back without dishonor. Alcohol played a similar role in religious ceremonies among the Sereer, where libations were used to call the "spirit powers" at village shrines. These ceremonies were the occasion for powerful public speech, the *xas ngoor*, in which senior men addressed the spirits and commented on public issues. The consumption of alcohol formed an integral part of these ceremonies.[13] Aristocratic drinking ceremonies were not religious events, but Wolof warrior culture preserved "archaic" customs condemned by Islam. Aristocratic traditionalism made it easy for Muslims to draw invidious comparisons between Wolof kings and nonbelievers.

Lat Joor's grandson gave one of the most detailed definitions of the *ceddo*. He began by defining the *ceddo* as the political class, those who exercised power through the monarchy and the aristocracy, including their slaves and their "clients." Then he turned to their relations with Islam. Most *ceddo* sought the aid and protection of Muslim holy men, by exchanging gifts (*xor*) for charms (Wolof *teere*, literally, a book, writings) that gave protection in battle, fertility in marriage, and success in politics. Nevertheless, most *ceddo* regarded Muslim holy men as "taboo" and "untouchable," and avoided close contact out of fear that they would lose the powers inherited from their ancestors. Other *ceddo* took Muslim holy men as advisors and followed Islam to the extent permitted by their political status. Such *ceddo* prayed and fasted when they could, but they also participated in warrior ceremonies and drank alcohol. Finally, a few individuals from the *ceddo* class converted completely and adopted the lifestyle of Muslim holy men.[14]

There was a tendency toward avoidance and segregation between *ceddo* and Muslims, even when there were important exchanges of services. Wolof saw the division between *sëriñ* and *ceddo* as a kind of pseudo-caste division, marked by social segregation and the exchange of services. The *ceddo* dedicated themselves to government and warfare, the Muslims to education and agriculture. Muslims received gifts of land, slaves, and cattle from the *ceddo* in exchange for rituals and prayers that legitimated their power. Both groups avoided close social contact with each other, as a general rule of thumb. Comparing the division between the monarchy and Islam to other inherited social divisions, court intellectuals argued that the privileges of the aristocracy were permanent features of the social order.

Ceddo identity can be seen as a conscious stance by the political class, putting a distance between themselves and Islam. The *ceddo* were nominally Muslims and many of them followed the precepts of Islam in their old age, after their retirement from politics.[15] *Ceddo* exempted themselves from the laws of Islam, based on their identity as warriors and servants of the king. They drank alcohol, fought the king's battles, and ate meat collected as tribute from peasant communities. Musicians and courtesans entertained them. Conspicuous consumption was crucial to the *ceddo* ideal and was opposed to the austerity of Islam.

THE CEDDO COURT

The legacy of the Atlantic slave trade was inscribed in the social structure of Wolof society in the nineteenth century. From the mid-eighteenth century onwards, the slaves of the Geej dynasty (*jaami-Geej*) decided the outcome of succession struggles for the throne. The royal slaves had a vested interest in dynastic stability, which was expressed when the military commanders of the royal guard threw their weight behind a candidate for the throne. Muslim critics of the Geej dynasty frequently targeted the royal slaves, who drank alcohol and fought for the king, as symbols of *ceddo* tyranny. Alongside the royal slaves, "caste" groups who inherited their occupations dominated the entourage of the king. As a result, both "caste" and "slavery" were strongly associated with the power of the monarchy and its struggle against political Islam.

Aristocratic power depended on slavery. The royal slaves of Kajoor and Bawol formed the fighting elite in the Wolof kingdoms and played important roles in the administration of the army and the state. These "privileged" slaves, many of whom inherited their positions of power, helped to police the wider institution of slavery and to manage the slave populations owned by their aristocratic masters. As with other historical examples of "privileged" slave warriors, the reality of "slavery" might be questioned. One thinks of the Sall family in Kajoor in the late nineteenth century. Technically "slave" in status, the Sall family completely dominated the key offices in the army and the state of Kajoor from 1859 to 1886 and continued to rule much of Kajoor for the French during the colonial era. Can the Salls, whose memory Wolof bards honor, and whose descendants today deny any "servile" status, be labeled "slaves"?

This confusion about slavery arises partly from the habit of seeing slavery primarily through the lenses of property and forced labor. Slavery was first and foremost a form of domination wielded by the master over his/her slave. As such it could be used for many ends. For the Wolof aristocracy, slaves played equally important roles as producers and as political dependents. Ordinary slaves grew crops for their masters and wove cotton cloth. They prepared food and worked as domestic servants. Their labors allowed aristocratic men and women to devote their time to warfare, politics, and the pursuit of pleasure. At the same time, privileged slaves played important roles as household and farm managers, as soldiers and government officials. They were the eyes and ears of the court, political confidants and enforcers, instruments of aristocratic power. They were trusted because of their slave status, which denied them any independent source of power. In theory, privileged slaves held power for their masters, although the reality was more complex than this.

Although slavery was the most important support of aristocratic power in the nineteenth century, it did not play a central role in the opposition between *ceddo* and *sëriñ*. Muslims complained about the power wielded by the king's slaves, but they were not opposed to slavery as an institution. After the aristocracy, Muslim scholars and merchants were the largest slave owners. If there was an "ideological" or "intellectual" battle in the nineteenth century, it was a battle for influence between Muslim scholars and Wolof bards, between the values of Islam and the values of the *ceddo* court. The intellectual of the Wolof court was the *géwél* or bard, the "organic" intellectual of the old regime. Bards followed their masters in public, singing their praises and witnessing their deeds. The office of bard was an inherited social position, so bard and aristocrat were linked through ancestry and tradition. The social role of the bard was rooted in the system of orders.

Wolof aristocrats lived according to a code of honor based on their vocation as warriors. Aristocratic "honor" (Wolof, *jom*) was rooted in noble birth, but it had to be sustained by acts of bravery in war and by generosity to clients and subordinates. Honor was rooted in the social structure of Wolof society, particularly the division between *geer* and *ñeeño*. This division created two distinct orders or status groups. The *geer* included all groups whose status derived from owning and working the land, from the poorest peasant to the king. The aristocracy differentiated themselves from the peasantry by their descent from kings and nobles, not by a distinct, named social status. The *geer* were opposed to the *ñeeño*, a category that included all inherited occupational groups in Wolof society: *géwél* or bards, *tëgg* or blacksmiths, and *uude* or leather workers. The *geer*'s higher status and claim to honor derived from their social independence as peasants, yeoman farmers, or landed aristocrats. The *ñeeño* had lower status because of their position as clients who labored for others. The system of orders was maintained by exclusive endogamy within the two groups: *geer* did not marry *ñeeño* and vice versa.

The "caste" system was an elaborate code that governed the exchange of gifts for service. There was an intricate web of ties between aristocratic patrons and their bards, blacksmiths, and leather workers. These ties of patronage and loyalty placed the *ñeeño* in the orbit of the monarchy. The Wolof shared this system of "orders" with fifteen other societies of the West African savanna.[16] Recent research on these so-called "caste" systems has stressed the ambiguous status of groups like the *ñeeño*. Early European observers and colonial scholars portrayed them as pariah-like groups who were despised by persons of higher status. In reaction to this rigid "caste" model, recent researchers have emphasized the influence and power wielded by specialists within the realms allotted to them by birth. The Mande blacksmiths, for example, were respected and feared for their control of fire and their ability to transform metals into tools and works of art. At the same time they played important social roles as circumcisers, as healers, and as advisors.[17] In Mande societies, the caste groups were also believed to have close connections with the spirit realm, which reinforced their inherited powers.[18]

In Wolof society, the *géwél* or bard is at the center of the system of orders. Most ethnographic research on the "caste" system tells us about perceptions today and cannot be used to understand the past. Today, Wolof "nobles" (*geer*) complain about the "greed" of bards and express resentment about *geer* obligations toward the bards. Nevertheless they respect the bards' power, based on the power of the bards' words to define social status. The nobles' complaints reflect the impoverishment of the aristocracy in the aftermath of slave emancipation. Caste "stereotypes" reinforce the superior status of nobles and place "caste" groups outside the orbit of Islam. "Nobles" speak slowly and softly, as is appropriate to their rank and sense of decorum. If they have a public statement to make, they need a bard to proclaim it. By contrast, bards and other *ñeeño* are stereotyped as loud and boisterous. Bards speak loudly and rapidly, with eloquence. Bard women dance frequently in public and are known for the lewd, sexually charged overtones of their performance. The stereotypes used for *ñeeño* are often used to describe slaves as well. Slaves and *ñeeño* are also stereotyped as lax Muslims. [19]

As an intellectual at court, the bard was in many ways the antithesis of the *sëriñ* or marabout. Bards celebrated a code of honor that predated Islam and justified monarchy. Bards saw themselves as witnesses to history and guardians of honor. In epic narratives, the role of the bard as the witness to words and deeds becomes a structural device which shapes events. Bards reminded aristocrats of the deeds of their ancestors and the honor of their families in the alcohol-charged setting of the *xas*. Demba Lamine Diouf, a contemporary bard, commented on the role of the bard at the *xas*. "Whenever they held a *xas* before going to battle, they called on the bard to participate. Because whoever spoke before the bard during the night of his future deeds could not go back on his words when the sun rose."[20] By the same token, the bard was also a witness to the deeds of the aristocracy on the field of battle. "Whenever they went to the field of battle on horseback the horse of the bard led the way. He was there between two warriors in battle, beating his drums, singing. He was the witness [*Kookoo daan fekke*]." After the battle it was the bard who gave testimony about what had happened. "When the battle was over and everyone returned home, they called him and said 'Come and tell us about the battle, as it happened.'"[21] Only the bard could testify to the conformity between deeds and words, which was central to Wolof conceptions of honor.

The Wolof made several social distinctions within the order of the *geer*. The term *baadoolo* described the peasantry, focusing on their poverty and lack of power. The grandson of Lat Joor, expressing aristocratic views, defined the *baadoolo* as "a person without any power at any level [of society]."[22] The powerlessness of the *baadoolo* was combined with a notion of poverty, because the word itself was derived from *ndóol* ("to be poor"). Although the peasantry were free and participated in the code of "honor" of the *geer*, they were politically subordinate subjects. While *baadoolo* status was defined negatively, the Wolof term *jaambuur* referred to free commoners with higher status: *jaambuur bi*, "an independent person," a "respectable person." In proverbs, the term *jaambuur* describes the social independence and respectability of the yeoman. "You must find two independent people [*jaambuur*] to judge between you,"[23] or "He has no honor, he won't look for work, but instead lives off the sweat of a *jaambuur*." *Jaambuur* also included the upper ranks of free commoners, who achieved higher status through their links to wealth and power, as titled landowners (*laman*), as village chiefs, and as persons of wealth or education. The term *jaambuur* reflects a state of honor, moral probity, and prosperity, and cannot be reduced to an economic class. Finally, the *geer* included the various ranks of the nobility, which were distinguished by their degree of noble birth.

These status groupings among free commoners demonstrated the way in which centuries of monarchical power and slave trading had reshaped Wolof society. In much of Kajoor, older, more egalitarian systems of land tenure had given way to a system of land grants (*lew*) in which peasants paid rents in exchange for land and protection. The lowly status of "peasants" (*baadoolo*) reflected this state of dependency. The middling ranks of Wolof society, the *jaambuur*, held some claim to land or labor that gave them more autonomy. Politically, the *jaambuur* had lost most of the power they had once wielded as electors of the monarchy.

Wolof kings did not concentrate their dependents in a central palace complex, as was the case in some West African kingdoms, where a royal city grew up around the king.[24] The ecology of the savanna did not permit large concentrations of population. In Kajoor, most kings constructed a royal residence in their central provinces, where they resided with the royal guard, their domestic slaves, and their important clients. In addition, the Kajoor king had a residence at Rufisque, the Atlantic port where most trade and diplomatic relations with Europeans were conducted. Many of the king's estates and royal slaves were scattered throughout the kingdom.

Kings represented a dynasty that included powerful interest groups, even though only a few nobles were eligible for the throne. The highest aristocratic rank was *garmi* for men or *lingeer* for women. A *garmi* could trace royal descent from both father and mother. A *lingeer* was a women from a royal matrilineage (there were seven of these) who could confer her noble status on her children. The most important lesser group of nobles was the *doomi-buur*, literally "children of the king." Most of these were the sons of kings with mothers of non-noble or slave status. Ultimately, aristocratic status was sustained and protected by the reigning dynasty. When the "son of a king" successfully usurped power, as Latsukabbe Faal did in Kajoor at the end of the seventeenth century, a new "royal matrilineage" was created. This Geej dynasty reigned almost without interruption until the French conquest.

Aristocratic dynasties maintained themselves in power by distributing lands and titles as rewards for noble birth and loyal service. When land grants were given they tended to become hereditary fiefs. Titleholders carved out a personal domain in which to settle their family and slaves, but also a territory from which they collected tribute and labor services from settled communities. Wolof kings had the right to remove many titleholders if they fell into disfavor, but such actions entailed political risks. New estates and titles were created from time to time, and old grants that had lapsed through the fortunes of war or migration were reclaimed. In the nineteenth century the competing factions of Wolof society all controlled some titles and land grants.

Ultimately, power came from the military power of the ruling dynasty, as brute force often overcame other claims to legitimacy. The Wolof kingdoms were dominated by a military aristocracy, which raises important questions about the importance of warfare to the social order. This is particularly true because for centuries Wolof kingdoms sold slaves to Atlantic merchants in exchange for firearms, Asian cotton cloth, alcohol, and manufactured goods. The Wolof kingdoms also traded slaves to Saharan merchants in exchange for horses, as part of a larger desert-savanna trade. This has led many historians to characterize the Wolof kingdoms as slave-raiding military states.

A review of the evidence will allow a more nuanced statement about the role of warfare in the Wolof states. In a previous book, I estimated that the export slave trade from the Wolof kingdoms formed only about 10 percent of the Senegambian slave trade for most of the eighteenth century. The one exception was the period from 1750 to 1756, when famine and warfare led to increased slave exports, and slave exports rose to 30 percent of the Senegambian total. This data is summarized in Table 1.1.

While the slave trade had political significance for the Wolof kingdoms, its importance was based on the convergence of several factors. The Wolof kingdoms profited from their geographic location by taxing Europeans in return for the right to establish trading forts and markets on the Atlantic coast.[25] They also played a predominant role in the provision trade in grain and other foodstuffs to Saint-Louis and Gorée. In the 1780s, when Saint-Louis and Gorée had a combined population of about 7,000, the islands required 2,000 metric tons of local grain per year.[26] The grain trade expanded rapidly, with minimal estimates of purchases by European and *habitant* (African and *métis*, native to coastal cities) merchants at 1,000 metric tons in the 1750s, 2,000 tons in the 1780s, and 5,000 tons in the 1840s, just to feed the urban populations. In fact surplus grain was also purchased for re-export to the desert, where it figured in transactions to purchase gum arabic. The Wolof kingdoms probably supplied about 75 percent of the grain purchased by French merchants, which does not include the direct trade in grain between the desert and the savanna. Slave exports were modest because there were other opportunities for acquiring European trade goods. On the other hand, the Wolof states depended on imported firearms from the end of the seventeenth century onward, creating a structural dependency on Atlantic commerce in the political system.

Table 1.1 Slave Exports (Atlantic), 1700–1800

	Wolof kingdoms	Senegambia
1700–10	3000–4000	22,230
1711–20	3000–4000	36,260
1721–30	3000–4000	52,530
1731–40	3000–4000	57,210
1741–50	3000–4000	35,000
1751–60	5000–6000	30,100
1761–70	2000–3000	27,590
1771–80	2000–3000	24,400
1781–90	2000–3000	15,240
1791–1800	2000–3000	18,320
Totals	28,000–38,000	336,880

Source: David Richardson, "Slave Exports from West and West-Central Africa, 1700–1810: New Estimates of Volume and Distribution," *Journal of African History* 30 (1989): Table 7, 17 for Senegambian estimates. James F. Searing, *West African Slavery*, 27–33, for Wolof Kingdoms.

In Senegambia, the Atlantic slave trade coexisted with an important trade between the desert and the savanna, which has led to debates about how the two sectors interacted. In my view, the development of gum exports brought the desert-side trade into the orbit of Atlantic commerce, but this interpretation has been challenged by scholars who see the desert-side sector as the dominant influence. In a recent book, James L. A. Webb has argued that Wolof slave exports to the Sahara and North Africa "equaled or exceeded the number of slaves sold into the Atlantic slave trade."[27] His interpretation is a critique of historians, beginning with Boubacar Barry, who have argued that the Atlantic slave trade ushered in a new era for Senegambian societies. In Barry's memorable phrase, the arrival of the European seaborne trade signaled the triumph of the caravel over the caravan.[28] In contrast, Webb argues that the export of slaves into the Sahara significantly exceeded Atlantic exports. In his view the state of Waalo, which sold only a few hundred slaves a year to Europeans, sold a minimum of 500 slaves but more likely 1,000–1,500 slaves a year in the Sahara to maintain its cavalry forces in the late seventeenth century.[29] The argument is based on what he calls the "horse and slave trade." Webb's thesis depends on a number of linked propositions. First, he argues that a "cavalry revolution" took place in Senegambia in the fifteenth and sixteenth centuries. Second, he describes the Wolof kingdoms as "cavalry states" and uses European estimates of "cavalry" forces. He concludes that Waalo had a minimum of "3000 horses in the Waalo cavalry" in the late seventeeth century, while Kajoor could field "2000, 3000 or even 10,000 horses" in the late eighteenth century.[30] Third, he argues that at least half of these "horses" were pure desert breeds, and that at least one-third of them had to be replaced each year due to mortality from disease.[31]

The thesis of a dominant horse and slave trade fails to stand up to closer scrutiny. While horses were important to aristocratic status, there was no cavalry revolution. If there was a revolution, it was based on firearms. Kajoor was the most powerful Wolof kingdom. The Geej dynasty introduced the systematic use of firearms at the end of the seventeenth century. Geej power arose in Bawol, on the periphery of the zone where horses were useful. Bawol had an Atlantic port at Portudal, however. The first Geej army was formed around a core of 300–500 riflemen, who exercised in formation. These were royal slaves and fought on foot. With this army, Latsukaabe Faal conquered Kajoor and annexed portions of Waalo, both of which had more horses, but fewer skills with firearms. In the early nineteenth century, infantry still formed the core of Kajoor's army. Dynastic traditions describe the royal guard of Birama Faatma Cubb (reigned c. 1809–1832) as "five hundred *fantassins* [infantry] armed with *dibi*, a long gun with a flint or piston firing mechanism."[32] In battle, the king and the nobles were mounted and directed the column of infantry. In the mid-nineteenth century, when the price of horses declined, the royal guard was transformed into a mounted unit. But the size remained about the same, at 500–600 horses.

Webb's second assumption is that European estimates of cavalry numbers are accurate. These estimates were made by European slave traders and company officials who had little occasion to observe what they described. It is unlikely that their estimates were accurate, because the numbers seem inflated by nineteenth-century standards when horses were cheaper. In 1860 an agent for the French estimated that the Dammel of Kajoor controlled an armed guard of 650, including 500 cavalry under his direct control, although more could be raised within his kingdom.[33] This estimate of the size of the royal guard seems entirely reasonable. A strong king with full support from the notables in the kingdom could raise between 1,500 and 2,000 cavalry. These estimates fit in with other data on the size of military forces in the 1860s. The Muslim rebels fielded 2,000 men in Kajoor in 1859, but they were infantrymen armed

with guns. According to the French, the rebels outnumbered the king's
forces, but they were soundly defeated. "They had more than 2000 men
armed with rifles and only faced several hundred cavalry."[34] In 1864
the French believed the combined forces of Lat Joor and Màbba numbered 4,000–5,000 men and commented: "Lat Joor possesses a certain
quantity of large horses (Arabian), but Màbba has few horses."[35] Again,
the bulk of soldiers were infantrymen. This evidence suggests that the
Kajoor monarchy controlled about 500 cavalry and that at most 2,000
could be raised in the entire kingdom.

Data on military engagements support the same conclusions. Kajoor's
cavalry fought like mounted infantry. They used their horses to escape
enemy troops and to position themselves for combat. Horses were crucial for secondary military operations, such as raiding for cattle and
taking prisoners. One of the most detailed accounts of Wolof warfare
describes the way armies marched back and forth in a kind of "parade."
One army would march toward the other's line and then discharge its
weapons. Speeches, music, and the display of battle flags accompanied
these parade movements. Then the other army would advance in the
same way. When one side gained a decisive advantage, the losers would
mount their horses and abandon the field of battle.[36] In battle, soldiers
relied on their guns, and could fight mounted or dismounted. In 1874,
during an invasion of Kajoor, members of the royal guard constructed
a fortification (Wolof, *tata*), that they defended against superior forces
until their ammunition was exhausted.[37] In Lat Joor's most successful
encounters with the French, Kajoor's army surprised French columns
on the march by attacking them from concealed positions that provided
cover.[38] The aim of the royal guard was to lay down an intense barrage
of fire at close range. These assaults were then followed by hand to
hand combat. Although Wolof narratives of battle focus on aristocratic
honor, occult forces, and feats of arms, they also provide many grue-
some descriptions of the casualties inflicted by gunshots in close combat.[39] All this evidence points in the same direction. Wolof armies
depended on firearms far more than on horses.

Finally, Webb's argument about slave exports to the Sahara is based
on the assumption that half of the horses in the Wolof states were pure
Arabians or crossbreeds sold by desert merchants, and that one-third of
this stock had to be replaced every year because of death from disease.
Based on Webb's assumptions, to maintain a cavalry of 3,000, Kajoor
would have sold 1,000–1,500 slaves a year. However, if the king only
maintained 500 cavalry, the number of slaves sold would have been
much smaller (160–320 a year). If, as is likely, only the king and his
inner circle of commanders and titled nobles rode desert horses, slave

sales in exchange for horses declined even further to the level of 60–120 slaves a year for the early nineteenth century.[40] Frédéric Carrère and Paul Holle, who were well-informed *habitants* from Saint-Louis, were explicit on this last point:

> Their horses are small, but full of fire. Those of a larger size, which are reserved for chiefs, are purchased from the Moors.[41]

The horse was a much-valued luxury for the Wolof aristocracy, a symbol of status and wealth, but it is silly to accept French propaganda that Kajoor was being "depopulated" by the sale of slaves for horses.[42]

The evidence suggests that the Wolof kingdoms sold hundreds (rather than thousands) of slaves per year to finance the purchase of firearms and horses from Atlantic and desert merchants. This does not mean that warfare was unimportant, but it reinforces the argument that the Wolof states were not expansionist slave raiding states. They raided the Sereer minorities who lived within the borders of their kingdoms in campaigns of "pacification" justified by Islam.[43] They punished political dissidence with enslavement, causing protest and rebellion among the Muslim populations of northern Kajoor.[44] Aristocratic violence also turned inward on itself. The genius of the Wolof aristocracy was for civil war. Each Dammel of Kajoor invaded Bawol, with the hope of uniting the two kingdoms. The praise poetry and epics of Wolof bards preserve the memory of these struggles for power. The king, egged on by his bard, calls on his champions and younger relatives to prove their honor and noble ancestry in feats of arms against Bawol, Jolof, Siin, or Saalum. The bard witnesses these feats of arms, naming the victor and his victims and describing the horses, which had their own praise names,[45] as did the guns.[46] These aristocratic wars provided an opportunity to seize slaves and cattle from the enemy, as the booty of victory.

The image of Wolof kings as ruthless slave raiders and slave traders has more to do with nineteenth-century domestic politics than it does with strict historical accuracy. Many contemporary academic interpretations echo the arguments of the Muslim party in the Wolof civil wars, which condemned Wolof kings as *ceddo* slave raiders who violated the laws of Islam.

ISLAM AND THE MONARCHY

The social pact that allowed Wolof aristocrats to live as *ceddo* in a Muslim society was ancient. Nineteenth-century Muslims condemned it as an anachronism. The struggle between the monarchy and Islam has colored almost all research on Islam in the Wolof states. Lucie Colvin described the Wolof case as an example of the failure of jihad, which postponed the triumph of Islam into the colonial period. She also argued that neither traditions nor written sources describe a "viable traditional African religion among the Wolof."[47] Colvin criticized previous researchers for interpreting the conflicts of the nineteenth century as movements of conversion, but emphasized the success of the monarchy in defeating militant Islam. The problem with this interpretation, which has become the basis for subsequent discussions, is that it captures only one side of the relationship between Wolof monarchy and Islam. In my discussion I will begin by emphasizing the long-standing accommodation between Wolof kings and Muslims, which was shaped by the presence of significant non-Muslim minorities within the kingdoms of Kajoor and Bawol.

Wolof Islam was the dominant religion in the nineteenth century, but it coexisted with the ancestral religion of the Sereer. In the Wolof kingdoms, the Wolof/Sereer dichotomy expressed the division between Muslims and non-Muslims. Wolof attitudes toward the Sereer minorities were summed up in the response of a royal official to French missionaries' requests to preach in Kajoor in 1851. He indignantly rejected the request: "Tell them that God alone is God and that Muhammad is his prophet, and that far from receiving God's law from others, we teach it. Kajoor is entirely converted and doesn't need anyone to instruct us." Then, as an afterthought he mentioned the Sereer. "If nevertheless God has sent them to teach his law, let them go into the forests of Njegem, in the country of the Noon [Sereer-Noon, Ndut] and the mountains of the Nase Cape; there they will find barbarous and unconquered peoples who do not recognize God, or monarchy or laws. Let them convert them if they can."[48]

Sereer populations who resisted Islam and the domination of Wolof kings existed in both Kajoor and Bawol. They were grouped around the Thiès escarpment and the massif of Njaas, elevated sandstone outcroppings that offered some defense against Wolof incursions. However, the balance of power between Wolof and Sereer was very different in the two kingdoms. Kajoor was almost entirely Wolof and Muslim in the nineteenth century, while Bawol had more substantial populations of independent Sereer. In western Bawol, the Sereer formed the majority of the population. The geography of religious belief exerted an important influence on the attitudes of Muslims and on the relations between the monarchy and Islam.

The alliance between Wolof kingdoms and Islam dated back to a period when Islam was a minority religion and Muslims welcomed even the nominal Islam of the Wolof court. Wolof kings supported Islam for political as well as religious reasons. This was based on the perception that Muslims accepted monarchy, while non-Muslims (the Sereer) did not. The distinction between the Wolof and the Sereer symbolized a complex set of opposed identities. The Wolof were Muslims who lived in compact villages in the open savanna. When they cleared an area for cultivation they cut down almost all the trees, symbolically stating their separation from the spirit powers, who inhabited the forest groves and were symbolized by snakes, birds, and other animals. The Wolof aligned their central mosque to the East. The Wolof paid tribute to kings and other overlords. The Sereer were not Muslim. They lived in dispersed settlements and village clusters in hilly and forested refuge areas dotted with sacred groves. The sacred grove or shrine in each village was the abode of the *pangol*, "spirits" who had formed a historic pact with the village community. Some Sereer regions were protected sanctuaries, in which barriers of forest were cultivated to keep out Wolof cavalry forces. French military officers surveyed Mbayar province in the 1890s and found Sereer villages surrounded by dense ramparts of impenetrable forest/bush, as wide as 10–20 kilometers in some places.[49] Many Sereer refused to pay tribute to kings and overlords of any kind. It is easy to see how Islam became an ally of the monarchy in the eyes of Wolof kings. The domain of the spirit powers was a potent source of opposition to Wolof rule.

The degree of distinction between Sereer and Wolof depended on the extent to which the Sereer had accepted monarchy. At the extreme of armed independence (Sereer Safèn, Joobas, Ndut, Sex), the Sereer did not recognize slavery, the system of orders ("caste"), or monarchy. When Sereer groups accepted monarchy, their societies then recognized slavery and hereditary orders, incorporating them into public ritual.[50] Wolof rulers adopted different strategies toward the Sereer populations living within their domains. If they refused to recognize the monarchy, they could be attacked and raided for slaves and cattle with impunity, in the name of Islam. On the other hand, Wolof kings were willing to negotiate agreements with Sereer populations, in which each side gained concrete advantages. A member of the royal family, who ruled through a slave minister (*farba*), controlled Mbayar province in Bawol. Within the province, Wolof officials (*sax-sax*) collected tribute and drafted animals and young men to fertilize and cultivate fields for their Wolof overlords. In exchange the Sereer were allowed to practice their religion and the Wolof king was required to appear before Sereer diviners at the beginning of his reign.[51]

The main point to be taken from this exploration of the Wolof-Sereer cultural divide is a reminder of how profoundly Wolof cultural identity was linked to Islam. The monarchy's defense of *ceddo* values has to be read against the background of a fundamental alliance between Wolof monarchy and Islam. Wolof kings initially promoted a universal religion that was opposed to the local powers of "Sereer" spirit sanctuaries and their diviners and war chiefs. Islamization was encouraged by the monarchy because, where it succeeded, it removed the "spirit powers" from the scene. But Islamization also created a new class of intellectuals, described in Wolof as *sëriñ si*. The *sëriñ* was essentially a teacher, someone who could read and teach the Quran. But the cultural logic of islamization made the *sëriñ* much more than a teacher. By the end of the seventeenth century, Wolof marabouts were powerful enough to form a counter-power to the monarchy.

The relations between Islam and the monarchy changed at the end of the seventeenth century when a new dynasty, the Geej, emerged in Bawol and conquered Kajoor. The Geej was an "Atlantic" dynasty, as *geej* means "sea" or "ocean" in Wolof. Geej power was based on the employment of slave soldiers and the use of firearms, and on skillful manipulation of the political advantages of participation in the Atlantic slave trade. In Wolof cultural terms, Geej power arose out of the struggle between the monarchy and the "spirit powers," between Wolof and Sereer in Bawol. Bawol's population was predominantly Sereer, and Bawol was a frontier zone of Wolof-Sereer interaction and conflict. The new dynasty had no Islamic credentials to speak of, when judged from the perspective of Wolof Muslims. But the Geej dynasty granted new powers of autonomy to Muslim communities.

The new deal between Islam and the monarchy created a group of "titled" Muslims. Latsukaabe Faal recognized the power of Muslim scholars as the rulers of autonomous village communities within the kingdom. Collectively known as *sëriñu-làmb* (literally, clerics of the drum), the leaders of these villages received titles which granted them a role equivalent to other title-holders in the kingdom. The titled clerics were known by appellations that linked their status as scholars (*sëriñ*) to control over a specific village: Sëriñ-Kokki, Sëriñ-Ñomré, Sëriñ-Luuga. While recognizing their power, the monarchy also gave them responsibilities. The "titled Muslims" were expected to aid in the defense of their territories and serve as the intermediaries between their communities and the monarchy. In exchange, the monarchy granted the Muslims dominion over the land they controlled and the populations who inhabited it. The monarchy also periodically gave new domains of land (*lew wi*) to Muslim scholars as charitable gifts that allowed them to found villages and schools.

The pact between the monarchy and Islam was made to win Muslim support. Latsukaabe came from the "frontier" of Wolof-Sereer interaction, a borderland where Islam was weak and the spirit powers were strong. Eventually he came to rule over the Wolof heartland through his conquest of Kajoor and through his expansion of Kajoor's borders to the north. Latsukaabe annexed Ganjool province, with its rich saltmines and close ties to Saint Louis, and Njambur province, the historic center of Wolof Islam. By granting titles and limited autonomy to Muslim leaders in the north, Latsukaabe hoped to win Muslim support for the new dynasty. As a Wolof king, Latsukaabe believed that Islam promoted submission to the monarchy.

Over time, the agreements of the eighteenth century took on new meanings. Kajoor was partitioned into spheres of influence, into territories of Islamic autonomy and territories of aristocratic dominance. These divisions reflected interlocking patterns of landownership and political organization. In Njambur province the *sëriñ* controlled the land (or more precisely the local tribute and taxes it produced) and held political office. Muslims there felt that they were living according to Islam, but resented their political subordination to the monarchy. In the rest of Kajoor, the aristocracy controlled most of the land, held the crucial political offices, and ruled directly or through slave officials. Under Geej centralization the tendency was for slave officials to take over important offices. By the nineteenth century, Muslims could portray Kajoor as partly dominated by free Muslims and partly dominated by the king's slaves. The division of lands and offices did not correspond to a map of Islamic belief. Many Muslims lived in royal and aristocratic provinces. The division between *ceddo* and *sëriñ* could refer to the political partition of the country or to the conflict of values it represented.

Muslims were divided over whether they could accept this division of power. Most Muslims accepted the status quo and hoped their cause would triumph in the long run. By seeking autonomy rather than control of the monarchy or independence, Muslims accommodated themselves to the political order while carrying out their work of education. Islam expanded over time by founding new villages and new schools and by negotiating the expansion of autonomous territories with the monarchy. Muslims working at the grass roots in areas such as Bawol, where Islam was expanding, benefited from new land grants. The most disaffected Muslims were those who already enjoyed autonomy, as in Njambur province. Muslims in Njambur rose in rebellion in 1790–1791 to protest the enslavement of Muslims by the king's slave warriors. They also called on a "foreign power," Fuuta Tooro, for aid after their initial defeat. Njambur Muslims aided the Lebu of Cap Vert when they rebelled and seceded from Kajoor.

As the events of 1790–1791 are often taken as a turning point in the relations between Islam and the monarchy, they deserve fuller discussion. Some Muslims remained neutral during the conflict, because they believed that Muslims could live in peace with the monarchy. The best example is from the family of Amadu Bamba. The village of Mbacké in Bawol was founded between 1790 and 1802 by Muhammad al-Khayr Mbacké, known in Wolof as Maharam. He received the land in grant from Amari Ngoone Ndella, best known for his brutal repression of the rebellion of the 1790s. The rebellion began when the slaves of the king killed Malamin Saar, a well-known Muslim scholar. Many of his friends and colleagues launched a rebellion, which they considered a holy war. Maharam Mbacké did not join the rebellion, even though he was a friend of Malamin, because he believed it was an act of vengeance rather than a jihad. When the king had defeated the rebels, Maharam asked him to pardon them and succeeded in having some of them freed. The king rewarded Maharam by granting him the land where he founded his village.[52] Maharam's descendants preserved a benign image of Amari Ngoone:

> Amari Ngoone loved the scholars and the pious and tolerated more from them than most kings could have borne. The more a scholar hated him and distrusted him, the more the king tried to improve relations and to satisfy him.[53]

This statement contrasts sharply with other accounts of Amari Ngoone Ndella. Lat Joor's grandson described the rebel marabouts led by Malamin Saar as bent on military rebellion. He noted that they imitated the *xas* of the nobility. The Muslims drank tamarind juice in public oaths to parody the alcoholic libations of the *ceddo*. But the Muslims were ill prepared for battle. Amari Ngoone defeated them and treated the survivors ruthlessly:

> He killed or sold as slaves the most important of them and only spared those who were simple schoolteachers, incapable, in his mind, of forming another coalition against him.[54]

Amari Ngoone also sold many Muslims as slaves when he defeated the invading Futanke Muslims from Fuuta Tooro. Mungo Park returned from West Africa on a slave ship that carried Muslims enslaved in Kajoor. He also reported that bards ("singing men") throughout Senegambia celebrated Kajoor's victory, which was seen as a setback for militant Islam.[55]

In her influential article on Islam in Kajoor, Lucy Colvin argued that after 1790 the rift between the monarchy and Muslims was irreparable and there was no effort at fence mending or compromise.[56] Her interpretation was based on the testimony of Muslim scholars from Muslim villages in Njambur (Kokki) and central Kajoor (Pir). Maharam Mbacké and his land grant shows that this attitude was not universal and reveals the division between advocates of jihad and defenders of orthodoxy. Muslim attitudes reflected the differing historic contexts of Islam within the Wolof kingdoms. In northern Kajoor, Islam was well established and Wolof Muslims there participated in the debates of a larger Sahelian Islam that encompassed the Sahara and Fuuta Tooro.[57] In Bawol, Muslims lived on a frontier of conversion to Islam where there were frequent conflicts between incoming Wolof settlers and Sereer villages. In this situation, Islam competed directly with the spirit powers. In consequence Muslims in Bawol judged the Islamic credentials of the monarchy from a very different perspective than their colleagues in Njambur. The geography of Islam had an important impact on Wolof attitudes.

In the long run the emergence of a new group of intellectuals, the *sëriñ*, challenged the Wolof monarchies. Muslims based their critique of the monarchy on Islam. Within the kingdom, they served as protectors and community leaders for those who lived on the lands they controlled. They articulated a system of values that conflicted with those of the court. Muslims did not drink and they valued labor and peace. They represented a worldly asceticism that led to accumulation. The aristocracy lived by warfare and violence, according to their own system of honor. They drank alcohol and lived off the fruits of others' work. They took what they wanted, consumed what they desired, and gave away gifts to demonstrate their generosity. By all indications, Muslims were winning over the people and therefore posed a direct threat to aristocratic power. The threat of political Islam was held in check by the superior military strength of the monarchy.

NOTES

1. The best study of Lat Joor is Diouf, *Le Kajoor*. For Diouf's interpretation of Lat Joor's commitment to Islam, see 257–61.

2. For Faidherbe's view of Kajoor see "Notice historique sur le Cayor," *Bulletin de la Société de Géographie de Paris*, series 7, vol. 4 (1883): 527–564.

3. Amadou Bamba Diop, "Lat Dior et le problème musulman," *Bulletin de l'Institut Fondamentale de l'Afrique Noire*, 28, B (1966): 497.

4. Interview, Serigne M'Baye Guèye Sylla, Darou-Mousty, July 28, 1995.

5. R. Rousseau, "Le Sénégal d'autrefois. Étude sur le Oualo. Cahiers de Yoro Dyâo," *Bulletin du Comité d'Études Historiques et Scientifiques sur l'Afrique Occidentale Française* 12 (1929): 169, note 1.

6. David Boilat, *Esquisses sénégalaises* (Paris, 1853), 308.

7. Vincent Monteil, "Lat Dior, Damel du Cayor, et l'islamisation des Wolofs au XIXe siecle," in Vincent Monteil, *Esquisses sénégalaises* (Dakar, 1966).

8. Lucy Colvin, "Islam and the State of Kajoor: A Case of Successful Resistance to Jihad," *Journal of African History* 15, no. 4 (1974): 587–606.

9. Colvin, "Islam and the State of Kajoor," 590.

10. Bassirou Dieng, ed., *L'épopée du Kajoor* (Dakar, 1993), Récits de Bassirou Mbaye, Récit XII: L'épopée de Lat-Dior, Wolof text, 378.

11. Colvin argues that use of the term pagan was restricted to informants from the "clerical community," "Islam and the State of Kajoor," 602.

12. Arame Fal, Rasine Santos, and Jean Léonce Doneux, *Dictionnaire wolof-français* (Paris, 1990), entries for *nijaay* and *jarbaat*. The dictionary gives "proverbial" uses where possible, based upon an extensive data-base.

13. Katherine R. Marcoccio, "Identity Conflict and Ceremonial Events in a Sereer Community of Saalum, Senegal" (Ph.d. dissertation, Brandeis University, 1987), 263–64.

14. Diop, "Lat Dior et le problème musulman," 498–99.

15. Frédéric Carrère and Paul Holle, *De la Sénégambie française* (Paris, 1855), 63.

16. Tal Tamari, "The Development of Caste Systems in West Africa," *Journal of African History* 32 (1991): 221–50.

17. Patrick McNaughton, *The Mande Blacksmiths:* Knowledge, Power and Art in West-Africa (Bloomington, Ind., 1988).

18. Sarah C. Brett-Smith, *The Making of Bamana Sculpture: Creativity and Gender* (Cambridge, 1994).

19. On the Wolof caste system, see Judith T. Irvine, "Caste and Communication in a Wolof Village" (Ph.D. dissertation, University of Pennsylvania, 1973). For comparative ethnographic data, see L.B. Venema, *The Wolof of Saloum: Social Structure and Rural Development in Senegal* (Wageningen, The Netherlands, 1978), 86, 127–28.

20. Dieng, *L'épopée du Kajoor*, 124. My translation from the Wolof.

21. Ibid. These passages comment on the declining status of the bard in Wolof society.

22. Diop, "Lat Dior et le problème musulman," 497.

23. Fal et al., *Dictionnaire*, 95.

24. For a good example of this, see Edna G. Bay, *Wives of the Leopard: Gender, Politics, and Culture in the Kingdom of Dahomey* (Charlottesville, Va., 1998).

25. Searing, *West African Slavery*, 71–74.

26. For a discussion of the assumptions behind such a calculation, see Searing, *West African Slavery*, 140, 142. For the population of Saint–Louis and Gorée in the 1780s, see ibid., 110, 165.

27. James L.A. Webb, *Desert Frontier: Ecological and Economic Change along the Western Sahel, 1600–1850* (Madison, Wis., 1995), 88.

28. Boubacar Barry, *Le Royaume du Waalo: Le Sénégal avant la conquête* (Paris, 1972), 55. Barry borrowed the phrase from Victorino Godinho, *L'économie de l'empire portugais aux XVe et XVIe siècles* (Paris, 1969). For a more recent statement of Barry's view, see Boubacar Barry, *Senegambia and the Atlantic Slave Trade* (Cambridge, 1998).

29. Webb, *Desert Frontier*, 82.

30. Ibid., 82, 81.

31. Ibid., 75.

32. Tanor Latsoukabé Fall, "Recueil sur la vie des Damel," *Bulletin de l'Institut Fondamental de l'Afrique Noire*, 36, B (1974): 127.

33. Oumar Ba, ed., *La pénétration française au Cayor* (Dakar, 1976), 394.

34. Ba, *La pénétration*, 247.

35. 13 G 304, Gorée: Correspondance, pièce 33, Oct. 22, 1864. All archival references are to the Archives Nationales du Sénégal (ANS), Dakar, D, E, G, J, and K series. Translations from the French are mine.

36. Carrère and Holle, *De la Sénégambie*, 70–71.

37. Fall, "Receuil," 133–34.

38. For a French perspective on these battles see A. Sabatié, *Le Sénégal: Sa conquête et son organisation*, (Saint-Louis du Sénégal, 1925), 150–53.

39. There are many examples in Dieng, *L'épopée*.

40. This is based on a figure of one hundred arabians and desert crossbreeds (as opposed to small local breeds), purchased for two to four slaves per horse.

41. Carrère and Holle, *De la Sénégambie*, 74.

42. This argument was made by Faidherbe, but is cited by Webb as a "prescient" comment, in *Desert Frontier*, 95. Much of Webb's thesis is based on the uncritical use of European sources.

43. For the role of the Sereer in the eighteenth-century slave trade, see Searing, *West African Slavery*, 35–38.

44. Ibid., 157–62.

45. Dieng, *L'épopée*, lists nineteen Wolof terms to describe the colors of a horse's coat (24), and the epics he transcribed contain numerous descriptions of horses.

46. Dieng, *L'épopée*, 421, for Lat Joor's gun and its name.

47. Colvin, "Islam and the State of Kajoor," 592.

48. Boilat, *Esquisses sénégalaises*, 174.

49. Jean-Marc Gastellu, *L'égalitarisme économique des Serer du Sénégal* (Paris, 1981), 278.

50. For this argument, see Gastellu, *L'égalitarisme*, 301–14.

51. Ibid., 284–97.

52. Serigne Bachir Mbacké, "Les bienfaits de l'Eternel ou la biographie de Cheikh Ahmadou Bamba Mbacké (translated by Khadim Mbacké) (1)," *Bulletin de l'Institut Fondamental de l'Afrique Noire* 42, B (1980), 577–78. The translator cites a poem by Muusa Ka as the source of this story.

53. Ibid., 578.

54. Diop, "Lat Dior et le problème musulman," 504.

55. Mungo Park, *Travels in the Interior Districts of Africa in the Years 1795, 1796, and 1797* (London, 1799), 511–13.

56. Colvin, "Islam and the State of Kajoor," 601, 603.

57. For a good discussion of the issues in that world, see David Robinson, *The Holy War of Umar Tal: The Western Sudan in the Mid-Nineteenth Century* (Oxford, 1985).

Figure 2.1   *Ceddo* (painting by Boilat) 1850s.

2

CIVIL WAR AND CONQUEST: MONARCHY AND ISLAM IN KAJOOR, 1859–1890

This chapter presents a new interpretation of the colonial conquest. I argue that the entire period from 1859 to 1886 was a Wolof civil war, with forces loyal to the monarchy battling insurgent Muslims determined to reform or destroy it. The war began with a Muslim rebellion in 1859. The rebellion failed, but left the monarchy crippled. By 1863 the first phase of the civil war had come to an end. The French took advantage of the conflict to place a new king on the throne of Kajoor, driving the partisans of the Geej dynasty into exile. The new king had sworn to uphold the goals of the Muslim party and rule for the French. His reign came to an end in 1865, in the midst of the worst famine in a century. The first experiment with colonial rule ended in failure and chaos.

The second phase of the civil war, from 1863 to 1869, coincided with a period of Muslim insurgency in the entire region. It was led by Màbba from a base in Saalum, to the south. The loyalists of the Geej dynasty joined Màbba as his disciples and allies. Demb War Sall led the exiles into this unusual alliance. He was the political leader of the royal slaves, who formed the core of the monarchy's inherited strength. Lat Joor, the king chosen by Demba War, was a teenager, freshly circumcised into manhood. These two men, first as allies, then as rivals, would lead a revived Geej monarchy back to power in 1870 and dominate Kajoor until 1886. Demba War Sall would rule Kajoor for the French until his death in 1902. The Geej loyalists also included prominent aristocrats, alarmed by French intervention and political instability throughout the region. Their later success was due to the Muslim credentials they earned fighting alongside Màbba, although skeptics believed they were more interested in pillage than religion.

The third phase of the civil war began with the return of the exiles to power in 1870, following negotiations with the French and with the Muslim party in Kajoor. The reign of Lat Joor was important, with impressive successes and failures. One success was the expansion of peanut exports, which brought prosperity. Much of this growth was fueled by state sponsorship. The Geej dynasty allied itself with powerful *habitant* merchants in Saint Louis, and slaves taken in recent wars were deployed on plantations producing peanuts. Peace and prosperity won broader support as well. The failures of Lat Joor began with his inability to win full support from the Muslim party. A new round of warfare began in 1875, when Kajoor was invaded by Muslims from neighboring Jolof, with the support of important segments of the Muslim party in Kajoor. Lat Joor's victory in 1875 was costly, leaving him with a political debt to the French, creating a rift with Demba War Sall, and earning Lat Joor the permanent hostility of many Muslims for his brutal execution or enslavement of his defeated enemies. In Murid traditions, 1875 is remembered as a turning point, transforming Amadu Bamba into an opponent of monarchy.

Lat Joor failed to secure his crucial alliance with the French, whose demands for a railroad became insistent after 1879. The French opposed his wars against Bawol and Jolof. He was ousted from power by Demba War Sall in 1883, replaced briefly by another king, and then replaced by Demba War Sall, who willingly accommodated to French colonial rule. Although Demba War Sall was a royal slave, he is better thought of as the representative of the slave-owning classes, whose interests he consistently defended. He was not an enemy of Islam, but he believed Lat Joor had gone too far in appeasing the Muslim party. He was vigilant against Muslims who threatened his power base, and he would help lead the attack on Murid Islam in 1895.

When the French opted for Demba War Sall to satisfy their quest for "hegemony on a shoestring," to use Sara Berry's phrase,[1] they yoked the colonial regime to a cart that carried considerable baggage. Throughout the civil war, one complaint was that the monarchy was dominated by "one family," the Geej and their allies, particularly their slaves. By attaching themselves to the same power base, the French colonial state inherited the opposition to a regime whose most enduring association was with slavery and the slave trade.

During the civil war, the terms of the debate about Islam and the monarchy were transformed. I have paid particular attention to debates about jihad, as depicted in Wolof sources. Many of the hopes invested in the rebellion of 1859 died with Njugu Lo, who held the title Sëriñ Luuga. He was killed in the first battle. What would have happened in northern Nigeria if Usuman Dan Fodio had been killed in the first confrontation with Gobir? After the failure of the rebellion, Muslim hopes focused on a series of regional leaders who waged holy war against *ceddo* rule and encroaching French power. However, the meaning of jihad began to change when aristocrats like Lat Joor joined the cause of militant Islam. By the 1880s there were signs that many Muslims had lost faith in jihad as a means of revitalizing Islam. This transformation set the stage for the emergence of new Sufi orders that would dominate Wolof responses to colonial rule.

The period of civil war was important because it shaped the history of colonial rule. French colonial officials believed that a new era of European power had begun. But nothing could undo the consequences of the French alliance with the royal slaves of Kajoor, which shaped Wolof understandings of colonial rule.

THE MUSLIM REBELLION OF 1859

In November 1859, the province of Njambur rose in rebellion against the Geej dynasty. The rebels, led by Sëriñ Kokki and Samba Maram Xaay, spread rumors that the rebellion had French support and would receive French military aid. Their tactics succeeded in convincing other Muslim leaders to join the rebellion. Their most prominent ally was Sëriñ Luuga, who was the most influential Muslim leader in this period.[2] He was killed while leading a charge against the army of Kajoor on December 25. The death of Sëriñ Luuga was the turning point for the rebels, whose military forces dispersed in confusion. By the end of 1859, 4,000–5,000 refugees fled to French-controlled territories along the Senegal River. The victorious *ceddo* burned dozens of Muslim villages in Njambur. Granaries that stored the recent harvest of millet and peanuts were burned to the ground.[3] The French authorities in Saint-Louis, who stood by while their "allies" suffered a humiliating defeat, used their influence to ensure that the refugees were allowed to return home.

The rebellion of 1859 failed, but marked a turning point in the history of Kajoor. The rebellion revealed the divisions in Kajoor's body politic and in the aftermath of the rebellion those divisions festered like an open wound. An analysis of the rebellion can begin with a portrait of the prin-

cipal conspirators and the factions they represented, but it must also consider the role played by the French, and the motivation of the rank and file
in the rebel forces.

The leadership of the rebellion represented a coalition of dynastic
rivals to Geej rule, led by Samba Maram Xaay, and Muslim community
leaders, represented by Sëriñ Kokki. Samba Maram Xaay was the leader
of a group of notables who wished to replace the Geej dynasty with a
king from the Dorobe royal matrilineage. No Dorobe king had ruled for
a hundred years, but the chief pretender, Maajoojo Dégén Koddu Faal,
had won support by promising positions of power to prominent families
alienated by Geej rule. Samba Maram Xaay had inherited the leadership of Maajoojo's faction after his brother was killed in a failed coup
in 1857. Maajoojo's supporters were openly pro-French. They corresponded with Governor Faidherbe, promising him that the French would
secure all the concessions they desired from Maajoojo. In concrete terms
this meant permission to construct a telegraph line between Saint-Louis
and Dakar.

Muslim support for the rebellion had more complex roots and was
more ambiguous in its political agenda. Sëriñ Kokki acted as the liai-
son between Maajoojo's supporters and the Muslims, and he accepted
the full implications of the Dorobe alliance. Muslim dissidence in
Njambur had deep roots, based on cultural conflicts between *ceddo* and
sëriñ. Muslims portrayed the Geej dynasty as anti-Islamic: a regime of
drunken nobles and warriors who pillaged and enslaved subject populations without mercy. They wanted a government that reflected Islamic
values. On the other hand the Muslims of Njambur did not declare an
all-out jihad, and the leaders of the rebellion seemed to think that they
could achieve their goals under a new dynasty headed by Maajoojo Faal.
Under the new regime, Njambur province would have achieved complete autonomy under the leadership of the *sëriñ*.

The official face of the Muslim party, represented by Sëriñ Kokki,
may have masked more radical agendas. In the military rebellion, Sëriñ
Luuga played the crucial role. He led a federation of villages centered
on Luuga. The French estimated that at the height of the rebellion the
Muslims had 2,000 men in arms, all equipped with firearms.[4] Most of
the rebels were free Muslim peasants from northern Kajoor. The French
believed that many rebels were migrants from Waalo, who had settled
in Kajoor during a cycle of ecological crisis and warfare along the
Senegal River valley.[5] Muslim peasants from northern Kajoor and Waalo
had joined rebellions against aristocratic rule in the 1790s and the 1830s.
Had the rebellion succeeded, it is unlikely that the grass roots would

have been satisfied with a change of regime that gave power to Maajoojo and Samba Maram Xaay. After the Muslims were defeated, many of them blamed Samba Maram Xaay for misleading them about French support.

During the rebellion rumors about the death of Dammel (King) Birama spread through Kajoor. The French gave enough credence to the reports to publish an article on his death in their official newspaper on December 13.[6] When he learned that the Dammel lived, Governor Faidherbe wrote to him on December 18, warning him that "trade liquor" (*eau-de-vie*) "kills quickly."[7] The French were convinced that the young Dammel, who was in his twenties, was drinking himself to death. The Dammel's infirmity did not aid the rebels. The Dammel's father, Makkodu, led the army during the campaign. Less than a month after the defeat of the rebellion, Birama died.

While the monarchy triumphed in 1859, the political costs were high. The young king of the ruling dynasty was dead, leaving no obvious successor to Geej power. His father, who had helped organize the victory, was not eligible to rule in Kajoor because he belonged to a different royal matriclan than his son. Nevertheless, Makkodu's interregnum won the support of state officials and the royal slaves of Kajoor. Makkodu's reign was a temporary expedient, but it would have lasted much longer if Makkodu had been able to reach a settlement with the French.

French colonial officials sat on the sidelines in 1859–1860, even though they were far from disinterested in the outcome. French inaction resulted from Faidherbe's uncertainty about how to achieve his goals. His plans for Kajoor represented a new departure for French rule in Senegal. Until 1860, Faidherbe's policies were designed to liquidate the remnants of the eighteenth-century trading system along the Senegal River and the Atlantic coast of Senegal. In a series of campaigns in the Senegal River valley from 1854 to 1859, Faidherbe inflicted important defeats on the Trarza emirate (the most powerful Saharan state) and the jihad of Al-Hajj Umar. The French no longer paid tribute to African states along the river and they controlled a series of fortified outposts from Saint-Louis to Médine. French military power had created pockets of French sovereignty and a zone of "free trade" for French merchants.[8] In 1859, Faidherbe led a campaign in Siin and Saalum, which created similar advantages for French and *habitant* merchants from Gorée, who controlled much of the trade in territories south of the Cap Vert peninsula.[9] None of these actions expanded French territorial control beyond the confines of French trading posts, except just outside Saint-Louis. Until 1860, the logic of conquest was mercantile, not territorial.

After these victories Faidherbe turned his attention to Kajoor. In October 1859, just before the rebellion in Njambur, he described the situation there. Faidherbe believed that the French had demonstrated their force to African populations who had "denied it till then," because they thought of Europeans as mere merchants.[10] Now the French controlled the Senegal River for 250 leagues and Kajoor was the one country on the river without a written treaty. Faidherbe believed the French would find willing support from the majority of the population, described as "peace-loving cultivators," if their policy was to "suppress the brigandage of the Dammel's *ceddo*" and to "regularize" his system of government.[11] If the French could achieve a change of regime, their essential goals would be accomplished. Faidherbe based his assessment on his belief that the Muslims of Njambur province, the core of the "peace-loving peasantry," would welcome the French as allies. Close trading ties and frequent correspondence between the French and the major Muslim towns underpinned the alliance.

The French viewed Kajoor as a strategic asset in 1859. The French possessions along the Senegal River and the trading posts linked to Gorée could be amalgamated into one colony if the French could secure their influence in Kajoor. The material embodiment of that influence was a projected telegraph line between Saint-Louis and Dakar-Gorée, to be followed by a railroad. As early as 1857, French military officers outlined the strategic importance of a railroad. French naval officers saw Dakar as the site of a military and commercial port. They noted with satisfaction the birth of a "small French city," based on the export trade in peanuts, and projected a "railroad between Saint Louis and Gorée" as a way of consolidating these developments.[12] A telegraph and a railroad would enable French forces to police the progress of Kajoor's "rationalization."

Faidherbe hoped to achieve his goals by getting the monarchy to approve a treaty allowing the French to construct and maintain a telegraph line between Saint-Louis and Dakar. He had negotiated with Birama, the Dammel who died in 1860, and he was prepared to negotiate with Makkodu. If negotiations failed, Faidherbe believed that a military demonstration would be sufficient to persuade the king to accept his plans. Finally, if all else failed, the French could impose a new ruler. With these plans in mind, Faidherbe requested military and financial support from Paris in 1859, but he took care to minimize anticipated expenses and to stress the modest nature of the changes he planned to impose.

Faidherbe emphasized his local support, based on his ability to recruit troops in the "colony." During his "military demonstration" in

Saalum in 1859, he announced the principle of military recruitment in the French "colony," essentially Saint-Louis and its suburbs and the Cap Vert peninsula. He told the assembled populations of Cap Vert that "they were French" and liable to serve in campaigns against "regimes" that harmed them by pillaging French commerce. According to Faidherbe, the crowd he addressed was "surprised" but "did not dare refuse."[13] In 1859 and again in 1861, Faidherbe recruited "volunteers" in Saint-Louis and Cap Vert. The "volunteers" were told that they were to protect French commerce and local populations from being pillaged by their own rulers. These new recruits supplemented the permanent garrisons under French command and new contingents arriving from France and Algeria.[14] Although the principle of military service was not new, for the first time it was linked with "citizenship" and "French" identity. In the eighteenth and early nineteenth centuries *habitant* merchants from Saint-Louis and Gorée had supported French military projects by lending them slaves who were trained to bear arms and fight to protect merchants' vessels and commerce. Slavery had been abolished in the colony in 1848, and Faidherbe's initiative reinstated military service on new terms.[15]

Faidherbe's decision had important ramifications, as in effect he created a pro-French "urban" party in the context of an emerging Wolof civil war. Faidherbe did not worry about the consequences of his acts, as he believed that the *habitants* were doomed to decline.

> The work of transformation underway in the colony of Senegal . . . has caused great consternation. . . . The part of the population which has demonstrated the worst humor has been those called the *habitants*. . . .They hold on to what they were in former times, the obligatory intermediaries between us and the states of the countryside not only for commerce but also for politics, which made them rich and powerful. Today, however, for the most part they are impoverished.[16]

With the merchant elite in decline, Faidherbe gave little thought to the consequences of recruiting soldiers from the population of fishermen, sailors, and artisans who made up the bulk of the male laboring population of the colony.

In November 1859, just as the rebellion in Njambur was beginning, the French minister of colonies approved Faidherbe's plans in Kajoor. Funds were allocated for the following year. The minister of colonies underlined the limited goals of French occupation. The minister did not want "another Algeria." Ownership of the land was to remain in the hands of the native population. French interests were commercial and could be achieved by protecting the population from the "rapine of their own chiefs" and replacing "hostile chiefs with others more devoted to our policies."[17] This description of what would later be called indirect rule echoed Faidherbe's own descriptions of his intentions.

The rebellion of 1859 may or may not have caught Faidherbe by surprise, but the French were surprised by the rapid and devastating defeat of the Muslims. Faidherbe decided to wait and see which faction emerged as the strongest. French intelligence described a number of competitors for the throne. One alternative, proposed by *lingeer* Debbo, was Lat Joor Joob, who was the ruler of Geet province and belonged to the Geej matrilineage. Princess Debbo volunteered to serve as Lat Joor's advisor. Samba Maram Xaay supported this idea in September 1860. Maajoojo Faal still had supporters among the rebels of 1859. The royal slaves of Kajoor were divided. One group cast its lot with Makkodu, the father of the dead king, in exchange for a promise to respect its members' positions. Another faction of royal slaves supported Lat Joor, because he was a member of the Geej matrilineage. After a struggle, Makkodu emerged as the strongest and was acclaimed king by the assembled notables of Kajoor.

Makkodu was a terrible disappointment to the French. This was expressed symbolically when he wrote to Faidherbe and told him: "You are the master of the sea but I own the mainland."[18] In this sentence, he summarily rejected the changes that Faidherbe had introduced since 1854. The French were dismissed as "mere merchants" who controlled the seas but could never claim power on land. His language reflected the eighteenth-century trade system and its protocols. Makkodu had not "heard" the message about French military power that Faidherbe had carefully constructed through his campaigns and propaganda. Makkodu reneged on all the agreements about the saltmines of Ganjool and the telegraph from Gorée to Saint-Louis. By the end of 1860 it was clear that Faidherbe had achieved nothing in Kajoor, and he prepared for war.

FROM REBELLION TO CIVIL WAR

At the beginning of 1861, Faidherbe described Kajoor to the minister of colonies as the one country in Senegal that had no peace treaty with the French, despite the fact that Kajoor occupied the lands between Saint-Louis and Gorée, "our principal establishments on the coast of West Africa." Kajoor's commerce was smaller than it should have been and French merchants were harrassed and pillaged. Faidherbe took a high moral tone and linked Kajoor to the savagery and injustices of the slave trade:

The greatest criticism one can make of the government of Kajoor is that the king or Dammel, when his ordinary revenues don't satisfy his needs and he wants to acquire horses, trade liquor, gunpowder, rifles or anything else, claims the right to use his *ceddo* to seize not only the cattle herds and property of his subjects, but his subjects themselves, free or slave. . . . This is the cause of a terrible depopulation and a lack of security for the producers which is equally harmful to our commerce.[19]

Faidherbe implied that the French had ignored this problem for too long, and that it was finally time to act:

For a long time we have limited our actions to complaints about this savage regime, a reminder of the era of the slave trade which only the Wolof and Sereer kings have preserved among all the Senegalese rulers.[20]

Faidherbe's rhetoric suggested that he had elevated his upcoming war against Kajoor to a "crusade" against the slave trade. His abolitionist discourse was directed at the French government, but it echoed Muslim critiques of the monarchy.

Faidherbe's actions in 1861 escalated the strife within Kajoor, transforming what began as a limited Muslim rebellion into a wider Wolof civil war. Faidherbe did this by his efforts to recruit Wolof allies, inside and outside Kajoor. Three key groups were immediately affected. First, the inhabitants of the colony itself were asked to aid the French in their war on Kajoor. Second, Faidherbe's plans for war included an appeal to the Muslims who had rebelled in 1859, and who might now achieve their goals with French support. Finally, by deciding to back a dynastic rival of the Geej, Maajoojo Faal, Faidherbe split the ruling classes of Kajoor into factions, based on their acceptance or rejection of his candidate.

By demanding military service from the inhabitants of the colony, Faidherbe raised the stakes for them. "Volunteers" from Saint-Louis, Rufisque, and other towns were told they were "French" and asked to fight against a common enemy. They were promised a new era of prosperity under more enlightened Wolof rulers. Since the "French" towns in Senegal were essentially merchant cities, the future described by Faidherbe had potential attractions. The population of the colony, made up largely of freed slaves, imagined that new opportunities would open up for them if the French dominated Kajoor. At any rate, from 1859 until 1890, the French enlisted soldiers from the colony in all the military campaigns against the Wolof kingdoms. Their role was symbolized by the leading role given to General Dodds, a *métis* from Saint-Louis, in the final campaign against Jolof in 1890. But the role of the ordinary soldier was more important. Expectations were raised among the African populations of the colony that they would benefit from the extension of French power. These expectations, which were largely frustrated, would have a lasting impact on the political role of the old colony in the new Senegal.

Faidherbe had difficulty organizing a decisive military encounter with Kajoor. His first attempt, in January 1861, was a total failure. Faidherbe entered Kajoor with a column of 2,200 troops, of which 675 or nearly a third were "volunteers" from the colony. Makkodu retreated into the interior, refusing all contact with the French. Then he sent an envoy to Faidherbe promising that he would agree to all the conditions Faidherbe desired if Faidherbe withdrew. While Faidherbe considered this proposal, he was met by envoys from Jolof and from the Bër-Geet, Lat Joor, offering support in his "war" on Kajoor. Faidherbe decided to trust Makkodu. Fearing that he would get caught in a "civil war," he returned to Saint-Louis.[21] Shortly afterward, Makkodu renounced his "treaties" with the French.

Faidherbe convened a war council in February 1861 to discuss the way the government should react to Kajoor's repudiation of the "treaties" authorizing the construction of a telegraph line and military posts. Faidherbe wanted war. The most vigorous opposition came from French and *habitant* merchants speaking for "commerce." Gustave Chaumet asked if the French could reach a peaceful settlement with Makkodu. Faidherbe replied that he couldn't neogotiate with "brutes" who were "always drunk" and who had recently rebuffed his emissary. Chaumet listened to the plans put forward by French military officers to impose the treaty by force. In his reply he argued that "commerce" and the "populations" of the French colony had suffered from the state of war on the river and its aftermath. They would suffer even more if Kajoor, "a rich province at our doorstep," which "had always been the breadbasket of Saint Louis and its suburbs" and which traded more with the French than any other region, now broke off relations. He cited detailed export statistics (carefully prepared in advance) that showed the importance of peanut exports from Kajoor. He found it strange that a "treaty" designed to "strengthen close ties" was now the cause of a complete rupture. He advised Faidherbe to be patient and to ignore the insults of the Dammel, who was "illiterate" and didn't understand the treaty negotiated in his name. France, as a "civilized" power negotiating with a "backward" country, had every reason to make sure both sides understood the treaty. Chaumet ended his speech with a plea for peace, based on his fear that war would destroy prosperity.[22] The military majority on the council ignored the fears of the representatives of commerce.

As he prepared to attack Kajoor and secure the election of a new king, Faidherbe maintained his contacts with prominent Muslim leaders. Faidherbe decided that the Muslims were too weak to rule Kajoor, but he made gestures in their direction. Before his first campaign in March, Faidherbe invited the population to overthrow their king and replace him with "someone who didn't drink."[23] Faidherbe was negotiating with various candidates for the throne, but his desire for Muslim support tipped the balance in favor of Maajoojo Faal, who had been the candidate of the rebels in 1859. Faidherbe supported Maajoojo and his ally Samba Maram Xaay on the assumption that they still had Muslim support. Faidherbe's new regime looked like an attempt to resurrect the coalition that had rebelled two years before.

During the March campaign, Faidherbe attempted to inflict heavy causalties on his enemy, in the hope that Makkodu would lose support. His column was an amalgamation of French regular forces and volunteers from Saint-Louis, who made up 25 percent of the 1,200 troops.[24] The campaign was a series of skirmishes, as Makkodu's forces withdrew, avoiding direct contact with French forces. Faidherbe estimated that he destroyed 25 villages, seized 500 head of cattle, and killed 300 Wolof soldiers, including some of the Dammel's army commanders.[25] The most effective French weapon was light field artillery, which wreaked havoc among African forces when flight was impossible. The French "victories," however, failed to produce any concrete political results. As a result, Faidherbe was forced to organize a third campaign in May, in which a similar French force joined up with 500 partisans of Maajoojo Faal. By this time the plans for Kajoor were clear. Maajoojo would be king. Maajoojo named Samba Maram Xaay as the head of the *jaambuur* and named the general who would command the royal slaves. As the French column pursued Makkodu, his hard-core contingent of supporters (which the French estimated at between 500 and 200 cavalry)[26] melted away, and the number of Maajoojo's partisans increased. By May 22, the French looked on as a majority of Kajoor's electors chose Maajoojo as the new king.[27]

By any standards, the reign of Maajoojo was a failure, both domestically and as a French effort to rationalize government. By December 1861, Maajoojo and Samba Maram Xaay were explaining their difficulties under the "new system," in which the right of the Dammel to pillage his subjects had been abolished. The villages of Taiba and Lao had refused to pay their taxes and to honor the rights of the king. The new king was a discontented convert to French ways of government. "Since we have renounced pillage and theft, we haven't been able to get anything out of our subjects."[28] The Dammel complained that the French had prevented him from "punishing" Lao, and then reported his plan to punish the Sereer, whom he described as "black savages who are our subjects." "They no longer obey me," he lamented, "instead of welcoming my envoys they beat them up and chase them out of their country."[29] Although Maajoojo complained that the French prevented him from doing as he wished, he in fact behaved according to the "old ways." At the end of December the French received a letter from Sëriñ Taiba, the leader of one of the villages cited by Maajoojo, who reported that the Dammel had pillaged his village, taking 70 rifles, 200 cattle, 100 goats, and 300 cloths that contained treasures of gold and silver. The troops of the Dammel were accused of expropriating food supplies, wrecking the fields under cultivation, and seizing twenty slaves, plus horses and donkeys, when they departed.[30]

Opposition to Maajoojo crystalized around Demba War Sall, the leader of the royal slaves of the deposed dynasty. Demba War represented a powerful family whose members dominated the slaves of the Geej and through them the state. Although they were "slaves" by status, their function as military commanders and overseers of the royal household better explains their social position. The royal slaves did not accept their ouster and sought a candidate to represent the Geej dynastic cause. By the end of 1861, Demba War had chosen Lat Joor, whom he visited in Kokki. Lat Joor was chosen for what he represented politically, a coming together of Geej royalism with Islam. Lat Joor's Islamic credentials, through his grandfather, a famous royal convert, and his mother, who was married to Sëriñ Kokki,[31] made up for his youth and the fact that he belonged to the wrong patrilineage. Lat Joor belonged to the Geej matriclan, but he was not a "Faal" who could trace his descent to the first king of Kajoor, as the rules of succession demanded. As a "Joob," Lat Joor had claims to rule over Geet province in eastern Kajoor, but not to reign as king. In epic celebrations of Lat Joor's memory by Wolof bards, the main narrative plotline between 1861 and Lat Joor's death in 1886 is the "friendship" of Demba War Sall and Lat Joor. Between 1861 and 1864, Geej forces inflicted several humiliating defeats on Maajoojo. Only French support of Maajoojo kept Lat Joor from being recognized as king. With two "kings," Kajoor suffered a state of prolonged war, until the French finally drove Lat Joor and his allies out of Kajoor in 1864.[32]

Demba War's decision to put Lat Joor on the throne was calculated to split the Muslim party. Demba War believed Lat Joor's candidacy would weaken Muslim opposition to the Geej dynasty. When chosen, Lat Joor was little more than a boy. Wolof bards recall that he still wore his boyhood locks and that Demba War Sall had to hold a circumcision ceremony in his honor.[33] The French estimated his age at sixteen or seventeen.[34] After the French drove Geej forces from Kajoor in 1864, the meaning of Lat Joor's candidacy was redefined in important ways. Demba War led his protégé into exile in Saalum and formed an alliance with Màbba Jaxu, whose jihad in Saalum presented a challenge to the traditional political order. This alliance between the Geej dynasty and Islam prepared the way for the restoration of Geej power at some future date.

The French did not immediately recognize the threat posed by these developments. They viewed the problem of "rationalization" as a question of replacing discredited or morally corrupt rulers with rulers more "favorable" to French interests. The French ignored the strength of the Geej dynasty, but noted the progress of Maajoojo's rehabiliation from *ceddo* depravity. French intelligence reported periodically on Maajoojo's behavior, as in June 1864:

> Madiodio [Maajoojo] remains sober and today one can affirm that he has entirely given up alcoholic drinks. He gives the example [to his people] of work by personally cultivating his vast domains.[35]

Maajoojo's sobriety was the good news. The main news was that Kajoor was suffering from a drought in June and July that threatened to bring famine to the country.[36] French merchants organized the distribution of emergency food relief for the famine victims in Kajoor in July 1864.[37]

For many decades the Wolof remembered 1865 simply as the "year of hunger" (*atumee xiif ba*).[38] The famine of 1865, which was the worst since the mid-eighteenth century, had multiple causes.[39] Widespread drought occurred for the second year in a row. As in the worst famines of the past, drought was compounded by war and by swarms of locusts. Warfare and locust swarms consumed much of the depleted harvest, as roving armies seized or burned grain reserves and locusts stripped the fields bare. In addition, an unidentified epidemic killed off the cattle herds, which normally served as a "reserve" of last resort during famines.[40] In 1865 the French organized famine relief on a much larger scale than in 1864. Thirteen French commercial houses pledged 30,000 francs to buy millet and to cover the costs of advancing peanut seed to peasants during the famine. The colonial authorities released supplies of millet and rice that they had collected in taxes or seized as fines in previous military campaigns. This "humanitarian" aid was seen as a means to consolidate French influence in Kajoor, even though it took the form of "loans" that had to be repaid from future harvests. During the famine relief efforts of 1865, French officials quietly suppressed the monarchy in Kajoor, judging their efforts to rule through Maajoojo a failure. They placed the best face on this series of disasters by seeing political reform and humanitarian assistance as two sides of the "regeneration" of Kajoor:

> We have succeeded in completing destroying banditry in Kajoor by getting rid of the Dammel and his *ceddo*, who previously controlled the central part of the country.[41]

In fact, the French efforts to rule Kajoor had failed. The worst nightmares of the French merchants had been realized. No one had any interest in advertising these setbacks, but in 1865 Kajoor was slipping into anarchy, with no central government. In some regions this meant that local rulers were virtually independent. In Njambur, Muslim community leaders achieved the kind of local self-government they had sought in the rebellion of 1859.[42] M'Barick Lo, the new Sëriñ Luuga, considered himself the governor of Njambur. In Sereer minority regions, which had always resisted the monarchy, the same state of virtual independence was achieved. In theory, French-appointed chiefs took control of the central provinces after 1865. But none of the rulers of Kajoor could protect its populations from periodic incursions by armed factions based in Bawol, Jolof, and Saalum, where Kajoor's civil war merged with larger conflicts between revolutionary Islam, aristocratic power, and the religion of the spirit powers.

THE JIHAD OF MÀBBA

Of all the religious conflicts of the nineteenth century, the jihad of Màbba Jaxu had the most direct impact on the Wolof kingdoms. As a result, Màbba figures prominently in Wolof historical memories and debates about holy war. Màbba's main target was the Sereer, but his conflicts with the French raised the question whether Muslims should fight colonial rule. The connection between Màbba and the Wolof states is based on his links with Lat Joor and with the family of Amadu Bamba. Màbba brought holy war waged in the name of Islam to the borders of the most important Wolof kingdoms, exacerbating divisions that had been laid bare during the insurrection of 1859. Three future Wolof kings, Lat Joor, Tanor Ngogne, and Alburi Njaay, fought with Màbba in the

1860s. Debates about Màbba's jihad were important at the time and helped define the attitude of a generation to holy war.

According to traditions preserved by Wolof bards, the decision to emigrate to Saalum was made by Demba War Sall. Màbba doubted the wisdom of welcoming Lat Joor, because he sought a "worldly kingdom" (*nguurug àdduna*). Màbba decided to welcome him only if he converted to Islam, shaved his head, and presented his shorn tresses to Màbba as a sign of his submission. When Demba War presented these conditions to Lat Joor he wanted to refuse on the grounds that he should not abandon his "character" (*jikko*). Demba War told him not to worry because conversion would be like cutting his hair. When it grew back no one would be able to tell it was ever cut.[43] The alliance between the Wolof aristocracy and Màbba was an alliance of circumstance, but it was more than an empty gesture. The future Wolof kings who fought for Islam believed that their commitment would bring them back to power. The survival of the aristocracy was at stake.

Epic traditions express a common judgment about the "conversion" of Lat Joor to Islam.[44] The alliance was political. The Kajoor exiles believed their adhesion to Islam would strengthen their claims to power when they returned to Kajoor. The political opportunism of Lat Joor's adhesion to Islam was real, but he maintained an Islamic commitment to the end of his life. The compromise that allowed the exiles to submit to Màbba was the work of Demba War Sall. He said: "Let us accept [Màbba's spiritual and military authority], but when we return [to Kajoor] we will do as we please." The agreement allowed the Kajoor exiles to live in residential segregation from Màbba's military forces, and to retain their own battle commands.[45] In his relations with Màbba, Demba War Sall never lost sight of his primary loyalty to Kajoor. In the critical battle against Siin in which Màbba was killed, Demba War Sall ordered the Kajoor exiles to stay back and reserve their forces. When the battle was lost and Màbba prepared for martyrdom, Demba War reminded Lat Joor of his duty to Kajoor and ordered his brothers Sangone and Bunama to remove him physically from the battlefield.[46]

Although Màbba's memory is celebrated today and historians have been sympathetic to the jihads of the nineteenth century, it is important to recall the controversies that surrounded Màbba's jihad in Kajoor and Bawol. Contemporary documentary sources give contradictory portraits of Màbba's jihad and its impact on Senegambia. French officials showed some sympathy for the jihad, convinced that Màbba and the Muslim party would prove favorable to the expansion of commerce and contribute to the destruction of the *ceddo* and the old regime. In 1864, just as Màbba made his prepa-

rations for the invasion of Siin, a French official in Kaolack reported hope-
fully: "Good relations will quickly be established between the followers of
Màbba and our traders, who are favorable to him in large part, being fed
up with the *ceddo*."[47] This optimism was based on the belief that the cultivation of peanuts and millet would expand rapidly under the influence of
Islam. Even when the extent of Màbba's military ambitions became clear,
the French were inclined to let him accomplish "the useful part of his
mission, the destruction of the *ceddo* of Sine and Saloum" and then deal
with him later.[48]

This favorable attitude to Màbba reflected French views of Wolof society, as divided between peaceful, industrious Muslims and brutal, pillaging
ceddo. This simple division between Muslim and *ceddo* failed to describe
the intense factional divisions that had been created by French intervention
in Kajoor. The civil war created a new constellation of factions and alliances that grouped together Muslims and aristocrats. French intelligence
reports captured the way these new alliances confounded a simplistic dichotomy between Muslim and *ceddo*:

> According to widespread reports Lat Joor has married the *lingeer* Debo
> to Màbba; at the same time he and his *kangam* [military command-
> ers], including Maye Sambaye [Meysa Mbaay],[49] have all become
> marabouts.[50]

The marriage of Màbba to the *lingeer*, like the "conversion" of Lat Joor
and his *ceddo* to Islam, forged a new alliance. At the same time there were
many Muslims who were openly critical of the jihad. An influential Muslim from Kajoor told the French:

> Màbba only makes war because of his ambition, to seize the country,
> slaves, cattle and money. There isn't a single Muslim in his army who is
> educated or inspired by true religious sentiment. They all are dreaming
> of pillage.[51]

The most critical European judgments of Màbba argued that he was
destroying the economy of Saalum and the Gambia River valley. When the
French asked the British for aid in their efforts to subdue Màbba in 1864,
the British were sympathetic. A British agent argued that Màbba's jihad
was destroying the commerce of the Gambia, but added that this was a
secondary consideration "in comparison with the ravages they have committed in destroying peaceable towns and villages, killing the male inhabitants, and taking the women and children into slavery."[52] After several
years of warfare, desolation now reigned in regions where cultivation had

been expanding for years. In some regions, desperate parents were offering "their children for sale for half a bag of rice" and in several towns people were dying from starvation.[53]

The Muslim leaders in the Wolof states were divided in their judgments of Màbba's jihad. Traces of these disagreements survive today. These memories provide important relfections on the meaning of this jihad. The best example is the attitude of Murid scholars. According to these scholars, Màbba recruited partisans for his jihad from Saalum, Bawol, and Jolof. His recruitment efforts in Bawol brought Amadu Bamba's father, Momar Anta Sali, to his court, along with other members of the family. Recruitment was modeled on the *hijra* (emigration) organized by Al Hajj Umar Taal and his successors to sustain Umar's jihad in the Niger River valley. Màbba was a disciple of Al Hajj Umar and a shaykh of the Tijani order. His goal was to organize a *hijra* to sustain his movement. The *hijra* was a call on Muslims to leave territories where they could not exercise their religion in freedom, and to take up jihad to protect a true Muslim state. In Umarian thought, *hijra* and *jihad* were linked together.[54] Màbba named his capital Nioro, in imitation of Umar. Most of his supporters were Wolof and Fulbe (Tukuloor) from Saalum, who were opposed to the way the Saalum monarchy compromised with the "spirit powers" of the non-Muslim Sereer. This local base for the revolution was buttressed by the active recruitment of Wolof and Fulbe "volunteers" and "recruits" from Bawol and Jolof.

Much of Amadu Bamba's family was caught unwillingly in Màbba's jihad. One of Amadu Bamba's grandfathers died during the emigration, although stories differ on whether this resulted from old age and health problems, or whether he was killed. The account by Bachir Mbacké focuses on the way Màbba recruited supporters for his jihad. Màbba "ordered all the Muslims in general and the *ulama* [scholars] in particular to emigrate to Saalum." Perhaps he did this to "save them from the vengence of the *ceddo*"; nevertheless, his orders "were disapproved of by some" who lived at peace with the rulers.

> Thus they all emigrated to Saalum, with the exception of those too weak to make the journey. These last were abandoned to themselves, and the religious commander forced their families to move to Saalum. That was one of the acts that certain people condemn. Nevertheless he [Màbba] can be excused for many of the errors committed by his clumsy policies and his refusal to consult, because his goal was to restore Islam and protect the Muslims.[55]

This is faint praise for a figure who has been revered as a crusader and as a "resistance" leader during the conquest of Senegal.[56] The same passage blames the lack of "true religious virtues" in the inner circle of Màbba's confidants for his failings. Then it concludes:

A fact has come to my attention that goes a long way to explaining the errors of Màbba: This man was not a scholar, he didn't have a deep knowledge of law, and he was completely inexperienced in politics.[57]

The discussion concludes with the wish that God pardon his faults and reward him for his efforts to revitalize Islam.

The same attitude toward Màbba was confirmed in interviews with Murid scholars in Darou-Mousty, a town in eastern Kajoor. Serigne M'Baye Guèye Sylla, when asked about Amadu Bamba's attitude toward the jihads that occurred during his lifetime, began by reminding me that Amadu Bamba's father was brought to Màbba's court in Saalum because Màbba wanted to rule according to Islam, "but he was not educated." Therefore he appointed Momar Anta Sali as judge, as did Lat Joor after him. Then he referred to the *qasida* (poem) that explained why Amadu Bamba refused to serve as a judge at court after his father's death. He would have been ashamed to be seen by angels at the court of a "worldly king." Finally, Sylla said: "For him there was only one jihad left, a struggle with the soul [literally, nose or breath], jihad al nafsi." [*Pur mom benn jihad moo desoon, mooy xeex ak sa bakkan, jihad al nafsi*].[58] He then elaborated on this idea, arguing that in truth [*ci batin*, in the Sufi sense of the "inner truth"] this was the only jihad. The age of the jihad of the sword [*jihad jaasi*] was over. The jihad of the soul was the only jihad recognized by the Murids. This doctrine was linked to Amadu Bamba's refusal to associate with worldly kings. They were, in effect, two sides of the same coin.

Another Murid scholar, Serigne Bassirou Anta Niang Mbacké, expressed the same idea in a more complex way. His teachings illustrate the way Sufi thought permeates the Murid tradition. Our discussion of jihad took place in a follow-up to our main interview and was held in front of his students. When asked what Sëriñ Tuuba [Amadu Bamba] thought about the jihads that took place during his lifetime, he began by saying that Màbba wanted to estabish Islam [*taxawaal*] throughout Senegal. He therefore gathered weapons and called on Muslims to join his struggle. He declared a jihad [*jiyaar*] against the unbelievers [*yéeféer*], in this case the Sereer, and in his wars he killed many unbelievers and many Europeans. Then Serigne Bassirou addressed the question of what Amadu Bamba thought of the jihad. He explained Bamba's teachings:

Màbba thought that through God he was guided to the right path, but it was not through God alone. There were slaves owned by free persons, slaves whose masters had bought them and who came with them and brought them into the war, and it was because of these slaves that God aided him to achieve victory, because of their labors.[59]

Serigne Bassirou's reference to the slaves contained a paradox of sorts. He later explained that their presence in the jihad came about through an error made by their masters.[60] Nevertheless he argued that it was the slaves' deeds and the fact that they won their freedom that made victory possible. After this apparent digression, Serigne Bassirou went on to list the reasons why Màbba's jihad was just and so was Amadu Bamba's agreement with it. "The war was sound, because Màbba did not fight because he wanted riches, he did not fight because he wanted slaves, he fought only for God." Serigne Bassirou continued: "God alone caused the war" [*Yalla rekk moo taxoon*]. He also stressed its legality: "He did it according to the law" [*Def na ko ci yoon*].[61]

Serigne Bassirou paused at this point. He had established the legal purity of the jihad, its fulfillment of the conditions required by Islamic law. The pause was interrupted by whispers from the students, who were concerned whether I had really understood what had been said. Serigne Bassirou then emphasized even more emphatically Amadu Bamba's agreement with the jihad, making an allusion once more to the "error" of bringing slaves into the war and its consequences. Then he abruptly shifted gears and asked, "But did Sëriñ Tuuba [Amadu Bamba] really agree, in his own thoughts [*ci boppam*]? No!"

He said [the age of] jihad is over. Because today jihad means . . . because today the jihad that is left is the jihad of the soul. The jihad of the soul means abandoning what God has forbidden and doing what he has recommended. . . . This is the greater, more difficult jihad.[62]

At this point he looked at me to see if I had understood and then he laughed.

Upon reflection, it became clear that Serigne Bassirou was giving a lesson about different levels of truth. From a legal point of view Màbba's jihad was sound, because it fulfilled the conditions imposed by Islamic law. The errors made involved the use of slaves in the war, but paradoxically, that became one of the reasons why God aided the jihad. It had become a means for slaves to achieve their freedom. But all this referred only to the external, legalistic level of reality, or *zahir* in Sufi thought. At the more esoteric, hidden level, *batin* in Sufi thought, the jihad of Màbba could not be supported, because the age of jihad was over.

THE REIGN OF LAT JOOR

Lat Joor has an important but ambiguous position in the history of Senegal and in Wolof memory of the past. Along with a handful of leaders from the last decades of precolonial independence, he has been adopted as a symbol of resistance to the French and figures prominently in popular interpretations of the conquest. Today many Wolof regard Lat Joor as a heroic symbol of the old regime. This contemporary image is based on a number of separate streams of evidence, written and oral, African and French. Many Wolof children can relate the story of Lat Joor and his horse Maawlaw and how Lat Joor refused the French railroad project. He vowed that he and his horse would die before seeing the railroad. This is a cliché that telescopes Lat Joor's reign into one image. Wolof bards perform an epic that celebrates Lat Joor because he died for honor. The praise-poem that begins and ends his epic recalls what the people of Kajoor say of Lat Joor:

> When we lost you we became soldiers [for the French], and paid our taxes; after you, all of these things.[63]

The bard's portrait of Lat Joor is only one of many. The contemporary image of Lat Joor also reflects the influence of the *habitants*. The *habitant* merchants of Saint-Louis adopted the cause of Lat Joor and an "independent" monarchy in the 1870s as a way of protecting their commerce. The *habitants* opposed the high-handed military policies of the French. They feared losing their position as intermediaries in Kajoor once the monarchy was destroyed and the railroad was completed. The "martyrdom" of Lat Joor in 1886 was already the occasion for nationalist protest.

Finally, Muslims, and particularly members of the Murid order, have important memories of Lat Joor based on his alliance with Màbba's jihad, his reign in Kajoor, and the fact that many members of his family became disciples of Amadu Bamba. Muslim memories are the most ambiguous. Lat Joor had difficult relations with Kajoor's Muslim community during his reign. Militant Muslims invaded Kajoor in 1874 and declared a jihad against Lat Joor. Many Muslims in Njambur province refused to fight or joined the invader. Lat Joor also had difficult relations with Amadu Bamba's father, Momar Anta Sali. What was true of the father was even truer of the son.

Much of Lat Joor's importance and ambiguity as a "symbol" derives from the fact that he figures prominently in the memory of all the parties who participated in the Wolof civil war. Many contemporary controversies draw their inspiration from the factional conflicts that wracked Kajoor in the 1870s and 1880s. When Lat Joor returned to the borders of Kajoor in 1869, he made overtures to the Muslim party and its allies. He hoped that his service with Màbba and his "conversion" made him an acceptable candidate for the throne. Nevertheless Lat Joor was still essentially the Geej candidate and the royal slaves formed the backbone of his army. Lat Joor was never able to overcome the contradictions between *ceddo* and Muslim in his own entourage. His reign can be divided into two periods. The first, from 1870 to 1875, was defined by conflicts over the place of Islam and the Muslim party in his reign. The issue of the railroad and French power in Kajoor dominated the second period of his reign, from 1875 to 1883.[64]

LAT JOOR AND ISLAM, 1870–1875

The return of Lat Joor and his partisans in 1869 came at a time favorable to their plans to restore the Geej dynasty to power. The French had overextended their military power in Senegal. Experiments with colonial rule in Waalo and Kajoor were judged as expensive failures that had produced few concrete results.[65] French and *métis* merchants were critical of military adventurism and its negative effects on commerce.[66] In these conditions it was not impossible for the former "enemies" of France to gain recognition once they had proven their local strength. French weakness gave Lat Joor and his allies the breathing space they needed. Nevertheless from the beginning they were forced to recognize that any "restoration" would not be a return to the past. The treaty that recognized Lat Joor as king in 1871 forced Kajoor to cede the northern and southern border provinces to the French and their allies.[67] However, even before Lat Joor could win French recognition he had to demonstrate his political strength. He did this in a series of military skirmishes that inflicted defeats on French forces. At the same time he opened negotiations with the notables of Kajoor.

In 1869 Lat Joor camped on the border of Kajoor and Bawol and began calling on his supporters to migrate to Bawol. Those who refused would be exposed to retaliatory raids. This threatened to destroy the trade of Kajoor, which was still recovering from the famine years of 1864–1866. To deal with this threat, the Muslim leaders in Njambur proposed in January 1870 to get rid of all the chiefs appointed by the

French and replace them with one ruler, the Lingeer Debbo.[68] As queen, she would rule in conjunction with the notables of Kajoor, in this case the Muslim party, acting as regent for her son, who was ten.[69] This impractical proposal was abandoned in April when the Muslim party rallied behind Omar Niang (Ñaan), who had served as chief of M'Bakol since at least 1866.[70] The new proposal was to elect Omar Niang as Jawriñ-Mbul, the highest traditional title held by a commoner, and to support Lat Joor. On April 24 an assembly of 300 notables met to deliberate. The group included the leaders of the Muslim party and supporters of Lat Joor. They voted to elect Omar Niang Jawriñ-Mbul. Lat Joor was offered the throne, if he agreed to rule in conjunction with Omar Niang. In June, Lat Joor was elected king.

Lat Joor came to power with the conditional support of the Muslim party.[71] The Muslims were not swayed by his past alliance with Màbba, but by the agreements negotiated in 1870. Omar Niang had been critical of Màbba. In 1866 he had complained to the French that Màbba's partisans had pillaged M'Bakol, seizing property, carrying away slaves, and enslaving free persons.[72] Màbba had been condemned by many of Kajoor's most prominent Muslims for the same reasons.[73] Nevertheless, the Muslim party was persuaded that Lat Joor had made a firm commitment to Islam. Omar Niang, who would lead the Muslim "betrayal" of Lat Joor in 1874, looked back on his decision, explaining: "We had heard that Lat Joor had become a Muslim and that is why we elected him."[74] Lat Joor's election had important political consequences. He could not replace the Muslims who had gained power under the French, and his powers of patronage were reduced.

Because Lat Joor's hands were tied in Kajoor, he adopted an aggressive foreign policy. As soon as he consolidated his power base in Kajoor, he attempted to conquer Bawol. Although Lat Joor was able to occupy the capital of Bawol in 1873, he was never able to secure his power there.[75] If he had been successful, the conquest of Bawol would have allowed Lat Joor to reward his *ceddo* chiefs with appointments. As it was, his invasion of Bawol only won him the hostility of Amadu Seexu, who was building a new jihad movement in Fuuta Tooro and Jolof. Amadu Seexu's jihad emerged in the aftermath of a devastating cholera epidemic in the Senegal River valley in 1869, winning support from Muslims convinced that the epidemics and famines that swept the region from 1864 to 1869 were signs from God. In Kajoor the movement won support from Muslims convinced that Lat Joor's reign was a return to aristocratic domination and continual warfare, as indicated by his invasion of Bawol.

All of these events led to a crisis in 1874–1875, when Amadu Seexu invaded Kajoor, declaring a jihad against Lat Joor and his allies. There is good reason to believe that members of the Muslim party invited Amadu into Kajoor. This was a renewal of civil war, with a substantial portion of the Muslim party defecting to Amadu. One of the first indications that something was afoot came in February, when Omar Niang warned the French that "something extraordinary" was about to happen in Kajoor.[76] Amadu Seexu occupied parts of Kajoor in the first months of 1874 and inflicted a first defeat on Lat Joor in July, when Omar Niang and Sëriñ Luuga joined forces with Amadu. Lat Joor was defeated again in October and forced to retreat. In his correspondence with the French, Lat Joor described Omar Niang and the chiefs of Njambur as "traitors" and blamed them for his difficulties.[77] The one bright spot was the successful resistance to Amadu by Demba War Sall, who fortified a position at Saq (in northern Kajoor) and killed a hundred of Amadu's men, while losing only five of his own soldiers.[78]

Lat Joor and his allies fled to French protection in Ganjool in October and asked the French for military aid. By December 1874, even some members of the Muslim party were worried about the continued occupation of northern Kajoor by Amadu. Sëriñ Luuga, who had aided Amadu, wrote to the French to express his concerns about the "destruction" of the country.[79] In January, the French organized a military column that fought alongside forces loyal to Lat Joor. Amadu suffered a serious defeat at Kokki in January and was killed a month later.

The events of 1874–1875 had serious consequences and are well documented in oral traditions linked to the main participants in the civil war. Wolof memories of the war against "Amadu the Tijani" provide insights into the internal politics of Kajoor under Lat Joor. Aristocratic traditions focus on the growing tensions between Lat Joor and Demba War Sall, while both Muslim and aristocratic traditions see the conflict as a turning point in relations between Lat Joor and the Muslim community. The war of 1875 also laid the groundwork for French colonialism. Because Lat Joor asked the French for aid, he would have to pay the price in the future.

Aristocratic memories focus on the consequences of the war. In Bassirou Mbaye's "epic" of Lat Joor, this is summed up by linking French military aid to the railroad project and to the end of the "friendship" between Lat Joor and Demba War Sall. After his defeat by Amadu, Lat Joor tells the French:

> Help me against Amadu Seexu.
> When he has been driven from the country,

the thing that you asked me for,
the rail between Saint-Louis and Dakar,
I will give it to you.[80]

Mbaye, a royal bard whose grandfather died at Sàq,[81] describes the conflict as a "civil war" [Wolof, *xeexub biirum réew*, "a war in the country"], and recalls that Demba War fought Amadu and Omar Niang while Lat Joor stood on the sidelines. More importantly, he says that Demba War rejected the agreement between Lat Joor and the French, which was witnessed by Lat Joor's new confidant, Masekk Ndóoy, and a Muslim scholar, Majaxate Kala. Lat Joor and Demba War quarreled and Lat Joor announced that Masekk Ndóoy would replace Demba War as the king's chief advisor [*farabiir-kër*].[82]

Because the "alliance" of Lat Joor and Demba War is the central narrative of the epic, the war with Amadu Seexu is the turning point in the story. For Wolof listeners, Masekk Ndóoy and Majaxate Kala symbolize the characteristics of the new government created by Lat Joor after the war. According to Lat Joor's grandson, Amadu Bamba Diop, the choice of Masekk was unfortunate, because he could not compare with Demba War. But Diop notes that Lat Joor made his decision after meeting with a group of notables who warned him against giving too much power to one family. Others were equally entitled to hold power.[83] Amadu Bamba Diop argues that Lat Joor was a reformer and a sincere Muslim, while Demba War was a traditionalist. In the aftermath of his near defeat, Lat Joor gave in to pressure to appoint officials from outside the inner circle who had returned from exile in 1869. This concession to the Muslim party was made at the expense of Demba War Sall. He kept his territorial command, but lost his position as the king's chief advisor.

The reference to Majaxate Kala has the same significance. Majaxate Kala replaced Momar Anta Sali (Amadu Bamba's father) as chief judge in the aftermath of the war with Amadu Seexu. Momar Anta Sali had returned to Kajoor with Lat Joor in 1869 and accepted a position as chief Muslim judge (Wolof, *xaali*). Momar Anta Sali founded a village near Lat Joor's residence, where he settled with his family and students. Lat Joor's grandson says that Momar Anta Sali was unpopular because his judgments were based on a strict interpretation of the Quran, but also because he was a "stranger," with no roots in Kajoor. He explains that pressure from Amadu Bamba forced his father to resign. Amadu Bamba left a note for his father that read: "Even the most honest judge has to settle his accounts with God."[84] The resignation of

Momar Anta Sali prepared the way for the rise of Majaxate Kala, a famous scholar with ties to the Muslim party. Kala had no close ties to Lat Joor and had warned the French in 1870 that Lat Joor was a "common liar."[85] Once appointed, however, Majaxate Kala became famous for decisions that served the interests of the court.

Memories of royal bards and family members present the narrative preserved by partisans of the Geej. Other Wolof sources reinforce the significance of 1875. Tanor Latsoukabé Fall, a descendant of the royal house of Bawol, recalled aspects of the war that led to a rupture between Lat Joor and Demba War Sall. Lat Joor was celebrating his victory in Bawol and had just formed a government with Demba War as the *farba kaba* (head of royal slaves and government minister), when he heard of the invasion of Kajoor. When he returned to Kajoor he suffered two military defeats and fled to Ganjool to ask for help from the French.

> But his valiant army commander, Farba Demba War, didn't agree. He regrouped his forces and constructed a fort at Sakné [Sàq] where he waited for the Tukuloor [Amadu Seexu and his Futanke soldiers]. All the princes of Kajoor aided him. They endured the struggle against the enemy from morning until night and completely exhausted their ammunition in their heroic defense against superior numbers. When night fell they escaped in the darkness and rejoined the Dammel, who was awaiting the outcome of the battle in his retreat at Ganjool.[86]

The details of the battle at Sàq underscore the growing tensions between the king and his chief minister and explain why Lat Joor has been accused of ingratitude. They also remind us that Demba War Sall was named to an important position in Bawol in 1873, shortly before he fell into disfavor.

Muslim sources also recall the conflicts of 1874–1875. Sources close to Lat Joor suggest that he responded to the defeat of 1874–1875 by opening his court to Kajoor notables who had been excluded until then. He did so to counteract the political weaknesses that had led to his defeat. The opening to "notables" began only after Lat Joor dealt with the "traitors" who had threatened his reign. Lat Joor's grandson recalls the repression of the Muslims who had sided with Amadu:

> A little while after the war Lat Joor set a trap for four marabouts from Louga who had sided with the invader. He had them killed to take the spirit of rebellion out of the other marabouts, because their rebellious spirit had harmed Kajoor and ruined the authority of the Dammel.[87]

Murid sources which trace the life of Amadu Bamba deal with these events because of their importance in the life of both Momar Anta Sali and his son. Here, it is the father who is important. The most important Murid commentary on 1875 begins with an account of the controversy among Muslims about the war between Kajoor and Amadu Seexu. The passage begins by casting doubt on the sincerity of the jihad. "Amadu Seexu, a man from the Fuuta, pretended to wage jihad against the rulers of Kajoor, to convert them to Islam in spite of the fact that they prayed, fasted, and made the declaration of faith. God understands better what it really was."[88] This statement is a reminder that not all Muslims supported the jihad in Kajoor. In the aftermath of the war, a controversy raged among Muslims over whether the victors could enslave their defeated enemies.

Amadu Bamba's father ruled that the war had been a war between Muslims, and that therefore no prisoners could be enslaved and the property of the defeated should be returned. The court ignored this ruling and found other Muslim judges who were willing to rule that it was legitimate to enslave the prisoners and seize their property. Murid sources also condemn the way Lat Joor repressed the Muslims of Kajoor who had sided with his enemy. Amadu Bamba told his son Bachir that one day he saw the bodies of Muhammad Fati and Alé Lô while visiting the court on an errand for his father. Both men were from prominent Muslim families in Njambur, families that held titles and positions of leadership. They had been executed after having been held bound in captivity. Amadu Bamba said: "When I stopped before the two corpses, I rejected whatever small attachment I still had to this world."[89] The story of the two corpses clearly relates to the aftermath of the war of 1875.

Murid traditions help to explain why Majaxate Kala replaced Momar Anta Sali. Majaxate Kala was renowned for his ability to reconcile Islamic law with the customs of Kajoor. Majaxate Kala authorized Lat Joor to collect the Muslim tax designed to provide alms for the poor (Wolof, *assaka*), in a controversial legal decision.[90] More importantly, Majaxate Kala's nomination could be seen as a gesture to the Muslim party.[91] The most important concrete issue was the status of war booty taken in Kajoor's conflict with Amadu Seexu. Majaxate Kala allowed that Kajoor's struggle was justified and he legitimized the seizure of war booty taken from fellow Muslims and the enslavement of the prisoners.

Lat Joor returned to power with the conditional aid of the Muslim party, but he was never able to win their full support. When he invaded Bawol in 1873, Muslims believed that he had betrayed the bargain that placed him on the throne. As a result, an important faction within the Muslim party supported the invasion of Kajoor by Amadu Seexu in 1875. By the end of the war, new issues and new conflicts had emerged. Lat Joor's brutal suppression of the Muslim traitors and his decision to enslave his defeated enemies were criticized. His efforts to win support from the Muslim party by removing Demba War Sall from power were criticized as spineless ingratitude by those who remembered Demba War Sall's heroic stand in the war against Amadu. His decision to appoint Majaxate Kala as chief judge won him some support within Kajoor, but was seen by others as a sign of opportunism and lack of real faith. Above all, Lat Joor faced the future without the support of Demba War Sall and the royal slaves, who had put him on the throne.

LAT JOOR AND THE RAILROAD, 1875–1883

The issue of the railroad dominated the second half of Lat Joor's reign. In the aftermath of the war with Amadu Seexu, Lat Joor made political concessions to the Muslim party, but he also renewed his efforts to satisfy his court by pursuing expansion. In 1875–1876, Kajoor once again invaded Bawol and Jolof. Although Lat Joor succeeded in placing his cousin Alburi Njaay on the throne of Jolof, he could not secure his power in Bawol.[92] This meant that he had to satisfy the demands by his entourage for titles and rewards from his power base in Kajoor, which was limited by his agreements with the French. For Lat Joor, the railroad might provide an opportunity to renegotiate. The issue that concerned him was the return of Ganjool and Jander provinces, which were controlled by the French under the terms of the treaty of 1871.[93] The railroad was on the French agenda after 1875, but no formal agreement was made until 1879 when Lat Joor signed a treaty authorizing the French to take possession of a thin strip of land in Kajoor and to build the railroad. However, the treaty failed to return Kajoor's lost provinces.

Lat Joor's "secret" agreement with the French, authorizing the construction of a railroad, became the focal point of factional strife in Kajoor.[94] In 1879, Lat Joor attempted to remove Demba War and his relatives from the positions they held in Kajoor. This proved to be difficult. Demba War Sall had been the chief military commander in Kajoor for over two decades, and he and three of his brothers held positions as province chiefs. When their power was threatened, Demba War Sall put forward Samba Lawbé Faal, Lat Joor's nephew, as a rival candidate for the throne.[95] If Kajoor had been independent, Demba War Sall could have engineered the deposition of Lat Joor in 1879. The electors of the kingdom met and voiced their support for Samba Lawbé as king.[96] Samba Lawbé was a young man, but he had proven his valor in Kajoor's recent war with Jolof. More importantly, he was both Geej (maternally) and Faal (paternally), which meant he had a stronger claim to the throne than Lat Joor. The election had no immediate effect, because the French now claimed the sole right to recognize a king. On the other hand, Demba War had revealed his political hand.

In 1881, Lat Joor began to distance himself from the railroad project, even though he now depended on French support. The evidence suggests that Demba War Sall and his allies pushed Lat Joor in this direction, knowing that it would lead to a crisis. The most important pressure came from Samba Lawbé, who announced his opposition to the railroad. Samba Lawbé was clearly following the instructions of Demba War Sall. The battle over the railroad was purely and simply a power struggle between Lat Joor and Demba War Sall. All the parties involved in the power struggle had "approved" the railroad in the negotiations of 1879.[97] By having Samba Lawbé declare his opposition to the railroad, Demba War Sall put pressure on Lat Joor to follow suit, knowing he would lose French support. At the same time, Demba War and Samba Lawbé privately assured the French that they supported the project.[98] If this was not clear enough, one of Demba War's brothers, Ibra Fatim Sarr, was the only important state official to openly support the railroad in 1881–1882.[99] Once Lat Joor publicly declared his opposition to the railroad he found it difficult to go back on his word. In 1882 Lat Joor vowed to fight to stop the railroad.

The decision to build a railroad linking Saint-Louis and Dakar forced the French to secure their position in Kajoor. The French parliament authorized funds for the railroad in 1882. French metropolitan visions of railroads opening up vast tracts of Africa to "civilization" provided a golden opportunity for French officials in Senegal. Kajoor's political struggle threatened these plans. Confident of their military strength, the French sent a column into Kajoor in 1882 and oversaw the election of a new Dammel, just as they had in 1861. This was an unexpected development for Demba War Sall. Samba Yaaya Debbo Sukko, who was proclaimed king by the French with the title Amari Ngoone II, had no support in Kajoor. He came from the Dorobe faction of the aristocracy that had sought power through the Muslim party since the 1850s. However, the Muslim party had now won its main demand, self-rule in Njambur province. Muslims had no reason to support Samba Yaaya, who had a reputation as a drunkard. French military intervention drove the partisans of Samba Lawbé and Lat Joor into exile and threatened the export economy of Kajoor. Far from being secured for the French,

Kajoor was paralyzed by political conflict. In 1882, the French administration faced potential disaster. Merchants in Saint-Louis protested against policies that would destroy commerce. Further turmoil could lead to the loss of metropolitan funds for railroad construction. Colonial officials were forced to make concessions to African realities.

The events of 1882–1883 clarified the position of the factions in Kajoor. Lat Joor remained intransigent in his defense of Kajoor's sovereignty and tried to use Islam to build a new coalition of support. Demba War Sall and Samba Lawbé began negotiations with the French over the issue of the railroad. They promised to bring the Kajoor exiles back before the planting season of 1883 if the French recognized Samba Lawbé as king and restored his allies to power. Demba War and Samba Lawbé agreed to cede the land necessary for the railroad, to cooperate with its construction, to police Kajoor for the French, and to encourage the development of peaceful commerce. The French accepted the offer of Demba War Sall, and Samba Lawbé was proclaimed king in 1883. As a concession to the Muslim party, Njambur province was given its independence under Ibramina N'Diaye, a chief acceptable to the Muslims in the province.

When Demba War Sall and Samba Lawbé made their deal with the French in 1883, they "rolled back" an unacceptable form of French colonial rule. France's chosen ally, Samba Yaaya, was removed from the throne and exiled to Saint-Louis. Demba War Sall and Samba Lawbé negotiated a settlement from a position of strength. They were still capable of military resistance, even if they understood its futility. They understood the importance of the export economy, using the threat of emigration and a boycott of commerce to get rid of the French regime. The treaty of 1883 resolved the most pressing issues between Kajoor and the French. After the treaty was signed, railroad construction made rapid progress. The Dakar-Saint-Louis railroad was completed without incident in 1885. In fact the French soon noted that the railroad and commerce were more secure in Kajoor than they were in territories under direct French administrative control. French merchants were pleased with the arrangement and forged close ties with Samba Lawbé and his *ceddo* allies.[100]

THE KAJOOR PROTECTORATE, 1883–1890

The political battle over the railroad is open to misinterpretation. Lat Joor's rejection of the railroad grew out of his efforts to maintain himself on the throne, rather than out of opposition to export agriculture. While French political intervention had nearly destroyed Kajoor's export economy

Table 2.1   Peanut Exports from Senegal (metric tons), 1870–1882

1870	22,598
1871	26,866
1872	22,431
1873	23,356
1874	37,279
1875	30,010
1876	23,409
1877	24,252
1878	55,000
1879	40,000
1880	52,816
1881	59,970
1882	83,000

Source: M. Courtet, *Étude sur le Sénégal* (Paris, 1903); Oskar Lenz, *Timbuktu: Reise durch Marokko, die Sahara und den Sudan* (Leipzig, 1884), vol. 2, 348 (based on meetings with Governor Bère de l'Isle); Xavier Guiraud, *L'arichide sénégalaise: monographie d'économie coloniale* (Paris, 1937); Jean Adam, *L'arichide: Culture, produits, commerce, amélioration de la production* (Paris, 1908).

in the 1860s, peanut cultivation flourished under Lat Joor from 1870 to 1882. By the time of the railroad crisis, the monarchy, the royal slaves, and the Muslim party of Kajoor were all deeply involved in the first "boom" of export production, which peaked during the crisis of 1882. Peanut exports expanded rapidly, beginning in the late 1860s, just before Lat Joor's return to Kajoor. Exports rose from around 8,000 metric tons in 1859[101] to 22,142 metric tons in 1867.[102] Exports doubled again in the second half of Lat Joor's reign, reaching levels of 50,000 metric tons for the first time. Peanut exports fell precipitously during the years of political conflict that began in 1883. Exports would not reach the 50,000 metric ton mark until 1893, and the peak year of 1882 would not be equaled until 1898.

Export data allow an estimate of Kajoor's and Bawol's contribution to total exports in the period 1886–1889. In 1886, Kajoor and Bawol exported 85 percent of the total crop (17,000 out of 20,200 metric tons), outproducing other regions by a wide margin.[103] Although there is little direct evidence about peanut cultivation, evidence from the 1880s and 1890s suggests that peanuts were produced both by free peasant households and by slave labor. One of the main themes of Lat Joor's correspondence with the French was his frequent complaints that his slaves were fleeing to French territory to obtain their liberty.[104] During the period from 1870 to 1882, a series of wars in the interior regions of Senegambia and the Upper Niger increased the availability of slaves throughout the region. There is little doubt that many slaves entered the peanut basin and contributed to the development of peanut exports. Demba War Sall intervened frequently to protect the slave trade to Kajoor and to prevent the flight of slaves to French territories and freedom.[105] It seems likely that slaves produced much of the export crop in this period.

The expansion of exports under Lat Joor calls into question some interpretations of the social base of the new export economy. In 1972, Martin A. Klein published an influential article, which argued that the abolition of the export slave trade and the growth of peanut exports were linked to the decline of aristocratic power and the rise of militant Islam. This was because Senegambian monarchies could no longer monopolize export earnings, and the sale of peanuts placed guns in the hands of ordinary peasants.[106] These arguments overstate the social impact of the new export economy at this point in time. Peanut exports favored small producers in the long run, but only after the decline of the internal slave trade and the beginnings of slave emancipation.[107] In addition, Klein's interpretation has a cultural dimension, based on the idea that the aristocracy was attached to slave raiding and pillage, while Muslims took advantage of the new cash crop. In Kajoor, both Muslim and *ceddo* saw the advantages of the peanut trade.

Two important issues remained unresolved in 1883. One was the right of Kajoor to wage war on its neighbors as it pleased, a right affirmed by Samba Lawbé, who led a disastrous attack on Jolof in 1886. The French regarded this as a violation of their treaty with Kajoor. The second issue was slavery and French policy toward runaway slaves who sought refuge and liberty on French soil. Slavery was a critical issue for the Wolof aristocracy. The colonial administration was willing to ignore the issue of domestic slavery, but was under intense metropolitan pressure in the 1880s to clean up the image of the French colonies. In 1880 the French government instructed the Senegalese administration to adhere to the letter of the law of 1848 that abolished slavery in French colonies and promised freedom to any slave who escaped to French soil. Slaves were no longer to be returned to their masters, as had often occurred in the past.[108]

The status of slavery was ambiguous under the treaty of 1883. In Kajoor, which was a protectorate, slavery was legal. Nevertheless, slaves only had to flee to Tivaouane or any of the other French posts along the railroad to reach French soil and liberty. Kajoor's ruling class believed that the treaty protected slavery. They were enraged when the French administration offered refuge to runaway slaves. This occurred in 1886 when the commandant at Tivaouane refused to give up slaves who had fled to the French post. His action provoked a confrontation with Demba War Sall and Ibra Fatim Sarr, who surrounded the French post with cavalry forces and ordered the commandant to release the runaway slaves.[109] The French interpreted this skirmish as a rebellion, and sent a punitive column into Kajoor. The column never made contact with the *ceddo* chiefs, but Samba Lawbé was found trying to collect taxes from the merchants in Tivaouane. In the encounter that followed, Samba Lawbé Faal was killed, even though he had played no part in the incident that led to the dispatch of the column.[110]

The death of Samba Lawbé was the first step in the abolition of the monarchy. The French refused to recognize the claims of Lat Joor, who was living in exile.[111] Instead they negotiated a new settlement with Demba War Sall. Slavery was the dominant issue in the negotiations. The French promised Demba War Sall they would not interfere with slavery, fearing his threats to lead a massive emigration from Kajoor.[112] Two weeks after the new agreement was signed, Demba War led the French to Lat Joor, who was killed at Deqlé in 1886 along with a small group of relatives and close allies. This battle has become a symbol of Wolof resistance to the conquest and is used to date the end of the old regime in the Wolof states. The monarchy in Kajoor died with Lat Joor.

Nevertheless, the transition to colonial rule was hardly a conquest. The battles between Kajoor and the French occurred from 1861 to 1871. Colonial rule did not emerge from the barrel of a gun, but from the smokestack of the railroad. Demba War's efforts to preserve some of the substance of the monarchy received political support from powerful *métis* merchants in Saint-Louis. The alliance between Saint-Louis merchants and the court of Kajoor began in the 1870s, based on mutual interests in the export trade in peanuts. In 1885 and 1886, two new newspapers were founded, *Le Réveil du Sénégal* and *Le Pétit Sénégalais*. These papers reflected the opinion of Saint-Louis' merchant elite, particularly as defined by Gaspard Devès and Jean-Jacques Crespin. *Métis*

politicians were determined to defend their own interests against the
large Bordeaux trading firms and to avoid a repetition of the commercial losses that had occurred when the French took over the gum trade
in the 1840s and 1850s.[113] They had developed special relations with
Kajoor during the reign of Lat Joor and were determined to maintain
them. When the French killed Samba Lawbé in 1886, there were bitter
protests. In Saint-Louis the death was described as an "execution."

> In Cayor, the Governor's policy has no name. . . . This policy has
> halted commerce in the country and seriously compromised its inter-
> ests, adding to the present crisis another dimension. . . . Will Cayor,
> placed under our protection, be better administered and produce as
> much as in the past? We hope so with all our heart, but when we see
> the state of material and spiritual misery which has characterized
> Waalo since our annexation . . . we can only doubt the future of
> Cayor.[114]

With the death of Samba Lawbé, the merchant community embraced
Demba War Sall as the next best thing to the monarchy.[115] Demba War
Sall maintained good relations with French and African traders from
Saint-Louis, whom he cultivated as political allies. This was facilitated
by his marriage alliance with the Descemet family of Saint-Louis, an
important political family with strong commercial connections.[116] Demba
War's relations with the commercial and political elite of Saint-Louis
were extensive. He dealt directly with trading firms like Devès et
Chaumet, and with politicians like François Carpot and Durand Valentin,
whose business interests he supported in exchange for credit and political support.[117]

Demba War Sall became the superior chief of the Cayor Federation,
a grouping of six provinces under the command of Demba War, his
brothers, and his closest allies. The Cayor Protectorate of 1886 was the
first successful exercise in state building in rural Senegal. The Protectorate of 1886 was an improvised solution to a specific problem. For
decades the French had vilified the *ceddo*. Faidherbe had described
ceddo-dominated Kajoor as a land afflicted by "the lawless violence of
a horde of drunken brutes."[118] The violence of the *ceddo* was contrasted
with the industry of the Muslim population. After 1886, French attitudes changed because the French now sought a way to translate military power into effective authority. With the abolition of the monarchy,
Demba War Sall ruled by portraying himself as the successor of the
Geej dynasty. By bringing permanent peace, he won the allegiance of
the *jaambuur*. Demba War preserved the Muslim organization of justice

that had been created by Lat Joor, although he replaced some of the judges with men of his own choosing.[119] This was a clear indication that there was no inevitable conflict between Muslim leaders and *ceddo*.

Demba War Sall and his *ceddo* allies were successful in adapting to the new demands of the cash-crop economy. The most common remark in the administrative files on the chiefs in Kajoor during the first ten years of the protectorate was that they devoted more time to cultivation than to administration.[120] Economic adaptation was facilitated by Wolof attitudes toward land and agriculture. Agriculture was regarded as a "noble" profession, and was the only form of manual labor that could be performed by members of the nobility and their warrior clients without shame or loss of status.[121] It is also clear that Demba War Sall and his chiefs were not working the land by themselves. They mobilized their clients and slaves, and developed a form of estate agriculture. The *ceddo* chiefs built their wealth on the basis on their ability to mobilize and control labor, which was reinforced by their political power. Cash-crop production was more important to their wealth than the salaries and remittances paid by the French. The greatest threat to this system was French hostility toward slavery.

Politically, the most striking success of Demba War Sall was his ability to make himself the uncontested master of Kajoor for the first decade and a half of colonial rule, and then to pass on much of his power to his successors. The economy recovered gradually from the collapse of production that followed the political instability of 1883–1886. Demba War became the most influential African advisor to the French. He provided troops and intelligence during the campaigns against Bawol and Jolof in 1890, and influenced the French choice of rulers for both protectorate regimes.[122] In Kajoor itself, Demba War's authority was virtually unchallenged. A series of French commandants tried to introduce reforms, but they failed because of Demba War's personal access to the upper levels of the administration and his political alliances in Saint-Louis.[123] In the 1890s, the French described Demba War as the wealthiest and most powerful chief in Senegal, although they already regarded him as something of an anachronism, a throwback to the era of the Dammels. With his death in 1902, an era in the history of Kajoor ended, but not the "Sall" dynasty.[124]

One final question should be raised. Did it matter that Demba War Sall and his chief allies were "royal slaves"? For almost all Wolof, it made no difference. The only complaints about Demba War and his allies came from the *garmi*, who protested that the French had granted power to their "slaves." Most Wolof viewed the *ceddo* elite as a subgroup of the aristocracy, not as "slaves."[125] This tendency to "erase" the memory of slave origins has continued. During the centenary of Lat Joor's death, the descendants of Demba War Sall protested when historians referred to their ancestor as a royal slave. In defense of their position they told a story about the origins of the Sall family. They claimed that the first Sall was a free noble who voluntarily served the Wolof king Latsuukabe. He became a royal slave through the duplicity of the king, who gave him a slave as a wife.[126] Therefore, slavery had been a technicality, rather than a reality, from the beginning.

In one sense it did matter. The ability of Demba War Sall to make concessions to the French was facilitated by his status. Both Lat Joor and Samba Lawbé Faal had seen the necessity for a settlement, but had been unable to make it work. The aristocratic code of honor, which was dinned into the nobility by the bards, make it extremely difficult for the *garmi* to relinquish territory and to renounce warfare. The royal slaves, who had managed the royal household, the court, and the army, found it easier to adopt a pragmatic attitude toward the advent of colonial rule. From their point of view, the French replaced the king, while they continued to manage affairs, just as before.

SLAVERY, DISANNEXATION, AND CONQUEST

By 1890 the Kajoor Protectorate had begun to influence French policy, as the French prepared to extend their conquest to the rest of Senegal. The French allowed the protectorate to live on, instead of annexing it to the colony of Senegal. By 1890 they were attempting to generalize from their experience in Kajoor. Governor Clement-Thomas described the new policy as "disannexation." The basis for the policy was an evaluation of the success of the Kajoor Protectorate and the failure of direct rule in Waalo.[127]

Governor Clement-Thomas's new policy rolled back some of the abolitionist principles that had been imposed by politicians in France in the 1880s. He could justify such a measure only by arguing that the "republican" victories of the 1880s were at the root of all his problems in 1890. In 1880 a republican campaign was mounted in the press and the French Chamber of Deputies against the practice of returning slaves to their masters from French soil. The minister of the navy, Jauréguiberry, came under personal attack for practices he had condoned when he was governor of Senegal from 1861 to 1863. In response, Jauréguiberry ordered the governor of Senegal to apply the law of 1848, including Article 7. This article declared that the presence of a slave on French soil automatically liberated the slave. Jauréguiberry specifically ordered the governor to put an end to the practice of returning slaves to their masters, in order to eliminate all ambiguity.

The result of these decrees was a massive movement of emigration away from the French territories that had been placed under direct rule.[128] This emigration, which was led by Fulbe pastoral herdsmen, was noted first in 1882 and continued steadily until 1890. In the area near Saint-Louis alone, 30,000 to 40,000 Fulbe had left French territory. Governor Clement-Thomas, who took office in 1888, launched a major inquiry into the causes of emigration. The conclusions of this study justified the policy of disannexation. Clement-Thomas condemned the Interior Bureau and its Department of Native Affairs, which had recklessly interfered with the traditions and customs of the peoples under their authority. One of his first acts as governor was to abolish the Interior Bureau, which had "completely withdrawn the inhabitants of the annexed territories from the authority of the Governor."[129] Yet, according to Clement-Thomas, these territories were less secure and more prone to unrest than the Kajoor Protectorate. If republican legislation prevented the governor from restricting the application of French law, then the geographical areas where French law was applied had to be limited to a strict minimum:[130]

> By substituting a liberally interpreted protectorate system for the regime of annexation and direct rule, we are abandoning a harmful policy, which alienated the native populations and was creating a desert all around us. . . . From now on they will live side by side with us, content to obey us because we will no longer be in a head-on clash with their ways and customs, and they will have confidence in our protection which will ensure their tranquillity and dependence.[131]

Disannexation provided a more general solution to the problem of slavery than had been achieved in Kajoor. During the conquest, the incidents that led to the death of Samba Lawbé Faal brought into focus the problem posed by the institution of slavery in rural Senegal. In 1892, Clement-Thomas signed a treaty on slavery with all the chiefs in protectorate states. The treaty abolished the slave trade and defined the conditions under which a slave could purchase his or her freedom. House slaves were referred to in the treaty as "servants" and their status was "clarified" in a way that satisfied the slave-owning chiefs upon whom the French had come to depend.[132] At the same time, the euphemism "servants" disguised the French recognition of slavery.

Disannexation had additional advantages to recommend it to the French. The separation of the rural areas from the old colony of Senegal drew neat lines between the realms of French law and African custom. In the 1890s this was valued chiefly because it allowed the French to tolerate slavery and harness the authority of Wolof aristocrats to the colonial administration. But it was soon valued as a way of excluding French law and democracy from the newly subdued territories of the protectorate.[133] Although disannexation was a specific response to a specific crisis, it had permanent effects because successive governors and governors-general felt the same need to protect the rural areas of Senegal from the "destabilizing" regime of French law and political liberty in the Four Communes. Disannexation created a permanent division between the rural districts ruled by African chiefs and the urban areas of the Four Communes. This distinction was paralleled by a further one between the "subjects" of the rural areas and the "citizens" of the Four Communes. The colonial towns had an intermediate status. They were placed under the authority of a French commandant, but the status of an individual depended on his place of birth.

The Conquest of Bawol

Disannexation paved the way for the conquest of Bawol. The French applied the protectorate policy in Bawol, but they were prepared to give local elites even more power than in Kajoor. The final conquest was anticlimactic. A French column deposed the ruling monarch and supervised the election of a ruler acceptable to the French. Few dramatic changes were made. The French did not even establish a permanent Residency in the new protectorate. The French sought collaborators who could render them real services, as Demba War Sall had done in Kajoor. By 1890, this was a proven policy, which had delivered maximum results at minimal cost.

Demba War Sall and his allies actively supported the French attack on Bawol in 1890. They provided military support and intelligence. They also advised the French on the choice of possible successors in Bawol. Thieyacine Faal, the ruling king, limited his diplomatic efforts to letters proclaiming his friendship with France. He also complained about the power given to "slaves" in Kajoor.[134] The French had their own reasons to desire a change of leadership. They regarded Thieyacine Fall, who was reportedly drunk all the time, as a weak leader who allowed his *ceddo* to pillage at will. On the other hand the French had no clear preferences for a successor and they followed the advice of Demba War Sall in the selection of Tanor Ngogne.[135]

Bawol did not put up much resistance in 1890. Before the French entered Bawol the "principal *jaambuur*" wrote a letter to Demba War Sall asking him to recommend the abolition of the monarchy, as in Kajoor. The letter, which was inspired by Meissa Anta Ngone, one of the province chiefs, expressed no hostility to Thieyacine Fall himself. But Meissa Anta denounced the younger *garmi* princes and their *ceddo*. When Commandant Villiers led a column into Bawol in March 1890, the French supervised the election of Tanor Ngogne, a *garmi* prince who had once fought alongside Màbba with Lat Joor and Demba War Sall. Tanor's election was opposed by the principal *jaambuur* of Bawol, who remained loyal to the Fall dynasty. The Great Jaraaf, who was the traditional delegate of the *jaambuur* within the state, led the opposition.[136] Although Tanor remained in power until his death in 1894, persistent opposition from some of the *jaambuur* troubled his rule. French influence in Bawol was more symbolic than real. Once the French had helped Tanor eliminate his domestic rivals, Tanor ignored French orders when he could get away with it, feigned sickness when summoned, and concentrated on eliminating his domestic enemies. Armand Armary, a *habitant* secretary who was the sole representative of French interests in this period, complained in 1892 that he was ill housed and fed and treated as the least of Tanor's slaves. He was frequently refused permission to see Tanor, who ignored French letters.[137]

CONCLUSION

The political regime created by Demba War Sall in 1886 satisfied the needs of the French for a cheap, efficient colonial administration. Demba War Sall and his allies reached out to the merchant elites of Saint-Louis and did their best to reconcile the moderate elements within the old Muslim party of Kajoor. However, whatever his successes as a colonial chief, Demba War could not lay to rest the tensions created by nearly thirty years of civil war. For many, his survival meant that the new colonial regime continued the worst features of the monarchy, the tendency for power to be concentrated in the hands of a few royal slaves.

Each party to the conflict could draw its own conclusions about its gains and losses. For the Muslim party of Kajoor the outcome was mixed at best. Njambur province had been separated from Kajoor in 1883 and was controlled by the Muslim party. The chiefs of Njambur were now agents of French colonial rule, with positions comparable to that of Demba War Sall. However, whatever advantages they derived from their position, Ibrahima N'Diaye and his allies could hardly claim to represent Islam. The most prestigious marabouts had not taken positions in the administration. The chiefs of Njambur represented the members of the old Muslim party most eager to take political office. In a period of rapid change, Ibrahima N'Diaye represented Muslim aspirations in 1859, not the realities of 1886. Powerful new voices would emerge in both Kajoor and Bawol in the 1890s, making the Muslim party of the nineteenth century, a coalition of nobles and titled Muslims, a relic of the past.

The "French" or "Senegalese" party, representing the interests of the Four Communes, was divided and in some disarray after 1890. The policy of disannexation had separated the Four Communes from the rural hinterland of Senegal, frustrating the ambitions of those who hoped that the French conquest would place the "Senegalese" in positions of authority. The merchants of Saint-Louis, who allied themselves with the monarchy in the hope of protecting their privileged position as commercial intermediaries, quickly realized that the protectorate policy gave no advantages to them. The French administration controlled all the towns in the interior and French merchants established trading posts in the railroad towns in Kajoor. The only concrete legacy of the colony's alliance with the French was the ambiguous status of the *originaires* as French citizens.

The party of the monarchy could take some comfort in the efforts of Demba War Sall to preserve the traditions of Kajoor. But Demba War Sall could easily symbolize the worst elements of monarchy. Muslims had complained in 1859 and again in 1875 that the monarchy put too much power in the hands of one family. The target of this complaint was the Geej dynasty and the slaves of the Geej. After 1886, Demba War Sall could only support a small fraction of the royal slaves, consisting of his own family members and loyal soldiers. During the conquest, many nobles and slaves had abandoned the court. Some had become disciples of the marabout Bou Kounta. Others had migrated to Bawol to join Amadu Bamba, who had criticized Lat Joor for his brutal suppression of the Muslim rebellion of 1875. All these dissidents represented a potential threat to Demba War Sall and his allies.

The smooth transition from monarchy to colonial rule was something of an illusion. Export statistics tell a different story about the turmoil of this period, as peanut exports declined from 83,000 tons in 1882, to 43,500 tons in 1883, to a low of 21,100 tons in 1886.[138] During this period, aristocratic factions from Kajoor led their followers into exile in Bawol. Not all of them returned to Kajoor in 1883 or in 1886. Their presence in Bawol contributed to the arrest and exile of Amadu Bamba in 1895.

The fact that Demba War Sall could claim the heritage of the monarchy confirmed the weak support for jihad in Kajoor. Many Muslims were satisfied by the peace that began in 1886, even though Demba War Sall enforced it for a French government. Jihad failed because it never won much support. The alliance between Lat Joor and Màbba confirmed the belief of many Muslims that warfare and jihad corrupted Muslims who followed that path. Wasn't it obvious that Lat Joor sought booty and power? The only other jihad in Kajoor occurred in 1875 when members of the Muslim party supported Amadu Seexu's declaration of jihad against Lat Joor. Didn't that prove that jihad led to civil wars between Muslims, in which Muslims killed, enslaved, and confiscated the property of other Muslims? These criticisms were raised at the time and they would be repeated by Muslims struggling to come to terms with the advent of colonial rule.[139]

NOTES

1. See chapter with this title in Sara Berry, *No Condition is Permanent: The Social Consequences of Agrarian Change in Sub-Saharan Afric*a (Madison, Wis., 1993).

2. *Moniteur du Sénégal et Dépendances* 1, no. 39 (Dec. 23, 1856). Sëriñ Luuga came from the influential Lo family.

3. Ba, *La pénétration*, 213–33.

4. Ibid., 247.

5. Ibid., 233–35. For the crisis in Waalo, see Searing, *West African Slavery*, 172–73.

6. Ba, *La Pénetration*, 218, for the article from *Moniteur du Sénégal et Dépendances*.

7. Ibid., 224.

8. Searing, *West African Slavery*, 187–93.

9. See Ba, *La pénétration*, 174–212, for documents on this campaign.

10. Governor to Minister, Oct. 13, 1859, quoted in Ba, *La pénétration*, 195.

11. Ibid.

12. 13 G 304, Gorée, Correspondance: Note sur la presqu'île de Cap Vert, Feb. 18, 1862, quoting a document of March 2, 1857.

13. Ba, *La pénétration*, 180.

14. For the column that invaded Kajoor in 1861, see ibid., 373–75.

15 On French military policy, see Myron Echenberg, *Colonial Conscripts: The "Tirailleurs Sénégalais" in French West Africa, 1857–1960* (Portsmouth, N.H., 1991), 1–24.

16. Ba, *La pénétration,* 283.

17. Minister to Governor, Nov. 21, 1859, quoted in ibid., 210.

18. Ibid., 331.

19. Governor to Minister, Feb. 5, 1861, quoted in ibid., 373.

20. Ibid.

21. Ibid., 374–75.

22. Ibid., "Procès-Verbal du conseil d'administration du Sénégal," Feb. 28, 1861, 396, 398–99.

23. Ibid., 405.

24. Ibid., 412.

25. Ibid., 412–14.

26. A *habitant* emissary, Louis Descemet, reported seeing 500 cavalry and 150 footsoldiers in January. He believed the Dammel could command larger forces, but this provides an estimate of those under his direct control. Ibid., 394. The lower figure, 200, was reported in May when Makkodu was pursued by the French. Ibid., 467.

27. Ibid., 467.

28. 13 G 57, Cayor, pièce 16, Lettre de Damel Madiodio et Diawdine Mboul Samba Maram Khay à Gouverneur, Dec. 12, 1861.

29. Ibid.

30. 13 G 257, Pièce 18, Lettre de Serigne Taiba, Dec. 23, 1861.

31. Amadou Duguay-Clédor, *La Bataille de Guîlé*, ed. Mbaye Gueye (Dakar, 1985), 74.

32. For a narrative of events, see ibid., 69–77.

33. Dieng, *L'épopée du Kajoor*, 378, 380–82. On the significance of Wolof hairstyles, see Niang Fatou Niang Siga, *Reflets de modes et traditions Saint-Louisiennes* (Dakar, 1990).

34. Ba, *La pénétration*, 260.

35. 13 G 257, Cayor, Correspondance: Pièce 66, June 1864.

36. Ibid., Pièces 65, 66, 68, 69, June–July 1864.

37. 13 G 257, Cayor, pièce 68, July 17, 1864.

38. Duguay-Clédor, *La Bataille de Guîlé*, 79.

39. On famine during the era of the slave trade, see Searing, *West African Slavery*, 132–44.

40. For French reports on the famine, see 13 G 257, Cayor, pièce 70, Rapport au Gouverneur sur la situation du Cayor, May 1865, which mentions *sauterelles* (locusts) and *epizootie* (cattle epidemic) as aggravating factors.

41. 13 G 257, Situation du Cayor, May 1865.

42. 13 G 257, Cayor, Correspondance, Lettre de Serigne Louga, M'Barick Lo, Nov. 20, 1866.

43. Dieng, *L'épopée* du Kajoor, 394.

44. Diouf, *Le Kajoor*, calls it a *jebbalu*, or act of submission to a religious guide, 252, citing Amadou Bamba Diop.

45. Diop, "Lat Dior et le problème musulman," 511–15.

46. Ibid., 517, 520–21. Diop's account is confirmed by sources recounting the battle from the perspective of Màbba's family: Ousmane Tamsir Ba, "Essai historique sur le Rip," *Bulletin de l'Institut Fondamental de l'Afrique Noire* 19, B (1957): 564–91; and Abdou Bouri Ba, "Essai sur l'histoire du Saloum et du Rip," *Bulletin de L'Institut Fondamental de L'Afrique Noire* 38, B (1976): 845–47.

47. 13 G 304, Gorée: Correspondance, A. Legourmand, Kaolack, July 18, 1864.

48. Ibid., pièce 18, July 29, 1864.

49. Meysa Mbaay was an older relative of Demba War Sall. He died in exile and has largely dropped out of Wolof oral sources.

50. 13 G 304, Gorée: Correspondance, pièce 27, Aug. 29, 1864.

51. Ibid., pièce 33, Oct. 22, 1864, reporting the opinion of Mademba Diop.

52. 13 G 304, Gorée: Correspondance, Colonel G. D'Arcy, Government House, Bathurst, June 24, 1864.

53. Ibid.

54. For these issues, see John H. Hanson, *Migration, Jihad, and Muslim Authority in West Africa: The Futanke Colonies in Karta* (Bloomington, Ind., 1996).

55. Mbacké, "Les bienfaits (1)," 580.

56. Martin A. Klein, *Islam and Imperialism in Senegal: Sine-Saloum, 1847–1914* (Stanford, Calif., 1968), is the standard work on Màbba.

57. Mbacké, "Les bienfaits (1)," 580.

58. Interview, Serigne M'Baye Guèye Sylla, Darou-Mousty, July 28, 1995. The *jihad al nafs* (Arabic) is often defined as a greater jihad, the war with the "base instincts." See Annemarie Schimmel, *And Muhammad Is His Messenger: The Veneration of the Prophet in Islamic Piety* (Chapel Hill, N.C. 1985), 53, for the *hadith* upon which this concept is based.

59. *Màbba, ci bopam, Yalla rekk moo ko tax jub, waaye du ko Yalla rekk taxa joge dafa am ay jaami-jaambuur, jaam yo xam ne seen boroom daan ko moomam jende ko ande ci biir xare bi, loolu moo tax Yalla dimbeli le bu mu ganye yeefeer, jaami-jaambuuru ku ligeey lo xam.* Interview, Serigne Bassirou Anta Niang Mbacké, Darou-Mousty, July 29, 1995.

60. This was a reference to Tijani practice, which allowed slaves to serve as soldiers in jihad under certain circumstances. See John Ralph Willis, "Jihad and the Ideology of Enslavement," in *Slaves and Slavery in Muslim Africa*, ed. John Ralph Willis (London, 1985), vol. 1, 16–26.

61. Interview, Serigne Bassirou Anta Niang Mbacké, Darou-Mousty, July 29, 1995.

62. *Dafa wax ne jiyaar jeex na. Ndax jiyaar leegi mooy . . . jiyaar bu des leggi, mooy jiyaar ak sa bekkan. Jiyaar ak sa bakkan mooy: baay li Yalla tere, def lu mu digle . . . jiyaar mo genn réy, mo genn mag.* Ibid.

63. Dieng, *L'épopée du Kajoor*, 374, 438.

64. The best account of Lat Joor is in Diouf, *Le Kajoor*. Although we differ on some points, Diouf's book offers a more detailed analysis of this period.

65. Barry, *Le Royaume du Waalo*, 152–53.

66. Ba, *La Pénetration*, 396–99; and the attacks on French policy in 1886 in *Le Réveil du Sén*égal, Oct. 10, Nov. 14, 1886.

67. Diouf, *Le Kajoor*, 238–43.

68. 13 G 258, Cayor: 1870–1874, Correspondance, pièces 1–2, Pétition signed by Serigne Merina, Serigne Coki, Serigne Niomrei (Ñomre), Serigne Louga, Serigne N'Guick, Jan. 15, 1870.

69. 13 G 258, Pièce 89, Lettre. Received by the French April 6, 1870.

70. 13 G 257, Cayor, Correspondance, pièce 89, Lettre de Omar Niang, chef de M'Bakol, Oct. 29, 1866.

71. I differ from Diouf's interpretation in *Le Kajoor*, 247–61. Diouf places more emphasis on the French and on external factors (Amadu Seexu).

72. 13 G 257, Cayor, Lettre, Omar Niang, Oct. 29, 1866.

73. 13 G 257, Pièce 88, Lettre de Serigne Pir, Boubacar Fal, Nov. 22, 1866.

74. 13 G 258, Cayor, pièce 160, Lettre de Omar Gnane [Niang], Diawdine Mboul. Received Feb. 11, 1874.

75. Diouf, *Le Kajoor*, 249–50.

76. 13 G 258, pièce 160, Lettre de Omar Gnane, Feb. 11, 1874.

77. 13 G 258, Cayor, pièces 169, 177, Lat Dior à Gouverneur, Oct. 6, 1874.

78. 13 G 258, Cayor, pièce 198, Lettre, Lat Dior à Gouverneur, Oct. 9, 1874.

79. 13 G 258, Cayor, pièces 192, 193, Lettres de Serigne Louga et Serigne M'Pal, Dec. 1874.

80. Dieng, *L'épopée du Kajoor*, 424.

81. Ibid., 422.

82. This is a titled position, typically held by a royal slave in charge of the king's household. It was only one of the titles held by Demba War Sall.

83. Diop, "Lat Dior et le problème musulman," 521.

84. Ibid., 525.

85. 13 G 258, Cayor, pièce 23, Letter de Madiakhate Cala.

86. Fall, "Recueil," 133–34.

87. Diop, "Lat Dior et le problème musulman," 522.

88. Mbacké, "Les bienfaits (1)," 604.

89. Mbacké, "Les bienfaits (2)," 56–57.

90. Amar Samb, *Essai sur la contribution du Sénégal à la littérature d'expression arabe*, (Dakar, 1972), 260. Amar Samb's chapter on Majaxate Kala is the most important discussion of Kajoor's qadi. Majaxate Kala is also discussed in Claudine Gerresch, "Le livre de metrique 'Mubayyin al-Iskal' du Cadi Madiakhate Kala: Introduction historique, texte arabe, traduction et glossaire," *Bulletin de l'Institut Fondamental de l'Afrique Noire* 36, B, no. 4 (1974): 714–68.

91. Diop, "Lat Dior et le problème musulman," 520.

92. See Fall, "Recueil," 133–35.

93. Julian Wood Witherell, "The Response of the Peoples of Cayor to French Penetration, 1850–1900" (Ph.D. dissertation, University of Wisconsin-Madison, 1964), 193, for the text of the treaty.

94. See discussion in Germaine Ganier, "Lat Dior et le chemin de fer de l'arachide," *Bulletin de l'Institut Fondamental de l'Afrique Noire* 27, B (1965): 223–81.

95. French sources indicate that Demba War and Samba Lawbé received the support of the major *jaambuur* electors in 1879. See letter of *jaambuur* to governor, quoted in Monteil, "Lat-Dior," 95.

96. Monteil, "Lat Dior," 95.

97. Demba War Sall and Ibra Fatim Saar supported the railroad project in 1879, before Lat Joor signed the treaty. See Ganier, "Lat Dior et le chemin de fer," 227, and the document quoted on 261.

98. Witherell, "Response of the Peoples of Cayor," 98, quoting archival documents.

99. Ibra Fatim Sarr Sall was the representative of the monarchy in Njambur for most of Lat Joor's reign.

100. See Paul E. Pheffer, "Railroads and Aspects of Social Change in Senegal" (Ph.D. thesis, University of Pennsylvania, 1975), 125–35.

101. Ba, *La pénétration*, 398.

102. M. Courtet, *Étude sur le Sénégal* (Paris, 1903), 24.

103. Mohamed Mbodj, "Un exemple d'économie coloniale. Le Sine-Saloum (Sénégal) de 1887 à 1940: Cultures arachidières et mutations sociales (thèse de troisième cycle, Université Paris VII, 1977–1978), 108.

104. This issue came up frequently, beginning with the return of Lat Joor to Kajoor in 1869: 13 G 264 and 13 G 265 contain correspondence on the flight of slaves from Kajoor. Once again, after the wars with Bawol and Jolof, from 1873 to 1877, there were similar complaints: 13 G 259, Lat Dior à Gouverneur, March 1877, and 13 G 260, Lat Dior à Governor, Dec. 1881.

105. See chapter 5, below, for examples and discussion.

106. Martin A. Klein, "Social and Economic Factors in the Muslim Revolution in Senegambia," *Journal of African History* 13 (1972): 419–41. For a similar argument, see Lucie G. Colvin, "Kayor and Its Diplomatic Relations with Saint Louis du Sénégal, 1763–1861" (Ph.D. dissertation, Columbia University, 1972), 293–95.

107. For a review of the "crisis of adaptation" in the nineteenth century, see the "Introduction" to *From Slave Trade to 'Legitimate Commerce': The Commercial Transition in Nineteenth Century West Africa* ed. Robin Law (Cambridge, 1995).

108. François Renault, "L'abolition de l'esclavage au Senegal: L'attitude de l'administration française (1848–1905)," *Revue Française d'Histoire d'Outre-Mer* 58, no. 210, (1971): 5–80, discusses these shifts in policy.

109. Pheffer, "Railroads and Aspects of Social Change," 215–35.

110. Samba Lawbé was accused of pressuring merchants to pay the fine imposed on him for his war against Jolof. Fall, "Recueil," 137, attributes his death to his refusal to pay the fine.

111. In 1885, Lat Joor was given permission to return to Kajoor to live as a simple subject: Mbaye Gueye and A. Adu Boahen, "African Initiatives and Resistance in West Africa," in *UNESCO General History of Africa* (New York, 1985), vol. 7, 117–19.

112. Ganier, "Lat Dior et le chemin de fer," 252.

113. On the campaign of the Saint-Louis merchants against the railroad and in support of Lat Joor, see Ganier, "Lat Dior et le chemin de fer"; and Moustapha Sarr, *Louga et sa région: Essai d'intégration des rapports ville-campagne dans la problématique du développement* (Dakar, 1973), 58–63.

114. See *Le Petit Sénégalais*, Oct. 14, 1886; and *Le Réveil du Sénégal*, Oct. 10 and Nov. 14, 1886. The *Réveil* of Oct. 10 described Samba Lawbé's death as an execution. The role of Devès and Crespin are discussed in Robert July, *The Origins of Modern African Thought* (New York, 1968), 242–47.

115. Gaspard Devès opposed the policy, in the hope that Lat Joor would be restored. Lat Joor was heavily indebted to Devès. See *Le Réveil du Sénégal*, Oct. 10 and Nov. 14 1886, for Deves' coverage of the affairs of Kajoor.

116. On the Descemet family, see Ba, *La pénétration*, 377–78. Demba War Sall had married Khady Diop, who was related to the Descemets. She is frequently mentioned in the administrative files and service files which record Demba War's relations with the French: 13 G 50, Chemise Demba War.

117. On the ties of Demba War to Carpot and Valentin, see 2 D 14-4, Cercle de Cayor, Corres. 1902, Commandant de cercle Vienne à Directeur des affaires indigénes, May 6, 1902; on his connections with Devès and Chaumet, see 2 D 14-

3, Corres. 1901, Rapport de tournée, June 25, 1901. See also his service files: 13 G 50.

118. Ba, *La pénétration,* 241.

119. On courts under Demba War Sall, see 2 D 14-2, 2 D 14-3. In 1901, Baba Jakhumpa was chief qadi of Cayor.

120. 13 G 50, Notes administratives sur les chefs du Cayor.

121. Assane Sylla, *La philosophie morale des Wolof* (Dakar, 1978), 128–29, 140–41.

122. 13 G 50, Chemise Demba War; James F. Searing, "Accommodation and Resistance: Chiefs, Muslim Leaders and Politicians in Colonial Senegal, 1890–1934" (Ph.D. dissertation, Princeton University, 1985), 77-85.

123. 2 D 14-3, Corres. 1901, Fevrier, Commandant Penel à Directeur des affaires indigénes, Feb. 16, 1901, et Directeur des affaires indigénes à Penel, Feb. 6, 1901.

124. For a more detailed discussion of Demba War's career and sources, see Searing, "Accommodation and Resistance," 152–58.

125. This same attitude prevails today in rural Kajoor. See Irvine, "Caste and Communication," 66. Most *ceddo* claimed to be nobles (*geer*) and their claims were accepted by all but the *garmi*. The main evidence is that *ceddo-geer* marriages were accepted, while the *geer* would not intermarry with descendants of "true" slaves (*jaam*).

126. Personal communication, Mamadou Diouf, October 1988. Diouf was one of the historians involved in the centenary debate.

127. Barry, *Le Rouyaume du Waalo.* On the new policy, see the documents in Yves-Saint Martin, *Une source de l'histoire coloniale du Sénégal: Les rapports de situation politique (1874–1891)* (Dakar, 1966), 146–50.

128. The accuracy of Clement-Thomas's analysis of the causes of Fulbe emigration has been questioned. See the discussion in Hanson, *Migration, Jihad and Muslim Authority*, where more emphasis is placed on Islam and Umarian influences. I am more interested here in disannexation as a political policy.

129. Saint-Martin, *Une source*, 150.

130. Ibid., 149.

131. Ibid., 151–52.

132. Saint-Martin, *Une Source*, 155–57.

133. A similar process occurred in Nigeria. Indirect rule began as an ad hoc solution to the problems of governing the Muslim North and forming alliances with the Fulani emirs. At the time of amalgamation in 1914, it was valued as a way of keeping "subversives" from Lagos out of the rural districts in the South. See the discussion in I.M. Okonjo, *British Administration in Nigeria, 1900–1950: A Nigerian View* (New York, 1974), 53–82; and J.A. Atanda, *The New Oyo Empire: Indirect Rule and Change in Western Nigeria 1894–1934* (New York, 1973.)

134. 2 D 9-4, Cercle de Louga, Corres. 1889; and 2 D 7-1, Baol, Corres. 1888–1890.

135. 2 D 9-4, Louga, Corres. 1889; and 2 D 7-1, Baol, Corres. 1888–1890. Demba War Sall had known Tanor Ngogne since at least the 1860s, when they had campaigned together with Màbba. In 1892 Tanor married a female relative of Demba War Sall, which suggests an alliance between the two men: 2 D 7-1, Baol, Corres. 1892, Tanor Ngogne à Gouverneur, May 27, 1892.

136. 2 D 7-1, Baol, Corres. 1889, Lettre de "Diambours" à Demba War, Jan. 1, 1889; and 2 D 7-1, Corres. 1890, Commandant Villiers à Gouverneur, March 16, 1890.

137. 2 D 7-1, Baol, Corres. 1892.

138. For a more detailed discussion of this decline, see the conclusion to chapter 5.

139. For a good discussion of the themes of this debate, see Dedoud ould Abdallah, "Guerre sainte ou sédition blamable? *Nasiha* de shaikh Sa'd Bu contre le *jihad* de son frère Ma al-Ainin," in *Le temps des marabouts: Itinéraires et stratégies islamiques en Afrique Occidentale Française v. 1880–1960*, ed. David Robinson and Jean-Louis Triaud (Paris, 1997), 119–53.

3

"GOD ALONE IS KING": RECONCEPTUALIZING MURID ISLAM

Historians and social scientists have interpreted the arrest and exile of Amadu Bamba in 1895 in the framework of French colonial policy toward Islam. Archival documents from 1895 have provided the evidence for these interpretations of the emergence of the Murid order, which link Amadu Bamba to Lat Joor, the last independent king of the Wolof kingdom of Kajoor. Murid Islam therefore appears to continue the resistance of the monarchy to colonial rule, with a new form of "passive resistance" replacing military resistance after Lat Joor was killed by French troops in 1886.

David Robinson's recent articles on the Murid order and French Islamic policy in Senegal and Mauritania are a good example of this archive-driven history.[1] In these articles we learn a great deal about the paths to "accommodation" between the French and various Muslim leaders and Sufi orders, and even more about the French Islamic experts who influenced policy. In the end what emerges is a history of how the French came to understand, accommodate themselves to, manipulate, or repress various Islamic movements. The focus is always on how the French related to "Islam." However well documented, this approach does not explain why Amadu Bamba posed a threat to the colonial order in 1895, when the French knew almost nothing about him, or why his mission and teachings attracted so many adherents. I focus on Amadu Bamba's relations with the monarchy, with colonial chiefs, and with Wolof peasants and slaves. I also place more emphasis on Murid sources and rely less on the colonial archives for my account of the triumph of Islam.

Figure 3.1 Amadu Bamba, 1913

I argue that the formal archival reports that have guided scholars are flawed. They contain not only factual errors based on French ignorance but also conscious deceptions written into the reports to reinforce the rumors and reports by informers that formed the sole basis for the charges put forward. Archival sources do not reveal either a coherent policy or an active role on the part of the French. They suggest that Wolof chiefs who had signed treaties with the French in 1883 were the real agents behind the arrest of Amadu Bamba.

Murid sources reveal a very different link between Amadu Bamba and Lat Joor than is presented in French sources. The two men were declared enemies from 1882 onward, when Amadu Bamba broke off his relations with the court. Despite close ties between their families, Amadu Bamba's attitude toward Lat Joor was highly critical. The Murid watchword "God Alone Is King" sums up this attitude, which was expressed in the defiant attitude of Murid disciples to colonial chiefs. By 1895 the repression of Murid disciples in Kajoor and the opportunities created by the founding of new Murid villages in Bawol led to a movement of emigration by Wolof peasants and slaves. This was the threat that Wolof chiefs in Kajoor tried to eliminate by using their influence with the French.

In addition to presenting a new interpretation of the events of 1895 and the meaning of the Murid challenge, I show how an uncritical faith in written sources as reliable guides to basic "facts" and "chronologies" has shaped previous interpretations of a seminal event in Senegalese colonial history. In this case, on a level playing field, Murid sources carry the day and open up new meanings for well-known events.

THE CHALLENGE OF ISLAM: 1895

In July 1895 a small French column set out on a mission to arrest Amadu Bamba, a Muslim scholar and Sufi shaykh who had attracted a large following among the Wolof in Bawol. Amadu Bamba was arrested, brought before the Privy Council of the governor, and deported to French Equatorial Africa. He was charged with planning a holy war against the French. The main proof of his guilt was the presence of enemies of French rule in his following, identified as the former partisans of Lat Joor, and Alburi Njaay. Amadu Bamba, Lat Joor and Alburi Njaay had been linked together in the past by their presence at the court of Màbba Jaxu, whose holy war had shaken the traditional Wolof political order to its foundations. Although the French had only sketchy intelligence on Amadu Bamba, they were alarmed by the apparent resurgence of Wolof resistance to colonial rule. French fears focused on the presence of *ceddo* warriors in Amadu Bamba's following. Unlike Wolof scholars and peasants, whom the French described as peaceful, the *ceddo* were the symbol of the old regime. As described by Commandant Leclerc, who led the column:

> In a word all the partisans of the Damels, all the *ceddo* who lived formerly only by war, pillage and rapine, and who have been reduced to poverty by our government, all of them have grouped themselves around the marabout-Mahdi, the destroyer of the whites.[2]

In many ways the arrest of Amadu Bamba was the final act in the conquest of the Wolof kingdoms. Martial Merlin, who wrote the brief justifying Amadu Bamba's deportation, argued that Amadu Bamba had taken up the banner of Wolof resistance to the French in 1886, immediately after the death of Lat Joor. At that moment, Amadu Bamba had migrated from Kajoor, which was coming under French control, and established a following in the interior of Bawol. From 1886 to 1895 Amadu Bamba had prepared himself to be the successor to the Wolof kings. His holy war, which the French believed their intervention had prevented, would have plunged Senegal into a new round of violence.

Most research on the Murid order has looked to French attitudes toward Islam to explain the events of 1895. They should be seen from the perspective of Wolof history, since the French knew almost nothing about Amadu Bamba except what their Wolof allies told them. Any historian who reads the archival sources about the arrest and deportation of Amadu Bamba is opening a dossier that contains the evidence for the prosecution. There is no record of what Amadu Bamba may have said in his own defense and no direct evidence of the statements of his accusers. The French administrators who ordered his arrest produced the whole dossier. Their main concern was to convince the Privy Council to approve the order of deportation.

The French sources of 1895 can be conceived as a textual pyramid, of which only the apex has survived. The base of the pyramid was formed by the reports of spies and informers and by accusations presented by Wolof enemies and rivals of Amadu Bamba, who were attempting to settle old scores. This information was presented orally to the French, and has to be reconstructed from surviving written sources. At the apex of the pyramid is the formal report of Martial Merlin, the director of political affairs, who ordered the arrest and presented the case to the Privy Council. Merlin's report draws upon two reports by Commandant Leclerc, the French administrator responsible for gathering information and carrying out the arrest. Most historians have paid too much attention to the apex of the pyramid and not enough to the base.

Wolof chiefs working for the French warned Leclerc and Merlin about Amadu Bamba. The most active informer against Amadu Bamba was Ibrahima N'Diaye. He was a member of the old Muslim party and was appointed Bour N'Diambour (king of Njambur) after Njambur province was annexed by the French in 1883. He was the source of almost all the information supplied by Commandant Leclerc in his first report on Amadu Bamba. His retainers told Leclerc that they had seen arms and munitions being shipped to Amadu Bamba. They also reported that Amadu Bamba had held a meeting for the Muslim New Year (Wolof, *tamxarit*), which 700 armed men attended. Ibrahima N'Diaye had sent "spies" to Jolof, where Amadu Bamba had established his residence. N'Diaye was probably also the source who informed Leclerc that Amadu Bamba could command 1,000 men and that he could count on the support of unnamed influential "chiefs" in Kajoor and Njambur.[3] Ibrahima N'Diaye played a key role in the arrest of Amadu Bamba. The column led by Leclerc left Saint-Louis and crossed Njambur province on its way toward Jolof. Ibrahima N'Diaye supplied the bulk of the troops that supported Leclerc's mission. The second informant mentioned by Leclerc was Ibra Fatim Sarr, a province chief in Kajoor.[4] No specific intelligence was attributed to Ibra Fatim Sarr, except that he too had sent spies to Jolof.[5] However, his close relations with Demba War Sall suggest that the royal slaves of Kajoor added their voices to the chorus denouncing Amadu Bamba.

Leclerc argued that Amadu Bamba was preparing a rebellion for the beginning of the dry season, in a few months' time. Leclerc admitted that he could not find any direct evidence for this charge, but he attributed the absence of proof to Amadu Bamba's guile:

> He will tell you he is poor and lives from the religious gifts he receives. But you should ask him: What was in the hundreds of trunks that he sent to his old residence at Mbacké as soon as he heard of my arrival on the borders of Jolof during the night of the 8th [of July]? There is nothing in his villages except hoes and if you find a rifle it is said to belong to visitors. All that is true, but what happened to the arms and munitions that he possessed six months ago when he came to Jolof and what happened to the cases of arms that were seen going through Coki and Djéwal several weeks ago? Does that mean that he has already distributed his arms and that, as I suggested in my previ-

ous report, he is only waiting for the end of the rainy season to begin his movement?[6]

Leclerc's speculations were based on the absolute trust he placed in the information provided by Ibrahima N'Diaye. This trust was so complete that it outweighed the evidence of Leclerc's own observations. Put another way, despite the fact that Leclerc found no evidence to support the charges against Amadu Bamba, he proceeded on the assumption that the spies were telling the truth and that Amadu Bamba was lying.

Amadu Bamba's guilt was embodied in the suspicious character of his following, described by Leclerc as a combination of *sëriñ* and *ceddo*. In Leclerc's opinion, this made Amadu Bamba more dangerous than Amadu Seexu, who had declared a jihad in Kajoor in 1875:

> There is a difference between them which works in the favor of Amadu Bamba. While Amadou Cheikhou only had the support of the *sëriñ*, our marabout has a real army of *ceddo*.[7]

The most detailed intelligence in Leclerc's report was a list of the relatives of Lat Joor who had joined Amadu Bamba. They were described as *ceddo* leaders who had rallied to Bamba's cause. Leclerc also gave the names of several prominent Muslim leaders who had joined the movement. The accuracy and detail of this information suggests that it came directly from a Wolof informant, most likely from Ibrahima N'Diaye. It is easy to imagine that Ibrahima N'Diaye convinced the French to take action by giving them the names of "*ceddo*" and Muslims who supported Amadu Bamba. By describing Amadu Bamba's following as a reincarnation of all the Wolof factions who had clashed with the French in the past, Ibrahima N'Diaye hoped to stir the French to action.

It is not difficult to understand the hostility felt by Ibrahima N'Diaye and his allies toward Amadu Bamba. They were members of the Muslim party who had accepted positions as colonial chiefs. According to Martial Merlin, the director of political affairs, Amadu Bamba's prestige reduced their authority to naught:

> In N'Diambour the chiefs are insulted. In the villages where the influence of Amadu Bamba is strongest, they feel contempt for the authority of the Bour [Ibrahima N'Diaye] and refuse to pay their taxes.[8]

The influence of Amadu Bamba in Njambur was a major worry for Leclerc. After he arrested Amadu Bamba, Leclerc sent Ibrahima N'Diaye ahead with his troops to occupy Kokki, where the column planned on spending the night. Leclerc arrived next, with a second group of troops, just before the arrival of Amadu Bamba. In spite of these precautions, an "outburst" was only narrowly averted. Hostile onlookers insulted the men guarding the saint. Villagers refused to allow interpreters working for the French to drink water from their well.[9]

Merlin's report on Amadu Bamba is based on Leclerc, but it also introduces new evidence. Merlin mentions one source of information not named in Leclerc: Demba War Sall, the president of the Confederation of Cayor.[10] Demba War was a trusted French ally in 1895, but he was also a man with a past. He had put Lat Joor forward as the candidate for king in 1861 and served under him for over twenty years. The part of Merlin's report that shows his hand is a long list of the "former warriors of Lat Joor," including "close relatives of the former Dammel" who had joined Amadu Bamba. The names are different from those in Leclerc's report, and could easily have come from Demba War, who was the "oldest companion" of all. Most of the rest of Merlin's report was based on Leclerc or on Merlin's own inventions.

Merlin's report has exerted a powerful influence on subsequent studies of Amadu Bamba and the Murids. Merlin's goal was to give the circumstantial evidence gathered by Leclerc more force. His report was addressed to the governor and the Privy Council and was essentially a political document. In my view his report contains both information that Merlin believed to be true and deliberate falsehoods that Merlin thought no one would notice.

Merlin's main strategy was to prove that Amadu Bamba was an enemy of French rule. Merlin's biographical sketch of Amadu Bamba contains a number of errors. The most important error is his statement that Amadu Bamba was born in Geet province of Kajoor. Although this may seem insignificant, it provides the beginning for Merlin's efforts to cast suspicion on the physical movements of Amadu Bamba after 1886. Amadu Bamba lived in Geet province from around 1869 until his father's death. According to Merlin, Amadu Bamba left Kajoor immediately after the death of Lat Joor in 1886 to escape French authority:

> The dismemberment of Kajoor, the direct influence that we would now have in the affairs of the country, no longer permitted Amadu Bamba to obtain the position that had always been the dream of his ambition.[11]

Frustrated in Kajoor, Amadu Bamba migrated to the extreme eastern region of Bawol. On the borders of Jolof, Kajoor, and Bawol, this new location was ideal for someone trying to escape attention and build up a movement.

Merlin's account of Bawol when Amadu Bamba arrived was calculated to arouse suspicion:

> This province was then ruled by Thieyacine Fall, a brutal, drunken *ceddo* whose authority was only supported by a few henchmen. They profited from his vices by constantly plundering the population. Therefore Amadu Bamba could hope that one day he would take charge of the Muslim part of the population and depose Thieyacine, whose power would by then be unbearable, and take his place; or failing that, place a chief loyal to him in power, Tanor Gogne [Ngogne], for example.[12]

This passage raises a red flag for someone familiar with the history of French policy in Bawol. Merlin had been in Senegal for four years, serving as the senior administrator responsible for relations with the Wolof kingdoms. He knew that the French had supported Thieyacine Fall as their ally in the 1880s. He also knew that the French had imposed Tanor Ngogne as the ruler of Bawol in 1890, after direct military intervention. Therefore he knew it was extremely misleading to pretend that Amadu Bamba had anything to do with Tanor's selection.

Merlin's error about Amadu Bamba's birthplace takes on new significance. Since his report failed to identity Mbacké-Bawol as Amadu Bamba's village of birth, he couldn't offer the obvious explanation for Amadu Bamba's migration from Kajoor to Bawol, which was his desire to return to his native village. Merlin continued, casting new suspicions on Amadu Bamba's move:

> Thus the marabout decided to settle not far from N'Gabou, where the assassin of Lieutenant Minet resided . . . in the neighborhood of M'Baké where he founded a large village called Touba.[13]

Merlin's report goes to considerable lengths to cast suspicion on Amadu Bamba's migration to Bawol, employing innuendo and outright falsehoods to achieve his goal.

Merlin treated Amadu Bamba's more recent movement from Bawol to Jolof in the same light. He interpreted it as a direct response to the death of Tanor and the threat of increased French power in Bawol. Merlin was speaking of French intentions rather than realities, since the "reorganization" of Bawol had not yet been completed. Nevertheless, he wrote:

> Today Jolof is in the same situation as Bawol was in 1887 when he arrived there.[14]

Merlin argued that Samba Laobé Penda, the king of Jolof, was weak, lacked authority, and was perhaps near the end of his life. Therefore Amadu Bamba's presence in Jolof, with what Merlin described as "thousands" of warriors, was suspicious. Merlin did not explain to the governor that Samba Laobé was a French ally and protégé, and that it could easily be argued that Jolof with a ruler was more stable than Bawol without one. Merlin was well informed about what was happening in both Bawol and Jolof. He had taken personal charge of the "reorganization" of Bawol after the death of Tanor. Bawol had no chiefs because the young Wolof princes whom Merlin had chosen to rule Bawol were still undergoing a period of intense education and training. Merlin knew these things, but he could count on the fact that the governor and the Privy Council were unlikely to take much interest in the details of French policy in the Wolof kingdoms.

Having cast suspicion on all of Amadu Bamba's movements and activities since 1886, Merlin proclaimed that everything he had done fitted into the pattern of Muslim leaders who had waged holy war against the French. This included associating himself with "Tijani doctrine" and "preaching holy war." It would be foolish for the French to show "excessive tolerance" and allow his embryonic rebellion to develop. There was no evidence to support these claims, which amounted to labeling Amadu Bamba a "dangerous fanatic."[15]

In their reports, Leclerc and Merlin referred to previous troubles between the Murids and the French administration in Njambur province in 1891–1892. Leclerc claimed that Amadu Bamba had visited the governor in Saint-Louis in 1891 and "denounced" many of his own disciples in exchange for his own freedom. Merlin gave a slightly different account. He said that Amadu Bamba had prevented his arrest in 1891 by sending his brother to Saint-Louis. His brother had assured the French of his loyalty and "delivered" the most compromised disciples.[16] There is little direct documentation of the troubles between the Murids and the French in Njambur province from 1889–1892. A letter from the Governor to Amadu Bamba from 1889 survives. It explains why the Governor expelled certain troublemakers from Njambur province. But the Governor's letter is written in a high-handed style used to "talk down" to Africans, and does little to clarify events.[17] It is clear that some of Amadu Bamba's disciples were expelled from Njambur province, that an exchange of letters and meetings took place between the French and representatives of Amadu Bamba, and that relative calm ensued thereafter. It is significant that Ibrahima N'Diaye and Majaxate Kala, both members of the Muslim party in Kajoor, provided most of the intelligence to the French in 1889.[18]

Merlin and Leclerc rehashed the events of 1889–1891 to discredit efforts by Amadu Bamba's family to defend him in 1895. Leclerc described the efforts of Amadu Bamba's brother, Ibrahim (Ibra Fati), to keep the peace and defuse tensions. Leclerc sent one of his interpreters to Touba to demand the surrender of Amadu Bamba. According to Leclerc, Amadu Bamba at first agreed to the French terms, and then made excuses and sent his brother, Ibra Fati, to Leclerc. Leclerc delivered an ultimatum to Ibra Fati. Either Amadu Bamba would surrender or Leclerc would attack Touba and seize him by force. Ibra Fati seemed indifferent to this threat, which he received with a quiet smile. Only later, when he observed that the military column was preparing to depart, did Ibra Fati plead with Leclerc and promise that his brother would surrender voluntarily. Leclerc agreed and there were no more misunderstandings.[19] Leclerc and Merlin treated the diplomacy of Ibra Fati as a "ruse" similar to those used in 1891. This time the French knew better than to fall for the same old tricks.

Leclerc and Merlin did everything they could to create the impression that Amadu Bamba was preparing a holy war, but their case was weak. It was based on rumor, on analogies with past events, and on efforts to associate Amadu Bamba with people who had opposed French authority in the past. One piece of evidence that Merlin did not mention was a report by a spy working for the French who visited Touba in 1893. Sidi Mohammed's main mission had been to report to Merlin on the activities and attitude of Tanor. During his mission Sidi Mohammed visited Amadu Bamba's village of Touba for three days. He arrived with a group he had met en route and was welcomed as a guest. He made an effort to talk to disciples of Amadu Bamba and reported:

> They told me that the marabout didn't like it when people joined him and then spoke badly of the whites. Such persons were told to leave and they were told to behave well toward the whites because they never harm those who submit to them. If they respect you, you are left in peace, but those who disobey them are punished.[20]

Sidi Mohammed also reported that Amadu Bamba only left his house to pray and that his disciples strictly controlled access to him.

The vacuum created by the death of Tanor provided the historic context for the alarm about Amadu Bamba. French sources indicate that the warnings came from Njambur (Ibrahima N'Diaye) and Kajoor (Demba War Sall) rather than from Bawol and Jolof. In fact, French sources point a finger directly at Ibrahima N'Diaye. Ibrahima N'Diaye began to sound the alarm about Amadu Bamba. His retainers reported seeing arms that were never found. He supplied most of the troops used during the operation. He ruled over a population that did not respect his authority. In 1889 and 1891 the French authorized him to arrest and expel followers of Amadu Bamba from his province. What was the threat Amadu Bamba posed to N'Diaye? Did he really believe Amadu Bamba planned to declare a jihad? Or did he simply feed false information to the French in the hope that they would remove his enemy from the scene?

One way to answer these questions is to examine Murid sources for the events of 1895. The basic explanation suggested to me by Murid historians was simple and fits much of the evidence. The Wolof chiefs who slandered Amadu Bamba feared him because he was "powerful." His power came from the numbers of people who flocked to him to become his disciples.[21]

Murid sources recall the troubled times in Njambur in 1889–1891 and the relative calm that followed. In Bachir Mbacké's biography of his father, *Blessings of the Eternal*, these troubles began when the "traditional chiefs and their collaborators" began denouncing Amadu Bamba to the governor. The governor gave the chiefs permission to expel the Murids from Njambur and force them to emigrate to Touba. The chiefs persecuted the Murids, burning down their houses and seizing their crops and property. Amadu Bamba wrote to the governor and the governor agreed to let the Murids live in peace if they obeyed the precepts of law and religion. These events are dated 1306–1307 in the Muslim calendar or 1888–1889.[22] French sources confirm this effort by the chiefs of Njambur province to outlaw the Murid order in their territory.[23] Murid recollections help explain why Amadu Bamba's followers in Njambur felt they had little choice except to emigrate to Bawol. Persecution by the chiefs created a movement of emigration. The continuation of this exodus to Bawol became one factor behind the events of 1895.

Murid sources depict a much more vigorous diplomatic effort by the Murids in 1895, led by Ibra Fati, who is known as Maam Cerno in Wolof. Ibra Fati first traveled with a letter for the governor. When he learned it was too late to stop the orders being given for his brother's arrest, he intercepted Leclerc en route. Murid sources focus on the duplicity of the Wolof interpreters and chiefs who worked for the French. They belonged to the faction behind Amadu Bamba's troubles with the French and did everything they could to frustrate Ibra Fati's mission. They mistranslated his words and the words of Leclerc, creating confusion and distrust on all sides.[24] Murid sources mention a figure they identity simply as the "secretary" (using the French word) of Samba Laobé Penda, the king of Jolof.[25] This man can be identified as Fara

Biram Lo. He was the French Resident in Jolof, sent there to advise Samba Laobé. He accompanied Leclerc on his mission, playing a crucial role. He was sent ahead to Touba to negotiate Amadu Bamba's surrender and was Leclerc's go-between in his discussions with Ibra Fati.

The informers who denounced Amadu Bamba in 1895 were principal figures in the colonial regime in Kajoor. Ibrahima N'Diaye represented the old-guard Muslim faction in Njambur province. The informers had tasted power from 1861 to 1869, only to be removed when Lat Joor returned from exile to become king in 1869. Many of them had supported the jihad of Amadu Seexu in 1875 as a way of getting rid of Lat Joor. This group gained definitive control of Njambur province in 1883.[26] Most of Ibrahima N'Diaye's allies were from the old Muslim elite of titled marabouts. They were threatened by the emergence of Amadu Bamba as a charismatic Muslim leader whose fame was leading Muslims to leave Njambur for Bawol. Demba War Sall and Ibra Fatim Sarr represented the royal slaves of Kajoor. The Wolof chiefs feared Amadu Bamba because his movement offered refuge to Wolof peasants and slaves eager to escape the authority of their masters in Kajoor and Njambur.

The arrest of Amadu Bamba had further repercussions in Jolof. The arrest and deportation of Samba Laobé Penda came in the wake of French action against Amadu Bamba. The French chose Samba Laobé to serve as king in 1890. In 1895 Samba Laobé was charged with offering to aid Amadu Bamba in his holy war against the French. The director of native affairs, Martial Merlin, presented these charges in a report to Governor-General Chaudié on January 2, 1896. The arrest of Samba Laobé was in some ways the comic epilogue to the exile of Amadu Bamba. All the dubious characteristics of the former decision were magnified in the case against Samba Laobé.

Fara Biram Lo, the *originaire* Resident in Jolof who served as chief interpreter during the arrest of Amadu Bamba, provided all the evidence against Samba Laobé. Fara Biram Lo had risen rapidly in the corps of interpreters. Born in 1869 in Saint-Louis, he had graduated from the *école secondaire* and served the French as an interpreter during the military operations in Jolof in 1890 and in a mission to the Ferlo in 1891.[27] In 1894 he was sent to Jolof by the French to observe and counsel Samba Laobé. Merlin described the relations between Fara Biram Lo and Samba Laobé in his report:

> The Burba Jolof, instead of taking into consideration the opinions and advice of this agent, as we had instructed, regarded him with

suspicion from the first day, and did everything he could to get rid of him.[28]

While Samba Laobé perceived Fara Biram Lo as an ambitious rival, the French naively viewed him as their loyal representative. His reports were considered trustworthy sources of intelligence. According to Merlin, Fara Biram Lo's reports

> showed each day more clearly the state of barbarism into which Jolof was submerged. Samba Laobé lived in a state of total degradation. Surrounded by his wives he took no interest in affairs of state and abandoned the direction of the country to a few *ceddo* of his entourage who took advantage of his indolence and indifference by continually plundering the unfortunate peasants and herders.[29]

This stereotypical portrait of the brutal *ceddo* was only a prelude to the real charge against Samba Laobé. He alone among the chiefs had neither denounced Amadu Bamba nor provided troops to aid his arrest. On the contrary, shortly before Amadu Bamba's arrest, Samba Laobé had become his disciple, an act which Merlin claimed "implied on the part of the political chief the offer of warriors for any undertaking whatsoever, which the religious chief wished to attempt." The final piece of evidence was even more spectacular:

> Our Resident and some guards on tour in Jolof discovered an abandoned chest containing a box of papers in the middle of the forest 30 kilometers from any habitation.[30]

Among these papers was a letter from Samba Laobé to Amadu Bamba promising him support in his jihad against the French.

These "proofs" were taken seriously in 1895, even though it is virtually certain that Fara Biram Lo had forged them. The French began to doubt them later, when they had ample evidence of the ambitions of Fara Biram Lo. Fara Biram Lo remained as Resident after the arrival of the new French-educated chief, Bouna N'Diaye. Fara Biram began a campaign of denunciation against the new Burba. Transfered to Kajoor, he then attempted to undermine French confidence in Demba War Sall. But Bouna N'Diaye, with his French education, and Demba War Sall, with over ten years of service, were able to expose the intrigues of Fara Biram Lo. In 1895, French fears of jihad precluded any serious examination of the evidence. The arrest and exile of the king seemed to confirm the justice of the action taken against Amadu Bamba.

Fara Biram Lo's effort to use his knowledge of the French to his own advantage was a sign of things to come. Although he worked for his own benefit, Fara Biram was typical of the *originaires*, who hoped to make gains from the conquest. French administrators were predisposed to believe reports given them by French-educated interpreters. *Originaires* spoke French and understood French values much better than Wolof aristocrats. An *originaire* as well educated as Fara Biram Lo could couch his reports in terms that appealed to deep-seated prejudices and beliefs. An interpreter charged with an inquiry into the abuses perpetrated by a Wolof ruler was handed a golden opportunity to further his own career.

In Wolof historical memory, the exile of Samba Loabé magnifies the importance of Amadu Bamba. He was sent into exile accompanied by a Wolof king, who became his disciple. In 1995 in Dakar I interviewed a well-known Murid painter who runs a workshop that produces paintings on glass and serves as a distribution center for Murid literature. I was shown two paintings that illustrated the events of 1895. One showed a scene in the governor's Privy Council where all the prominent Muslim leaders signed a statement acknowledging that the governor "was the only king." Amadu Bamba had refused to sign the statement and this was the reason for his arrest. The scene did not depict a historical event, but illustrated the Murid slogan "God Alone Is King." The second painting showed Samba Laobé sitting beside Amadu Bamba as his humble disciple in Gabon.[31] The Murid pop singer Cheikh Lo also drew on this image in his song "Bamba sunu Goorgui." The refrain emphasizes that Bamba went to the sea [i.e., into exile] accompanied by Samba Laobé Njaay.[32] The marabout was now the master and the king was the servant.

THE DRAMA OF 1886

The French sources for the arrest of Amadu Bamba may be a classic example of a "poisoned well," but this has not stopped them from exerting a predominant influence on subsequent research. Later researchers read the documents of 1895 with the hindsight created by the dramatic expansion of the Murid order in Senegal.

The most influential interpreter of things Murid was Paul Marty. Marty was an expert on African Islam who worked for the Government-General of French West Africa and wrote extensively on Islam in the period from 1907 to the outbreak of World War I. Marty reworked the raw data of the archival reports into a coherent interpretation of what he called "Muridism." In doing so, he gave new life and vigor to some of the most dubious charges brought against Amadu Bamba in 1895. Marty never questioned the analysis presented by Merlin and Leclerc, which linked the "Murid threat" to the crisis created by the French occupation of Kajoor in 1886. Marty repeated Merlin's assertion that Amadu Bamba left Kajoor in 1886 for Bawol to escape French authority, and that he migrated from Bawol to Jolof in 1895 for the same reason.[33] In fact, Marty's biographical sketch of Amadu Bamba is a paraphrase of Merlin's indictment. In 1886 and "for a long time thereafter" Amadu Bamba believed he was destined "to restore, for his own benefit, [independent] local authority."[34] For that purpose, he gathered around him the partisans of the old regime, who lived at his expense. Marty believed that French repression had convinced Amadu Bamba to limit his ambitions to the religious sphere, but his following still embodied a kind of Wolof patriotism. The die-hard partisans of Wolof independence had converted to Muridism as a way of expressing "passive resistance" to the colonial regime.[35]

Marty's discussion of the Murids embodied other, more subtle assumptions, which have influenced later research. Marty wrote: "In this vast political drama, the principal actor is not Amadu Bamba. It is the chorus that plays the leading role."[36] The chorus consisted of Amadu Bamba's brothers and his most prominent disciples, especially Shaykh Ibra Fall. Marty presented the founder as an enigmatic, mysterious figure, and one, furthermore, who was little involved in the dramatic expansion of the Murid order. Marty paid little attention to Amadu Bamba's family background and life before 1886. In two pages Marty presented a rapid overview that focused on Amadu Bamba's father's close relations with Lat Joor. This reinforced the connection between Amadu Bamba and the partisans of the old regime.[37] Marty's writings create the impression that Amadu Bamba emerged into history in 1886 during the conquest of Kajoor and that he embodied Wolof resistance to the conquest in a new Islamic guise.

Marty's writings have influenced all subsequent research. This influence is particularly striking in treatments of the life of Amadu Bamba. Marty's basic narrative has been accepted without question in most works. The crisis of 1886 and the link between Amadu Bamba and Lat Joor is central to Donal B. Cruise O'Brien's interpretation of the Murids. Cruise O'Brien transformed Marty's stage directions, his hints about the "condottieri of the old regime," and his argument that the "chorus" plays the leading role, into the "drama of 1886." This drama focuses on three characters, Lat Joor, Amadu Bamba, and Shaykh Ibra Fall. As he developed his interpretion, Cruise O'Brien gave the leading role to Shaykh Ibra Fall, the semi-pagan *ceddo* who embraced Amadu Bamba in 1886.

The most significant link between Marty and Cruise O'Brien is the latter's interpretation of the migration from Kajoor to Bawol in 1886. "The battle of Dekkilé, in the year 1886, was the final defeat of the Wolof armies at the hands of the French conquerors."[38] In O'Brien's view, the death of Lat Joor created a crisis and the Murid order was created in this moment of defeat and humiliation. French sources suggested that Amadu Bamba made the move when he did to escape French authority, which cast suspicion on his intentions. O'Brien accepts this but adds a new element by drawing upon the traditions of Wolof bards, who describe a meeting between Lat Joor and Amadu Bamba on the eve of the battle. In O'Brien's synthesis, this meeting symbolizes the transition from active to passive resistance to the French. Amadu Bamba is linked firmly with Lat Joor. More importantly, Amadu Bamba inherits the following of those displaced by the conquest.

There are a number of problems with this synthesis. The "battle of Dekkilé" was a police operation to remove Lat Joor from the scene rather than a major military confrontation. Lat Joor had been deposed three years earlier. It was Samba Lawbé's death in 1886 that made Lat Joor once more a threat to the colonial regime in Kajoor. Wolof bards celebrate "Déqle," but only to emphasize that Lat Joor died almost alone, with a small group of followers, abandoned by his old allies. His martyrdom was a gesture of "honor." Demba War, his old ally, led the troops that tracked him down.[39]

Wolof sources provide multiple accounts of the meeting between Lat Joor and Amadu Bamba. The grandson of Lat Joor, whose name, Amadu Bamba Diop, symbolized his family's new Murid identity, argued that Lat Joor hoped to obtain a blessing for his actions and to see his martyrdom endorsed as that of a holy warrior killed in a jihad. Instead Amadu Bamba offered him "more than a kingdom" if he stayed with Amadu Bamba as a follower. Lat Joor refused this offer, but accepted the gift of a *boubou* (Muslim cloak), which became his funeral shroud. Amadu Bamba also prayed for him.[40] Lat Joor's grandson emphasized the fact that most of Lat Joor's immediate family became followers of Amadu Bamba after Déqle.[41] Murid sources recall the meeting, but stress Amadu Bamba's efforts to persuade Lat Joor to stay with him. Amadu Bamba offered to teach Lat Joor and to guide him, and wanted him to give up his plans for a confrontation with the French. Lat Joor refused.[42] For Wolof bards this refusal is charged with meaning. Lat Joor was an aristocrat, he had vowed resistance; his word and honor had been engaged. The epic also focuses on the ironies that bind the two men and their families. As he takes leave of Lat Joor for the last time, Sëriñ Bamba, Xaadimu Rasool (the servant of the Prophet), forgives Lat Joor's son in advance for the persecution he will suffer at the son's hands.[43]

Cruise O'Brien drew upon the "traditional history" of Kajoor for his account of 1886, but he ignored the context of the meeting between Amadu Bamba and Lat Joor.[44] For the bard, the drama of Lat Joor was the "betrayal" of the king by his oldest friends and allies. The principal "traitor" was Demba War Sall. Demba War engineered the coup that forced Lat Joor into exile in 1883 and he led the French patrol that tracked Lat Joor down at Déqle in 1886. After Lat Joor's death, Demba War assumed power in Kajoor and held his position until his own death in 1902. In the final encounter between Amadu Bamba and Lat Joor, Amadu Bamba asks:

> Am nga nguurug àdduna ba mu doy;
> Naa la defal nguurug Barsaq?

> You have had a worldly kingdom already;
> How have you prepared for the kingdom of Barsaq (the other world)?[45]

In the epic, the meeting demonstrates Lat Joor's loyalty to the values of the court and the aristocracy. Whatever his religious beliefs, he was still bound primarily to his word of honor. When he refused Amadu Bamba's offer to stay and study, he chose honor (*jom*) over submission to God.

By removing the story from its context, Cruise O'Brien changed its meaning. The message was not the movement from one dynasty to another, but Lat Joor's martyrdom in the cause of an aristocratic code of honor opposed to Islam. The bard emphasizes the conflict of values. Not only does Lat Joor refuse Amadu Bamba's offer, but Amadu Bamba must forgive Lat Joor's son for persecutions yet to come. In the bard's narration, time is porous, and the future illuminates the past. Mbakhane Diop, Lat Joor's son, will play a crucial role in the second arrest and exile of Amadu Bamba in 1903. It is these future events to which the bard alludes.

Murid sources have had little influence on what scholars have written about Amadu Bamba. The main reason is the difficulty of gaining access to the Murid tradition, which is communicated in Wolof and Arabic. Researchers have been given a false sense of security by the abundance of materials in French. Few French language sources, however, reflect the Murid tradition. This applies to French language materials by Senegalese authors as well as to works by French colonial experts. Scholars have not been careful enough in establishing the provenance of their sources.[46] One author, Fernand Dumont, has written an intellectual biography of Amadu Bamba based on a study of some of his *qasida*.[47] Dumont's research is valuable, but it was undertaken without consulting the traditions and commentaries in Wolof that accompany the *qasida*. The selection of *qasida* Dumont used was just that, a selection, which omits many poems cited by Murid authorities.[48]

In summer 1995 I went to Darou-Mousty, a large town in Geet province in the kingdom of Kajoor. Darou-Mousty was founded in 1912, but it is now the center of the Murid order in Kajoor. Not far from Darou-Mousty is the village of Mbacké-Kajoor, which was founded by Amadu Bamba's father around 1870, just after Momar Anta Sali was appointed judge at the court of Lat Joor. Not far from Mbacké-Kajoor is Déqle, a village that houses the tomb of Lat Joor and the tomb of Amadu Bamba's father. Déqle is also the battlefield where Lat Joor was killed by French troops in 1886. Darou-Mousty, the town that now dominates the region, was the principal residence of Ibrahim Mbacké, Amadu Bamba's brother. Ibrahim, known to the French as Ibra Fati and remembered in Wolof as Maam Cerno, was the closest disciple of Amadu Bamba within his immediate family. His descendants dominate the town today, and I went to Darou-Mousty to interview them about their history. I chose this landscape rich with memories of Wolof history because of its close ties to the events of 1886 and 1895.

When I arrived in Darou-Mousty, the Murid commemoration of the hundredth anniversary of the exile of their founder had just come to an end. Needless to say, for the Murids, the events of 1895 have an intense religious meaning. One way this is expressed is through the notion that the exile was a test. Because God intended great things for the founder, because he intended to raise him up, it was necessary for "the servant of the Prophet" [Wolof, *Xaadimu Rasool*] to be put through an earthly trial.[49] Stories, some of them based on the poetry of the founder, some of them popular tales, tell of the sufferings and dangers that Amadu Bamba overcame. One disciple in Darou-Mousty informed me that Sëriñ Tuuba, as Amadu Bamba is commonly known in Wolof, underwent 286 trials during his exile, a number identical to the number of verses in the second sura of the Quran.[50]

In Darou-Mousty I was on the track of Murid memories, interpretations, and narratives. I was received at the house of Moustapha Apsa Mbacké, one of Maam Cerno's many sons. I explained my intentions, hoping my explanations in Wolof would produce results. I was then sent to see the head of the town, Serigne Abdou Khoudosse, who is the current successor of Maam Cerno. After our meeting, he authorized my research.

One of the questions I hoped to answer in my fieldwork concerned how the Murid order preserved its history. The answer was not long in coming. I was directed to address myself to particular individuals in Darou-Mousty. These were the historians of the order. One of Abdou Khoudosse's sons told me: "We don't need *géwél* here. We write our own history."[51] An explicit contrast was being made between the memories of the bards (Wolof, *géwél*) and the memories of Muslims. I was told that the foremost historian of the town and of Maam Cerno was Serigne Bassirou Anta Niang Mbacké. He was one of Maam Cerno's sons and had written a book about his father in Arabic, with a translation in *wolofal*, Wolof written in Arabic characters. I was also referred to Serigne M'Baye Guèye Sylla, an enterprising young scholar in the town who had established a foundation in honor of Maam Cerno. Finally, I was advised that I should travel to Darou-Marnane, a village near Mbacké-Kajoor, to speak with Pathé Dieng, an older man who had written *wolofal* poetry about Maam Cerno. As I completed this tour of those who had been recommended to me as "historians," I learned more about the intellectual traditions of the order.

By pursuing the memories of the Murids I hoped to find a different master narrative than the one in the French archives. I was looking for history as commemoration, maintained by repeating stories about Amadu Bamba, by reciting his poetry, by recalling his words. This realm of memory is not quite the same as the "history" of the academy. Amadu Bamba was spoken of in what might be called the "sacred present" and his words were not recalled as history but as religion. But these memories did record what the Wolof chose to remember about their own history, not what the French chose to document in their archival files.

Murid sources about Amadu Bamba have been shaped by the intellectual traditions of Islam. The study of the Quran is the foundation of Islamic education, but Islamic intellectual traditions were shaped by the way the life of the Prophet was studied. Because the Prophet's life was a noble example, scholars studied narratives or traditions (called *hadith*) that contained sayings or actions of the Prophet. These traditions were analyzed as sound or unsound by studying the chain of transmitters that led back to one of the companions of the Prophet. Biographical dictionaries, which paid particular attention to the connections between individuals, flowed naturally from the study of *hadith*. The scholars of Islam soon extended this form to include biographical dictionaries about themselves, paying particular attention to the wanderings of itinerant scholars pursuing their education. Alongside the *hadith* and biographical dictionaries, popular biographies of the prophet Muhammad and of Sufi saints shaped the way history was remembered in Muslim communities.

The biographies of Amadu Bamba have been shaped by these ways of preserving the past. The life of the founder begins with an account of his ancestors and their achievements as Muslim scholars. It then treats his education, including a mention of his teachers and those who guided him in his spiritual quest and education. The biography then turns to some of the turning points in his life. One of these turning points has direct relevance to what Cruise O'Brien calls the "drama of 1886."

In Murid traditions, the first turning point of Amadu Bamba's adult life involved the decisions he made when his father died. These stories explain the emergence of his mission and his decision to leave Kajoor for Bawol. Momar Anta Sali died in December 1881 or December 1882, depending on the account. The most precise date given is "Tuesday, 20 Muharram 1299" in the Islamic calendar,[52] a date which converts to December 12, 1881.[53] Other sources give Muharram 1300,[54] that is, December 1882. In the simplest narrative, Amadu Bamba is invited by one of his father's friends to present himself at the court of Lat Joor to offer his services to the king. This invitation is given just after his father's funeral services have come to an end. Because his father served the king, he is assured his request will be well received. Bamba replies:

> As for the prince, I declare to you that I will not pay visits to princes, that I desire nothing of their worldly goods. I will only seek honors from God, the master of masters.[55]

In the assembly of mourners, some expressed surprise and admiration at this refusal of worldly wealth. Others were amazed and wondered if he was stupid or crazy.[56] After this revelation of his intentions, Amadu Bamba called the students who had been studying with him and his father and told them that there would be a dramatic change:

> Those who keep my company to learn should look inside themselves. You are free to go elsewhere or to return to your families. But if you want what we want, do as we do.[57]

This laconic announcement caused a number of students to leave. Afterwards Shaykh Bamba kept silent, asking no questions for an extended period of time, until only a minority of the disciples remained. These events were the prelude to his departure from Kajoor and settlement in Bawol.

Despite the assurances given to me that Murids did not need bards, some of the most important Murid sources on the life of Amadu Bamba are performances by converted bards. On religious holidays, "popular preachers" speak before crowds of the faithful. Most of these popular preachers are from bard families. They have converted to the Murid path and created a new form of employment for themselves as preachers. This professional adaptation requires literacy in Arabic. The popular preachers translate Arabic texts, especially the poetry of Amadu Bamba, into Wolof and make them accessible to the mass of Murids, who at best have a ritual command of Arabic for the purposes of prayer.

The reason why bards, rather than Murid scholars, fulfill this social role has much to do with the value system of the Wolof old regime and the place of the bard within it. In Wolof society the bard witnessed to social status in a society in which honor was the core value. Bards were public speakers who witnessed to honor and courage, cowardice and shame. Bards, as masters of public speech, spoke for other groups. The bard performed an important social function, but had a low status in society. As clients, bards were inferior. One result is that rhetorical, artful speech is a sign of low social status. In public settings, aristocrats whispered to their bards and the bards spoke for them.

Popular preachers in the Murid order speak artfully and loudly before the public, using microphones to amplify their speech. This kind of performance is respected when a preacher shows his knowledge of Arabic and can interpret and contextualize the text that is translated. But such performances are not perceived as "dignified" teaching like that carried out by high-status scholars. For my purposes, the popular preachers' performances were important sources. They came closer to a historical narration of the life of Amadu Bamba than any other Murid sources. They also supplied a tradition of explication and commentary. These performances, which I purchased as audiocassettes from specialized traders in the marketplace, had the additional advantage of being addressed to a contemporary Wolof audience. They were sources I had found, rather than sources that I had helped to create.

In accounts of Amadu Bamba's life, the narrative serves as a general framework that allows a writer or performer to elaborate and comment on the message in the events. Murid commentators insert *qasida* into the narrative to explicate events. A good example of this occurs in Mbaye Ngirane's (a converted bard's) treatment of the events surrounding the funeral of his father. He begins by noting that Amadu Bamba was thirty years old when his father died and that he had already acquired a reputation as an important scholar and teacher. After his father's funeral, a friend of the family asks Sëriñ Touba to present himself at the court of Lat Joor. He refuses. Mbaye Ngirane explains Bamba's refusal by quoting extensively from his *qasida*. His refusal of worldly honors is based on his sole allegiance to God alone. The assembly promptly replies, "He's crazy!"(*Ñu dalde ne dafa dof!*) This leads to a long reflection, based on another *qasida*, on "Murid craziness." Shaykh Bamba is proud to accept the charge that he is crazy if it describes his uncompromising devotion to God alone. In the Wolof translation of the *qasida* there is a recurring refrain, "I am crazy" (*dema dof*) and statements such as, "I am fine in my craziness" (*Mangiy sant Yalla ci suma dof*).[58]

In Mbaye Ngirane's narrative, one further event occurs between the funeral and the summoning of the disciples. Shaykh Ibra Fall, one of the central figures of the Murid order, arrives and pledges himself to Bamba or literally "gives him his head" (*jox ko boppam*), setting a new pattern of obedience for Shaykh Bamba's disciples. Then Amadu Bamba calls the disciples together and tells them that if they have simply come to study, they should seek out a new teacher. But if they want to follow his steps (*dox*) and his madness (*dof*) they can come with him. Many leave and many stay, and the group moves from Kajoor to Bawol.[59]

In popular biographies this turning point is a discrete event that explains Amadu Bamba's break with the court of Lat Joor. In other sources, the relation of Amadu Bamba to the court is a key theme, but the explanation is more complex. The most detailed Murid source on the life of Amadu Bamba is the biography that one of his sons, Bachir, wrote in the 1930s, shortly after his father's death in 1927. *Blessings of Eternity* is a complex work. It is more a meditation on the principles of Islamic mysticism than a narrative. But it contains several anecdotes that parallel in meaning the stories that cluster around the death of Shaykh Bamba's father. One passage tells how Amadu Bamba began to attract the attention of his father's patrons and friends in Kajoor, including members of the court of Lat Joor. Amadu Bamba disliked meeting with the nobles of Kajoor and the king. He did so only to please his father. This gave him a reputation which people commented on:

> This behavior toward worldly rulers was the strangest thing in that period. People secretly commented on how little interest he showed in the princes and his repugnance toward them. Some said "Maybe he is crazy" and others affirmed "He's an idiot. We will beg pardon for him."[60]

At the same time this strange behavior gave him notoriety at a young age.

In *Blessings of Eternity,* Amadu Bamba's attitude toward the court is illustrated by a story about how Bamba was courted by Samba Lawbé

Faal, who would oust Lat Joor and become king. Bamba is called by his father and told: "Samba Lawbé wants you to leave with him and become his Shaykh, just as I was the Shaykh of his Uncle Lat Joor."[61] Later, Samba Lawbé visits Bamba and finds him at prayer. Samba Lawbé refuses to sit on the bed that is offered and sits on the floor out of respect. He repeats his request that Amadu Bamba follow him. Amadu Bamba replies: "I cannot leave and abandon these students who have come to learn the precepts of religion. Far from me, such an idea!" Samba Lawbé accepts his refusal. He gives Shaykh Bamba a horse as a gift. As soon as the prince leaves, Shaykh Bamba sells the horse and divides the money between three Muslim creditors who have vainly been following Samba Lawbé.[62]

The most important commentary on Amadu Bamba's relations with the court in *Blessings of Eternity* begins with an account of the controversy about the war between Kajoor and Amadu Seexu. Amadu Bamba's father, Momar Anta Sali, ruled that the war was a war between Muslims, and that therefore no prisoners could be enslaved and the property of the defeated should be returned. As noted earlier, the court ignored this ruling and found Muslim judges willing to rule that it was legitimate to enslave the prisoners and to seize their property. The court regarded the issue as settled until one of Lat Joor's cousins became a disciple of Amadu Bamba in about 1882. As a condition of his conversion, Amadu Bamba made him give up all property and free all slaves acquired as the result of the war in 1875. When Lat Joor heard of this, he was displeased and ordered Amadu Bamba to come to court and to debate the question with the religious scholars. Amadu Bamba refused, invoking the traditions of Islam:

Neither pride nor vanity has prevented me from replying to your convocations. I don't fear to encounter you and since I have no doubts about the validity of my argument, I don't fear a debate with the scholars. But tradition says that one must visit a scholar and not order him to court. . . . I would be embarrassed if the angels saw me before the door of the king for a purely secular affair.[63]

The traditions that Amadu Bamba invoked were Islamic traditions, not Wolof traditions. Amadu Bamba alluded to a *hadith* about the Prophet that said: "The best kings are those who visit the 'ulama' [scholars] and the worst 'ulama' are those who visit the kings."[64] Similar sentiments were expressed by Al Ghazzali, one of Amadu Bamba's favorite authors, who once said that all benefits from rulers were illicit, because everything they owned was either stolen or suspected of being so.[65]

Amadu Bamba's refusal to visit the court was considered disrespectful and might have led to action against him if Lat Joor had not been preoccupied by his troubles with the French over the railway in Kajoor. This allows a fairly precise date to be given for these incidents, since the French troubles with Lat Joor began in early 1882, and by December 1882 the French had decided to drive Lat Joor from Kajoor.[66]

Other Murid accounts of the dispute with Lat Joor emphasize the role of Majaxate Kala, a famous scholar with close connections to both the court and Amadu Bamba. Majaxate Kala had been one of Amadu Bamba's teachers, giving him instruction on the art of writing poetry in Arabic. Majaxate Kala was also the judge who replaced Amadu Bamba's father as Lat Joor's chief judge after the war of 1875. When Lat Joor heard that Amadu Bamba had criticized the enslavement of prisoners taken in 1875, he summoned Bamba to court. Amadu Bamba wrote a letter to Majaxate Kala, in which he quoted a well-known authority who had written: "A learned man in the court of a king is like a fly on excrement." Lat Joor and Majaxate Kala pondered this metaphor, discussing who had fared worse. In the end they decided to ignore the insult, comparing Bamba to the unfertile ground in a field that the owner decided to leave uncultivated.

A few days later, Lat Joor and his judge passed close to Mbacké-Kajoor, the residence of Amadu Bamba. Feeling it was his duty to greet his former teacher and his father's friend, Amadu Bamba met them. Majaxate Kala immediately brought up the war booty taken from Amadu Seexu. He argued that Amadu had falsely proclaimed himself to be a prophet and attacked Kajoor, so it was legitimate to fight him, to take booty, and to reduce to slavery the prisoners taken in combat. "Who told you that he claimed he was a prophet?" asked Bamba. "The people of Kajoor," responded Kala. Bamba replied: "They were his enemies, his adversaries who fought him in war, and you, as a judge, only took into consideration the accusations brought by the people of Kajoor against their enemy." Neither Kala nor anyone else spoke in reply.[67]

Murid sources consistently present Amadu Bamba's break with the court of Kajoor as having occurred during the reign of Lat Joor (prior to 1883). They also argue that the death of his father freed Bamba from his ties to the court. Murid sources indicate that Amadu Bamba left Kajoor after the death of his father, probably sometime in 1882 or 1883. They call into doubt the whole notion that 1886 and the death of Lat Joor constituted a turning point in Amadu Bamba's spiritual career.

Murid sources also offer insights into the immediate background to Amadu Bamba's arrest. The events are treated in Murid commentaries on jihad. Murid sources emphasize Amadu Bamba's rejection of the "jihad of the sword" in his adult life. This theme appears frequently in the performances of popular preachers. The message is clear: Amadu Bamba practiced and taught the greater jihad, the jihad of the soul, and he warned people against the jihad of the sword. Popular preachers draw upon the poetry of the founder to teach these lessons.

M'Baye Ngirane presents the warnings about jihad just after he describes the "awakening" of Amadu Bamba to the supreme status of "master of his time" (Wolof, *boroom jamanoo*, a translation of the Sufi term *qutb al-zaman*, or "pole of the era"). The proof of this awakening was Amadu Bamba's vision of the prophet while he was awake. In Sufi tradition such a vision was a sign: "Everything has its distinguishing sign, and the sign of attainment by the worshipper is seeing the Prophet while awake."[68] This vision is also the basis for the Murid's belief that their order was linked directly to the Prophet Muhammad.[69] The vision occurred in 1893 or 1894, in Amadu Bamba's spiritual retreat at Mbacké-Bari in Jolof, where the French would arrest Bamba in 1895.[70] The encounter of Prophet and shaykh is given an intimate tone, with Amadu Bamba addressing the Prophet as a friend and lover. He would rather stay with the Prophet and never again part from him than become the "master of his time." Mbaye Ngirane explains this vision as the attainment of *ixsaan* (from Arabic *ihsan*), the third phase of truth in Sufi thought, which he explains as a union (Wolof, *jaxasoo*) with God.[71] Amadu Bamba's teachings on jihad were directed to those who pressed him on the issue. When Amadu Bamba rejects jihad he does so by citing a litany of his contemporaries who fought and died: Al Hajj Umar, Màbba Jaxu, Amadu Seexu, listing the places where they died.[72] This litany of tragedy is followed by a listing of the places that Amadu Bamba built during his lifetime and the trials he overcame.

Other popular preachers approach this theme more directly. When Amadu Bamba is asked if he wages jihad, he responds affirmatively: "I wage the [greater] jihad, against what is forbidden and what is pleasing."[73] Alternatively, emphasis is placed on rejection of the jihad of the sword by stressing that there is only one jihad left, the jihad of the soul [*jiyaar ak sa bakkan*], which is greater and more difficult.[74] Amadu Bamba practiced this greater jihad with a single-mindedness that set him apart from his contemporaries. His vision of the Prophet in 1893 or 1894 was proof of his extraordinary mystical knowledge of God. This "charismatic" illumination preceded his arrest and exile.

French archival reports from 1895, Paul Marty's study of the Murids, and Cruise O'Brien's analysis all suggest that the influence and success of the Murid order derived from the close relationship between Amadu Bamba and the family of Lat Joor. This argument was first used to show that Amadu Bamba posed a threat in 1895, because he had an entire *ceddo* army at his command. But it is also central to Marty's argument that the chorus played the leading role in the Murid order. While the founder himself did nothing, Marty argued that Amadu Bamba's following demonstrated that the order was a continuation of Wolof resistance in a new, passive form. Marty assumed that the adhesion of Wolof nobles and princes enhanced the authority of Amadu Bamba. Marty argued that the conversion of the Wolof to Islam was the direct result of Lat Joor's conversion:

> His conversion was followed by that of his subjects, whom he ordered, as is the case with all black princes, to embrace his religion.[75]

Because Lat Joor represented those who opposed French rule, his relations with Amadu Bamba attracted these die-hard patriots to the Murid order:

> The unyielding patriots ran to join the Murids of Amadu Bamba, because this religious chief, the friend and marabout of the fallen Damels, visibly aspired to their succession and became the symbol of their lost independence.[76]

While Marty and Cruise O'Brien explain the success of Amadu Bamba as a result of his relations with the court, Murid sources focus on the conflicts between the monarchy and Islam. Cruise O'Brien ignored his informants' "vehement denials" of Lat Joor's importance to the order and based his interpretation on French colonial sources.[77]

Conflicts did not disappear with the conversion of Lat Joor's family to Islam and affiliation with the Murid order. This can be seen in the portrayal of royal converts in Murid sources. Converts, particularly idle nobles who converted to find a means of supporting themselves, are presented to teach lessons in humility. The new dependency of the converts is a punishment for past misdeeds. After citing precedents in Islamic history for rulers and ministers who were punished for their persecution of scholars, *Blessings of Eternity* relates the story of a "minister" or "adviser" of Lat Joor who mocked Amadu Bamba's legal judgment and incited the king against him. He lived most of his later life in poverty tending his cattle. One day he saw Amadu Bamba, followed by an impressive crowd of disciples. The "minister" rushed through the crowd and forced his way to the front so he would have the chance to touch the palm of the shaykh.[78]

Bachir Mbacké also relates his personal recollections of Lat Joor's sister, a royal princess (*lingeer*) who participated in the intrigues against Amadu Bamba:

> As for the princess, the *lingeer*, I saw her begging before the doors of our Shaykh and before our house and the houses of the Murids. Thanks to their aid she ended by converting to Islam along with other members of the now powerless royal house. Think of the useful reflections that could come from this example.[79]

For the Murids, the lesson to be drawn from the conversion of the nobility is encapsulated in these stories. They show the humiliation of the mighty and the generosity of the shaykh, who forgave his tormentors.

CONCLUSION

French archival sources from 1895 suggest that Wolof chiefs in Kajoor and Njambur engineered the arrest of Amadu Bamba. The most obvious source of the chief's hostility was their fear that the Murid order would undermine their power by attracting peasants and slaves, who migrated to Bawol to seek a better life. Murid sources cast serious doubt on the thesis put forward by Merlin, and elaborated by Marty and Cruise O'Brien, which identified the connections between Amadu Bamba and Lat Joor as the source of Bamba's charisma. The Murid order was not a "rebirth" of the aristocratic party, but a new incarnation of Wolof Islam. Amadu Bamba's reputation derived from his outspoken hostility to the monarchy, which was symbolized by Lat Joor. The aristocrats and *ceddo* who joined the order did not define its meaning. They had to renounce their past and were regarded with suspicion by the scholars who led the order.

Outwardly, the Murid order maintained a position of political orthodoxy and submission to power. Orthodoxy was based on the Quran: "O you who believe, obey God, obey the messenger and those in authority" (4:59). The Murid order affirmed orthodoxy, but did so in a provocative manner. The Murid slogan, "God Alone Is King," (*Yalla rekk moo buur*) sums up this attitude. Today this slogan can be seen on Senegalese taxis and minibuses, but it was once yelled in defiance at aristocrats and colonial chiefs in imitation of Amadu Bamba's break with the court.

Amadu Bamba's life and actions before 1895 help to explain the crisis that led to his arrest and exile. In 1883 Amadu Bamba had broken off his relationship with the court of Kajoor and returned to his homeland with a small group of disciples. This move took Amadu Bamba away from the "Atlantic" core of the Senegalese colony, where the export economy was most developed, to its more independent Wolof hinterland. His departure was a gesture of hostility to the court, since Amadu Bamba left with a reputation based on his refusal to endorse the enslavement and persecution of Muslims by Lat Joor. In the Wolof hinterland, the following of Amadu Bamba expanded rapidly. Between 1883 and 1895, Amadu Bamba and his followers founded or rebuilt three major settlements, Darou-Salam, Touba, and Mbacké-Bari. The new order had positive relations with the Wolof kings of Bawol and Jolof, based on a cultivated indifference to the "things of this world." Lat Joor's grandson relates how Tanor's retainers were allowed to take whatever they wanted from the worldly possessions of Amadu Bamba. They took advantage of this opportunity, passing on much of the wealth to their master, Tanor. Finally, however, they felt shame for taking advantage of Bamba's generosity. At this point Tanor declared himself a follower of Amadu Bamba.[80]

Murid historical memories heap scorn on the Wolof courts. When I asked him what Amadu Bamba thought about Wolof kings, Serigne Bassirou Mbacké reminded me that Muslims had a "constitution" (he used the French word) in the Quran. He peppered his comments on Wolof kings with remarks like "We didn't need kings" (*Soxlauñu buur*), "We didn't need [distinctions] between free persons and slaves" (*Soxlauñu jaambuur, soxlauñu jaami-jaambuur*).[81] On one level, what the Murids asked of Wolof kings was to be left on their own, to live according to their own path.

This was not to be. One interesting aspect of the storm of denunciation that overcame the Murids in 1895 was that it all came from Kajoor, the center of the expanding colonial state and economy. The colonial chiefs of Kajoor and Njambur had inherited what was left of the power of the monarchy in 1886. By 1895 they felt threatened by the growth of a Muslim movement that was settling new villages just beyond their borders. Their opportunity came in 1894 with the death of Tanor, who had ruled Bawol from 1890 to 1894. In 1895, Wolof chiefs began to feed French administrators in Kajoor and Saint-Louis with rumors of holy war. They reinforced the fears they evoked with false reports of weapon shipments and with lists of the dangerous men who had joined Amadu Bamba. The French were taken in by these reports and arrested Amadu Bamba to protect their Wolof allies. The Wolof chiefs also helped create the crisis of 1895, since their persecution had left the followers of Amadu Bamba little choice except migration. It was this flight of men, women, labor, and tax revenues to Bawol that they now wanted to be stopped by French action.

The Murid role in the events of 1895 was their provocative attitude to the colonial representatives of the old Wolof monarchies. The political attitude of the Murids was summarized in their slogan, "God Alone Is King," which combined Islamic orthodoxy with a deep contempt for the court. The political implications of the Murid path had been spelled out over time. The Murid order rejected the jihad of the sword. Amadu Bamba was disturbed by the state of Wolof society, by Wolof ignorance of Islam, and by the vicious social habits inherited from the old regime. The Wolof were ignorant and lazy. The Murid order prescribed hard work for all and serious study for a select few.[82] The flexibility of the order was symbolized by the attitude toward Shaykh Ibra Fall, a converted *ceddo* from the old regime. He worked hard for the founder, leaving diligent prayer and study to others. This heterodox attitude was not condemned, but incorporated into the mission of the new order. The message was clear. The new order was for all, even those with a dubious past. Amadu Bamba's son praised Shaykh Ibra Fall by saying that it was through him that "thousands of scoundrels" who had served the royal courts of Kajoor, Bawol, and Siin had converted to Islam.[83] However, the presence of former *ceddo* in Amadu Bamba's following did not justify the rumors of holy war in 1895. Their conversion and hard labor symbolized their rehabilitation and redemption, their parting with a past of violence and pillage that survived mainly within the French colonial state after 1895.

NOTES

1. Robinson, "Beyond Resistance and Collaboration"; Robinson, "An Emerging Pattern of Cooperation between Colonial Authorities and Muslim Societies"; and Robinson, "The Murids: Surveillance and Collaboration."

2. Oumar Ba, ed., *Ahmadou Bamba face aux autorités coloniales (1889–1927)* (Dakar and Paris, 1982), 42.

3. Ibid., 29–32.

4. 13 G 50, Dossier Ibra Fatim Sarr, chef du Baouar et Gueoul.

5. Ba, *Ahmadou Bamba*, 31.

6. Ibid., 38–39.

7. Ibid., 40.

8. Ibid., 51.

9. Ibid., 37.

10. Ibid., 43.

11. Ibid., 44–45.

12. Ibid., 45–46.

13. Ibid., 46.

14. Ibid., 49.

15. For a discussion of "Tijani" as a code word in French policy, see Robinson, "French 'Islamic' Policy," 415-35; and Robinson, "Ethnography and Customary Law in Senegal," *Cahiers d'Études Africaines*, 32, 2 (1992): 221-37.

16. Ba, *Ahmadou Bamba*, 38, 48.

17. Ibid., 28.

18. They are both named in 1 G 136, Rapport d'Angot, for which, see ibid., 26-27.

19. Ibid., 34-37.

20. 2 D 13-14, Cercle de Thiès, Rapports, tournées, missions. Rapport Sidi Mohammed, 1893.

21. Interview, Serigne Bassirou Anta Niang Mbacké, Darou-Mousty, July 25, 1995.

22. Mbacké, "Les bienfaits (1)," 613-14.

23. This is the view of Paul Marty, *Études sur l'Islam au Sénégal* (Paris, 1917), vol. 1, 225.

24. Mbacké, "Les bienfaits (1)," 616-17.

25. Bouchera Samb, *Waxtaan ci mbir tuuki Sëriñ Tuuba yoonu geej,* audiocassette, tape 1, side 1.

26. See Sabatié, *Le Sénégal*, 331-32, and Diouf, *Le Kajoor*, 274, 284.

27. On Fara Biram Lo, see Ba, *Ahmadou Bamba*, 176; and 2 D 9-13, Rapport de mission de M. Bancal, 1891, which gives details of his early career.

28. Ba, *Ahmadou Bamba*, 78-80, reprints Merlin's report. The passage quoted is on page 79.

29. Ibid., 79.

30. Ibid.

31. The painter's name is Mor Gueye. The interview took place on July 20, 1995.

32. Cheikh Lo, *Né la thiass*, World Circuit, 1996, CD.

33. Marty, *Etudes sur l'Islam au Sénégal*, vol. 1, 230-31.

34. Ibid.

35. Ibid., 251. The phrase "passive resistance," first used by Marty, became a key concept of later writers, especially Cruise O' Brien.

36. Ibid., 281.

37. Ibid., 222-23.

38. Cruise O'Brien, *The Mourides of Senegal*, 11.

39. Dieng, *L'épopée du Kajoor*, 432-36.

40. Diop, "Lat Dior et le problème musulman," 526.

41. Ibid., 526.

42. Interview, Serigne Bassirou Anta Niang Mbacké, Darou-Mousty, July 25, 1995.

43. Dieng, *L'épopée*, 432.

44. In a recent article, David Robinson follows Cruise O'Brien but compounds his error by describing the bards' account as "Murid tradition": Robinson, "Beyond Resistance and Collaboration," 157.

45. Dieng, *L'épopée du Kajoor*, 432.

46. For example, the work of Cheikh Tidiane Sy, *La confrérie sénégalaise des Mourides* (Paris, 1969), is Senegalese, but does not reflect the Murid tradition.

47. *Qasida*, from the Arabic, describes a kind of poem that praises its subject.

48. Fernand Dumont, *La pensée religieuse d' Amadou Bamba: Fondateur du Mouridisme sénégalais* (Dakar, 1975). Dumont's work is still useful, but did not have the impact it might have had.

49. For example, see Mbacké, "Les bienfaits (1)," 619.

50. Notes of meeting with Serigne M'Baye Guèye Sylla.

51. Field notes on visit to Abdou Khoudousse, Darou-Mousty, July 1995.

52. Mbacké, "Les bienfaits (1)," 587.

53. For conversion, I used G.S.P. Freeman-Grenville, *The Muslim and Christian Calendar: Being Tables for the Conversion of Muslim and Christian Dates from Hijra to the Year A.D. 2000* (London, 1963).

54. Mouhamed Moustapha Ane, *La vie de Cheikh Ahmadou Bamb*a (translated by Amar Samb) (Dakar, n.d.), 6.

55. Ane, *La vie*, 7.

56. Ibid.

57. Ibid., 9.

58. Mbaye Ngirane, *Waxtaan ci Sëriñ Tuuba*, audiocassette, no date. Judging from internal references, this recording dates from before 1989, because it was recorded while Abdou Lahatte Mbacké was the head of the Murid order.

59. Ibid.

60. Mbacké, "Les bienfaits (1)," 586.

61. Ibid.

62. Ibid., 586–87.

63. Ibid., 605.

64. Quoted by Henry Munson, Jr., *Religion and Power in Morocco* (New Haven, Conn., 1993), 44.

65. Ibid.

66. See the account in Diouf, *Le Kajoor*, 270–74.

67. Samb, *Essai sur la contribution du Senegal à la littérature d'expression arabe*, 429–30, quotes this conversation from a work in Arabic by Mamadou Lamine Diop.

68. See Louis Brenner, *West African Sufi: The Religious Heritage and Spiritual Search of Cerno Bokar Saalif Tal* (Berkeley, Calif., 1984). Brenner quotes this from Umar's writings and comments on the concept, 41–42.

69. The best study of Muhammad in Islamic thought is Schimmel, *And Muhammad Is His Messenger*.

70. The French refer to a "second Touba" in Jolof. Murid sources refer to this village as Mbacké-Bari, and explain that Amadu Bamba rebuilt an abandoned village that had been founded by his grandfather.

71. Mbaye Ngirane, *Waxtaan ci Sëriñ Tuuba*. The stages of truth are explained in Mbacké, "Les bienfaits (2)," 48: Islam (submission) is the first phase, manifest in Islamic law (*shari'a*); faith (*amin*) is the second phase, manifest in the Sufi way (*tariqa*); and *ihsan* is the third phase, manifest in the absolute truth (*haqiqa*).

72. This litany is quoted first in Arabic and thus derives from the *qasida*.

73. Samb, *Waxtaan ci mbir tuuki*, tape I.

74. Moumar Mamoun Amar, *Waxtaan ci yoonu geej*, audiocassette.

75. Marty, *Études sur l'Islam au Sénégal*, 250.

76. Ibid., 251.

77. Cruise O'Brien, *Saints and Politicians*, 24.

78. Mbacké, "Les bienfaits (1)," 606–07.

79. Ibid., 607.

80. Diop, "Lat Dior et le problème musulman," 530–31.

81. Interview, Serigne Bassirou Anta Niang Mbacké, Darou-Mousty, July 25, 1995.

82. Mbacké, "Les bienfaits (1)," 596–97.

83. Mbacké, "Les bienfaits (2)," 70.

4

CREATING COLONIAL ORDER: STATE AND SOCIETY IN BAWOL, 1894–1903

In the 1890s, the French colonial authorities implemented an important series of political reforms in Bawol. Since the French had made few demands during the conquest, these initiatives can be considered a "second conquest." The motivating factor was the death of Tanor Ngogne, the king of Bawol, in 1894. The choice of a successor was an obvious opportunity for the French, but its impact was amplified by the arrest of Amadu Bamba. The political reconstruction of Bawol that followed the conflicts of 1895 was the most significant in the colonial period and had long-lasting effects. This is one of the few times in which French authorities acted on a coherent set of principles. Most research on French administrative policy has focused on the better-documented period that began with the creation of a powerful Government-General in 1902. By that time, however, the outlines of the colonial state were well established in Senegal. With a few exceptions, the policies articulated in Dakar after 1902 had little impact on the basic structures of colonial rule. The reforms of the period after 1895 were based on the policies of disannexation and protectorate rule that emerged in 1890. The French decided to achieve their goals by placing French-educated aristocrats in charge of smaller versions of the traditional Wolof kingdoms. This was an extension of Faidherbe's attempt to rationalize government by replacing "corrupt" kings with kings who accepted French leadership.

From a political point of view, the efforts at reform failed. French ignorance of and indifference to the "traditions" of Wolof politics contributed to this failure, as did poor management of the program by individual French administrators. French-educated Wolof aristocrats failed to perform as expected, which was blamed on their atavistic attachment to the old regime. But the greatest threat to the French-educated aristocrats who took command of Bawol came from within Wolof society. Their failure is interesting because they were under attack from many quarters. "Senegalese" citizens denounced them as feudal exploiters and tyrants, zealous "republican" commandants investigated them for corruption, and militant Murid disciples insulted them and refused to obey their orders unless told to by their religious superiors. In the end, the French reforms accelerated the triumph of Islam that was already evident by 1903, when Amadu Bamba was arrested and exiled for a second time to protect the prestige of Mbakhane Diop, the son of Lat Joor.

The conflicts that undermined French reforms were driven by the same factions and parties that had struggled for advantage during the conquest. Because the state was dominated by aristocrats representing a reformed monarchy, the most important critics of these aristocrats were urban representatives of the "Senegalese" party and the new Sufi orders that replaced the old Muslim party. The populations of the Four Communes emerged from the conquest with an ambiguous status as French citizens and heightened expectations that they would reap the benefits of colonial rule. A diaspora of urban-based merchants, politicians, and French-educated clerks and commercial employees saw Bawol as a frontier of opportunity whose doors could be opened with an organized attack on *ceddo* tyranny and oppression. At the same time they learned that the protectorate regimes could be used to exclude them from landownership and political power in the Wolof countryside. Their privileges were also their liabilities. Their predicament was summarized by the new term used to describe their status, *originaire* (that is, from the Four Communes). The term for the status that gave them special rights also labeled them as outsiders. At the same time, the Murid order was building a new social order in eastern Bawol, based on its ability to recruit disciples. The second arrest and exile of Amadu Bamba in 1903 revealed the decline of aristocratic power and prestige. The conflicts that undermined the authority of colonial chiefs reflected deeper social changes taking place within Wolof society, as peasants sought out new patrons in a rapidly changing social order.

This chapter begins with a brief discussion of Bawol under Tanor from 1890 to 1894. The discussion then turns to French efforts to reform Wolof monarchy. The expectation that exposure to French education and administrative practice would transform Wolof aristocrats into bureaucrats serving the colonial order was naive. French administrators rarely followed the protocol of the protectorate policy, which conflicted with deep-seated republican prejudices against aristocracy and monarchy. However, the French efforts to create a system of indirect rule in Bawol also failed because aristocratic authority was under seige from within. The chapter concludes with a discussion of the new position of Islam in colonial society, which is one measure of the social transformations underway.

THE END OF THE OLD ORDER:
THE REIGN OF TANOR NGOGNE

The reign of Tanor Ngogne Dieng brought an aristocrat from the same generation and background as Lat Joor to the throne. Tanor had campaigned with Màbba and Lat Joor in his youth. His "election" in 1890 was more a result of his friendship with Demba War Sall than a result of local support. Like Lat Joor, Tanor restructured the kingdom to accommodate Islam without sacrificing aristocratic power. He appointed Muslim judges to administer justice for the Muslim community and expected political support from the Muslims in return. In Bawol these reforms had much less support than in Kajoor. At least a third of the population was made up of non-Muslim Sereer, who looked to the titled representatives of the *jaambuur* for political protection. Tanor's rule was steadfastly opposed by members of the Fall dynasty, who regarded Tanor as a usurper. While Demba War Sall benefited from the dethronement of the Fall dynasty, which might claim rights in Kajoor, Tanor's rule was weakened by his lack of local support. The French were hardly aware of the political dimensions of Tanor's election, although they would have a major impact on Bawol.

Bawol was on the periphery of the areas controlled by the French in the 1890s. The governor corresponded with Tanor through his *habitant* secretary. Tanor's letters to the governor were written in Arabic by the chief qadi, Matoufa Sylla, and translated by the head interpreter in Saint-Louis. Apart from this correspondence, the French sent out occasional missions of inspection from Thiès, the nearest French post.[1]

French policy soon brought about the situation predicted by the *jaambuur* in 1890 when they counseled Commandant Villiers to abolish the monarchy. They told Villiers:

As soon as Tanor feels secure, we will be eaten [pillaged] by him just the same as by another king. Why doesn't the Governor want to orga-

nize us as in Kajoor? Then we would be done once and for all with
thefts and pillage and we could cultivate in peace.[2]

The dissident *jaambuur* led 1,500 to 2,000 supporters into exile in 1891
to protest Tanor's "election." Patterson, the commandant at Thiès, saw
this as a political maneuver designed to provoke the dismissal of Tanor.
He viewed it as a threat to French authority and helped Tanor disarm
the dissidents, believing that he was disarming the *"ceddo* party," a
group of diehards committed to the old order. Meissa Anta Ngone, the
leader of the *"ceddo,"* was arrested and exiled to Waalo.[3] In 1891
Patterson saw events in Bawol as Tanor wanted him to see them. He
soon changed his mind, but Tanor retained the support of the governor
until his death in 1894.

Once the French had helped Tanor eliminate his rivals, he began to
ignore the orders he received. In 1892 Patterson noted that the "Sultan
of Bawol" rarely responded to French requests. He had refused to compensate Meissa Anta Ngone and other *jaambuur* whose property he had
seized in 1891 and ignored summonses to meet with French representatives.[4] By 1893, Patterson turned against Tanor. In a report to the
director of native affairs he accused Tanor of complicity in thefts and
murders carried out by his slaves and his chiefs, of slave raiding, and
of attempts to bribe Patterson. Patterson denounced the "horrible and
barbarous" crimes that were carried out under the cover of French rule.
The Sereer minorities of Bawol were the victims of the worst abuses.
Relations between Tanor and Patterson became tense, and Tanor came
to regard Patterson as his personal enemy.[5]

Under French pressure, the king punished the worst abuses of Wolof
rule over the Sereer. For example, in 1892 soldiers employed by the
Bar Diack, a province chief, stole seven sheep from a Sereer. When he
complained they seized him, bound him, and hung him upside down
from a tree. When fellow Sereer from the village of N'Diemane tried to
rescue him they were shot down in cold blood, leaving four dead and
three seriously wounded. In spite of the steadfast denials of wrongdo-
ing by the Bar Diack and his retainers, Tanor removed the Bar Diack
from office.

The authorities in Saint-Louis regarded Tanor's reign as an improvement over the situation under Thieyacine, whose intrigues they blamed
for much of the unrest. This interpretation came from no less a source
than Tanor himself, whose letters to the governor went directly to the
director of native affairs. Patterson was replaced by Louis Molleur as
commandant, but relations between Thiès and the king did not improve.
G. Donis, an assistant administrator, conducted inquiries into abuses of

power under Tanor in March and May 1894. Donis detailed the exploitation of the Sereer by Tanor's retainers and condemned the "corruption" and "extortion" common in the administration of justice. These problems were particularly noticeable in the Sereer provinces because Wolof chiefs regarded the Sereer as a source of plunder. The Wolof aristocracy despised the stateless and "pagan" Sereer as "savages." Migration from the province of Ngoye and revolt in the village of Mbambey alerted the French to widespread unrest.[6]

Donis reported that Tanor had confiscated all the horses owned by the Sereer, because their "race" was unworthy. Sereer villages were forced to lavishly entertain Tanor and his retainers when they visited a region. Tanor and his officials imposed heavy fines for minor infractions and lived at the expense of the population while the money was being collected. Tanor's officials investigated each childbirth to see if they could impose fines for out-of-wedlock birth or adultery. Harsh treatment of the Sereer was given a veneer of legitimacy by Tanor's committment to Islam.[7]

Donis tried to convince Tanor to alter his methods of government, at a meeting (*palabre*) in March:

> All afternoon was passed in a *palabre* during which I attempted to make this chief understand that the abusive treatment to which the population of Bawol was constantly subjected was the cause of migration from Ngoye, the revolt of Mbambey. Even if he, Tanor, was not responsible for these acts, it was his duty to find the culprits among his retainers—the source, in my opinion, of all the trouble—and to put an end to all these extortions, which could only harm him and turn the French government against him. He made me understand that the principal cause of all the conflicts was the division of the population into two camps, some loyal to him, and another still under the yoke of the Ex-King Thieyacine.[8]

More was at issue than a dispute over "facts." Signs of unrest disturbed the French, but they expected African chiefs to adopt the French notions of an overarching state power serving the public good. This notion was foreign to France's African allies in the 1890s. They understood politics as an effort to reward allies and eliminate enemies. Conflict was almost inevitable between these two conceptions of power.

Before the French had time to act on Donis' recommendation that Tanor should be deposed, Tanor Ngogne died on June 15, 1894. The governor, Henri de Lamothe, saw an opportunity to bring Bawol more directly under French control without altering its status as a protectorate. He decided to divide Bawol into two provinces under the control of two French-educated Wolof princes. Salmon Fall, the son of Thieyacine Fall, and Mbakhane Diop, the son of Lat Joor, were chosen to command West and East Bawol. Governor de Lamothe convoked the principal *jaambuur* of Bawol to a *palabre* at Thiès on July 3, 1894, recognizing their traditional role as electors during a succession. He explained that the French intended to divide Bawol into two provinces, abolishing the monarchy. Bawol would be ruled by two superior chiefs comparable to Demba War Sall in Kajoor and Yamar Mbodj in Waalo, whom he cited as examples. He promised that crown properties would remain in the hands of their possessors, invited political exiles to return, and promised to maintain district chiefs in their current positions. He tried to explain the reasons for the decisions:

> Real improvements have been made since the time of Thieyacine, but many more are still to be realized. To arrive more promptly at our goals, it is absolutely necessary that the chiefs of the protectorate areas, while being chosen according to the traditions honored by the populations they will govern, be familiar with the ideas and favorable to the interests of the protecting power. It was to further this program that the School for Sons of Chiefs was reestablished. It is from the young people who have attended this school that the candidates will be chosen to fill the positions that become vacant among the current native chiefs.[9]

In a more accurate summary of the "progress" achieved under Tanor, the French governor argued that "every [chief] pillaged at will under Thieyacine," while under Tanor, "only the king and a few of his men" were allowed to abuse their power. The French believed that the ordinary *baadoolo* had benefited from this "regularization" of oppression.[10]

African chiefs were not responsible for all wanton acts of oppression in Bawol. In May 1895, the French administrator at Thiès ordered the "destruction" of the village of N'Dioung for refusing to supply him with fodder for his horses. During the incident, a hostile crowd of armed villagers surrounded him. Under the direction of Tanor's chief retainers, a hundred horsemen burnt the village to the ground after seizing all the property they could carry. According to the French, the villagers were then resettled elsewhere, although there were accusations of enslavement. Later, the brother of the village chief said that the trouble began when Louis Molleur, the French commandant, ordered the arrest of the chief on a "personal whim."[11]

The reforms followed the reopening of the School for Sons of Chiefs and Interpreters in 1892. Governor Clement-Thomas had attempted to re-open the school in 1890, but the General Council had refused to provide the funds he needed.[12] The hostility of the *originaires* to the school was part of the fallout over disannexation. The General Council refused to vote funds for a school designed to educate the sons of chiefs from the "interior." A separate budget was created for the protectorate and the school was reopened. Unlike the budget for the Four Communes, the new budget was under the direct control of the governor. As a result, the rural areas were removed from the sphere of influence of politicians elected in the Four Communes.

The School for Sons of Chiefs and Interpreters trained the collaborators needed to implement indirect rule. The education provided was practical and adapted to local needs. The curriculum included instruction in French, French history and geography, African geography, Arabic, and elementary mathematics, sciences, agriculture, and comparative French and Muslim law.[13] The Native Affairs Department ran the school. This promoted contacts between future chiefs and French administrators and segregated the chiefs from the school system that served French merchants and *originaires* in Saint-Louis. The school continued Faidherbe's policy of winning over African allies and spreading French influence gradually through the co-optation of the local elite.

The decision to educate future chiefs and expose them to the principles of French civilization answered charges that disannexation had been a retreat from the principles of French colonization.[14] It reconciled the protectorate policy with the colonialist ideology of the *mission civilisatrice*, which justified French intervention in the name of the "universal principles of French civilization." The administration of Senegal, which had been attacked for turning over the protectorate to chiefs from the traditional political class, could point to the School for Sons of Chiefs as proof that the French conquest would lead to the gradual improvement of the lot of Africans in French territory. This would occur as French-educated chiefs replaced their "feudal" predecessors. The means chosen to achieve this end had simply been adapted to local social conditions.[15]

In 1894 the French planned a simple administrative reorganization of Bawol. The French were dissatisfied with Tanor and hoped to achieve more rapid "progress" through the appointment of French-educated chiefs. Nothing indicated that the French planned more than this. Delcassé, the minister of colonies, specifically counseled the administration in Senegal not to abandon the protectorate policy for direct rule.[16] Nevertheless, the reform brought rapid change as rival Wolof groups tried to take advantage of the new situation.

FRENCH-EDUCATED ARISTOCRATS IN BAWOL

The French plans to rule the protectorate through French-educated descendants of the traditional ruling class were implemented in 1895. Two young princes who had been captured by the French in the campaigns of the conquest were appointed "superior chiefs" in Bawol. Mbakhane Lat Dior Diop became the superior chief of East Bawol, and Salmon Fall became the superior chief of West Bawol. Both chiefs were sons of precolonial monarchs, but neither had a strong hereditary claim to the position he received. Salmon Fall was the son of Thieyacine Fall by a concubine (*tara*), so traditionally he was a *doomi-buur*, son of a king, but not a *garmi,* or royal prince. Without French support he might have expected to command a subordinate province. As a result his appointment as superior chief aroused controversy within the Fall family.[17] Mbakhane Diop was the son of Lat Joor, but he was given a command in Bawol rather than in Kajoor. His stongest claim was in Geet province (Kajoor), where the Joob (Diop) had their fiefdom. Both superior chiefs were placed in charge of canton and province chiefs whose appointments predated the newcomers' arrival and whose loyalties lay elsewhere. The French did not allow the superior chiefs to make up for their lack of traditional legitimacy through force, nor did they allow them to place their own men in key positions.

The French were not bothered by the fact that these appointments violated Wolof traditions. Their knowledge was imprecise, but they viewed aristocratic prestige as a portable asset attached to a family name and lineage. The French assumption that any Wolof aristocrat could rule any Wolof province undermined the reforms. Salmon Fall and Mbakhane Diop were so young when they were assigned to positions in Bawol in 1895 that it was decided to let them continue their education in Tunis for a few years. The young chiefs returned to Senegal in 1898. The French expected them to act as agents for the dissemination of French ideas and methods of administration. The crash course they had recieved in French civilization and French administrative practice was supposed to guide them and they were expected to introduce more enlightened methods of rule. The French barely acknowledged the enormity of the task that they entrusted to two youths under twenty years of age. In fact they judged the young chiefs' "lapses" all the more harshly because of their education.

Wolof expectations conflicted directly with French ones. The young chiefs were under pressure from the entourage of relatives, clients, *ceddo,*

Figure 4.1 Mbakhane Diop, son of Lat Joor (1920s). (Courtesy of the National Archives of Senegal. Reprinted with permission.)

and *géwél* that quickly formed around them. Relatives and clients expected gifts, patronage, and employment. Because of their youth, the chiefs were expected to listen to the demands and counsel of their older relatives and clients. Some of the French commandants who supervised them were aware

of these pressures and commented on them in their reports, but they regarded these "atavistic" customs and social relations as something to be
combated rather than tolerated. The unrealistic expectations of many French
commandants became a source of tension between them and the superior
chiefs.

The French appointed two assistant administrators as Residents at
Lambaye and Sambe in East and West Bawol to supervise the chiefs, but
they were instructed to stay in the background and allow the chiefs as
much autonomy as possible. The superior chiefs were given a fixed salary
of 10,000 francs a year from the proceeds of the head tax. This was a
generous individual salary, but it was inadequate to meet the many expenses of the superior chiefs, who were expected to support their retainers
from it. The superior chiefs headed their provinces and commanded the
canton chiefs. They were aided by a Council of Notables, which represented the more important canton chiefs and the Qadis of each province.
Canton chiefs were allotted salaries of 3,000 to 4,000 francs if they served
on the Council of Notables and 1,500 if they did not. The Council of
Notables was primarily judicial in function. It was presided over by the
superior chief, and the other members were assessors, performing a role
that combined the functions of assistant judge and jury. The French intended to create a budget for each province, but this experiment was abandoned because the young chiefs were unable to manage the budget. Apart
from their salaries, the chiefs shared some of the proceeds from judicial
fines with the French.[18]

The French regarded the new organization in Bawol as a minor variation on the previous arrangement and believed that the royal origins of
the new chiefs were sufficient to command respect. This proved to be
a serious miscalculation. Under the old regime no ruler could expect
automatic support from provincial commanders. The canton chiefs under Mbakhane Diop and Salmon Fall owed their appointments to local
influence or to the patronage of Thieyacine Fall or Tanor Ngogne, not
to the new chiefs. Salmon Fall might have inherited the support of the
"Fall clan," but he faced the opposition of some of his own relatives,
who held equal or superior title to office. The two most powerful "clans"
in Bawol at the end of the nineteenth century were the Falls and the
Diengs, the political allies of the last two independent monarchs.[19] The
French considered the Dieng family and its allies to be the more important because they retained many of the positions they had gained under
Tanor. The Falls also held a number of important territorial positions.[20]
Some of the subordinate chiefs were powerful and had distinguished
records of service with the French. Salla Dior had volunteered for mili-

tary service outside Senegal in the 1890s and had been wounded leading Wolof troops in a charge against the army of Dahomey. He had been decorated with the Legion of Honor.[21] Neither aristocratic "clan" accepted the authority of the superior chiefs.

Aristocratic opposition was only part of the problem. Peanut cultivation was expanding rapidly and had important ramifications. Two new groups symbolized the change: the Murid community and the *originaires* from Saint-Louis and other coastal settlements who had come to Bawol to profit from trade and related developments. Because Murid leaders tried to cultivate good relations with the French during the exile of Amadu Bamba (1895–1902), the *originaires* contested the power of the chiefs most openly from 1898 to 1902. They regarded the reorganization of Bawol as only a timid step toward direct French rule and pressured the administration to extend French law and abolish "feudal" exploitation. As early as July 1897 the administrator at Thiès, Farque, wrote to express his concern that pressure from the *originaires* would lead the French to intervene directly in the internal affairs of Bawol:

> A certain current of opinion in Senegal has taken the view that the Administrator at Thiès and the two Assistant Administrators at Lambaye and Sambe are the true chiefs of Bawol, even though in reality they are only regulators and inspectors. . . . That would be a dangerous error: these people have already forgotten the only too recent consequences of our direct intervention in the affairs of the natives in the suburbs of Saint-Louis. The consequences would be much more dangerous in Bawol, with a population of 120,000.[22]

The political role of the *originaires* was typified by a demand by Hyacinthe Devès, a member of an influential *métis* family from Saint-Louis. He asked the administration to abolish the *assaka*, a Muslim tax for alms, in the village of N'Dioung where Devès had established his residence. This was the same village that had been destroyed on French orders in 1895. In 1897, Devès claimed to be the village's protector, although his ultimate goal was control of land, labor, and commerce. Devès presented his demand as an attempt to defend the peasantry of Bawol from exploitation by the *ceddo* chiefs. The legal petitions he filed indicate that he worried that the right to collect *assaka* established a claim to landownership. Devès mobilized his network of friends and allies, which included his brother, François Devès, a politician from Saint-Louis, and François Carpot, a lawyer who was politically active in the protectorate. These men had local agents in Bawol who provided them with information on the abuses of the chiefs. In the 1890s they were constantly testing the new administration, particularly the alliance between the French and the aristocracy.[23]

The colonial administration viewed Devès' initiative with suspicion, because an *originaire* with political connections could become a counterforce to the administration in the countryside. *Originaire* politicians threatened the neat separation between the protectorate and the Four Communes created by the policy of disannexation. Politicians from the Four Communes never accepted this artificial division of the colony. Before his election as the first *métis* deputy in 1902, François Carpot practiced local politics in the *cercles*. He sold his legal protection, offered to intervene with the administration to reopen judicial disputes already settled in the native courts, and sent agents into the countryside to solicit complaints against the administration and the chiefs. One of Carpot's favorite claims was that he could make or break a chief employed by the administration.[24]

Notables such as Devès and Carpot relied on the services of lesser agents, often *originaires* employed by the administration, who provided them with intelligence. The *originaires* showed remarkable solidarity. The French were often embarrassed by leaks from African agents in the administration that found their way into the political networks centered in Saint-Louis. Mody Mbaye, a young *originaire* from Saint-Louis, began a career in Bawol in the 1890s that established his reputation as a political advocate and troublemaker. Mody Mbaye first came to Bawol in the 1890s as Tanor's French secretary. He used this position to ingratiate himself with the French and by 1898 he was working as a schoolteacher in Fandène in West Bawol. Along with this function he was charged with supervision of the post and telegraph service, and served as secretary to the Council of Notables headed by Superior Chief Salmon Fall. These jobs provided Mody Mbaye with valuable intelligence on what was happening in Bawol. This information provided the foundation for Mody Mbaye's career as a crusader for justice in "*ceddo* dominated" rural Bawol.[25]

Mody Mbaye was a French-educated intellectual, a public letter writer (*écrivain public*) who combined the functions of notary public and legal advocate for his clients. His trademark was the anonymous letter of denunciation, outlining the crimes of his enemies. His enemies were principally the superior chiefs, because he believed that if the aristocracy fell from power, Mody Mbaye and his allies could take their place.[26] As an employee of the administration, he used his insider knowledge as a weapon. Mody Mbaye is fascinating for what he reveals about the politics of colonial rule in rural Senegal. An underground intellectual opposition to the protectorate policy, based in Saint-Louis, continued to fight for the goals of the "Senegalese" party in the Wolof civil war. They demanded rights to land and power in the countryside, but could do so only indirectly, in covert opposition to aristocratic rule.

The only counterweight to the difficulties facing the superior chiefs was the support of the colonial administration, but this was lukewarm at best. The French commandants in Thiès and Bawol expected the superior chiefs to act like French bureaucrats. G. Adam, the administrator at Thiès, wrote an extremely critical report on the administration of Mbakhane Diop after a tour of Bawol in 1898. He thought he had detected signs that Mbakhane was trying to revive the "spirit of the Dammels":

> Mbakhane, the young chief, is gifted with a keen intelligence. Unfortunately, if left to himself, or rather under the influence of certain of his counselors, the inclinations that are sleeping in him will be awakened quickly and we will be obliged to intervene in a brutal manner. He loves griots, horses, women, royal compounds, etc., etc. He is told that he has the right to all these ornaments because his father was a king.[27]

Mbakhane Diop may have been under the influence of his entourage. Certainly, Adam was influenced by information fed to him through the networks controlled by the *originaires*. In August, Adam investigated charges that Mbakhane was extorting money from his subjects by accepting gifts of millet and animals for himself and his retainers while he was on tour. Mbakhane was also accused of accepting gifts of sheep on the Muslim holiday of Tabaski, and for his wedding. These charges, which were confirmed by Adam's inspection tour, were first made in an anonymous letter addressed to the administrator at Thiès. Adam reprimanded Mbakhane, first in private, and then in public in front of an assembly of notables and chiefs. This, he noted with apparent satisfaction in his report, was an extreme wound to Mbakhane's pride. During the investigation, Mbakhane did not deny any of the charges brought against him, but he excused himself by explaining that the gifts were customary. This was true, but it did not interest Adam, who expected Mbakhane to use his French education to fight the spirit of the old regime.[28]

Adam's relations with Mbakhane Diop revealed the difficulties that plagued French efforts to rule the Wolof states as protectorates. The administration chose to rule through aristocrats in order to tap their prestige and influence, but opposed the aristocratic spirit as corrupt and as a sign of nostalgia for the old order. The French appointed the sons of kings as superior chiefs, but they became alarmed when the chiefs began to assemble a court and retinue, and they saw the actualization of prestige in the form of gifts and tribute as "extortion" and "rapine." They ignored the Wolof nobility's cult of honor and did not hesitate to humiliate the young princes before their subordinates, many of whom were potential rivals. Most of these acts were not based on policy, but reflected the personal relationship between the chiefs and their immediate superiors, the French commandants. French prejudices were manipulated by the *originaires*, who hoped to be the beneficiaries of direct colonial rule.

There is little doubt that many chiefs were "corrupt" and sought unofficial sources of income to supplement their salaries. The chiefs did not use their entire income to maintain a clique of flatterers and courtesans, as some reports suggested. In a typical comment, the director of native affairs told Adam to invite Mbakhane Diop to "dismiss the griots and *ceddo* he had gathered around himself, because if he no longer has to support them he will have fewer expenses."[29] The chiefs paid for the cost of a parallel administration. Their retainers collected taxes, policed the territories, maintained the census rolls used for taxation, and recruited laborers to maintain public roads. The chiefs paid their retainers, but these "wages" were never included in the French budget or in the calculation of the salaries allotted to the canton and province chiefs. Such expenses were a major incentive for "corruption." Expenses of honor such as the maintenance of *géwél*, horses, and polygynous households, which visibly displayed wealth and symbolized chiefly status, compounded the chiefs' financial needs. Maintaining status was an obligation, not a choice.

Different French commandants interpreted the protectorate policy in radically different ways. Under Decazes, who commanded the *cercle* of Thiès from 1899 to 1902, there was a serious effort to work through the superior chiefs. Decazes attempted to reinforce their authority for the first time. He ignored his subordinate in East Bawol when he suggested that Mbakhane Diop be removed from office for his lassitude and lack of authority. Decazes conducted an inquiry into the administration of East Bawol that led him to criticize the Resident, Rocaché, rather than the superior chief. Rocaché had bypassed the superior chiefs and given orders directly to the canton chiefs. This affront to the prestige of the superior chief and Rocaché's lack of tact in his dealings with Mbakhane Diop were singled out as the real cause of the problems in East Bawol. Decazes also tried to pinpoint the sources of opposition to the superior chiefs among their subordinates. In February 1902, Boido Gay, the head of the royal slaves under Tanor, and other chiefs of the "Dieng clan" were removed from office for their systematic attempts to undermine the authority of the superior chiefs.[30] Decazes' more tolerant attitude toward the chiefs was revealed by his investigation into their use of labor *corvées* for the cultivation of their fields. He excused this as a traditional practice, which the French should gradually abolish through the introduction of wages, rather than as a criminal offense.[31] Resistance to Mbakhane Diop was pervasive among the old guard. In 1903, Thieyacine Tiong Fall, the chief of Ngoye, arrived in Diourbel in a drunken rage when he heard that Mbakhane was investigating his administration. Thieyacine Tiong Fall was accompanied by twenty armed cavalry. Although the French could not get a coherent report from him, he protested his innocence and he told Mbakhane repeatedly "that he had campaigned with his father before he [Mbakhane] was born."[32]

The policies of Decazes were abruptly reversed when Vienne replaced him in April 1902. Vienne was an inexperienced newcomer, but he was eager to make his mark. Following up reports of abuses in the administration of West Bawol, he began an investigation that led to the dismissal of Superior Chief Salmon Fall in July 1902. The trial and dismissal of Salmon Fall demonstrated the power of a commandant to make crucial policy decisions. They also demonstrated how the most resolute administrator, particularly one who saw himself as a crusader for justice, fell prey to manipulation. Until his dismissal in 1902, Salmon Fall had received good reports from his superiors. He was often favorably contrasted with Mbakhane Diop, praised for his more modest lifestyle, and described as extremely loyal to the French. In 1902, Salmon Fall was charged with fraud in the collection of judicial fines, misappropriation of public funds, and numerous "extortions." Most of the key testimony against Salmon Fall was given by Mody Mbaye, the *originaire* schoolteacher serving as secretary and treasurer of the Council of Notables of West Bawol. Vienne never questioned the motives of Salmon Fall's accusers. During his trial, Salmon admitted to some minor "extortions," which he described as customary gifts. He admitted that he had been misled at times by his older relatives, but denied the more serious charges. Salmon also admitted to "having collected 1158 francs [in head tax] which he confounded with his personal resources." He promised to pay this sum back after the peanut harvest.[33]

Certain aspects of the trial and its aftermath revealed the political nature of the accusations. Salmon Fall had to be brought before the Council of Notables twice to obtain a conviction. This was achieved because the second council had been purged of all his relatives, clients, and allies. Vienne was so sure that he was liberating the population from exploitation that he dismissed as "childish inventions" the reports from the Resident of West Bawol that Salmon's dismissal was causing unrest. A few months after the trial, the evidence was called into question when Mody Mbaye, the key witness, was fired from the positions he held for embezzlement of funds and other abuses of power. Vienne replaced Salmon Fall, a French-educated aristocrat, with an older brother, Canar Fall, who lacked his education and spoke almost no French. This decision made little sense. The French reforms were designed to replace the old guard with a new generation of French-educated chiefs. Within less than two years, Canar Fall was involved in a slave trading scandal known as the "Chautemps Affair," which led to the death of a French administrator. The dismissal of Superior Chief Salmon Fall reopened all the political conflicts in the *cercle* and went a long way toward undermining the authority of the other superior chief, Mbakhane Diop.[34]

By 1904, the French regretted the "errors" made in 1902. They criticized the irregularity of the trial, the faulty evidence, and the stupidity of the appointment of Canar Fall. Martial Merlin, who returned to Senegal in 1903 to serve as secretary general in Governor-General Roume's cabinet, expressed his regrets and did what he could to salvage the career of Salmon Fall. As one of the architects of the protectorate policy, he regarded the dismissal of 1902 as a mistake. Salmon's wife, Dior, wrote letters to the governor-general in which she pleaded that her husband be given some job and blamed "a certain Mody Mbaye" for his downfall.[35] Salmon Fall was hired as a clerk in Dakar in 1903, where he worked for a meager salary. His financial desperation can be seen in the numerous letters he wrote to have his mother's widow's pension (only 360 francs a year) restored.[36] He was recommended for reappointment as a canton chief by Merlin's office beginning in 1905. He obtained a post in Bawol as canton chief in Mbayar province in 1907, but he died suddenly on October 18, 1911, leaving behind many debts. An inquest determined that poison was the cause of death, but there was no determination as to whether it was a case of murder or suicide.[37]

The story of Salmon Fall is a sad commentary on French policy in Bawol. His dismissal hastened the demise of the aristocracy. Over the long term, the major reason for this decline was the growing influence of the Murid order, but the incoherence of French policy played its role. First, the French appointed teenage princes as superior chiefs in provinces where they had only weak traditional claims. They were expected to command older canton chiefs whose power was well entrenched. Instead of recognizing the difficulty of their position, the

French alternately harrassed them and supported them. More importantly, French administrators were manipulated by the *originaires*, who were waging a covert war against aristocratic power.

This incoherence continued after 1902. Mbakhane Diop was allowed to influence a key decision in 1903. He was the main inspiration behind the second arrest and deportation of Amadu Bamba. Then he was summarily dismissed in 1906 as a corrupt relic of the old regime. Mbakhane Diop was removed from office and his position was abolished after a "severe and competent investigation conducted by M. Molleur led to the recognition of innumerable abuses."[38] Molleur reported that Mbakhane Diop had spent 43,550 francs on horses alone from 1898 to 1901, that his wedding had led to extravagant expenditures, and that he was unable to support his esti- mated 150 dependents (family and retainers) on a yearly salary of 14,000 francs. The evidence was indirect, because it had proven difficult to find witnesses or proofs.

> It was his subjects, the country which paid the costs of this court, and in spite of the greatest surveillance it was difficult to prevent all these people [Mbakhane's dependents and retainers] from forcing the native to con- tribute in order to participate in the prestige of their chief. Mbakhane, who is very proud by nature, could not imagine that the era of the *ceddo* and of numerous escorts was over and that our representatives no longer needed *griots* to sing their praises.[39]

Despite some fear on the part of the French, Mbakhane's dismissal caused no major incidents. Mbakhane Diop, a Tunis graduate, then entered the colonial administration as a clerk and interpreter.[40]

By 1907, when Bawol became a separate *cercle*, it had no superior or province chiefs, in contrast to the other Wolof states. For a brief time the French were pleased with this, but administrative reports from Bawol are filled with complaints about the canton chiefs' lack of real authority. Be- cause of their declining authority, the canton chiefs were unable to resist new challenges to their power.

THE MURID CHALLENGE

Amadu Bamba was arrested and exiled for a second time in 1903, less than a year after his return from exile. A number of similarities seem to invite a comparison between 1895 and 1903. As in 1895 the key French official was Martial Merlin, who was now serving as acting governor-gen- eral. Merlin had written the report that led to the first exile of Amadu Bamba. Fara Biram Lo, who had served as the interpreter in 1895, returned to play the same role in 1903, even though both the French and the Murid community had good reasons not to trust him. More fundamentally, Islam still posed the greatest threat to the Wolof chiefs who formed the core of the colonial state.

The "crisis" of 1903 began in April when Saint-Louis began to receive reports that Amadu Bamba was defying French authority. "Rumors" suggested that his followers were contemplating armed resistance to any attempt to remove him from the village of Mbacké in Bawol. Amadu Bamba had been allowed to return from exile because of his good behavior in Gabon and in response to repeated lobbying on his behalf by his partisans in Senegal. After 1902, his supporters included the newly elected *métis* deputy, François Carpot, who had received financial aid from some of Amadu Bamba's prominent disciples in return for his promise to intervene with the French authorities.[41] The French regarded their decision to pardon Bamba as an act of clemency. In Senegal it was widely interpreted as Amadu Bamba's miraculous victory over his French oppressors. His return was cited as a concrete manifestation of his unparalleled spiritual powers. After his return to Mbacké in East Bawol, Amadu Bamba's presence attracted a large number of visitors who came to give gifts and pay their respects. Some settled permanently as members of the Murid community. This influx of persons and wealth began to cause concern. In April the Resident of East Bawol sounded the alarm. He reported that the presence of Amadu Bamba was undermining the authority of the chiefs and compromising the security of the province.[42]

As in 1895, the French intelligence was based on reports from chiefs under their command, in this case Mbakhane Diop, the superior chief of East Bawol. As the son of Lat Joor, he had a particularly close and difficult relationship with Amadu Bamba. Amadu Bamba had prayed for Mbakhane's father, unable until then to have a son, before Mbakhane was born.[43] Mbakhane knew that Amadu Bamba was one of the last persons his father spoke to before his death. He also knew that many members of his family, including several uncles, had become Bamba's disciples.

Mbakhane Diop was charged with a special mission to gather information on the marabouts of his province in 1903. He came to Mbacké on April 17 and demanded to see Amadu Bamba. He was refused access and told to conduct his business with Shaykh Anta or Ibra Fati, Amadu Bamba's brothers. Mbakhane insisted on seeing Amadu Bamba because of orders from the commandant and he was finally granted permission. According to Mbakhane's report, Amadu Bamba responded to Mbakhane's explanation of his mission in the following terms:

Since my return from Gabon I no longer want to have dealings with chiefs, nor with those called commandants; I will only conduct business with their chief, the Governor, whom I saw in Saint-Louis. You who dare to speak with me like this, if I have not yet rendered you miserable it is only because I pity you: I knew your father. . . . If not for that you would not leave here safe and sound. Beware that nothing befalls you as you leave. Mbakhane, depart and leave me in peace. I am not a man of this world, but of the other; I see only God, my vision passes over men.[44]

Even this one-sided account shows that the encounter between the two men was charged with meaning. Mbakhane Diop was the son of a king, but his father had died as a martyr fighting the French. Amadu Bamba had offered Mbakhane's father refuge at the end of his life. Bamba was now one of the most powerful religious figures in rural Senegal. Many of Mbakhane's elders were his disciples. Although it is difficult to believe that Amadu Bamba spoke in the manner described, it is easy to see why Mbakhane thought the French had put him in an impossible position.

Whatever the details of the encounter, Mbakhane Diop felt that his prestige was jeopardized. He described his dilemma to Martial Merlin, whom he had known since the 1890s when Merlin had supervised his education at the School for Sons of Chiefs. After describing the growing power of Amadu Bamba and the Murid order he concluded:

You can verify that Amadu Bamba plays a role much greater than mine, that his influence impairs my authority and my prestige. Some canton chiefs have reported that their subjects no longer listen to them because the influence of Muridism dominates their cantons. You can understand how difficult it will be for me to command this part of my province where I can no longer go without risking another affront and humiliation. . . . I would therefore be grateful to you for examining the situation in which I now find myself, because the French government appointed me and has the duty to support me.[45]

The meeting between Mbakhane Diop and Amadu Bamba set the stage for the crisis of 1903. One further "incident" occurred before the French decided to act. Amadu Bamba refused to come to Thiès to meet with the French commandant: he wrote that he was in religious retreat and was too ill to leave Mbacké.

Merlin showed greater caution and sophistication than he had in 1895. He demanded more detailed information, and in May he dismissed reports of rebellion and jihad as exaggerated rumor. Because he considered the commandant at Thiès, Vienne, inexperienced, he asked the administrator at Tivaouane, Allys, to send a trusted agent to Mbacké to collect information on the spot.[46] Merlin himself sent Fara Biram Lo, the government's head interpreter, to Mbacké. His mission was to convince Amadu Bamba to come to Saint-Louis. Fara Biram Lo carried a letter from Shaykh Sidiyya, a pro-French marabout from Mauritania. The French had calculated that he was Amadu Bamba's spiritual master, based on his position in the Qadiri order. Shaykh Sidiyya counseled obedience to the French.[47] When Amadu Bamba refused to leave for Saint-Louis, Merlin began preparations for his arrest.

Even after the decision to dispatch a column, Merlin took precautions to avoid military confrontation and unnecessary bloodshed. Shaykh Ibra Fall, who had a residence at Thiès, was contacted by the French and sent ahead with a letter from Merlin explaining the reasons for the arrest. This letter, entrusted to one of Amadu Bamba's closest disciples, explained Merlin's plans to send Amadu Bamba to reside with Shaykh Sidiyya in Mauritania. Bamba was asked to surrender peacefully to avoid bloodshed. In the end, Amadu Bamba was taken into custody without a shot being fired. He was exiled to Mauritania in the hope that the influence of Shaykh Sidiyya would lead to a resolution of the conflicts between the Murids and the French colonial authorities.[48]

The arrest of Amadu Bamba was motivated by fears that inaction would lead to a collapse of French authority. The rumors circulating in 1903 were considered extremely dangerous. People reported that Amadu Bamba had defied French authority with impunity, that the French feared him and were powerless, and that the *tubab* (Europeans) would soon be forced to leave Senegal.[49] Merlin decided that these rumors presented a real threat to French interests. Even if they were grossly exaggerated, they could affect the population and lead to trouble. Merlin feared that the actions of a "few hotheads" would be sufficient to provoke serious incidents and threaten the lives of French traders in Bawol. Given the social psychology of colonial Senegal, the refusal of one marabout to leave his village resulted in near hysteria and the dispatch of a major military column.

As in 1895, the Murids seemed ill prepared to deal with the crisis. Amadu Bamba underestimated the seriousness of the situation, as it was seen by the French. At first he tried to respond to the French summons through his brothers Shaykh Anta and Ibra Fati. They were sent to Saint-Louis with letters assuring the French of his loyalty and peaceful intentions. On June 3, Amadu Bamba wrote a letter to Merlin explaining that his refusal to go to Saint-Louis was not a sign of hostility to the French.

He claimed that his only desire was to be left alone to pursue his religious studies. He asked Merlin to disregard the charges of his enemies. He had not and would not defy French authority. By the time Merlin received this letter, the preparations for Bamba's arrest had already been made.[50]

After his arrest, Amadu Bamba blamed his difficulties on the lack of discipline of some of his disciples. They were responsible for the rumors that encouraged a spirit of disobedience to the French authorities. Before leaving for Mauritania he left instructions for his *taalibe*. For the first time he counseled obedience to the colonial chiefs as well as to the French authorities:

> From now on he who puts me in difficulty with the Government and the chiefs by his words will be abandoned in this world and the next.
>
> Here are the instructions that you should follow: He who wishes to read and write in Arabic should address himself to my brother Ibrahima, called Ibra Fati. He who wishes to work without studying should address himself to my brother Sidi El Moctar, called Shaykh Anta. He who wishes to combine study and work should go to Ibra Fati.

In the same letter, Amadu Bamba warned his brothers and prominent disciples to expel any disciples who caused trouble with the French authorities, including the chiefs.[51]

In the aftermath of Amadu Bamba's arrest, the French believed that they could detect signs of tension in the inner circle of the Murid order. Some members of Amadu Bamba's family reportedly blamed Shaykh Anta for Amadu Bamba's troubles with the colonial chiefs. Ibra Fati, the brother closest to Amadu Bamba, requested and received permission to emigrate to Kajoor. According to Commandant Allys' report, "He only wants to live in peace with us and cultivate his fields, but no longer wishes to have anything to do with Shaykh Anta Mbacké."[52] Ibra Fati's decision to move was opposed by Shaykh Anta, who regarded himself as the head of the community in his brother's absence. Ibra Fati believed that the French might allow Amadu Bamba to live with him in Kajoor as an alternative to exile in Mauritania. The French arranged for Meissa Mbaye Sall, the chief of West Saniokhor in Kajoor, to concede sufficient lands to Ibra Fati and his followers. Within a short period of time, the region settled by Ibra Fati became one of the richest peanut exporting centers in Kajoor. Along with Ibra Fati, Amadu Bamba's older brother, Moumar Diara Mbacké, Touba's village chief, actively sought to repair relations with the French. Moumar Diara served as the guide to Commandant Prempain when the latter toured the Murid community in Bawol in August 1903, demonstrating his willingness to cooperate with the French authorities. During the crisis of April–May he had reportedly said: "I knew we would get into trouble, because our conduct is not that of a marabout but that of a king."[53] The French believed that both brothers regarded Shaykh Anta as the source of trouble with the French and the chiefs, although Wolof custom allowed them to suggest this only indirectly in their conversations with Prempain.

The French agreed that Shaykh Anta was the main source of conflict between the Murids and Mbakhane Diop, the superior chief. In the period preceding the crisis, Shaykh Anta had become the enemy of Mbakhane Diop. He had written numerous complaints against the superior chief, which he sent to the French administration. At first, the bad relations between Shaykh Anta and Mbakhane Diop pleased the French. Their conflict signaled the end of a dangerous "friendship." Pior to their falling out, Shaykh Anta had tried to win Mbakhane's friendship through gifts of horses and other acts of generosity.[54] After Amadu Bamba's arrest, Shaykh Anta maintained a provocative attitude toward the French and Mbakhane Diop. Shaykh Anta believed that his political connections in Saint-Louis made him immune to punishment, and he promised to use his influence to secure his brother's release. When Prempain toured the Murid community, Shaykh Anta was absent, letting it be known that he was making "political calls" in Saint-Louis. When he returned, he made a public show of his reluctance to shake hands with Mbakhane Diop, who had accompanied Prempain on his tour. One of Prempain's goals was to reaffirm French confidence in Mbakhane Diop and to explain to the Murids their duty to obey the chief as the representative of French authority. Prempain emphasized his point by telling Shaykh Anta that, in contrast to the superior chief, no one owed Shaykh Anta any deference except as a wealthy man. Outwardly Shaykh Anta accepted this explanation, but he was the Murid leader who asserted that the Murids were the true successors of the aristocracy in Bawol.[55]

By all accounts Shaykh Anta was an ambitous man. His demand to be treated like a great lord was a source of conflict in 1903. Shaykh Anta demanded respect and deference not only from the Murid community but also from the colonial chiefs. Mbakhane Diop felt humiliated in 1903, and suspected that someone was inciting the Murid community to show disdain for the superior chief. The defiant speech that Mbakhane Diop quoted in his letter to Merlin sounds more like Shaykh Anta than Amadu Bamba. Mbakhane's humiliation came from the refusal of Amadu Bamba's brothers to let him see the shaykh. In 1903, Amadu Bamba may have paid the price for his brothers' ambitions.

Murid sources give a different picture of the events of 1903, with the blame placed squarely on Mbakhane Diop. Like the Wolof chiefs in 1895, Mbakhane feared Amadu Bamba because of the strength and faith of his followers. He therefore spread slander and lies to provoke the French into action.[56] In Darou-Mousty, I asked the scholars of the town about Maam Cerno's (Ibra Fati's) decision to emigrate to Kajoor in 1903. Their immediate response was that it was not Maam Cerno's decision, but the result of an order (*ndigal*) from Amadu Bamba.[57] Someone was needed to take charge of the Murid community in Mbacké-Kajoor. The leader of the community in Kajoor had died recently and Maam Cerno's family had close connections with Mbacké-Kajoor.[58] He also went there to create new settlements for the order.

Murid sources downplay conflicts within the family; they indicate that the expansion of the order in Kajoor came out of a sense of new opportunities there. Demba War Sall died in 1902 and his sons and nephews were trying to establish themselves as his successors. The Sall family took advantage of the conflict between Mbakhane Diop and Amadu Bamba because it was an opportunity to weaken the family of Lat Joor, which had ambitions in Kajoor. Amadu Bamba's son recalled the extraoridinary behavior of Meissa Mbaye Sall, Demba War's son, during the crisis of 1903:

My uncle told me that when Meissa came to greet the Shaykh and receive his blessing he found him preparing to depart. He joined with the Murids who were carrying the baggage just as if he was one of them.[59]

The gesture of Meissa Mbaye was not forgotten, but taken as a sign. When Maam Cerno settled in Kajoor he developed a close relationship with the Sall family.[60]

The exile of Amadu Bamba reveals characteristic aspects of French policy toward Islam. The French overreacted to a struggle over prestige and influence between French-appointed chiefs and Murid leaders. Because they did not understand the nature of Amadu Bamba's authority and stature, the French reacted in near panic to unverified rumors and to Amadu Bamba's refusal to leave his chosen retreat. The dispatch of a military column and the arrest of Amadu Bamba hardly seem justified. The Murids misjudged the importance of prompt compliance with requests to meet French representatives. The events of 1903 suggest that the French accepted the consequences of their alliance with the aristocracy and were prepared to back the colonial chiefs. If so, the French quickly abandoned this policy. In 1905, Mbakhane Diop was "blacklisted" by Governor Camille Guy along

with other prominent representatives of the aristocracy, and he was summarily removed from power in 1907.

French reports on the exile of Amadu Bamba indicate the absence of
any well thought-out policy toward the Murid order. Most reports con-
fine themselves to comments on the "rebel" marabout and his reported
activities. Most of the information was gathered second hand from the
chiefs, even though they were direct parties to the conflict. There was
no attempt to move beyond these stereotypes and analyze the Murid
movement as a social phenomenon. Almost a decade passed before the
French began the systematic study and surveillance of Islam under
Governor-General Ponty.[61]

The decision to exile Amadu Bamba had important consequences for
both the French and the Murids. Amadu Bamba lived under house arrest
and surveillance for the rest of his life, since the French never again took
the risk of letting him live outside their control in rural Senegal. His exile
increased his stature as a religious leader and "martyr of Islam." Amadu
Bamba maintained correct relations with the French for the rest of his life
and cooperated with the colonial authorities when they made specific demands of him. At the same time, Amadu Bamba seemed to understand that
his stature depended on his refusal to seek out direct relations with French
authorities.

AMADU BAMBA, MALIK SY, AND THE TRIUMPH OF ISLAM

The second exile of Amadu Bamba symbolized many of the changes
taking place in Wolof society at the turn of the century. Its full significance appears most clearly when seen in the larger setting of Kajoor
and Bawol. In 1902, the year that Amadu Bamba returned from exile,
Al-Hajj Malik Sy took up permanent residence in Tivaouane, in the
heart of Kajoor. The two "renewers" of Wolof Islam in the twentieth
century had taken their place as the successors of the nineteenth-century
Muslim party. The contrasting careers of Amadu Bamba and Malik Sy
reflected the very different positions they occupied in the Wolof landscape of colonial Senegal. Malik Sy based his career in the cities and
towns of the Four Communes and Kajoor. Amadu Bamba created a series
of new settlements in rural Bawol, attracting migrants who wanted to
live under his authority. Malik Sy did not pose a threat to the Wolof
aristocracy and openly accepted French rule. Amadu Bamba was in a
position where he competed for the allegiance of Wolof peasants and
attracted runaway slaves, even if he tried to maintain peaceful relations
with those in power.

Malik Sy returned from the pilgrimage in 1891 and settled in Saint-Louis, where he taught for a number of years. Malik Sy founded schools or lodges for the Tijani order in Saint-Louis, Dakar, and Tivaouane, the capital of Cayor District (*cercle de Cayor*). In all of these places, Malik Sy lived in territories ruled directly by the French. His affiliations with the Tijani order included a direct link to Al-Hajj Umar (and therefore to jihad), but these ties were moderated by Malik Sy's affiliation with branches of the order in the Sahara and North Africa that had never supported jihad and had submitted peacefully to French colonial rule. [62] Malik Sy devoted most of his attention to education and the schools he ran were reputed to be the best in Senegal. This was the opinion of Paul Marty, who also took note of Malik's Sy's strong following among the "citizens" of the Four Communes. In Kajoor, Malik Sy won the support of the Muslim party, as exemplified by the fact that a majority of Muslim families and scholars joined his branch of the Tijani order. This was a significant change. In the nineteenth century, Islam had a territorial organization symbolized by the role of the *sëriñ*, who commanded specific villages and districts in Njambur and held titles to lands scattered throughout Kajoor and Bawol. This territorial organization co-existed with Sufi Islam, which in the early nineteenth century meant the Qadiriyya order. At a time when the monarchy could still threaten Muslims with pillage and enslavement, the protection offered by the territorial authorities was important. During the colonial period, protection was no longer a major issue. The *sëriñ* who became colonial chiefs in Njambur under the patronage of Ibrahima N'Diaye quickly lost their religious authority. Learning, mysticism, and charisma became the new signs of religious authority. Most Muslims rallied to the new Sufi orders that were emerging, and the Tijani branch founded by Malik Sy was the most successful.

In contemporary Senegal, Malik Sy's pro-French stance seems more suspect than it did at the time. Postcolonial scholarship and nationalism have both emphasized jihad. In this context, the French persecution of Amadu Bamba gives a nationalist aura to his order. Malik Sy's support of French rule was couched in language that appealed to the sentiments of Muslims in Kajoor. In 1912, Malik Sy addressed a letter to the Tijani order and all Muslims in Senegal that called on them to support French rule. French victories during the conquest were a sign of God's will. Part of his letter specifically addressed the history of the monarchy:

Remember, before they came [to rule] amongst us, we were killing one another, we were enslaving one another and we were pillaging one another, whether we were Muslims or infidels. And if they had not come, we would still be in that state, today more than ever.[63]

This judgment must be read as a condemnation of the monarchy echoing the position of the old Muslim party. Malik Sy's position in support of French rule was similar to that taken by other scholars who condemned jihad and argued that French rule provided better guarantees for the practice of Islam than the old regime ever had. Sa'd Bu, a prominent scholar in Mauritania, had taken this position publicly in 1909 when he condemned armed resistance to the French and argued that Muslims who followed jihad always ended by shedding Muslim blood and living from pillage.[64]

Malik Sy's mission as a teacher in Tivaouane posed no threat to the French or to the traditional Wolof hierarchies in Kajoor. Unlike Amadu Bamba he did not found new villages or settlements and therefore he was never accused of trying to "steal" other people's children, slaves, or dependents to build up his own following. On the other hand, Tivaouane was strategically positioned in relation to the Wolof heartland in Kajoor and to the Four Communes. It was located in the corridor created by the railroad between Saint-Louis and Dakar, where towns like Louga, Tivaouane, and Thiès were growing rapidly, attracting a mixed population of rural migrants and "citizens" from the Four Communes. Malik Sy's branch of the Tijani order played an instrumental role in diminishing the cultural rift that might have emerged between Wolof Muslims and the "citizens" of the Four Communes. In the Four Communes, Malik Sy came to represent an educated and progressive Islam that had nothing to fear in dealing with the "civilizing mission" of the French colonial state. Wolof Muslims who had lived with a *ceddo* monarchy could come to terms with a secular colonial regime that protected their freedom to worship as they wished.

In its time, Malik Sy's Islam was socially conservative, but open to the "modern" world as represented by French colonialism. Malik Sy argued that Muslims could take advantage of modern technologies like the telegraph to transmit important religious messages, such as announcing the end of Ramadan to fasting Muslims. His disciples came from many of the wealthiest, established families in Kajoor and the Four Communes. Some of his judicial decisions supported the status quo with learned arguments. He ruled that Muslims should pay the obligatory alms on the peanut crop, because it was the basis of the economy, even though other jurists argued that alms tax should be confined to basic subsistence crops (and not levied on cash crops).[65] In its historic context Malik Sy's ruling supported demands for *assaka* on peanuts, which was collected by titled Muslims and other titled "landowners," including chiefs like Ibrahima N'Diaye and the Sall family in Kajoor. Malik Sy argued from principle, not on the basis of French interpretations of land tenure law, but his ruling was probably welcomed by landowners. The most progressive aspect of Malik Sy's mission was his emphasis on rigorous educational standards.

Amadu Bamba's position in the Wolof landscape could not have differed more. The Murid order was rural. It was formed in opposition to the court and the monarchy. It expanded by drawing in new converts, migrants who uprooted themselves and moved to Bawol, on the periphery of Wolof society. Most scholars have tried to explain the arrest and exile of Amadu Bamba in 1895 and again in 1903 by analyzing French "Islamic" policy. I have tried to show that French decisions were made in direct response to promptings from Wolof aristocrats. In 1895, Wolof chiefs in Kajoor and Njambur denounced Amadu Bamba as a dangerous fanatic preparing for holy war. The charge was false, but it reflected the fears generated by the emergence of a new pole of charismatic authority in the aftermath of civil war.

More specifically, the Murids were identified with a faction from Kajoor's civil war: those who supported Lat Joor in 1886 and who opposed the settlements of 1883 and 1886 that gave power to Muslim notables in Njambur and royal slaves in central Kajoor. Although this claim had some truth to it, it does not really explain the hostility and fear behind the charges. Was there anything in the teachings of the Murid order to justify the hysteria? One possibility is the Murid *ndigal*, a term used to describe a religious recommendation or order coming from a person of authority. A *ndigal* from Amadu Bamba must be obeyed, according to Murid belief. If he had ordered a holy war, there is no doubt that his followers would have obeyed. French sources show no awareness of this doctrine. Amadu Bamba's enemies in Wolof society would have known about it. In contemporary Senegal, Murid and non-Murid alike often see the *ndigal* as the defining characteristic of the Murid order. Tijani Muslims explain the political and economic power of the Murid order by pointing to the *ndigal*, since the Tijani successors of Malik Sy in Tivaouane have no comparable authority over their disciples. In the early colonial period, Murid disciples frequently refused to obey orders from canton chiefs until they received a *ndigal* from their religious superiors telling them to do so. This, combined with the slogan "God Alone Is King," created an attitude of disobedience to "political authorities" (representing the corrupt powers of this world) that enflamed the hostility of Wolof chiefs. In 1903, Mbakhane Diop tried to use the power of the French colonial state to overcome the disrespect rooted in Murid beliefs.

Although the *ndigal* may have seemed subversive and dangerous to those in power, it cannot entirely explain the events of 1895 and 1903. The migrations set in motion by the Murid order posed a real threat to aristocratic power. Wolof religious scholars, aristocrats, peasants, and slaves began migrating to the new settlements created by the Murids in the 1880s. From the perspective of the Wolof rulers in Kajoor, this movement posed a double threat. The Murids created a dissident religious community just beyond the borders of Kajoor, based on an ideology that threatened the legitimacy of those in power. At the same time, migrants from Kajoor made up a large proportion of the new converts. Their departure weakened the social basis of aristocratic power, which depended on the labor and obedience of peasants and slaves. This theme will be explored further in subsequent chapters on slavery and emancipation.

Finally, one might ask what the role of French Muslim policy was in 1895 and 1903. It played no real role in 1895, but in 1903 it led to the decision to exile Amadu Bamba to Mauritania, where he was to reside with Shaykh Sidiyya Baba, a prominent scholar who supported French colonial rule. The rationale for this decision was that Sidiyya Baba occupied a higher position of authority within the Qadiri order, to which Amadu Bamba also belonged. The French hoped Amadu Bamba would behave as Sidiyya Baba's disciple and absorb his teachings, obeying him "as one would the orders of a father toward a son."[66] Although this reflected a more sophisticated understanding of Islam than previous French decisions, it was based on a false premise and did not achieve its desired goals. Amadu Bamba created no trouble in exile, but he never behaved as the disciple of Shaykh Sidiyya. Murid sources emphasize Amadu Bamba's independence and his claim to a greater spiritual power than that of his host. Bachir Mbacké tells an anecdote about how his father was separated from Shaykh Sidiyya and then delayed rejoining him, despite receiving several commands. One of Shaykh Sidiyya's messengers suggested that Bamba's act was spiritual disobedience to his superior. In response, Amadu Bamba wrote a letter to Shaykh Sidiyya that said: "I am not your disciple—as you know well—because I am forbidden from attaching myself to anyone on this earth. This is not because I disrespect or underestimate Shaykhs, but because the Messenger of God turned to me to educate me and promote me and there is no way that I can turn away from him."[67] This passage alludes to Amadu

Bamba's vision of the Prophet in 1893 and Murid belief in a direct connection between the order and the Prophet Muhammad.

Other Murid sources make the same point in another way, by noting that Amadu Bamba first revealed a distinct *wird* or ritual prayer for the Murid order while he resided in Mauritania.[68] This was the final step in formalizing the distinct identity of the Murid path as a separate Sufi order, independent of the Qadiri or Tijani orders. It was, in effect, a declaration of independence made while Bamba was in exile. Once again, there is a striking contrast between Amadu Bamba and Malik Sy. Malik Sy devoted considerable energy to acquiring prestigious links to the Tijani order in Mauritania and Morocco. Amadu Bamba claimed a direct link to the Prophet Muhammad that freed him from such connections and rooted his order in Senegal.

CONCLUSION

The political conflicts that undermined French reforms and aristocratic power had their roots in the Wolof civil war that began in 1859 and ended with the colonial conquest. The issues, factions, and personalities that crystallized at the conquest continued to dominate the conflicts between the colonial state and Wolof society. Although colonial sources depict these conflicts in political terms, the conflicts revealed more profound transformations in the Wolof social order.

The second arrest and exile of Amadu Bamba in 1903 revealed a new balance of power in the ongoing conflict between aristocratic authority and Muslim authority. The superior chief of East Bawol, Mbakhane Diop, was the son of Lat Joor, but he also represented French efforts to create a reformed version of aristocratic power. In 1903 he begged the French to do something to restore his prestige, as Amadu Bamba was more powerful in every way than he was. He was insulted and intimidated by the behavior of Murid disciples and members of the inner circle around the founder, who had refused Mbakhane's requests to visit Amadu Bamba. The French obliged, as they were also alarmed by the influx of people and money. They reported a mood of religious hysteria, wild preaching about how Amadu Bamba "defeated" his exile, and therefore the French. The events of 1903 revealed the incipient collapse of aristocratic power, which became more and more evident over time. The Murid order embodied many of the most threatening changes, in the eyes of the aristocracy. Mbakhane Diop was in debt. He was threatened with investigations if he accepted gifts or bribes from his subjects. He couldn't afford his entourage of griots, retainers, and loyal slaves, and he couldn't have purchased slaves to work for him if he had wanted to. By contrast, peasants and slaves from the entire surrounding region were settling in East Bawol as Murid disciples. Many of them behaved insolently, and refused to obey orders unless told to by their religious leaders. Money was also piling up around Amadu Bamba, who received donations from pilgrims who flocked to see him and receive his blessing.

In French sources, these crises appear to be political threats to colonial law and order, dressed in the clothing of holy war and rebellion. Murid sources reveal an altogether different constellation of forces, with Murid Islam calling for a radical reconstruction of Wolof society from the ground up. The monarchy was corrupt, guilty of enslaving Muslims and repressing Islam. Muslims were asked to abandon their attachment to kings and aristocrats, to free slaves taken in unjust wars, and to join communities where God alone was king. The new social order was based on communal self-reliance and hard work, turning its back on the distinctions of class and birth that dominated the old regime. Although the Murid order attracted some adherents from the highest ranks of society, its mass support came from peasants and former slaves, who sought a better life in a new peasant society. The social meaning of Islamic renewal was directly linked to aristocratic decline and slave emancipation, which is the subject of the next chapter.

NOTES

1. 2 D 7-1, Corres. 1890–1892.

2. 2 D 7-1, Corres. 1890, Villiers à Gouverneur, March 16, 1890.

3. 2 D 7-1, Corres. 1891, Patterson à Gouverneur, July 21, 1891; 2 D 7-1, Rapport: Désarmement des tiedos, 1891, n.d.

4. 2 D 7-1, Corres. 1892, Dossier: Meissa Anta.

5. 2 D 7-2, Corres. 1893, Rapport de Patterson à Directeur des affaires indigènes, April 30, 1893.

6. 2 D 7-2, Corres. 1894, Rapport de tournée de G. Donis, May 13, 1894.

7. 2 D 7-2, Corres. 1894, Rapport de tournée de G. Donis, March 5, 1894.

8. Ibid.

9. 2 D 7-6, Clipping from *Journal Officiel du Sénégal et Dépendances*, July 7, 1894.

10. 2 D 7-2, Letter de Gouverneur à Ministre des Colonies, July 9, 1894.

11. 2 D 7-2, Baol, Correspondance, May–June 1895.

12. The original school, created by Faidherbe, was closed for budgetary reasons in 1871. See Denise Bouche, *L'enseignement dans les territoires français de l'Afrique Occidentale* (Paris, 1974), vol. 1, 343–44.

13. Bouche, *L'enseignement* I, 344-49; and J 7 (9), Rapport sur le Collège des fils de chefs, 1892.

14. These attacks came from Gallieni, among others. See Saint-Martin, *Une source*, 143–59; and J 7.

15. Governor de Lamothe emphasized this theme: see J 7. See the speech of de Lamothe at the inauguration of the school, in *Journal Officiel du Sénégal*, April 9, 1892, 152. For a good discussion of French colonial ideology, see Alice L. Conklin, *A Mission to Civilize: The Republican Idea of Empire in France and West Africa, 1895–1930* (Stanford, Calif., 1997).

16. 2 D 7-2, Corres. 1894, Gouverneur Henri de Lamothe à Ministre, July 9, 1894, and Delcassé's response.

17. 1 G 296 (4), Monographie: Cercle de Thiès 1903–1904, p. 18, discusses the Fall and Dieng "clans" in this period and the split in the Fall family over the appointment of Salmon as superior chief.

18. On the plan, see 2 D 7-6, Chemise 1, Rapport de l'Administrateur Farque à M. Merlin, Directeur des affaires indigènes, July 11, 1897. The reorganization of Bawol was the work of Merlin. Some features, such as the Council of Notables, became models for later French initiatives.

19. 1 G 296 (4), Monographie: Cercle de Thies 1903–1904.

20. Salla Dior Dieng was Bar Diack, or canton chief of Diack. Biram Bigué Dieng, the son of Tanor, was canton chief of Ndondel. Boido Gueye, the head of the royal slaves under Tanor, was chief of the Fulbe, Kael-Kantor region. The chief qadi of Bawol, Matoufa Sylla, had been appointed by Tanor and was still influential. In the Fall clan, the Bay Mbayar was Ely Manel Fall. Latsoukabe Thilor Fall was chief of Ndandene. Thieyacine Tiong Fall was chief of Ngoye or Bur Ngoye. On the chiefs in 1897, see 2 D 7-6, Chemise 1, Rapport de Farque, July 11, 1897; for 1899, see ibid., Rapport de Rocaché, August 14, 1899. 13 G 51 contains the service records of some of the chiefs, e.g., Boido Gueye, Dossier Boido Gueye.

21. 2 D 13-14, Cercle de Thiès, Rapports, tournées, missions. Louis Molleur, May 7, 1895.

22. 2 D 7-6, Chemise 1, Rapport de Farque, July 11, 1897.

23. 2 D 7-10, Chemise 3, contains the documents on Devès' demand and French responses.

24. On Carpot's activities in Bawol 1900–1902: see 2 D 13-4, Corres. 1902, Rapport de Vienne, August 29, 1902; and 13 G 71 (12), Poulet à Gouverneur Général, 1904.

25. Mody Mbaye's role as Tanor's secretary is noted in 13 G 51, Dossier Tanor Ngogne. 13 G 77, Dossier Mody Mbaye, is devoted to his activities: Piece 30, Lieutenant Gouverneur Peuvergne à Gouverneur Général, Feb. 10, 1909, gives a detailed summary of his career, including his activities in Bawol from 1898 to 1904.

26. Mody announced this ambition during the "Chautemps Affair" of 1904. On the "Chautemps Affair," see chapter 5.

27. 2 D 7-7, Baol, Chemise 2, Rapport de tournée de G. Adam, August 18, 1898.

28. Mody Mbaye may have written the anonymous letter that began the investigation. See 2 D 7-7, Chemise 3, Rapport de tournée de G. Adam, Oct. 10, 1898. The director of native affairs, Farque, was equally suspicious of Mbakhane Diop. He had Mbakhane's relations with his family and allies in Kajoor under close surveillance: 2 D 13-3, Corres. 1898, Directeur des affaires indigenes à Commandant de cercle, Nov. 8, 1898.

29. 2 D 13-3, Corres. 1898, Nov. 8, 1898.

30. 2 D 7-10, Chemise 5, Rapport de Rocaché, Dec. 30, 1899, and Decazes' response.

31. 2 D 13-4, Corres. 1901, Decazes à Directeur des affaires indigenes, Dec. 23, 1901. On the investigation into chiefs who defied the superior chiefs and the measures taken against them, particularly Boido Gueye, the head of the "Dieng clan", see 2 G 2-34, Rapport mensuel, Baol Oriental, Feb. 1902; and 2 G 2-35, Rapport politique, 1er trimestre 1902.

32. 2 G 3-35, Rapport politique, Résidence de Diourbel, Dec. 1903.

33. On the dismissal of Salmon Fall, see 2 D 13-4, Corres. 1902, Vienne à Directeur des affaires indigènes, Sep. 7, 1902; 13 G 51, Dossier Salmon Fall; 2 G 2-32, Rapport mensuel, Cercle de Thiès, July 1902. Mody Mbaye's role is noted in 13 G 77 (30), Dossier Mody Mbaye, Lieutenant Gouverneur à Gouverneur Général, Feb. 10, 1909. Salmon Fall's wife protested the role of Mody Mbaye in a letter to the Governor-General: 2 D 13-5, Corres. 1903, Dior Fall à Gouverneur Général, Jan. 27, 1903.

34. The decisions of 1902 were criticized in two later reports: 13 G 76 (35), Dossier Salmon Fall, Note de l'administrateur en chef Peuvergne, May 10, 1905; and 13 G 296 (130), Affaire Chautemps, Georges Poulet à Lieutenant Gouverneur, April 30, 1904.

35. 2 D 13-5, Cercle de Dakar-Thiès, Corres., 1903. Dior Fall à Gouverneur Général, Jan. 27, 1903.

36. 13 G 78 (9), Correspondence on petition of Fatim Diara, a widow of Teeñ Thieyacine Fall, 1905.

37. 2 D 7-10, Chemise 7, Succession de Salmon Fall.

38. 13 G 71 (63), Rapport sur les chefs indigenes, p. 15.

39. Ibid.

40. Ibid., p. 16. Mbakhane Diop was sent to serve in Casamance, outside the Wolof region of Senegal. From 1906 to 1911 he served as a *commis expéditionnaire hors cadre* in Casmance, Salde, and Bakel, and then in Lieutenant Governor Peuvergne's cabinet. He was appointed canton chief of Jaol-Gohe in Thiès in 1911, and became province chief of Keur Bacine in Luuga in 1915: 2 D 9-8, Cercle de Louga, Corres. Affaires Divers: 1915, Nov. 15, 1915.

41. The role of Carpot is mentioned in a letter from Commandant Allys to Martial Merlin dated June 1, 1903, cited in Ba, *Ahmadou Bamba*, 104. The role of Carpot is also mentioned in oral tradition according to Cruise O'Brien, *The Mourides of Senegal*, 44–45.

42. Le Résident du Baol Oriental, R. du Laurens, à Commandant de cercle de Thiès, April 25, 1903, reproduced in Ba, *Ahmadou Bamba*, 94–95.

43. See Dieng, *L'épopée*, 432; and Diop, "Lat Dior et le problème musulman."

44. ANS Dossier Amadou Bamba, Lettre no. 13, Mbakhane Diop à Commandant de cercle, April 25, 1903. Quoted in Ba, *Ahmadou Bamba*, 188–90.

45. Dossier Amadou Bamba, Mbakhane Diop à M. Merlin, April 25, 1903. This letter is quoted without attribution in Ibid., 24.

46. Ibid., Gouverneur Général p.i. Merlin à Commandant de cercle de Tivaouane, May 1903, 99.

47. Ibid., Commandant de cercle Allys à Gouverneur Général, May 28, 1903, 101–2.

48. Ibid., Gouverneur Général p.i. Merlin à Amadou Bamba, June 10, 1903, 111. For reports on the military and political preparations for his arrest, see ibid., 103–10.

49. These rumors were reported by the Resident of East Bawol in Résident du Laurens à Commandant de cercle, May 22, 1903, and in an unsigned letter addressed to Merlin on June 3. See ibid., 100, 105.

50. Amadou Bamba à Gouverneur Général (Arabic and translation). See ibid., 114.

51. Ibid., 123–24.

52. 2 D 14-4, Corres. 1903, Commandant de cercle Allys à Gouverneur Général, July 6, 1903.

53. Résident du Laurens à Commandant de cercle, May 22, 1903, reprinted in Ba, *Ahmadou Bamba*, 100. For Moumar Diara's efforts to mend relations with the French, see 2 D 13-14, Rapport de tournée de M. Prempain, August 14–20, 1903.

54. On Shaykh Anta's role in the events of 1903, see 2 D 13-14, Rapport de tournée de M. Prempain; and 2 G 3-35, Rapports politiques, Résidence de Diourbel, Sep. 1903 and Dec. 1903.

55. 2 D 13-14, Rapport de tournée de M. Prempain.

56. Interview, Serigne Bassirou Anta Niang Mbacké, Daour-Mousty, July 25, 1995.

57. Ibid.

58. Ibid.

59. Mbacké, "Les bienfaits (1)," 631.

60. See chapter 7.

61. In 1903 the French were only beginning to show awareness of the Murids as a religious community. The term "Mouride" or "Mourite" had just come into use in administrative reports, such as the "Monographie sur le cercle de Thiès," in ANS 1 G 296 (7), but it was used as a synonym for "fanatic."

62. For a discussion of Malik Sy's position in the Tijani order, see Said Bousbina, "Al-Hajj Malik Sy: Sa chaîne spirituelle dans la Tijaniyya et sa position à l'égard de la présence française au Sénégal," in *Le temps des marabouts: Itinéraires et stratégies islamiques en Afrique Occidentale Française v. 1880–1960,* ed. David Robinson and Jean-Louis Triaud (Paris, 1997), 181–98.

63. Ibid., 192.

64. Abdallah, "Guerre sainte ou sédition blamable," published the text of Sa'd Bu.

65. See Amar Samb, *Contribution*, 345–46, for the text and other legal opinions.

66. Ba, *Ahmadou Bamba*, letter from Merlin to Shaykh Sidiyya, June 20, 1903, 119.

67. Mbacké, "Les bienfaits (2)," 107.

68. Bouchera Samb, *Waxtaan ci mbir Maam Cerno ak Seex Ibra Faal*, audiocassette. Also interview, Serigne M'Baye Guèye Sylla, Darou-Mousty, July 28, 1995.

PART II

SLAVERY AND EMANCIPATION

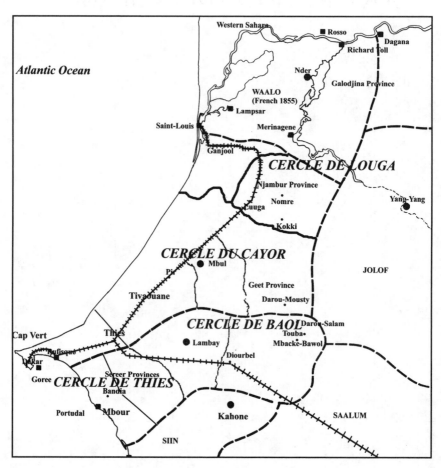

Map 5.1 Colonial Kajoor and Bawol, 1912

5

SLAVERY UNDER SIEGE, 1890–1905: COLONIALISM, RESISTANCE, AND RUNAWAYS

In the nineteenth century, slavery was the most important basis for aristocratic power. The sale of slaves taken in wars and punitive raids financed the purchase of firearms, horses, and luxury goods. Privileged royal slaves formed the backbone of the state and the army. Ordinary slaves grew food crops and cash crops for their masters, performed domestic chores, and wove cotton cloth. During the conquest, French policies toward slavery were one of the main obstacles to a durable alliance between Wolof aristocrats and French colonial rule. Despite metropolitan pressures to suppress the slave trade and take action in favor of runaway slaves, French colonial officials managed to negotiate a series of compromises to protect the interests of Wolof slave owners.

Historians of slavery and Islam have offered different perspectives on the power and authority of Wolof chiefs in the decades following the conquest. Historians and social scientists who have focused on Sufi Islam have argued that the old regime collapsed rapidly, creating a vacuum of authority that was filled by the emergence of new Muslim leaders. In their view, colonial chiefs had no real legitimacy after 1886, as they were merely paid servants of the French, minor bureaucrats in the new colonial order.[1] While such a view assumes part of what it is supposed to explain, the rapid consolidation of new Islamic movements lends plausibility to the emphasis on radical historical change.

Historians studying the institution of slavery have stressed the continuity of aristocratic power. Martin Klein's recent survey of slavery and emancipation in French West Africa provides a good example. Klein argues that the French census of slavery was exceptionally inaccurate in the Wolof regions of Senegal, producing an undercount that he attributes to the lassitude of French officials and the deceptive attitude of Wolof slave owners and chiefs. He argues that slaves accounted for nearly one-half of Wolof rural populations in 1903–1904, with the implication that slaves produced many of the peanuts grown for export. The vitality of slavery was linked to the persistence of a large-scale slave trade into the peanut basin well into the colonial period. Klein also emphasizes the persistence of "slaves" (*jaam*) as a status group in contemporary Wolof society, suffering certain forms of social discrimination even though they no longer work for their masters. While I offer a different interpretation of the same data, Klein's view is notable for its emphasis on continuities in aristocratic power and social hierarchy.

This chapter begins with a discussion of recent studies of slavery and emancipation in West Africa, and debates about the relative importance of colonial policies and actions versus the initiatives taken by slaves. The chapter then explores a series of battles that were fought around the issue of slavery. French efforts to suppress the slave trade, without alienating slave owners or touching the institution of domestic slavery, were counterbalanced by the efforts of Wolof aristocrats and *métis* merchants to defend the slave trade. In 1900–1904, "slave trading scandals" forced the issue of slavery onto the colonial agenda, but also revealed that slave trading was clandestine, dangerous, and small in scale by this time. I try to date the "effective" ending of slave imports, which is crucial to any interpretation of the census data gathered by the French from 1903 to 1905. Whatever their limitations, these sources are fundamental to any discussion of slavery in the colonial period. Over time, the battles over slavery shifted from the slave trade to the problem of runaways. In my discussion I integrate slave emancipation into the broader stream of Wolof history. In simple terms, this means aristocratic decline and Muslim ascendance. The chapter concludes with a review of the evidence on the economic impact of emancipation. My discussion brings together topics that are usually treated separately. I try to bridge the gap between interpretations that focus on the radical transformation of Wolof society by Sufi Islam and those that focus on the continuities embodied by slavery and the slave trade.

COLONIAL POLICY AND RUNAWAY SLAVES

At the turn of the century, slavery moved from the bottom to the top of the colonial agenda in French West Africa. During the conquest, pressure from the French government had led to efforts to suppress the slave trade, but "domestic slavery" was taken off the agenda as too "sensitive." The existence of "slaves" had been papered over with obfuscation designed to make slavery invisible to French political opinion. In that obscurity, slavery lingered on until the issue was taken up on the orders of the new governor-general, Ernest Roume, in 1902.

Roume took command of French West Africa as a representative of the Colonial Party. He was a civilian with business connections in the French Empire. His mandate was to clean up the mess left by decades of military control. Roume's first task was to reorganize the federation to provide the financial resources he needed to launch an ambitious program of railroad and port construction. His interest in slavery grew out of his economic program. Would French action against slavery lead to social chaos and economic decline? The surveys of slavery undertaken between 1903 and 1905 on Roume's orders were supposed to answer this question. At the same time, Roume feared that "scandals" about slavery would ruin any chances of raising a loan in France.

After the French parliament authorized French West Africa to raise a loan of 65 million francs in 1903, Roume made the reorganization of the federation his top priority. A new charter for French West Africa was issued on October 18, 1904. The decree gave the federal Government-General control of customs receipts throughout the federation. Senegal was organized as before: it included the Four Communes and the protectorate areas and was under the authority of a lieutenant governor in Saint-Louis. The Government-General of the federation was not responsible for the administration of any territory and the federal capital was transferred to Dakar. Dakar became an imperial city and the center of a vast communications network reaching into the heart of the Western Sudan. The charter of 1904 gave the Government-General the basic structure it retained throughout the colonial era. Its primary function was to promote the economic development of the federation as a whole.[2]

Roume reached the summit of administration in French West Africa through his connections in the Ministry of Colonies and the Colonial Party.[3] The appointment of an "outsider" with no African experience was unusual. Business interests and politicians in the Colonial Party had been critical of the military direction of expansion in the 1890s.

After 1898, they were led by Théophile Delcassé, an ardent nationalist and colonialist, who believed that the future of the colonies depended on "rational economic development" (*mise en valeur*). Delcassé was foreign minister from 1898 to 1905, directing foreign affairs longer than any other politician in the Third Republic. Delcassé criticized the "Sudanese officers" because he believed French expansion should be based in the wealthier coastal colonies rather than in the interior of the Sudan. He oversaw a number of efforts to restructure the French empire in West Africa, culminating with the appointment of Roume and the federal reorganization of 1904.[4]

Roume first established a sound financial basis for the development of the federation. By 1905 he was satisfied that these concerns had been met. Roume then directed his attention to the internal organization of the federation. His policies reflected the ideology of the Colonial Party and the domestic orientation of the "radical" governments under which he served. Roume and his lieutenants were intent on destroying the power of what they called the "great chiefs": the African kings and aristocrats whose power had survived the conquest. As a good republican, Roume saw vestiges of "feudalism" as obstacles to progress. Education was "laicized" in West Africa, following the separation of church and state in France in 1905. Roume's most important initiative was his decision to investigate "domestic slavery" with an eye toward its abolition. The era of pragmatism was over. From 1902 until World War I, France's African policies were shaped by the dictates of republican imperialism: France had a mission to liberate it from the vestiges of a "barbaric" past and to give Africa the imprint of French civilization.

Roume and his successors gave a new orientation to French policy.[5] In principle, it was anti-aristocratic, and it favored measures that would lead to slave emancipation. The new tone was important. It made it difficult for aristocratic chiefs to defend slavery, while it encouraged slaves who sought their freedom. However, it would be a mistake to give too much credit to these changes in French policy. The issue of slavery forced itself upon the French. In the period from 1900 to 1904, there were a number of "scandals" that demonstrated the French failure to end the slave trade. Two of these occurred in Senegal, which was supposed to be a "showcase" of French achievement. Roume ruled out any radical change in the instructions guiding the investigation of slavery. He and the Government-General sought the "reform" of a social condition "that could not be changed immediately and radically by a revolution without leading to substantial and dangerous economic upheaval." Such an "upheaval" would destroy the "work of civilization" that was the goal of French policy.[6] The French authorities did not want radical change, but they did want to extricate the colonial government from any complicity in maintaining slavery or the slave trade.

Radical agendas of slave emancipation must be sought in the actions of slaves rather than in colonial policy. During the last twenty years, slave emancipation has become an important topic of research and debate for historians of West Africa. A number of important studies focus on how slavery came to an end under colonial rule. Nevertheless there is little consensus on how to answer crucial questions. In 1988, Suzanne Miers and Richard Roberts described the spectrum of interpretation as ranging from belief that slave emancipation was a "non-event" to belief that it was a major crisis for colonial rule and the beginning of a social "revolution."[7] There is now more agreement about the importance of emancipation, but differences of interpretation and emphasis remain. My discussion begins by describing these debates, in order to place the Wolof experience in a larger context.

For purposes of comparison, the Wolof can be grouped with the Islamic societies of the West African savanna, where slavery played a fundamental role in the social order. For these societies, Martin Klein, Paul Lovejoy, Jan Hogendorn, and Richard Roberts have proposed interpretations placing runaway slaves at the center of the narrative. They have called attention to the large-scale exodus of slaves during the period of the conquest and its aftermath in Mali and Northern Nigeria. In both regions a substantial portion of the slave population fled when warfare and disruption caused by colonialism gave them an opportunity. For French West Africa as a whole, Martin Klein estimated that between 20 percent and 40 percent of the slave population fled, or 300,000 to 500,000 slaves out of an estimated slave population between 1 and 1.3 million.[8] Paul Lovejoy and Jan Hogendorn reached similar conclusions for Northern Nigeria.

The "exodus" school places the slave's own efforts to win freedom at the center of the narrative because colonial officials reacted to "initiatives from below." There were differences between French and British reactions. The French decided to acquiesce and let slaves leave their masters. In formal terms, the French decided that they would not recognize the legal status of slavery or any claims based on it. Although they worried about the social and economic consequences of slave departures, the French were not committed to maintaining aristocratic power and they hoped the mobility of labor would benefit the federation as a whole. With a few exceptions, they put up few barriers to slaves leaving their masters and acquiring access to land elsewhere.[9] The British in Northern Nigeria had a nearly identical policy, which Paul Lovejoy described as "legal status abolition," but put more roadblocks in the way of slaves who wanted to flee their masters. The British did this because their alliance with the emirs was the foundation of indirect rule. The powers granted to Islamic courts made it more difficult for slaves seeking freedom, because "self-purchase" contracts were enforced as the legal route to freedom. The British also tried to deny runaway slaves access to land in other regions of Nigeria.[10]

Colonial policies were secondary to the initiatives taken by slaves. Slavery in Maraka towns and the Sokoto Caliphate was harsh, and "departures were most numerous from those societies that were harshest in their exploitation of slave labor."[11] The "exodus" had a common ground in "plantation" systems that exploited slave labor and in high concentrations of slaves captured in recent wars, who hoped to return to their homelands. Slaves that stayed behind during the conquest and its aftermath, often because they had no "home" to return to, renegotiated their relationship with their masters. Their goal was more autonomy, more freedom to work for themselves by reducing their obligations to their masters. With some exceptions, the status of slaves changed dramatically during the early colonial period.

Critics of the "exodus" thesis have focused on the slaves who stayed with their masters, pointing out that these slaves formed a large majority. Igor Kopytoff has suggested that the emphasis on runaway slaves is misguided, because it is based on the "Western" opposition between "slavery" and "freedom." In his view a more ethnographic perspective would show that Africans defined identity through household and kinship networks. Most slaves did not run away because they would have become "non-persons," atomized individuals with no social identities, a fate akin to "social death." Therefore, most of them chose to better their status from within the networks they belonged to. Slaves were "clients" as well as slaves and they needed the protection and security that derived from their "client" status. Kopytoff's view of emancipation derives from his vision of slavery in Africa. Slavery was open-ended and flexible, because slave status was compatible with many social roles. The status of slaves varied from one society to the next. It could evolve over time as well.[12]

These opposing perspectives on slave emancipation are not incompatible. In previous publications I have argued that Wolof slavery transformed slaves into clients over time. This transformation came about because of the dynamic interaction between the slave life cycle and the ways slave owners managed slave labor. I have argued that a more ethnographic perspective on slavery blurs the neat lines between slavery and freedom that shape many discussions. I have also questioned the utility of the "plantation model" for Wolof slavery. Slaves who labored under their master's supervision formed only one segment of the slave population. Other slaves paid "rents" in the form of labor or grain. Differentiation among slaves was an integral part of the system of slavery as a whole.

If one applies a more "ethnographic" vision of slavery to the evidence presented by historians of the "exodus" school, it intensifies some of that school's findings. If one assumes that Maraka or Hausa slavery contained an internal dynamic similar to Wolof slavery, then one must conclude that a very high proportion of "true" slaves (first generation) fled their bondage in the early colonial period. Such a conclusion justifies the emphasis on runaway slaves in those regions, but raises new questions about slaves who stayed with their masters and about regions where no exodus occurred. Wolof society is a good case in point.

There was no measurable, massive departure of slaves in the Wolof kingdoms, no "exodus" comparable to those in other regions. Administrative reports record complaints about runaway slaves by aristocratic chiefs working for the French, but the flight of slaves was small in scale and spread out over time. Why? Based on comparisons with other regions, a number of possible explanations come to mind. It could be that Wolof slavery was less "harsh," but that seems unlikely. More plausibly, it might be argued that there were fewer "first generation" slaves or that these slaves had been moved too far from their homelands to return there. The Maraka and Hausa regions had high concentrations of recently enslaved persons from neighboring regions. In the Wolof states, warfare in the 1860s and 1870s had created similar slave populations, but in the 1880s and 1890s most slaves were imported from the Niger River valley. For this reason, the slaves most likely to run away faced a very long journey home.[13]

The most important difference between Wolof society and the regions that experienced a "slave exodus" was economic. The export economy of the Wolof states grew dramatically between 1868 and 1883 and again between 1892 and 1914. Economic expansion created important opportunities. Migration became an important phenomenon within the Wolof kingdoms, but most Wolof migrations were over short distances and were related to the expansion of agriculture and cash-crop cultivation. Migrants from outside the region entered the Wolof kingdoms as "migrant farmers" to take advantage of the possibilities of earning cash incomes. Runaway slaves merged into these two streams of migration, joining new Wolof settlements where labor was short and few questions were asked, or taking up positions as "migrant farmers" alongside migrants entering the region for the first time.

While such a reconstruction is plausible and fits the evidence, it has important implications for the study of slave emancipation. Slaves who joined new Wolof settlements in the early colonial period or migrated to the city had no interest in calling attention to their origins and their descendants have no interest in telling their stories. This means that the most interesting stories about slave emancipation will never be told. No amount of fieldwork is likely to penetrate this silence, because the status of slaves who stayed with their masters is a compelling cautionary tale. Ethnographic research on Wolof society "today" or "since independence" paints a depressing picture of slave emancipation as a "nonevent." The slaves who stayed with their masters still form a separate status group.

Judith Irvine's ethnographic study of the caste system shows that in Kajoor, "slaves" have been assimilated into the system of orders as a "pseudo-caste." They can only marry amongst themselves and slave-descendants are considered subordinate "clients" of their masters. If a slave-descendant marries a "noble" (*geer*), the children are considered "slaves" (*jaam*). Although "slaves" do not work for their masters, they, like *ñeeño* (hereditary occupational groups), can be asked to perform "services" that lower-status persons perform for higher-status persons. Their claim to the land that they farm is based on their status as "clients." Even "slaves" who purchase their freedom from their masters are said to be wasting their money, because it will make no difference.[14] In Kajoor, descendants of slaves are poorer than free people.[15] Venema's fieldwork among the Wolof of Saalum only examines economic issues in detail. Venema concludes that slave-descendants do not suffer economically from their low status. Many of them devote more time to work and are more open to innovation than "nobles." This reflects the differing economic histories of Kajoor and Saalum. Kajoor pioneered the export economy, but later became a region of out-migration and declining opportunities. Saalum was on the frontier of migration and economic growth, especially after World War I. However, slave-descendants in Saalum have the same social status as in Kajoor. Other groups treat them as a "caste." The stereotypes of "slave" behavior resemble the stereotypes of other caste groups. "Slaves" are loud, sexually promiscuous, undignified. They love drumming and music, have ties to "spirit" powers, and are poor Muslims.[16]

The reinterpretation of "slavery" as "caste" created a distinct status group for the descendants of slaves who stayed with their masters, but should not be confused with the persistence of slavery. West African "caste" systems were unaffected by the end of slavery.[17] What occurred in Wolof society is paralleled by developments in other "caste" societies. In his recent study of slavery and emancipation, Martin Klein puzzled over the evidence for the persistence of slavery (or at least the social stigma associated with slave descent) without noting that almost all his examples come from so-cieties where "caste" coexisted with slavery.[18] In these societies, the rein-terpretation of slavery as "caste" shows that not all negotiations benefited slaves. Slave owners lost their control over labor, but imposed a social status that prevented complete emancipation. The services and deference demanded from slave-descendants are, however, related to "caste" rela-tions, not to slavery.

Any discussion of slave emancipation must deal with the difficulties inherent in the topic. From a methodological point of view, this means that ethnographic data must be historicized and archival sources must be read ethnographically. It is important to recognize that the story of slave emancipation cannot be separated from the dominant historic conflicts in the Wolof kingdoms, which began in the civil wars of the nineteenth century.

SLAVE TRADE IN SENEGAL, 1880–1903

At the beginning of the colonial period, the legal status of the slave trade to Senegal was ambiguous. The ambiguity derived from contra-dictory proclamations and acts by France and its representatives in West Africa during the period of the conquest. The debate on the slave trade and French policy toward fugitive slaves began in earnest in 1880, when the minister of the navy, who was responsible for France's West Afri-can colonies, was attacked in the Senate for circumventing French laws against slavery by returning runaway slaves to their owners.[19] As a re-sult of public debates in France, the government in Senegal was or-dered in 1882 "to put an end to all acts that might give credibility to the belief in any tolerance by your administration for the shameful traf-fic in slaves."[20] The governor of Senegal responded by warning the minister that the new policy might lead to war with all the states on the Senegal River. In addition, runaway slaves in Saint-Louis were described as a danger to the city, as sources of crime, disorder, and arson. Finally, the governor lectured the minister on the dangers caused by the inter-vention of Paris in African affairs. "It is easy to say at the rostrum of the Chamber of Deputies, 'We don't want anything more to do with slavery,' but it is extremely difficult for the Government of Senegal to execute the instructions it receives on this subject."[21] Colonial officials in West Africa argued that an activist policy would harm French com-merce.

In the 1880s the most active center of the slave trade was the Senegal River. Small flat-bottomed riverboats (*chalands*) were used to bring slaves down-river from Bakel and Médine. In 1880, the French arrested five slave traders on the lower river near Dagana for trafficking in slaves. The slave cargoes consisted almost entirely of young children under twelve years of age, most of them young girls. The slaves spoke "Bambara" (Bamana or some related Mande language) and reported that they had been seized while gathering wood on the outskirts of their village. When captured by the French, the children were completely naked and in poor physical health. They had been poorly fed and many showed signs of beatings. The commandant at Dagana emphasized the difficulties of suppressing the slave trade on the river. The boats used were small and could be hidden in side channels of the river to escape detection. The slave traders were often aided by local populations in their efforts to escape French patrols. "Citizens" from Saint-Louis used their privileged legal status and political connections to protect themselves from prosecution.[22]

One of the most important markets for slaves, especially for young girls, was Saint-Louis itself. In a report intended to document the progress made in implementing the "tougher" policy articulated in Paris, the Court of Appeals in Saint-Louis was profoundly pessimistic:

> In conclusion . . . it is unfortunately too certain that slavery still reigns in Senegal, not only in French territory, in the ports [on the river], but also in the city of Saint-Louis and its suburbs. On this point, it must be stressed, there has been no improvement over the last few years. It is true that at Saint-Louis the shameful habits of slavery are kept hidden. . . . It is in the suburbs of Saint-Louis, at the very gates of the city, at Leybar and at Gandiole, that the Moors come to sell their human merchandise.[23]

French efforts to control the illegal influx of slaves to Saint-Louis resulted in ninety-one liberations in 1882. Thirty-eight males and fifty-three females were freed from slavery. Forty of the liberated slaves were children under eighteen years of age.[24]

During the conquest, the problem of slavery had exerted a decisive influence on French policy. The policy of disannexation had been formulated in 1889–1890 to respond to the threat of massive emigration from French territory. The distinct legal status created for the Senegalese kingdoms brought under French rule was designed to quiet the fears of slave owners, who believed that conquest would lead to a policy of emancipation:

> The only means at our disposal for stopping these movements of emigration, which have already created such harm to the colony, and for per-

manently preventing their return, is the policy of disannexation and the creation of small principalities placed under a protectorate and under the sovereignty of France.[25]

The primary reason for disannexation was "the disaffection created by the emancipation of the slaves of the inhabitants of our territories."[26] During the inquiries that led to the formulation of the new policy, the French had received dozens of letters in Arabic from the notables of Waalo. One letter protested:

> We buy slaves with our savings and these slaves work for us. Today you are taking them away and freeing them. This will be our ruin. We also ask that you let us judge our affairs as our fathers always did in the past.[27]

In the treaties negotiated with the chiefs of Waalo, Jolof, and Njambur in 1890 and extended to Kajoor in 1892, Governor de Lamothe made explicit guarantees on the question of slavery. Article 5 of the Treaty of February 15, 1890, stated:

> Slaves [*captifs*] will no longer be sold in the countries placed under our authority. Slaves of all origins will be treated as those which we call house slaves [*captifs de case*], who are not slaves [*esclaves*], but servants [*serviteurs*] like those spoken of in chapters 24 and 43 of the book of God.[28]

This smoke screen of terminology and references to Islamic law created confusion about the meaning of the treaty. In addition, Article 5 went on to legalize the slave trade to Senegal under certain conditions:

> Nevertheless our subjects preserve the right to repurchase slaves [*racheter des captifs*] from foreigners in countries where they continue to be sold; because it is preferable that slaves coming from far and barbarous countries be brought into the houses of those who will treat them as servants, rather than being sold to those who will treat them as slaves.[29]

The treaty stipulated that all slaves had the right to purchase their freedom for a sum that could not exceed 500 francs.

Throughout the period from 1892 to 1905, French policy toward slavery was fraught with ambiguity. Based on the treaties signed with African rulers in the "protectorate," the French colonial government recognized the legitimacy of slavery under Muslim law and authorized the continuance of

Table 5.1   Slaves Emancipated in Senegal, 1894–1895

Post	1894	1895	Total
Matam	29	200	229
Kaedi	28	25	53
Podor	51	201	252
Dagana	--	75	75
Richard Toll	31	36	67
Saint–Louis	1064	847	1911
Tivaouane	14	21	35
Thiès	--	20	20
Foundiougne	1	13	14
Total	1218	1438	2656

Source: Archives Nationales du Sénégal, K 13, pièce 127, État des captifs libérés dans diverses
postes de la colonie en 1894 et 1895, Dec., 5, 1895.

the slave trade for a limited period of time. As long as there were territories outside French or British jurisdiction in West Africa, the treaties of
1892 allowed the importation of slaves. Since in fact the confrontation
between French troops and independent African states continued until 1898,
many slaves were available for purchase. The merchants of Saint-Louis
and the rulers of colonial Kajoor took advantage of this situation by im-
porting slaves.

At the same time, the French authorities continued to issue freedom
papers to slaves who fled to Saint-Louis and to the towns and posts
under direct French administration in the interior. The numbers of slaves
freed were never important enough to threaten the institution of slavery, but they were far from insignificant. They are documented in Table
5.1.

Acts of emancipation were concentrated along the Senegal River and
in Saint-Louis. Most slaves were seized from slave traders operating on
the Senegal River. The rest fled to French posts along the river. The
vast majority of slaves received their freedom in Saint-Louis, where the
French courts were under pressure to implement policies imposed by
the antislavery lobby in Paris. By contrast, very few slaves were freed
in the *cercles* of the peanut basin, where demand for slave labor was
high.

One result of the concentration of antislavery efforts along the river was an increase in the number of slave caravans delivering slaves overland to markets in Kajoor and Bawol. These caravans appeared in French records when Wolof chiefs began obstructing their passage. In 1893, Tanor Ngogne seized a number of slave caravans on their way to Kajoor. According to testimony gathered from the slave traders, they entered Bawol in January and paid Tanor a tax (*coubal*) of 150 francs for the right to travel through Tanor's territory and trade. Two days later the caravan was stopped by seven cavalrymen in Tanor's employ, who announced that the caravan traders had no right to trade in slaves. By that time, 2 slaves had been sold.[30] Shortly thereafter, more caravans were seized and a total of 27 slaves were turned over to the Qadi, to be given to Tanor for safekeeping. The most complete list of the slaves seized in Bawol gives the names and ages of the 27 slaves: 13 girls between the ages of 6 and 13; 11 women between the ages of 15 and 30; and 3 males, one boy of 8 years, and two men (aged 16 and 30). The caravan leader claimed that the group of caravans originally possessed 44 slaves.[31] After their seizure, the caravans became the subject of a protracted dispute between the slave traders and the French administration.

Justin Devès, the most prominent *métis* merchant-politician in Saint-Louis, intervened on the side of the caravan leader, Mody N'Diaye. Devès described the caravan leader as "an interpreter working for my commercial firm who was accompanying *jula* (Dioulas, i.e., merchants) from the Upper Senegal who came here to trade their products for merchandise."[32] The slave traders believed that their actions were perfectly legal. They had purchased their slaves at Banamba in the French Sudan and had received permission from the French administration there. The slave traders emphasized their close personal connections with the most influential *habitant* merchants in Saint-Louis. Yoro Diallo, the leader of one of the smaller caravans, explained that he had received "une balle de guinée, filature x," worth 1,000 francs, on credit from a M. Descemet, who had also paid his passage on the steamer Anna to Médine. At Banamba this cloth had been used to purchase seven females and one male slave. Yoro Diallo claimed it was his intent to settle in Bawol with the slaves, where he would have them cultivate for him.

Martial Merlin, the director of native affairs, refused to let the commandant at Thiès send the slaves to Saint-Louis or Dakar to receive liberty papers, because they would "expand the number of vagabonds and prostitutes . . . in those cities." He ordered the commandant to turn the slaves over to Tanor, who could act as their "tutor," treating them as his "house slaves" while the administration examined their case.[33] While the French temporized, they continued to receive letters from lawyers and merchants in Saint-Louis, who defended the slave traders. The supporters included J.J. Crespin, one of the most prominent *métis* businessmen and politicians, and Jules Couchard, a French lawyer chosen as mayor of Saint-Louis in 1890 and elected as deputy in 1893.[34] Under these pressures, the commandant at Thiès was ordered to return the slaves to their owners. The order was based on the owners' claim that they were not professional slave traders, but simply wanted to settle down and farm with the help of their slaves. In the end the commandant refused to hand over the slaves because of the scene that occurred when he tried to carry out his orders:

> As soon as they caught sight of their former masters they began to sob out of fear that they would once again fall under the domination of the cruel men who had mistreated them before and who are nothing more than slave traders and not farmers as they claimed in Saint-Louis.[35]

Louis Molleur, the commandant, expressed shock that someone with the reputation of J.J. Crespin had intervened on behalf of slave traders. By July 1894, the slaves had received liberty papers. The governor decided that the adults would be allowed to go wherever they wanted, while the children would be taken to Saint-Louis and given to families who were willing to serve as tutors.

The seizure of the slave caravans in Bawol was not an isolated event. The Bour [king of] Saloum, another French ally, was also stopping slave caravans passing through his territory on their way to Bawol and Kajoor. In June 1893, Demba War Sall complained to the director of native affairs that four slave traders from Kajoor had lost twenty-eight slaves and other goods when their caravan was seized in Saalum. The *jula* (Dioulas) who had been arrested by the French and who were imprisoned in Saalum were acting as agents for merchants in Kajoor. Almost all of the slaves were children and they had been given to the Bour Saloum for safekeeping. Ernest Noirot, the commandant, advised the Bour Saloum to make the "liberated" slaves work for him. In *petit nègre*, the broken French he used in his letters to his chiefs, he wrote: "In the meantime, you are feeding those people; make them work in your fields, as that is better than leaving them with nothing to do."[36]

When Noirot examined the slaves from the captured caravan, he expressed surprise at seeing "only a few women, a number of teenage girls who were extremely thin, and eleven children from 8 to 10 years old, including two boys, in all twenty-three persons." Four slaves, all girls, had been given to a local man in payment for a debt owed him by the slave traders, with the approval of the administration, and one slave had died.

Noirot's investigation revealed that the whole caravan came from the same village in the Upper Niger region. They had been seized and sold by Samori when their village was destroyed.[37] A prolonged effort was made by Demba War Sall to have the slaves sent to their purchasers in Kajoor. With the support of Justin Devès, Demba War almost convinced the French to release the slaves to his agents. Noirot had persuaded himself that the slaves would be safer from the threat of resale in Kajoor than in Saalum, but in the end, protests from the slaves themselves again prevented their transfer to Kajoor.[38]

One of the most revealing comments on the events in Saalum was a comment from the Bour Sine to Noirot:

> The Bour Saloum can have slaves because the caravans travel through his territory, but I don't have any luck because the Dioulas avoid Sine, which is too close to the *toubab* [Wolof, "Europeans," "whites"].[39]

For the Bour Sine it was clear that the seizure of slave caravans was a new way to acquire slaves, especially attractive because it could be carried out under the cover of antislavery activity. The French authorities in Saint-Louis encouraged this interpretation of events. The chiefs who seized caravans were allowed to have custody of the slaves, encouraging them to serve as self-interested agents in the suppression of the slave trade.[40] Caravan leaders, who undertook the difficult overland journey to Kajoor to avoid French patrols on the Senegal River, would be discouraged by the losses inflicted by zealous chiefs in Bawol and Saalum.

The seizure of slave caravans in Bawol and Saalum in 1893 provoked a debate between commercial interests and French colonial authorities about the slave trade. The mayor of Saint-Louis, Crespin, orchestrated the defense of the slave trade. One of his aides argued that the continued supply of slaves was of vital interest to Senegalese commerce. "If the regions that supply us with peanuts are unable to supply themselves with workers, we must recognize that the owners of the land will not cultivate it themselves; as a result the principal resources of the colony will be diminished."[41] Martial Merlin, the director of native affairs, rejected these arguments. France had to favor the cause of humanity and civilization, and there was no evidence to support the claim that a shortage of labor would result from the suppression of the slave trade. The chiefs in the protectorate regions had acted within their sovereign rights when they stopped the caravans, and the colonial government would do nothing to compensate slave traders who had lost property.[42]

In 1895, Merlin wrote a memorandum on the problem of the slave trade, focusing on the relations between the colonial government and its African allies in the protectorate. Merlin described the slave trade as "one of the most important political problems in Senegal" and "one of the most difficult to resolve."[43] Slavery formed an integral part of the social structure and was recognized by Islamic law. "In Senegal France found herself in the presence of populations committed to Islam, which already possessed a solid organization."[44] This reality was reinforced by bargains made with African rulers during the period of the conquest. "Treaties were made with the chiefs which gave them certain guarantees and which forbid us to make any changes in the conditions of the country without their consent. The same treaties require us to negotiate any major changes with them."[45] Merlin recalled the difficult negotiations between Governor de Lamothe and the rulers of Kajoor and Fuuta Tooro over the question of slavery, but argued that the treaties signed in 1890 and 1892 were the first steps toward emancipation. African rulers had accepted the principle that their slaves would be transformed into "simple tenants for a period of indenture" of ten to twelve years, after which they would be completely free, although they would have to pay rent on the land given to them.[46]

French sources on the slave trade reveal underlying patterns that persisted up to the turn of the century. Two trading networks supplied slaves to Saint-Louis and the Wolof states. Desert traders in Mauritania controlled one of these. They smuggled kidnapped or purchased slaves across the Senegal River into the suburbs of Saint-Louis, where they were sold. The second trading network was based in Saint-Louis itself and in Kajoor. Wolof and *métis* merchants financed the purchase of slaves in the Niger River valley, as they had since the eighteenth century. To avoid scrutiny and capture, many slaves were transported overland rather than down the Senegal River. The merchants of Saint-Louis maintained that this trade was legal, under the treaties signed during the conquest, just as the importation of "liberated" slave children for adoption was legal in Saint-Louis itself. The most vocal defenders of the slave trade were merchants who had allied themselves with Lat Joor in the 1870s and who now allied themselves with his "successor," Demba War Sall. Their politics and rhetoric had a "nationalist" edge to it, as they saw themselves as the defenders of "Senegalese" commerce against the growing monopoly of power exercised by French merchants. Saint-Louis and Kajoor were the major markets for slaves. What distinguished them from other regions was their wealth, as earnings from commerce and peanut exports provided them with the cash to finance slave imports and purchase slaves.

French sources provide little information on the scale of the trade. Martin Klein and Bernard Moitt have argued that it was large in scale.

The main evidence comes from French sources reporting on the "slave trade passing through Médine" in 1888–1889. A French administrator reported that "10,130 slaves" passed through the region in one year, between December 1888 and November 1889.[47] The French assumed that these slaves were headed for Senegal. Even if these reports were accurate, there is little evidence to suggest a massive influx of slaves into the Wolof states. No slave "exodus" occurred during the colonial era, and the French created only one "liberty village" to house runaway slaves in the Wolof states. This contrasts sharply with other regions in French West Africa that had large populations of recently enslaved persons.[48] The French may have exaggerated the size of the slave trade and been wrong about the destination of the slaves. Evidence from within the Wolof states suggests that the slave trade was small in scale and semi-clandestine by the 1890s. The small caravans of young girls that reached Kajoor and Saint-Louis suggest that the trade was becoming risky and that it could not satisfy the demand for slaves.

It is important to fix some date for the "effective" ending of the slave trade to the Wolof states, because the choice of date will influence the interpretation of the archival surveys of domestic slavery which were made in 1903–1905. The year 1895 seems a reasonable choice. Slaves continued to be imported after that date, but not on the scale needed to sustain old slave-holdings or create new ones. The French shut down the slave markets in the Niger River valley between 1898 and 1900, putting an end to the open purchase of slaves. After 1899, the French authorities in Mali feared the flight of runaway slaves to Senegal and noted the beginnings of seasonal migration, but the slave trade itself was vigorously suppressed.[49] Rivalries between colonial chiefs also hastened the demise of the trade. Stopping slave caravans was a way to curry favor with the French authorities and might lead to surreptitious slave acquisitions. Even the support of Saint-Louis politicians could not protect the slave trade to Kajoor after 1895. The young girls who suffered abuse and mistreatment in the 1890s were among the last victims of the slave trade. Slave trading scandals after 1900 demonstrate the strong demand for slave labor, but also reveal the difficulties of obtaining slaves.

SLAVE TRADE SCANDALS, 1900–1904

Between 1900 and 1904, two major "scandals" revealed the failure of the French colonial authorities to put an end to the slave trade in Senegal, their oldest, best policed, and most prosperous colony. What set these "scandals" apart from other slave trading incidents was the simple fact that they became public knowledge, were discussed in the press, and therefore had a political impact. The first centered on the trade in young girls to Saint-Louis, a "French" city of 20,000, which was the capital of both Senegal and French West Africa in 1900. The trade in slave children had been legalized after emancipation in 1848 under the cover of "adoption" (*tutelle*) and "apprenticeship." New evidence emerged in 1900 that some young girls were being forced into prostitution and that "apprenticeship" had been transformed into true slavery. The second scandal involved slave trading by Wolof chiefs in Bawol, including the superior chief of West Bawol. Together these incidents, along with similar events in other colonies, explain how slavery forced itself onto the colonial agenda. They revealed that the persistence of "domestic" slavery and the demand for slaves generated a "clandestine" slave trade.

The traffic in young girls, which implicated some important *métis* and French merchants in the city, was most embarrassing, because it was legal. The attorney general's office in Saint-Louis investigated the matter, due to reports of prostitution, forced marriages, and the sale of slaves and slave children.[50] What was really going on is difficult to determine, but there is some evidence for a worst-case scenario: important "persons" were using the institution of "adoption" to sell slaves outside Saint-Louis. The attorney general took the position that the institution of adoption was sound. "Hundreds of young children" without any parents had been transformed into "good farmers or skillful workers." Without "adoption" (*tutelle*) they would never have known "the benefits of liberty or of civilization." At the same time he admitted serious abuses, which he blamed on African customs:

> Blacks in general and even certain persons of the country [*certaines personnes du pays*, i.e., *métis* or French resident merchants] do not explain to their young charges that they have simply been placed in their custody for a limited time. They try, on the contrary, to convince them that they were purchased with the permission of the government, that they are slaves, slaves until they die.[51]

Masters who convinced their charges that they were "slaves" were guilty of the most serious abuses. Some masters treated their slaves as concubines. Others tried to sell them outside Saint-Louis, or to sell their children. Other slaves were forced into prostitution in the city. If the girls were married off, the masters collected their bride price.

The attorney general noted that a "clandestine" or semi-legal trade in slave girls had existed since the mid-nineteenth century.[52] He attributed

Table 5.2 Saint-Louis, Imports of "Liberated Slaves," 1898–1903

1898	201
1899	183
1900	126
1901	145
1902	139
1903	112

Source: Archives Nationales du Sénégal, K 16, Enquête sur la captivité, pièce 6.

this to a high demand for household servants within Saint-Louis itself. The demand for slave girls was intensified by the fact that they could also serve as concubines, wives, or prostitutes. How many girls were imported into Saint-Louis and where did they come from? In a separate report, the governor argued that most of the girls had been stolen or seized by "Moors" (desert merchants from the Sahara). The traffic in young girls constituted "one of the principal elements of the Moors' commerce with Senegal and one of the causes of their frequent abductions."[53] The colonial government kept records of the legal trade in "freed slave children" who were placed in "apprenticeship." The figures are given in Table 5.2.

These official figures represent the visible portion of a much larger trade in slave girls, because the figures were presented with an important disclaimer: "Most children imported in these conditions [as "freed slaves" in *tutelle*] are not reported to the Attorney General's office."[54]

Whether the French admitted it or not, the trade in slave girls showed that slavery had reasserted itself in Saint-Louis. In all likelihood, *métis* and desert merchants were also using "adoption" as a cover for a larger clandestine slave trade in Njambur and Kajoor that placed slaves in *métis*-owned farms and businesses. French hopes for a quiet and gradual death for slavery were misplaced.

The "Chautemps Affair" began when the French investigated charges that Canar Fall, the superior chief of West Bawol, and some of his canton chiefs were guilty of trafficking in slaves. The complaints came from royal slaves who had been given to Diery Fall as part of the bride price paid to him when Canar Fall married his sister. Diery Fall had not kept the slaves, but had sold them. His act was a clear violation of the laws outlawing the slave trade. The royal slaves complained because they were "household slaves," born into slavery. Their sale violated their traditional rights as well as French colonial law. In April, Commandant Prempain summoned Canar Fall and Diery Fall to the French Residency at Thiès, where they were to be notified of the administration's decision with regard to their case. By giving them notice of his intent to judge their case, Prempain gave the accused the opportunity to plan their response as well.[55]

On April 7, Canar Fall, Diery Fall, and Canar's uncle, Bokar Thillas, the canton chief of Ngueoul, arrived at the French Residency accompanied by a large number of armed retainers. The three men were brought before Prempain and his assistant, Donis, on the second floor of the Residency. Socé Sow, the principal guard at Thiès, served as interpreter during the meeting. Prempain stated his case against the men, focusing on the relative gravity of their offenses. He blamed Canar Fall for giving royal slaves to Diery, but focused on the more serious charge of trafficking in slaves. The trouble began when it became clear that Prempain intended to punish Diery more severely than Canar. They began to argue. Diery said that Canar knew he intended to sell the slaves, but Canar denied it. Prempain fined both men 100 francs, and sentenced Diery Fall to fifteen days in jail, the maximum discretionary sentence under the *indigènat* ("native" code of law).[56]

Diery Fall protested and asked Prempain to convert the prison term to a large fine. He tried to convince Prempain that he could not go to prison because he was a *garmi*, but Prempain ignored this appeal to "honor." When the guards attempted to take Diery Fall into custody, he pulled a revolver from under his tunic and shot two of the guards. Prempain and Donis fled the room to seek help, while Socé Sow tried to subdue Diery Fall. In the ensuing confusion, Chautemps and Castel, two junior administrators, ran into the room from the ground floor of the Residency. They were followed by a large number of Diery Fall's retainers, who had heard the gunshots and rushed up the stairs. One of the retainers, Sarithia Dièye, killed Chautemps with a knife thrust while he was trying to subdue Diery Fall. During the struggle, Canar Fall and Bokar Thillas watched passively. Afterwards they waited in the garden while Diery Fall fled with his retainers.[57]

The scene outside the Residency revealed the disarray of the French. Diery Fall, who believed he had been betrayed by Canar, prepared for his death. As Diery Fall retreated, one of his retainers "brandished the bloody knife that struck Chautemps and cried":

> "We've killed a commandant, we will get another." Diery Fall for his part told his griot: "I'm going to die. Sing my praises." The witnesses of

these events did not immediately understand what had happened, habituated as they are to seeing native chiefs traverse the town with their armed retinue and griots singing. . . . Canar Fall and his uncle [Bokar Thillas] remained at the Residency until M. Prempain ordered them to pursue the assassins. They left immediately, loudly promising to arrest and bring back the guilty parties.

M. Prempain has explained that he intended at that moment to arrest Canar Fall, but in the presence of the numerous armed retinue which accompanied the chief he feared a rebellion that he did not feel he could resist with the means at hand. Such a rebellion could have led to the massacre of all the personnel at the Residency and of the unarmed European merchants who had gathered there.[58]

These events took place at Thiès, the largest French administrative center in rural Senegal, with a large "European" population and the largest concentration of African soldiers outside Saint-Louis. In spite of this, the canton and province chiefs of Bawol and the neighboring districts carried out the pursuit of the fugitives without French help. The forces under French command were useless for the pursuit of small groups of fugitives in the "bush." The canton chiefs used their influence over local populations and their familiarity with the terrain to pursue and arrest Diery Fall and Sarithia Dièye. The French were supposedly all-powerful, but they were powerless without allies who could establish direct contact with the population.[59]

The conclusion of the Chautemps Affair resembled a play in which aristocratic chiefs weighed their future careers and loyalty to the French against family ties and the aristocratic code of honor. Diery Fall was pursued by Canar Fall and a canton chief not allied with the "Fall clan," Ibrahima Ngoné, into Kajoor where he sought refuge with his cousin, Samba Niébé Bethio. Samba Niébé was a graduate of the School for Sons of Chiefs and the canton chief of Mboul in Kajoor. Samba Niébé convinced Diery Fall to turn himself in at Tivaouane just before Canar Fall and Ibrahima Ngoné arrived with their followers. At first, Diery refused to leave with Canar. He claimed that Canar had broken a pact they had made to resist the French if threatened with punishment, a pact that only he, Diery, had honored. Finally the group left together. During the journey, one of Canar's retainers suddenly shot and wounded Diery Fall. Diery leapt from his horse and was shot again. Diery begged his retainers to kill him, in the account given by Samba Niébé:

"Finish me off, my slaves! Finish me off!" When no one shot he put the barrel of his gun in his mouth and pulled the trigger.[60]

Samba Niébé, who observed all these events, noted the feeling of shame he felt when he returned to his compound. "At my compound the women were crying and they told me that I had delivered [into French custody] my kinsman. I let them speak."[61]

Canar Fall brought Diery's head to the French post at Thiès. He was now accused of ordering Diery's execution to protect himself. The most eager informants against the "Falls" were rival chiefs from the "Dieng" clan.[62] Thiès was now under the command of Peuvergne, an inspector of native affairs sent by Acting Governor-General Merlin. Peuvergne ordered the display of Diery Fall's head in the public square at Thiès for one hour. Peuvergne later argued that circumstances forced him to combat wild rumors that Diery Fall was "protected by Allah." The crime had been committed with extraordinary ease and the fugitives had escaped under the eyes of the guards at Thiès. Peuvergne believed that the events at Thiès "had created a strong impression on the superstitious spirit of the natives," and that only physical proof of Diery Fall's death could prevent further trouble. His decision embarrassed the Government-General. Reports of the display of Diery Fall's head reached the French press, and led one paper, *La Liberté des Colonies*, to report on August 14, 1904, that "those who had the mission to civilize have demonstrated to the population that they are more savage than the blacks." With Diery Fall dead, French attention turned to the pursuit of Sarithia Dièye and the collection of testimony on the events of April 7. Canton chiefs pursued the fugitive assassin to the Gambian border and prepared the way for his arrest by English officials.[63]

Like most political disturbances, the Chautemps Affair provided an opportunity for political intrigue. Mody Mbaye tried to use it to promote his own career. Mody Mbaye had been instrumental in provoking the dismissal of Superior Chief Salmon Fall in 1902, but Mbaye was subsequently dismissed from his position as a clerk with the administration on charges of embezzlement. During the Chautemps Affair, Mody Mbaye was acting as an agent for M. Briffaut, an examining magistrate at Thiès. After the murder of Chautemps, Mody Mbaye cabled information to the administration on several occasions and took credit for the capture of some of Diery Fall's retainers. He tried to ingratiate himself with the French administration. He also sent dispatches to the French press, in which he portrayed himself as the "hero" of the affair and condemned French collaboration with "native feudalism."

These efforts were the most public but least interesting of Mody Mbaye's activities during the Chautemps Affair. In July he began to send a series of anonymous letters to the administration, laying the groundwork for his bid to have himself appointed superior chief of West

Bawol. He denounced Salla Dior, now the senior chief in West Bawol, for complicity in the slave trading that caused the Chautemps Affair. His reasoning was simple: Salla Dior was now the chief most likely to succeed Canar Fall. Using his own name he wrote a number of letters to the administration, presenting his candidacy for the position of superior chief. He promised to serve as an enlightened and loyal representative of French authority, one who would end the abuses of native feudalism. This attempt failed when the French discovered that he had written the letters denouncing Salla Dior. Mody Mbaye's reputation alone would have been enough to exclude him from consideration for appointment as a chief, let alone superior chief of West Baol.[64] However, Mody Mbaye's intervention reminded the French that *originaire* politicians were ready to take advantage of any sign that the French alliance with the aristocracy had weakened.

The Chautemps Affair was a major scandal for the Senegalese administration, magnified by the fact that Chautemps was the son of a prominent French politician. The French reacted by punishing all those deemed guilty or negligent. Commandants Prempain and Donis were suspended for one year and six months respectively. Canar Fall, Bokar Thillas, and several of their retainers were arrested, tried, and condemned along with Sarithia Dièye for complicity in Chautemps' murder. The Chautemps Affair strengthened Roume's hand and discredited the "protectorate policy" which he had inherited. The old-hand "Africanists" in Roume's cabinet, led by Martial Merlin, put the best face on the scandal. They praised the loyalty and zeal shown by the canton chiefs in their pursuit of Diery Fall and his accomplices. In their opinion the Chautemps Affair was caused by the dismissal of Salmon Fall in 1902, and his replacement by an old-regime aristocrat with no exposure to French civilization. They blamed Prempain for mishandling the slave trading charges. But the protectorate era was over. As a result of the affair, Governor-General Roume and Camille Guy, Roume's personal friend and choice for lieutenant governor of Senegal, pressed forward with plans to abolish domestic slavery and end the abuses perpetrated by the aristocratic chiefs.[65]

From a Wolof perspective there are a number of points of interest about the "Chautemps Affair," which is remembered by Wolof bards in the tale of "Jeeri Joor Ndella."[66] First of all, this "epic" tale deals entirely with events during the colonial period. Second, the hero of the tale is Jeeri Faal (Diery Fall), the aristocrat most implicated in slave trading. Wolof bards fill us in on Jeeri's background. He was the son of Samba Yaaya Faal, who was proclaimed Dammel by the French in 1882 and then forced to abdicate. The second role in the tale is given to Sarica Jéey (Sarithia Dièye), the loyal slave retainer who stays by Jeeri's side to the bitter end. Jeeri and Sarica become symbols for the aristocratic code of honor. The Wolof tale amplifies their deeds by adding Chautemps' wife to the list of their victims. Before they kill Muse Sataa (Monsieur Chautemps), Jeeri and Sarica go on a drinking spree to display their loyalty to the ways of the *ceddo*. They are dressed luxuriously, drink and eat with great abandon, seek out the company of *géwél* and women, and publicly display their contempt for the French and their laws. Near the bloody climax, Jeeri explains to the commandant:

> My sister received ten male slaves and ten female slaves as bride-
>   wealth;
> Those slaves that I took I sold.
> I am the son of a king;
> I cannot farm, I cannot clear land.
> *Géwél* follow me and my slaves depend on me;
> I must capture slaves and sell them to buy alcohol and take care of
>   those who trust me.[67]

In the tale, Jeeri and Sarica kill Sataa (Chautemps) and his wife, who is beheaded after one of her breasts is cut off. The execution and mutilation of a French woman symbolizes total contempt for colonial law and authority. What the tale celebrates is the Wolof aristocrat who would rather die than compromise his honor serving the French.

Although neither French sources nor Wolof accounts focus on the slaves who protested against their sale, the "Chautemps Affair" marks a moment of slave resistance. The "household" slaves who were given to Diery Fall and then sold by him considered themselves "clients" of Canar Fall, with rights that placed them above newly purchased slaves. They refused to be treated as "true" slaves and their protests touched off the whole series of incidents. The risky actions of Canar Fall and Diery Fall reinforce the evidence that the slave trade had ended well before 1904. Their behavior proves that there were few "true" slaves left in 1904, willing to be sold as part of the bride-wealth for an aristocratic marriage.

SLAVERY IN THE WOLOF STATES

The most important sources for the history of slavery are the district reports compiled by French administrators under the supervision of the Government-General in 1903–1905. The purpose was to give French authorities the information they needed to assess the impact of abolition on the economy and on the societies under French rule. Unlike other sources on slavery, which were generated by specific crises or incidents, the reports of 1903–1905 present a systematic survey of slavery. Commandants were asked to provide as complete a census of slavery as possible, and to comment on the work regime of slaves, their treatment by their masters, the number of runaways, and the importance of the clandestine slave trade.[68] As a result these sources have played a crucial role for historians of slavery in West Africa.

Even at the time the survey was taken, the French authorities were aware that the information obtained was flawed. Most of the reports filed by administrators in Senegal were criticized for "lack of detail and analysis" in the answers given to the questions asked. Commandants were blamed for the "small amount of work" they put into their reports, for letting junior administrators do much of the work, and for giving too great a role to the African chiefs under their command.[69] Only two reports (Tivaouane and Dagana) and one sub-report (Résidence de N'Diourbel, cercle de Thiès, i.e., East Bawol) were described as "good" in the entire colony. Two of the three reported on Wolof districts.

Some of the difficulties faced by administrators investigating slavery resulted from the fears of slave owners. René Manetche, whose report on slavery in Dagana was praised for its thoroughness, admitted his failure to obtain an accurate census of slavery in spite of several tours of his district:

> The reason is clear: the natives, fearing that the administration intends to take away their slaves by freeing them, employ all their wiles to hide the truth. When they are asked how many slaves they own, they reply with confidence that they don't have any, that they only have free servants. Many slaves, under interrogation, give the same response.[70]

The fears of the slave owners were justified by past experiences with French policy toward slavery. After a respite of little more than a decade, they feared that the French were returning to a policy of "abolition." Manetche's solution to this problem was to "estimate" that slaves formed 50 percent of the population in the *cercle* of Dagana, in all, 26,000 slaves, the second largest slave population reported for any district in Senegal, but the highest as a percentage of the population.

It is clear that the census data on slavery represent an undercount, because African slave owners did not trust the French. But it is less clear how fears of French intentions affected the surveys of slavery for specific districts. Dagana may have been an extreme case. Much of the

Table 5.3 Slaves in *Cercle* of Tivaouane

Provinces	Men	Women	Boys	Girls	Slaves
Saniokhor Occidentale	320	430	190	192	1132
Saniokhor Oriental	619	697	366	271	1949
Mbouar	460	668	217	181	1526
M'Boul	398	612	243	229	1482
Guet	392	681	700	692	2385
Peuls [Fulbe]	293	309	128	48	778
Laobés	29	99	29	23	180
Totals	2951	4236	2485	1962	11634

Source: Archives Nationales du Sénégal, K 18, pièce 10, Cercle de Tivaouane, Jan. 1904.

cercle had experienced direct French rule in the period from 1855 to 1890. Because of its location along the Senegal River and its proximity to Saint-Louis, Dagana had felt the effects of earlier French efforts to suppress the slave trade and to free runaway slaves. There were large numbers of liberated slaves in the district. Freed slaves formed the majority of the population in Galodjina province, with a population of 1,982 in 1903.[71] While the commandant in Dagana was forced to "estimate" the number of slaves, on the assumption that the population was hiding the truth, other districts returned census data that gave precise details of slave-holdings for each canton, with a breakdown of slave-holdings by gender and age, as requested by the French. Some areas, such as Njambur province in the *cercle* of Louga even gave the names of slave owners. Did the slave owners of Njambur province trust the French or their African chiefs more than the slave owners in Dagana did? If the same fears prevailed everywhere, what categories of slaves were reported or omitted in the census data compiled by the French?

Although these questions cannot be answered with precision, the contrast between stonewalling in some districts and complete census data in others reflected the recent historical experience of rulers and slave owners with French policy toward slavery. In Kajoor, where the French had given specific guarantees to slave owners during the conquest and turned a blind eye to the slave trade organized by Saint-Louis merchants until quite re-

Table 5.4 Slaves in *Cercle* of Louga

District	Men	Women	Children	Total
N'Diago	--	--	--	--
N'Guick-Merina	255	357	225	837
Gandiolais	163	262	119	544
N'Diambour	798	1187	1249	3222
Djollof [Jolof]	1490	1823	1024	4337
Total	2696	3629	2615	8940

Source: K 18, pièce 13, Captivité: Cercle de Louga.

cently, there was little fear of giving data about slavery to the French. In districts that had lost large numbers of slaves during the conquest, the fears of French intentions were much greater.

The *cercle* of Tivaouane, which contained the core provinces of Kajoor, reported a slave population of 15,000. This was based on a census of the provinces in the district, which reported the data presented in Table 5.3. This data is particularly interesting, because it provides information on gender for all age groups in the slave population.

In reporting the data from the census, the commandant decided to increase the total number of slaves from 11,634 to 15,000, based on his conviction that the survey represented a substantial undercount of the slave population.

The *cercle* of Louga, which was made up of the northern provinces of Kajoor and the kingdom of Jolof, reported a slave population of 8,940, as listed in Table 5.4. The slave population was divided into men, women, and children, with data provided for each major administrative division.

The absence of slaves in N'Diago and the small numbers of slaves in N'Guick-Merina and Gandiolais were explained by the proximity of these districts to Saint-Louis. Many slaves had fled to Saint-Louis permanently, or had obtained freedom papers and resettled in the district. This resistance to slavery continued. The commandant received thirty-five demands for freedom papers in 1903 from slaves who complained of "beatings, being deprived of food, excessive demands and insults."[72]

One of the most interesting aspects of the data from Louga is that it was one of the few districts that provided any information on the size of individual slave-holdings. The most detailed information was reported for

Njambur province, a strongly Muslim region with a long history of in-
volvement in trade with Saint-Louis. Njambur was a Muslim, rather than
an aristocratic province. The province was dominated by *sëriñu-lamb* from
villages like Louga, Niomré, and Kokki. The power of the titled marabouts
had been consolidated during the conquest, when Ibrahima N'Diaye became the figurehead "king" in a province where Muslim leaders held political power and controlled much of the land.

The census data from Njambur list slave-holdings by village and by
household. Non-slave-holding households were omitted from the census. In one sample group of 14 villages there were 53 slave-owning
households, which meant that the typical village had between two and
four slave owners. In one village from the sample there were no slave-
owning households. The 53 slave owners of the sample owned a total
of 386 slaves: 100 men, 134 women, and 152 children. Typical slave-
holdings ranged from 3 to 10 slaves per household. The census data
from Njambur also provides examples of large slave owners. The most
obvious example was Ibrahima N'Diaye, the province chief of Njambur.
His household included 75 slaves: 15 men, 24 women, and 36 children.
The typical large slave owner owned fewer slaves. Examples were Ibra
Anta Gueye, with 27 slaves (5 men, 11 women, 11 children); Khaly
Fall, with 32 slaves (7 men, 12 women, 13 children); Makhoudja Sène
with 14 slaves (4 men, 7 women, 3 children); and Seny Seck with 24
slaves (6 men, 9 women, 9 children).[73]

Finally, the *cercle* of Thiès (Bawol) reported a slave population of 26,054,
with 754 slaves in the Sereer provinces, 20,000 in West Bawol, and 5,300
in East Bawol. The report from West Bawol gave the largest slave population in a Wolof region, but it was criticized as the "worst" report of the
lot. The commandant had not answered any of the questions about slavery,
and his census was based on an estimate of the slave population as "at
least one-quarter" of the population. East Bawol broke down slave-holdings by ethnic group. The Sereer cantons, with a population of 45,000,
owned 1,000 slaves; the Wolof cantons had 3,000 slaves out of a population of 21,000; the Fulbe cantons, with 8,568 inhabitants, owned 1,300
slaves. The total slave population was 5,300.[74]

The census material on slavery in the Wolof states raises a number
of questions. In addition to its other inadequacies, the survey data presents only a "snapshot" of slavery at one moment in time. Historians
who wish to reach conclusions about slave reproduction, gender ratios,
and other questions must keep this fact in mind. A number of scholars
have argued that the archival data proves that slave populations did not
reproduce themselves. They have pointed to two facts: slave women
outnumbered slave men almost everywhere, but the number of children

is relatively small (slightly more than one child for each woman of childbearing age).[75] However, if the data are "adjusted" to take account of the end of the slave trade, the picture becomes more complex. If the slave trade ended around 1895, then one would expect to find a larger number of women than men in the adult slave population. Many of the women (women being defined as any female over fourteen years old) of 1904 had been imported as girls in the 1890s. Data from the Wolof regions consistently show this pattern. On the other hand, there is little evidence to support the thesis that slaves did not reproduce themselves. Although one finds only "one child per woman" in many Wolof districts, this proves little. One must take into account the fact that many of the slaves listed as "women" were just entering their childbearing years. The young girls imported in the 1890s were now young women. But the data are too fragmentary to tell us very much about slave reproduction.

The sexual ratios of slave children in the Wolof districts were either nearly balanced, as one would expect if the slave trade had ended in 1895, or show an excess of boys, which requires some explanation. This pattern is the opposite of that which prevailed when slaves could be purchased. Girls always outnumbered boys in the nineteenth-century slave trade and in slave-holdings.[76] The same pattern prevailed in most regions of French West Africa, as revealed by the French census data. The excess of "boys" in 1903–1904 was probably the result of the "clandestine" sale of girls to Saint-Louis. Sales of girls were easier to disguise as "marriages," and girls entering puberty brought a higher price than any other slaves.[77] The French reported the price of a male slave as 250 francs, while a female cost 500 francs. Children were sold for 200 francs, but the most desirable slaves were girls reaching puberty, who sold for 500 francs or more. The other possibility is that a significant number of young girls were taken as concubines by their masters and were not counted in the slave population.

If the census data on slavery are compared with the census data for the population as a whole, an estimate of the percentage of slaves can be calculated for the *cercles* of Tivaouane and Louga. In 1900 the French reported the population of the *cercle* of Tivaouane as 119,601.[78] The slave population was 11,634, which was adjusted to 15,000, or roughly between 9 percent and 12.5 percent of the population. The population of the *cercle* of Louga was 108,118 in 1900,[79] with a population of 8,940 slaves, adjusted to 10,000. The adjusted slave population amounted to just under 10 percent of the population. These percentage estimates are lower than might be expected. During the conquest, some French sources placed the number of slaves at somewhere between one-half and two-thirds of the population. However, these were impressionistic estimates. They were not based on a census of slavery.[80]

My view is that the French sources that reported a majority of slaves are misleading. Some districts dominated by the monarchy and its closest allies may have had slave majorities, but I doubt this was true of the overall population. I would estimate the overall slave population in Kajoor in 1880 at somewhere between one-quarter and one-third of the population, with fewer slaves in Bawol. Colonial census data reported slave populations of only 10–12 percent in Kajoor in 1904. Even if the real percentage was closer to 15–20 percent at that time, my conclusion is that many slaves had won their freedom by that date.

All the reports on slavery in Kajoor and Bawol emphasized the division of slaves into a number of distinct categories, representing different forms of dependence on their masters. The terms used by the French were translations of distinctions made in Wolof. The report on slavery from the *cercle* of Tivaouane divided slaves into three groups: crown slaves, household slaves, and slaves of the land.[81] The terms in French were "Les captifs de la couronne," "Les captifs de case," and "Les captifs de terre," which were presented as translations of "Diam Bour" (Wolof, *jaami-buur*), "Diam Dioudou" (Wolof, *jaami-juddu*), "Diam Sayor" (Wolof, *jaami-sayóor*). French reports on slavery devoted considerable attention to the analysis of these different categories of slavery.

Crown slaves "were not really slaves, or even servants." As owners of slaves, land, and herds, they were wealthy; as retainers and henchmen of the king, they formed an integral part of the ruling class. The imposition of colonial rule had brought some changes in the status of the royal slaves. Many who had previously served as soldiers or administrators now cultivated the land. Although they did not work for their masters, they were required to provide them with gifts and aid when it was needed. This aid was requested when their masters were required to pay bride-wealth, for circumcision ceremonies, or for any other "serious purpose." When these demands were made, the slaves collected contributions until they could pay the sum required.[82] Royal slaves had become clients of their masters, and showed no interest in changing their social status, which was a source of pride.

Newly purchased slaves, "slaves of the land." or *jaami-sayóor* in Wolof, were commonly referred to as "trade slaves" in French documents. They suffered the worst conditions:

> The newly purchased slave is purely and simply a slave; the fruits of his labors belong exclusively to the master. These slaves experience abusive treatment of all sorts.[83]

Newly purchased slaves worked exclusively for their masters; they could not own property; and they were entirely dependent on their masters for food, clothing, and other necessities. They were given the most difficult tasks in farm work and in the household. The result, whatever slave owners said, was a harsh form of bondage.

> Most slaves work only for their masters; they don't always receive enough to eat; they sleep with the farm animals and are almost never given any clothes to wear. . . . Masters treat their slaves harshly; they give them nothing and mistakes are punished without mercy.[84]

The result of this situation was clear, in terms of slave responses to emancipation. Newly purchased slaves "would greet any measure of liberation with joy."[85]

The most ambiguous category was that of "household slaves," a term translating Wolof expressions that described slaves born in the master's household.[86] The status of slaves born in the household seemed ambiguous to the French because it changed during the life cycle of the individual. In addition, the social position of an individual slave depended on his position in a larger slave family. Household slaves could be granted the privilege of marriage and residential separation from the master's household, but their ability to win this autonomy required them to abandon one or more of their children. The fluidity in the relations of masters and slaves, over time and in space, requires further analysis.

Historians writing about slavery in West Africa have focused on problems of labor and work regimes, on the treatment of slaves, and on slave resistance, particularly on the patterns of desertion during the colonial period.[87] Although historians differ in their emphasis, there is some degree of consensus on these issues. Slaves in Islamic West Africa labored under a work regime that divided the day and the calendar week into times when slaves labored for their masters and times when they could work for themselves. Work regimes varied depending on the size of slave-holdings and the amount of supervision. Less attention has been paid to the life cycle of the slave and the slave family.

The report on slavery from Eastern Bawol is particularly detailed on the importance of the life cycle for "household slaves." In a summary of the evidence, the report observed:

> Young, they are fed and housed by their masters; at an older age, when they are married and become heads of families, they are free to choose a place of residence where they live in freedom with their family members.[88]

This apparently rosy portrait of slave autonomy was severely qualified by the conditions imposed on slaves who wished to establish their own residence. First of all, a slave had to receive the permission of the master to leave his household. The general requirement for this was that the slave leave "one or several of his children in the service of his master or his mistress." In addition, slaves had to pay their masters an annual tribute of a granary of millet.[89] When these conditions were satisfied, the slave and his wife and any remaining children could establish their own household. In essence, a slave family could purchase greater autonomy by giving the master control over one or more children. The same cycle was repeated by the next generation. "The slaves ceded to the master, when they reach maturity, do exactly the same as their parents if they wish to create an independent family."[90]

In short, married slaves who wanted more autonomy had to cede their children to the master. Such a possibility was available only to slaves who had already satisfied a difficult set of obligations that preceded marriage. Before a male slave could marry he had to obtain permission from his owner:

> The house slave may marry a slave woman with the permission of the master who owns the women. He is required to give a gift to the owner of his wife in addition to the bride-wealth, which he pays to the family of his bride.[91]

Other sources insist that the slave husband paid bride-wealth to the owner of his wife, so the slave groom could be required to pay twice.[92] These obligations shed new light on the labor regime of young household slaves. They lived with the master, were fed and housed by the master, and owed him their labor from sunrise until two o'clock in the afternoon six days a week. In the late afternoons and evenings, household slaves were allowed to work on a plot of land allotted to them by their masters. With the harvest from these plots, slaves fed themselves during the periods when they worked for themselves. Young slaves who wished to marry had to save their earnings from the time they could work for themselves. When not engaged in agricultural labor, slaves tended their masters' herds, carried out domestic tasks, and produced cotton cloth.

The structure of the slave life cycle helps explain important features of slavery. Historians have noted that slave families were small, and have proposed different explanations.[93] Slave women were deeply involved in "reproductive" labor, such as child-care, for the benefit of their mistresses, but often at the expense of their own family life.[94]

Because the children born to slave women were the property of their masters, and were controlled by them, it has been suggested that slaves consciously refrained from bearing children.[95] The data collected by the French in 1903–1904 suggest additional factors that shaped the formation of slave families. Slave children were taken from their parents as the price of establishing a separate slave residence. Difficult conditions were imposed on young male slaves who wished to marry and establish their own households. At the very least these conditions must have delayed marriages for men. Unlike free persons, slaves could not expect help from their fathers or maternal uncles in preparing for marriage.

Most importantly, the slave life cycle reveals the intimate link between slave status and the denial of the norms of kinship and family, as understood by the Wolof. Slave men paid bride-wealth, but did not gain paternal rights over their wives' children. Slave parents bore the responsibility of raising their infants, only to lose their children to the master's household at an age when their productive labor might have helped their parents. A married couple who wished to gain autonomy by building a separate residence, becoming slave tenants on the master's land, had to abandon one or more of their children to the master. From the master's point of view, this control over the slave family was essential to maintaining control over household slaves who were allowed to spatially distance themselves from the master's household. The affective ties between parents and children were the best guarantee that household slaves would not run away.

The dynamic which transformed slaves into "clients" over time also grew out of the methods used to manage slave labor. A prosperous household that accumulated slaves through purchase would also tend to spin off client households of slave tenants on the master's land. These slave "clients" began as married couples who paid a ransom in labor (their children) and grain after having spent their youth in their master's service. Over time these families became "tenants" of slave origins who paid tribute to their masters and served them in more indirect ways. The end of the slave trade accelerated this process of transformation, creating "client" groups who resembled the "slaves" observed in the ethnographic present, who owe no labor but retain a subordinate social status.

The efforts of masters to retain control over household slaves by controlling their children was played out most clearly in the bitter "family" dramas that occurred when slaves ran away. French archival sources allow intimate glimpses into a few of these dramas. An analysis of them reveals that there were strategic moments in the slave life cycle that shaped patterns of resistance to slavery in the colonial period.

PATTERNS OF RESISTANCE TO SLAVERY

Women and Children

The most detailed evidence about individual runaways comes from Saint-Louis in the period between 1880 and 1890, when the French authorities were under pressure to abolish slavery. Slaves who fled to Saint-Louis joined an urban population with a majority of freed slaves. Although this made Saint-Louis an attractive destination for runaways, their first experience was the trauma of flight from the master's household and the fear of expulsion. Slaves who fled to Saint-Louis took risks that affected the family members who were left behind. Runaways contested the institution of slavery and the paternalism of masters, who claimed that slaves were treated as family members. French judicial records document the experiences of runaways and the dangers they faced, and the ways they contested slavery. Slaves and masters shared a way of talking about slavery, but disagreed about the meaning of the words that they used.

Since most slaves had no homeland to return to, what concerned them most was the master's power to threaten the ties of kinship and family they left behind. Marriage and the birth of children were crucial steps in the formation of family ties. An unmarried slave was a "child" in the master's household and was under the direct control of the slave owner. Marriage was the most significant amelioration possible in the lifetime of a slave. Marriage and the formation of a family were steps toward more autonomy, but also the beginning of new forms of control. Slaves who married and had children were less likely to think of flight, unless they were willing to give up their children to the master, exposing them to possible retaliation.

These tensions in family life produced specific patterns of flight. The slaves with the least to lose and the most to gain were young adults reaching the age when they could marry and establish households. If they remained in slavery and married, marriage would bind them more tightly into bondage. Men and women slaves faced different choices and different risks. These issues of generational age and gender appear in the patterns of flight from slavery in the Senegal River valley.

Women who fled slavery had to consider the risks that flight posed to their children. The position of slave children went to the heart of the slave's condition. The children belonged to the master and worked for the benefit of the master. If women with children fled from their masters, they left their children at the master's mercy. Slave women who fled to Saint-Louis to obtain their freedom brought desperate pleas to the French courts to help them find their children. In almost every case, masters sold off the children to punish women slaves who dared to run away.

In 1883 a thirty-year-old woman who fled to Saint-Louis and obtained her freedom brought a complaint before the French administration. She testified:

> I was a slave of Abdou Sarr, a farmer at N'Diebene. I escaped and received my freedom at Saint Louis. As soon as my flight was known my master in Kajoor sold my son, named Demba Bitaye Ba, in order to take his revenge on me. This news was brought to me by my husband, Samba Diala, who lives in Gandiole [N'Diebene]. I want to ask for your assistance in this matter.[96]

The son, who was ten years old, had been beaten by his master after his mother's flight and then sold.

This was not an isolated case, but illustrated one of the ways masters punished runaway slaves. The case of another woman who fled to Saint-Louis illustrated the same pattern. Mairam Ba fled to Saint-Louis from the village of Leona in the canton of Gandiole and received her freedom papers on May 19, 1883. After her liberation she returned to her former village to visit her children, whom she described "as still the household slaves of my former master," Amadou Fall. When she returned to her village she found that her two children were no longer there. After quarreling with her former master, who attempted to beat her, she went to visit his brother. He told her that her children had been sold, but he did not know where or to whom. On her way back to Saint-Louis she narrowly avoided capture by three armed men who were following her tracks. She escaped by hiding in the bush. She assumed that her master had sent the men and that their intent was to reenslave her and sell her into slavery. She too sought help from the French administration in her search for her children.

Both cases illustrate how masters disregarded "customs" that should have protected slave children from punishment and sale. Because their children were born into slavery, mothers assumed their children's status as household slaves would protect them against sale. They learned that what slaves believed to be their rights were seen by their masters as concessions that could be withdrawn at will. From the master's point of view, a runaway slave destroyed the basis for accommodation between masters and slaves. Runaways had to be ruthlessly punished if the master was to retain any control over the slaves in his household. Selling the children and relatives of a runaway provided a powerful warning to slaves who contemplated flight. If recaptured, runaways were beaten and sold.

The Subversive Slave

Runaways took risks and could be punished by their masters. Nevertheless, some runaways took considerable risks to liberate family members. The most dangerous act was to return to the master's village. Not content with obtaining their freedom as individuals, runaway slaves sometimes acted in ways that made them appear to be social rebels, intent on subverting the system that had exploited them. However, like slave owners who attempted to punish runaways by striking at their families, subversive slaves sought revenge against their former masters as individuals. One well-documented case of this kind involved a Tukulor slave named Samba Boubou, who had lived in slavery near the French post at Dagana.

Samba Boubou was a runaway slave from Dialmath, who obtained his freedom in Saint-Louis and worked as a weaver. After living for several years in Saint-Louis, Samba made plans to liberate the members of his family, who were household slaves of his former master. He presented six Tukulor acquaintances to the French authorities in Saint-Louis, claiming they were his relatives, and received six certificates of liberty. He then took the papers to Dialmath, where he attempted to free the members of his family. His arrival and activities created a considerable stir, leading the French authorities in Dagana to intervene. They feared that Samba's activities would lead to emigration out of French territory. In the end, the French confiscated the liberty papers and forced Samba to return to Saint-Louis. The most interesting aspect of the case is the testimony which presented the perspective of Samba Boubou and his master, Abou Dada.

When asked why he tried to free his relatives with certificates obtained in Saint-Louis, and why he presented himself to the French authorities as a relative of Abou Dada, his former master, Samba replied, "I am not exactly the son of the same father and mother as Abou, but we are household slaves and we should be treated as members of the family. However Abou makes us work and treats us like slaves that he purchased yesterday. That is the reason I wanted to put an end to the situation." Before returning to his village, Samba had taken the precaution of paying for his own liberty. He did what he did because he could not afford the price that was asked for his family.[97] His inability to purchase his family's freedom created a feeling of desperation that led to his subterfuge.

Samba's master, Abou Dada, said that Samba had arrived in the village and presented his liberty certificates to the village chief, who refused to accept them. The village chief knew that the slaves had not gone to Saint-Louis and presented themselves to the head of the judicial department. According to Abou Dada, the village chief then began to cry. Abou interrupted him and pointed out that he was the one who was wronged. The chief said: "I am not only crying about what has happened to you, but because I will be ruined in the same way one of these days if our slaves can receive liberty papers from Saint Louis. I will be ruined, my family will be ruined, the notables and all the heads of families will be ruined. There is nothing left to do but to leave this country, even though we were promised that our status and our customs would be respected." After this encounter Samba Boubou began to incite the slaves in Abou Dada's household to run away. According to Abou, his slaves "were living peacefully with me, occupied with the work of the harvest." Abou described his slaves as household slaves who had long belonged to his family. He claimed that he treated them as members of his family and that they had never complained.[98] These statements were carefully crafted to appeal to French fears and establish a benign portrait of slavery.

The two accounts differed in their interpretation of events, but agreed on most facts. One of the few factual disagreements was over the price that Samba had paid for his freedom. According to his master, Samba had paid two slaves for his freedom four years after he ran away, while Samba claimed that he had paid four slaves and a horse. It is significant that Samba paid anything at all, considering that he had received liberty papers in Saint-Louis and had lived there for several years. The freedom conferred by the French did not satisfy his desire to end his condition of bondage, so he paid his master the price of his liberation. Paying for his own freedom was also the first step in his attempt to liberate the rest of his family.

The most interesting aspect of the testimony is the shared discourse about the proper relationship between a master and his household slaves. Both Samba and Abou agreed that a master should treat his household slaves as members of his family. They disagreed sharply over how slaves were actually treated in Abou's household. According to Samba, the household slaves were treated as if they had been purchased yesterday, in violation of their status as members of the family. According to Abou, his household slaves were content and the household reflected the paternalist ideal of slavery.

Samba's efforts to liberate his relatives showed the strong ties of kinship and family that bound him to the siblings he left behind in slavery when he escaped to Saint-Louis. But his actions also expressed a wider tie of kinship that he felt with all the household slaves of his former master, since he encouraged all of them to flee when he returned to his village. His sense of a "slave community" was very personal and limited to his master's household. He encouraged his brothers and sisters in servitude to flee a cruel master who mistreated his slaves, but he did not hesitate to purchase his freedom by giving slaves to his master.

Flight from Slavery in Kajoor (1900–1904)

The stories of individual slaves round out the portrait of slavery in the surveys of 1903–1904 by providing glimpses of the fault lines of conflict between masters and slaves. In a similar way, the information provided by French administrative correspondence helps historicize the snapshot of slavery by providing information on the efforts of Wolof chiefs to prevent the flight of slaves in the period just before 1903. The evidence from Kajoor is particularly interesting, as it provides evidence that Demba War Sall and his allies considered runaway slaves a serious problem at the turn of the century.

Demba War Sall's efforts to protect the institution of slavery are reflected in the reports filed by French administrators in Tivaouane between 1900 and 1903. They reveal that Wolof chiefs in Kajoor tried to close two specific escape routes for slaves. One route led to the city, where slaves sought their freedom by obtaining liberty papers from the French authorities. The second route led from Kajoor to the Murid settlements in Bawol, which were denounced by Demba War Sall as havens for runaway slaves.

In July 1901, the French administrator in Tivaouane was forced to examine the problem of runaway slaves. From a legal point of view, the case forced a reexamination of the ambiguous status of "domestic slavery" in the protectorate. Demba War Sall took the initiative by asking the new commandant, Vienne, to examine the issue shortly after his arrival in Tivaouane. The case revolved around a freed slave named Ganour Dieng. He had employed the services of a *métis* lawyer named Louis Huchard, who practiced law in Dakar. Ganour Dieng's goal was the emancipation of two of his relatives, who were owned by Manguelay Fall, a resident of Kajoor. The French administrator at Tivaouane refused to act when Ganour Dieng approached him. Ganour Dieng came to the French post with a letter from Huchard. Huchard demanded the release of the slaves and asked for two certificates of emancipation. Huchard based his demand on the law of 1848, which ended slavery in the colony of Senegal. Vienne based his refusal on the treaty of 1893 with the chiefs of the protectorate. The treaty defined domestic slaves as servants, cited Islamic law, and still had the force of law in the protectorate. Huchard's demand for immediate emancipation without compensation was contrary to existing practice and law, but Huchard won in the end because he threatened to bring the matter to the attention of the deputy for Guadeloupe and to protest in France.[99] Although Huchard's motives are unclear, the conflict was another skirmish between the Wolof aristocracy and the *originaires*.

Demba War Sall did not give up without a fight. He forced the French to restate their policy toward slavery in the protectorate, with support from the chiefs and qadis of Kajoor. Demba War gathered support for a letter of protest against Huchard, which was endorsed by all the chiefs and qadis. They argued, on the basis of treaties with the French, that domestic slavery was legal in the protectorate because it formed an integral part of Wolof custom and Islamic law. French administrators were more circumspect in their defense of slavery. They cited the political dangers of emancipation, which they believed would undermine the authority of the chiefs. On the other hand they argued that domestic slavery was a benign institution, and cited the examples of slaves who refused emancipation, or stayed in the master's households even when they were granted their freedom. The administrators didn't want to create a precedent by allowing Huchard to assert the claims of French law in the protectorate. They believed that such a step could undermine the entire edifice of rural administration.[100]

In 1902, the French administrator at Tivaouane, Vienne, relayed a typical complaint that reflected the attitudes of the chiefs:

> I take this opportunity to inform you that the chiefs of Kajoor report that many slaves of the interior have fled to Dakar and Saint-Louis where they can obtain, without investigation, a certificate of emancipation. Half of the population of Kajoor consists of household slaves and the liberation of these natives could cause great damage to the country, which is essentially agricultural. Most liberated slaves refuse to work in the fields and are so many hands lost to agriculture.[101]

French policy toward slavery had not yet taken the new direction decided on by Roume, which did not become official until 1905. As late as March 1903, the administrator at Tivaouane defended the thesis that slaves originating outside French territory could be legally imported, although they could not be resold.[102]

Demba War Sall was also the leading influence behind reports on the "Murid" threat that were written up by French commandants in Tivaouane at the turn of the century. Administrators in Tivaouane were fed intelligence about dangerous Muslim fanatics who were draining the country of its people. The reports were full of tales of runaway slaves, but they also complained that free children and women were fleeing their families and making tracks to the Murid settlements in Bawol. These complaints document the failure of the Wolof aristocracy to end the Murid threat by having Amadu Bamba arrested and exiled in 1895. Even with Amadu Bamba in exile, Wolof chiefs found themselves unable to stop the exodus of the faithful to the Murid heartland in Bawol. The rivalry between Islam and the aristocracy was a battle for the hearts and minds of Wolof peasants and slaves.

The first important report was filed in February 1901, by the commandant at Tivaouane. He reported that two of his chiefs feared the consequences of Muslim "agitation" in their provinces. The chief of Mboul reported that marabouts claiming religious inspiration were preaching revolt:

> The youth and particularly the students in Quranic schools are strongly influenced by these teachings. Some have abandoned all work and beg for alms, which is a pretext for not paying the head tax.[103]

Although there were rumors of revolt and holy war in this and later reports, they were embellishments by chiefs trying to interest the French in a more mundane problem: the loss of labor to Muslim leaders, almost all of them Murids. Penel regarded the rumors of holy war as an exaggeration, but he promised to investigate through inquiries among the chiefs and qadis of the district.

In March 1901, Penel filed two reports on the Muslim agitation in Kajoor. One was a translation of intelligence gathered by Demba War Sall and the chief qadi of Kajoor. The second was Penel's commentary on this document, based on conversations with the chiefs and the qadis of the province. Demba War Sall's report identified all the *seriñ* involved in the agitation as disciples of "Ibra Fall of Guet N'Dar at Saint-Louis, who also possesses compounds at Dakar, at Boukou Diara, in Gandiole province, at Thiès and other areas." This clearly identified the group as Murid.

> We know many other things about leaders in other territories, but we can only give you the names of those who live in our country [Kajoor]. I will tell you what I know about them: They have eaten all the property of the people by tricking them; they have also taken away children and many other persons and they make them work for them. They take the

wives of others and make them their wives; they emancipate slaves be-
longing to others and make them their wives. They organize the kidnap-
ping of girls in order to give them to their followers without the
permission of their parents.[104]

This passage is particularly interesting for its focus on women slaves: "They
emancipate slaves . . . and make them their wives."

In addition to being denounced as stealers of slaves, children, and wives,
the Murids were attacked for their heterodox views, which were alledgedly
rejected by all good Muslims in Kajoor:

All educated Muslims who abide by the law agree in criticizing them,
because their acts are absolutely contrary to Muslim law. They promise
paradise to their followers.[105]

Demba War Sall and the chief qadi portrayed themselves as the defenders of orthodoxy against heresy. All good Muslims rejected the idea that a
shaykh could promise paradise to his followers. Salvation came from following the law, not from the spiritual grace of a saint.

Penel's commentary began by noting that the agitation was not a new
phenomenon, but went back some time. Most of his report elaborated on
the themes of Demba War and the chief qadi, including their claim that the
Murids (who were never identified by name, the term not yet being current) had no religious legitimacy. One member of Amadu Bamba's family
was identified by name: Amadu N'Doumbé Mbacké, residing at N'Diassane
in Kajoor. Penel's report also examined the recruitment of young men and
women:

The principal marabouts have installations in the principal towns; Alioune
Touré, at Pire, Momar Fall, at Kébémer. They do not live there, but
come to make purchases. . . . The marabouts have become masters of the
youth whom they fanaticize; they persuade young people to abandon
their families, and to give them all their possessions, and they make
them work exclusively for themselves. They tax people and impose enormous contributions on them. In this way they accumulate considerable
riches and provisions of all kinds: grain, horses, etc.[106]

The rest of Penel's report echoed the charge of Islamic heterodoxy that
formed the main theme of the chief qadi's denunciation of the Murids.

Repeated charges by hostile outsiders, particularly by the canton
chiefs, that the Murid order was a haven for runaway slaves, children,
and women, have to be seen in the context of the social changes taking

place within Wolof society. In the older settled districts of Kajoor, colonial chiefs tried to protect the institution of slavery and the rights of
titleholders to collect fees and services from peasants living on the land.
On their borders a new religious order offered food and refuge to all
who joined the order and submitted to its rules. The Murids were famous for their bursting granaries and generosity to guests. The Murids
repeatedly opened new lands for settlement, digging wells and founding villages on unoccupied land. New recruits donated their labor in
exchange for food, shelter, and spiritual guidance for a period of years.
At the end of their service they were rewarded with a compound and
the means to marry and found a family. At the end of the day, the Murids
paid fewer taxes and duties on their land than the inhabitants of aristocratic provinces in Kajoor.

CONCLUSION

One of the problems with archival evidence about slavery is that it con-
sists of a series of snapshots rather than a continuous stream of evidence
over time. The "snapshot" provided by the survey of 1903–1905, which is
the only attempt at a complete census, has shaped most discussions. This
snapshot confirms certain fundamental contrasts. The census showed that
there were almost no slaves in regions where Sereer minorities formed the
core of the population. In the "Sereer provinces" of the *cercle* of Thiès,
with a population of 46,000, there were only 754 slaves.[107] Almost all the
slaves belonged to Wolof and other strangers residing in the district. On
the other hand, the percentage of slaves in the Wolof districts seems "too
low" and requires some discussion.

In his recent book, *Slavery and Colonial Rule*, Martin Klein decided
to revise upwards the census figures on slavery for the Wolof districts,
because the figures were "poor." He argues that "No one counted slaves
and few wanted to know how many there were." On the basis of this
and other arguments, he raises the number of slaves in three districts by
84,600, changing percentages from less than 10 percent to 20 percent
or from 12 percent to 40 percent.[108] Klein's revisions are for the districts (*cercles*) of Louga, Tivaouane, and Thiès.[109] Two of these districts
were Wolof and the third (Thiès) was formed out of the Wolof kingdom
of Bawol, which had a large Sereer population. Klein's "correction" of
the census figures is radical: he adds 84,000 slaves to three districts
where the French only counted 51,000 slaves. In the end he describes
his revisions as "cautious," citing Cruise O'Brien's suggestion that in
the old peanut basin (Kajoor), slaves made up half to two-thirds of the
population.[110] But O'Brien's number is little more than an "informed

guess" based on French estimates. The crucial question is, when did slavery begin to decline? My argument is that slavery was already a dying institution in 1903, because many slaves made their move to freedom during the conquest and many more followed them in the period from 1886 to 1903. While it is true that 12 percent seems too low a percentage of slaves for the central districts of Kajoor in the precolonial period, revising the 1905 census precludes other explanations. The census figures for the Wolof districts may be inaccurate, but they are probably just as accurate as the figures for other districts. Some of the census returns are detailed, as indicated previously, and cannot simply be dismissed. The census figures have to be put in historic context, not discarded. This problem returns the discussion to the "slave exodus" that has dominated recent discussions of the end of slavery in West Africa.

One of the questions that worried colonial administrators at the turn of the century was the economic impact of slave emancipation. Based on what had happened in Caribbean colonies, they feared prolonged economic decline. Georges Poulet, who wrote one of the major studies of emancipation commissioned by Roume, believed that a radical policy of emancipation could cost a "half a billion francs" in lost revenue.[111] The severe economic decline that the French feared never materialized, but the question they asked has importance for understanding the development of peasant farming in West Africa. French fears were based on their understanding of the process of emancipation in the Americas. In the Americas, the economic decline that followed slave emancipation was linked to the resistance of former slaves to the plantation system. If other alternatives were available, slaves refused to work for wages on plantations. They were reluctant to work under supervision producing the same crops they had formerly produced as slaves. As a result, plantations declined or substitute forms of contract labor were imported to sustain the plantation system. In some colonies, former slaves became peasants, withdrawing much of their labor from the market economy. Where sharecropping replaced slavery, as in the southern United States, former slaves gained some control over the labor process.

An important body of research has argued that a slave plantation system emerged in the nineteenth century in parts of West Africa.[112] The analogy between West African slave plantations and New World slave plantations allows for some important variations, rooted in cultural differences and a lesser degree of economic rationalization in West Africa. Nevertheless, the analogy suggests that West African economies must have experienced the shock effects of slave emancipation. Little evidence for such a decline exists in most regions of West Africa, be-

cause of the discontinuities between the precolonial and colonial economies. Senegal may be an exception to this rule, but the evidence is
indirect and can be assessed only by reconsidering the chronology of
slave emancipation in the Wolof kingdoms.

Martin Klein's skepticism about the census figures for slaves in the
Wolof kingdoms derives from his understanding of the slave exodus in
Mali and other parts of French West Africa. In Mali, the slave exodus
occurred during and immediately after the French census of slavery.
Seen in a different way, the exodus occurred within a decade of the
conquest. Fighting with the Umarians ended in 1893, but conflicts with
Samori continued until 1898.[113] As a result of these wars, there were
many more newly enslaved persons in Mali than in the Wolof kingdoms, where the last large-scale war had occurred in 1875 and where
the "conquests" of 1883, 1886, and 1890 were negotiated settlements.
Comparisons with Northern Nigeria, based on the work of Paul E.
Lovejoy and Jan S. Hogendorn, also suggest that most slaves who ran
away did so in the first decade of colonial rule.[114] This chronology makes
sense. Disaffected slaves who remembered their homeland did not wait
on colonial policy. They fled during the chaos of conflict and war, at
every opportunity when they sensed the inability of their masters to
resist.

This chronology suggests that disaffected slaves in the Wolof kingdoms would have fled in the period from around 1882 to 1892, in a
period of warfare, uncertainty, and disorder. It is true that slaves continued to be imported into the Wolof kingdoms in this period, but in my
view the numbers were relatively small.[115] These newly imported slaves
probably accounted for a substantial portion of the runaways in the early
1900s. For the earlier period there is insufficient evidence to document
a slave exodus, but there is some evidence. The removal of Lat Joor
from the throne, warfare between Kajoor and Jolof, and the creation of
the Kajoor Protectorate under the leadership of Demba War Sall marked
the period from 1883 to 1886. The best data concern the royal slaves of
Kajoor, an atypical group. One faction of privileged slaves and slaves
owned by the royal house remained under the authority of Demba War
Sall. Another group of royal slaves became disciples of the marabout
Bou Kounta in this period.[116] Finally, it was this same period that saw
the emergence of the Murid order, which criticized the corruption of
Islam in the court of Kajoor. If we assume a broad pattern of slave
flight in this period, we can explain the low percentage of slaves in the
population by 1903–1905. The census was taken when the institution of
slavery was in decline. It counted only those slaves who stayed with
their masters during the first two decades of colonial rule.

Table 5.5 Peanut Exports, 1882–1891

Year	Metric Tons	Value (fob Senegal)	Price (Local Markets)
1882	83,000	26,500,000	20.80 fr
1883	43,500	10,373,000*[1]	14–16
1884	36,790	8,806,000*	14–16
1885	45,061	10,730,000*	14–16
1886	21,100	4,998,000*	14–16
1887	25,100	5,950,000*	14–16
1888	40,342	9,520,000*	14–16
1889	31,906	7,558,656	14–16
1890	27,221	5,426,000	15
1891	26,391	5,479,000	15

Source: Adam, *L'arachide*, 136–45; Courtet, *Étude sur le Sénégal*; 18–25.

Note: [1] * Indicates that the sources did not provide information on the value of the crop, which had to be calculated from price estimates.

This interpretation receives support from the economic data concerning peanut exports in this period. There is indirect evidence that the first shocks of slave emancipation produced a downturn in export production. The most prolonged downturn in the export economy occurred between 1883 and 1891, in the immediate aftermath of the conquest.

French experts were aware of the decline, which they attributed to competition from India, which began in 1883. They argued that Indian production caused the price of peanuts to fall in Europe. The price paid for 100 kilograms of peanuts fell from 20.80 francs to 15 francs in 1883. This drop in price was long-lasting and prices fell further from 1895 to 1899, by which time the volume of exports had recovered to the level first reached in 1882. The value of Senegal's peanut exports did not reach the level of 1882 again until 1900. However, there is little evidence that the drop in peanut prices was solely responsible for the decline in production. Producers may have reduced the acreage allotted to peanuts after the price dropped, but this trend quickly reversed itself as the new price was accepted. Other factors were clearly at work, including the chaos created by the conquest and the flight of slaves in this period. Colonial experts focused on prices as a good technical explanation for what had occurred. They did not want to admit that the *habitant* merchants and politicians of Saint-Louis were right when they argued that French military intervention would harm the economy and commerce. They also failed to notice that the export boom that occurred under Lat Joor relied heavily on the exploitation of slave labor. As aristocratic power waned, a new peasant economy began to replace an older slave economy.

My interpretation of slave emancipation in the Wolof districts of Senegal differs from that presented in the recent synthesis by Martin Klein. His interpretation assumes that nothing much happened to alter the incidence of slavery between 1883 and 1903. My interpretation is that slavery had already substantially declined by 1903. This fits in with the decline of aristocratic power and the rise of Sufi Islam. Would Mbakhane Diop have begged the French to aid him in his confrontation with Amadu Bamba in 1903 if aristocratic power and slavery had still been intact? Why would Wolof aristocrats undertake the risky sale of household slaves that led to the Chautemps Affair if many first generation slaves were still available? Many slaves fled during the political turmoil from 1883 to 1895 and slaves continued to flee thereafter. Although the direct evidence for this is anecdotal, it offers a better explanation for the census figures than does Martin Klein's interpretation.

My explanation is also consistent with an emphasis on slave initiative. While French inquiries into slavery may have provided a trigger for slave flight in Mali, there is no reason to believe that all slave initiatives were direct responses to colonial policy. Slaves seized opportunities when they presented themselves. In the Wolof states, the early development of an export economy provided slaves with just such opportunities. A full understanding of emancipation is only possible when the developing peasant economy is taken into consideration. That is the subject of the next chapter.

NOTES

1. Cruise O'Brien, *The Mourides* of Senegal, 13–34. For further discussion, see chapter 7.

2. Colin Newbury, "The Formation of the Government General of French West Africa," *Journal of African History* 1, no. 1 (1960): 111–28; and Colin Newbury, "The Government General and Political Change in French West Africa," *St. Anthony's Papers*, No. 10, *African Affairs*, no. 1, London, 1961. ANS archival sources on the creation of the Government-General are 18 G 1 to 18 G 5.

3. Roume was a graduate of the École polytechnique and belonged to dozens of colonialist organizations. According to C.M. Andrew, P. Grupp, and A.S. Kanya-Forstner, "Le mouvement colonial français et ses principales personalités," *Révue Française d'Histoire d'Outre-Mer* 62 (1975): 640–73, Roume was one of the forty-

five leaders of the colonial movement in France. For information on Roume's early career, see *Annuaire du Ministére des Colonies*, 1904, 760.

4. On Delcasse, see C.M. Andrew, *Theophile Delcassé and the Making of the Entente Cordiale* (London, 1968). On French policy, see A.S. Kanya-Forstner, *The Conquest of the Western Sudan: A Study in French Military Imperialism* (Cambridge, 1969). On the Parti Colonial, see C.M. Andrew and A.S. Kanya-Forstner, "The French 'Colonial Party': Its Composition, Aims and Influence 1885–1914," *Historical Journal* 14 (1971): 99–128, C.M. Andrew and A.S. Kanya-Forstner, "The *Groupe Colonial* in the French Chamber of Deputies 1892–1932," *Historical Journal* 17 (1974); and Stuart Michael Persell, *The French Colonial Lobby 1889–1938* (Stanford, Calif., 1983), 75–114.

5. See Conklin, *Mission to Civilize.*

6. Quotations from K 16, Enquête sur la captivité, 1903–1905, pièce 1.

7. Richard Roberts and Suzanne Miers, "The End of Slavery in Africa," in Suzanne Miers and Richard Roberts, eds., *The End of Slavery in Africa* (Madison, Wis., 1988), 3–68.

8. Martin A. Klein, "Slavery and Emancipation in French West Africa," 188, in *Breaking the Chains: Slavery, Bondage, and Emancipation in Modern Africa and Asia* ed. Martin A Klein (Madison, Wis., 1993).

9. Roberts, "The End of Slavery in the French Soudan, 1905–14"; Roberts, *Warriors, Merchants, and Slaves;* and Manchuelle, *Willing Migrants*, 118–45.

10. Lovejoy and Hogendorn, *Slow Death for Slavery.*

11. Klein, "Slavery and Emancipation in French West Africa," 188–89.

12. Igor Kopytoff, "The Cultural Context of African Abolition," in *The End of Slavery in Africa*, ed. Suzanne Miers and Richard Roberts (Madison, Wis., 1988) 485–503.

13. The journey was difficult, but not impossible. Migrant laborers traveled just as far in the early colonial period. See Manchuelle, *Willing Migrants.*

14. Irvine, "Caste and Communication," 100–11.

15. Ibid., 372–433.

16. Venema, *Wolof of Saloum*, 86, 129–44.

17. Ousmane Silla, "Persistance des castes dans la société wolof contemporaine," *Bulletin de l'Institut Fondamental de l'Afrique Noire*, B, 28 (1966): 731–70.

18. Klein, *Slavery and Colonial Rule*, 240–47.

19. This debate was provoked by Victor Schoelcher, the leading French abolitionist. See Victor Schoelcher, *L'Esclavage au Sénégal en 1880* (Paris, 1880).

20. K 12, Ministre à Gouverneur, Paris, Jan. 31, 1882.

21. K 12, Gouverneur à Ministre, Réponse no. 34, March 20, 1882.

22. K 11, Commandant de Dagana à Gouverneur, Oct. 13, 1880.

23. K 12, Cour d'Appel à Gouverneur, March 4, 1882.

24. Ibid., Libérations, April 1, 1882.

25. K 12, Gouverneur à Ministre des Colonies, Lettre no. 2042, Dec. 18, 1889.

26. Ibid.

27. K 12, Lettres arabes: Dagana, Jan. 17, 1889, Jan. 21 1889, and Feb. 2, 1889.

28. K 12, Traité du 15 février 1890.

29. Ibid.

30. K 13, Affaire Mody N'Diaye.

31. K 13, Captifs: Affaire de traite, Sénégal, 1893–1894.

32. Ibid., Pièce 4.

33. Ibid., Pièce 10, Merlin à L. Molleur, June 7, 1893.

34. Ibid., Pièces 23, 24 (Couchard), and 25 (Crespin). For background on the two men, see G. Wesley Johnson, *The Emergence of Black Politics in Senegal: The Struggle for Power in the Four Communes, 1900–1920* (Stanford, Calif., 1971), 52–54.

35. K 13, Pièce 32, L. Molleur à Directeur des affaires indigènes, April 21, 1894.

36. K 13, Noirot à Bour Saloum, June 13, 1893.

37. K 13, Pièce 14, L'Administrateur du Sine-Saloum à Directeur des affaires politiques, August 12, 1893.

38. K 13, Pièces 49, 68, 69. Demba War was still trying to get the slaves sent to Kajoor in May 1894. The ultimate fate of the freed slaves is unclear.

39. K 13, Pièce 54, Noirot, Dec. 21, 1893.

40. K 13, Pièce 48, Directeur des affaires politiques à Noirot, Sep. 21, 1893.

41. K 13, Lettre de M. A. Le Savoreux, July 26, 1893, and Note de J.J. Crespin, Nov. 3, 1893.

42. K 13, Note de Merlin, Directeur des affaires indigènes, n.d., c. 1894.

43. K 13, Pièce 126, Note sur l'application de l'acte [d'abolition], Dec. 5, 1895.

44. Ibid.

45. Ibid.

46. Ibid. Merlin's phrase is "simples tenanciers engagés à temps," a phrase full of ambiguity.

47. Bernard Moitt, "Peanut Production and Social Change in the Dakar Hinterland: Kajoor and Bawol, 1840–1940" (Ph.D. dissertation, University of Toronto, 1985), 226. See also Bernard Moitt, "Slavery and Emancipation in Senegal's Peanut Basin: The Nineteenth and Twentieth Centuries," *International Journal of African Historical Studies* 22 (1989): 32–36. For similar statements by Klein, see *Slavery and Colonial Rule*, 56, 64–65, 100.

48. For the French Sudan, see Roberts, *Warriors, Merchants and Slaves;* and Roberts, "The End of Slavery in the French Soudan."

49. On the worries of French authorities in the Sudan about the flight of "runaways" to Senegal and efforts to suppress the slave trade between the Sudan and Senegal, see K 15, Captivité et esclavage, 1900–1903, pièce 1, Lettre de Mori Keyta à M. le Gouverneur, May 18, 1899; pièce 2, Lieutenant Gouverneur du Soudan français à G.G. de l'AOF, Sep. 15, 1899; pièce 3, Procureur G. du Sénégal à Gouverneur du Soudan; pièces 5 and 6, Circulaire du Gouverneur Ponty, Feb. 1, 1901 and Oct. 11, 1900.

50. The main report is K 15, Pièce 13, Procureur Général, chef du Service Judiciaire à M. le G.G., Dec. 20, 1900.

51. Ibid., pp. 10–11.

52. He quoted an article in *Moniteur du Sénégal et Dépendeances*, Dec. 15, 1857, describing a similar trade.

53. K 16, Enquête sur la captivité, quoting a report by the Lieutenant Governor of Senegal, p. 8, Nov. 1903.

54. K 16, Pièce 6.

55. 13 G 296 (7), Affaire Chautemps, Rapport de Poulet, April 20, 1904. There are two dossiers on the Chautemps affair: 13 G 296 and 13 G 297. The two best reports

are those of Georges Poulet, who succeeded Prempain as commandant (13 G 296 (7), April 20, 1904, 24 pages), and Peuvergne, the inspector of native affairs sent to manage the crisis after the death of Chautemps (13 G 296 (6), April 14, 1904, 21 pages).

56. 13 G 296 (7), Rapport Poulet, pp. 2–6.

57. 13 G 296 (6), Rapport Peuvergne, pp. 1–6.

58. Ibid., pp. 7–8.

59. This is clear from the records in 13 G 296.

60. 13 G 296 (103), Déposition: Samba Niebe Bethio, April 11, 1904.

61. Ibid.

62. 13 G 296 (108), Déposition: Mari Fall, suivant de chef de canton Biram Bigue [Dieng], April 11, 1904. Biram Bigue was the son of Tanor Ngogne Dieng, the last king of Bawol.

63. Peuvergne justified his decision in his report, 13 G 296 (6), pp. 13–14, and 16–17. On the role of the chiefs in the pursuit of Diery Fall and Sarithia Dieye, see 13 G 296 (112), April 16, 1904.

64. *La Dépêche de Toulouse*, May 18, 1904, published an article giving an account of Mody Mbaye's "heroic" exploits. 13 G 296 (9) and 13 G 297 (86, 87, 90, 93) give details of Mody Mbaye's campaign against Salla Dior and his efforts to get himself appointed as a chief. Pièce 90, July 18, 1904, is the anonymous letter Mody wrote denouncing Salla Dior. He later confessed to having written this letter. Pièce 93 is Mody Mbaye's letter announcing his candidacy for superior chief.

65. 13 G 297 contains the records of the disciplinary action taken against Prempain and Donis. Poulet's report recommended the reinstallment of Salmon Fall. He was seconded by Martial Merlin. One historian, Mbaye Gueye, in "L'Affaire Chautemps et la suppression de l'esclavage de case au Senegal," *Bulletin de l'Institut Fondamental de l'Afrique Noire*, B, 27, nos. 3–4 (1965): 543–59, tried to link the Chautemps Affair directly to the abolition of slavery in 1905, but the evidence for this is weak.

66. See Dieng, *L'épopée*, 440–73, "Jeeri Joor Ndella," by the royal bard, Bassirou Mbaye.

67. Dieng, *L'épopée*, 458.

68. The documents generated by the survey are contained in different dossiers in the K series of the AOF archives. The more general synthetic reports are in K 16, Enquête sur la captivité, 1903–1905, and K 17, Rapport sur la captivité de M. Poulet, 1905. The responses from individual administrators in the *cercles* of Senegal are in K 18.

69. K 16, Pièce 17, Rapport à M. le G. G. sur les réponses des administrateurs et commandants de cercle au questionnaire relatif à la captivité en AOF, Dakar, Feb. 1905.

70. K 18, Pièce 20, Cercle de Dagana, Captivité, René Manetche.

71. K 18, Pièce 20.

72. Ibid.

73. K 18, Pièce 14, Province de N'Diambour, Nombre de captifs, Louga, Jan. 25, 1904.

74. K 18, Pièces 4, 5, 7, 8.

75. Claire C. Robertson and Martin A. Klein, eds., *Women and Slavery in Africa* (Madison, Wis., 1983) provide examples ranging from the "laws of slave reproduction" (more accurately "non-reproduction") discussed by Claude Meillassoux, "Female

Slavery," to the more balanced assessment by Martin A. Klein, "Women and Slavery in the Western Sudan."

76. See Searing, *West African Slavery*, 182, for a nineteenth-century example.

77. For prices, see K 16, Pièce 45, État synoptique des renseignments fournis par les commandants de cercle sur le régime de la captivité dans l'AOF.

78. Courtet, *Étude sur le Sénégal*, 140.

79. Ibid.

80. See the conclusion of this chapter for further discussion of this question.

81. K 18, Pièce 10, Captivité: Tivaouane.

82. Ibid.

83. K 18, Pièce 13, Captivité: Cercle de Louga.

84. K 18, Pièce 20, Captivité: Cercle de Dagana.

85. K 18, Pièce 18, Cercle de Louga.

86. The Wolof expressions are *jaami-juddu*, literally "slaves by birth," or *jaami-néeg*, literally "slaves of the house."

87. I refer to studies by Klein, Roberts, and Lovejoy, cited earlier.

88. K 18, Pièce 7, Baol Oriental.

89. Ibid.

90. Ibid.

91. Ibid.

92. K 18, Pièce 20, Cercle de Dagana.

93. For this debate, see Robertson and Klein, eds., *Women and Slavery in Africa*.

94. This is one of the points made by Margaret Strobel, "Slavery and Reproductive Labor in Mombasa," in *Women and Slavery*, ed. Robertson and Klein.

95. Robert Harms, "Sustaining the System: Trading Towns along the Middle Zaire, in *Women and Slavery*, ed. Robertson and Klein, 105.

96. K 12, Procès verbal, March 14, 1883.

97. K 12, Dagana, Procès verbal, Dec. 13, 1885.

98. Ibid., Procès verbal, Dec. 14, 1885.

99. 2 D 13-4, Cercle de Dakar-Thiès, Corres. 1901, July 18, 1901; 2 D 14-3, Cercle de Cayor, Corres. July 1901.

100. These are the arguments presented by Vienne: 2 D 14-3, Vienne à Directeur des affaires indigénes, July 10, 1901.

101. 2 D 14-3, Cayor, Corres. 1902, Vienne à Directeur des affaires indigénes, May 8, 1902.

102. 2 D 14-4, Cercle de Cayor, Corres. March 1903, Allys à Directeur des affaires indigénes, March 14, 1903.

103. 2 D 14-3, Cercle de Cayor, Corres. 1901, Commandant Penel à Directeur des affaires indigénes, Feb. 28, 1901.

104. 2 D 14-3, Cercle de Cayor, Corres. 1901, March 14, 1901. This is the date of the translation of the original report, which was written in Arabic by the chief qadi, who was a close ally of Demba War Sall.

105. Ibid.

106. Ibid., Lettre no. 287, Commandant Penel à Directeur des affaires indigénes, March 15, 1901.

107. K 16, Pièce 17, Feb. 1905.

108. Martin Klein, *Slavery and Colonial Rule*, 256.

109. Ibid., Appendix 1, 256.

110. Ibid., citing Donal B. Cruise O'Brien, *Saints and Politicians. Essays in the Organization of a Senegalese Peasant Society* (Cambridge, 1975), 27.

111. K 17, Rapport sur la captivité de M. Poulet, 1905, p. 31. Poulet cited the Caribbean precedent, pp. 5–6, and the less threatening analogy with Russian serf emancipation, p. 40.

112. For the general argument, see Paul E. Lovejoy, *Transformations in Slavery: A History of Slavery in Africa* (Cambridge, 1983).

113. Klein and Roberts, "Banamba Slave Exodus"; Roberts, "The End of Slavery in the French Sudan." See also Martin Klein, *Slavery and Coloniali Rule.*

114. Paul E. Lovejoy and Jan S. Hogendorn, "The Reform of Slavery in Colonial Northern Nigeria," in *The End of Slavery*, ed. Suzanne Miers and Richard Roberts (Madison, Wis., 1988) 395–96. For the conflicts of this period, see also Lovejoy and Hogendorn, "Revolutionary Mahdism," 217–44.

115. In this I disagree with Martin Klein, who has argued that "massive numbers" were imported. For an earlier statement of my position and the relevant evidence, see Searing, *West African Slavery*, 198–99.

116. This is discussed in chapter 7.

Figure 6.1 Weighing peanuts at a trading post (c. 1907).

6

EMANCIPATION FROM BELOW: THE EMERGENCE OF A MUSLIM PEASANTRY, 1890–1914

Nineteenth-century descriptions of Wolof society focus on the plight of the *baadoolo*, a term emphasizing "powerlessness" as the essential character-istic of the peasantry. This old-regime stereotype reflected the bias of the aristocracy. In the aristocracy's view, peasants earned their living by the sweat of their brow, did not bear arms or participate in power, and owed tribute and taxes to their overlords.[1] Peasants contradicted this stereotype by rebelling against the monarchy on more than one occasion. In today's Senegal the term *baadoolo* has an archaic ring. Peasants refer to them-selves more readily as *beykat*, a word with connotations much like the English word "farmer." The transition from *baadoolo* to *beykat* describes one of the most important transformations of Wolof society.

In the nineteenth century, the *baadoolo* lived in communities that owed allegiance and tribute to political overlords. Whether these were aristocrats, royal slaves, or titled Muslim leaders, they inherited their authority and represented the peasantry in the larger political world. Peasants did not choose their overlords; they inherited them. Peasants lived alongside substantial slave populations, sharing a similar way of life but with no political or societal rights of their own. This rural so-ciety was radically transformed in the years between the conquest and World War I. The main impetus from below for change came from the cash-crop economy.

In my view historians have focused too narrowly on masters and slaves, slave resistance, and colonial policy in discussing emancipation, and not enough on peasant society. Peasant cash cropping has not been a central theme in studies of slavery, but it has appeared in discussions of Islam and the Murid order. Colonial studies focused more on peanuts than on peasants.[2] Recent economic studies have taken a macroeconomic perspective that emphasizes the decline of African merchants, the domination of European commercial firms, and the long-range, negative consequences of mono-crop agriculture. There is substantial truth to all these points, especially if one examines the Senegalese economy from the perspective of the 1930s or the 1960s.[3] I will focus on the social transformations that occurred at the grass roots of rural society during the first cash crop "boom," from 1890 to 1914. Cash cropping played a crucial role in the transition from an economy based on slavery to a peasant economy. The chapter begins with a discussion of the "vent for surplus" model. My analysis focuses on the peasant household as the central actor in the colonial economy. Generation and gender created hierarchies within the household, but the household was the essential unit of production and consumption. The dynamic growth of the peasant economy explains the rapid decline of slavery in the peanut basin. Peasant households employed many "seasonal migrants." Many were long-distance migrants, but many others were runaway slaves. There are parallels between the roles of unmarried dependents (especially bachelors), slaves, and migrant farmers, which appear when the household is examined from within. The dynamic growth of the peasant economy played a crucial role in emancipation.

While peasant households responded to the opportunities created by cash cropping, they were also enclosed within new colonial hierarchies. The most important was the commercial system, which I explore by examining the important role of credit and debt in the peasant economy. The credit hierarchy reveals the chain of command in the colonial economy, which began with the big European import-export firms, and worked its way through a chain of European, Arab, and African merchants until it reached the village peddler and the peasant household. The proliferation of merchants trying to profit from peasant production led petty traders working at the village level to offer high-risk credit to households, accompanied by usurious rates of interest. This in turn provoked the intervention of the colonial state, which was concerned that peasant debt would undermine the export economy.

THE TRANSITION FROM SLAVES TO CASH CROPS

Wolof peasants grew peanuts for export, but historians have debated why they grew them and what they gained in return for their efforts.

Some explanations are inadequate. One common theme is the coercive stimulus of the head tax, which had to be paid in cash. But Mohamed Mbodj pointed out that the rate of taxation averaged only around 10 percent of peasant cash earnings, so it is difficult to explain the vigorous development of peasant farming on the basis of the head tax alone. Similarly, administrative coercion played only a small role.[4] Other explanations, such as those that focus on the role of Islam, and particularly the Murids, are too limited in scope. Even if they are valid for the Murids, they cannot explain peasant farming in the peanut basin as a whole.

In the 1950s, Hla Myint proposed one of the most influential explanations for the cash-crop "booms" of the colonial period.[5] His "vent for surplus" model argues that land and labor were underutilized assets in West Africa and that export economies developed in response to the stimulus of world market demand. One feature of these "export booms" was the rapid expansion of production without significant technological innovation. Myint's explanation is that African societies put new land into production using existing labor supplies and technology. Historians have criticized Myint for neglecting labor and migration. Export booms often occurred in the midst of rapid social change, symbolized by slave emancipation and migration. Myint gives the impression that previously "lazy" Africans worked harder because of the incentives created by the world market, while in fact new lands were settled and many social battles were fought over labor. The model suggests that African households reduced their leisure time and mobilized family labor, with existing peasant households providing a mass base of small producers for the "take off" of export production. A. G. Hopkins, whose interpretation of cash cropping began with the "vent for surplus" model, argued that peasants responded to the opportunities of the world market. West African peasants produced for the market to pay for the goods sold by European merchants, which allowed them to diversify their consumption. Peasants produced peanuts for their exchange value, on their own initiative, while European merchant firms and colonial railroad construction gave them access to the world market.

Hopkins' reformulation of the vent for surplus model has been both praised and criticized. Hopkins has been lauded for rejecting the model of a closed peasant society, unable to make rational market decisions, and for his efforts to historicize Myint's schema. At the same time Hopkins' analysis has been criticized as an abstraction based on neoclassical economic theory, rather than a historical explanation of peasant farming.[6] Critics of colonial economic development have argued that peasants rarely benefited from market production, because European merchant firms monopolized profits and accumulation. Historians influenced by Marxism and world-systems analysis have focused on new forms of exploitation rather than on peasant initiative.[7]

While the "vent for surplus" model was criticized for its assumptions about labor, it is worth reformulating another aspect of Myint's argument, which deals with the connection to the world economy. Behind the "vent for surplus" model are two conceptually distinct changes associated with colonial rule. One was the development of the transportation network of steamship companies, ocean ports, and railroads. The other was the "currency revolution," also explored by Hopkins, which made European currencies the measure of economic value and productivity.[8] This second aspect needs to be explored in more detail. Colonial currencies measured the value of African exports in money, reflecting the prices of raw materials in European markets.

Myint's concept can be historicized by asking what changed in West Africa's connection to the world market in the transition between the slave trade and the era of export agriculture. The change was fundamental. During the era of the slave trade, world market prices operated on the margins of the domestic economy. Europeans judged the price of slaves to be "low," based on comparisons with the price of slaves in the Americas, and this price differential was fundamental to the possibilities of trade. The "low" price of African slaves in European currencies permitted slave traders to absorb high costs of transporting slaves across the Atlantic and other risks.[9] When European slave traders purchased provisions such as grain on the African coast, prices were "local" and goods were judged to be "cheap" except during periods of crisis and famine when supplies dried up and prices soared. During the era of the slave trade, markets were unconnected and prices in West Africa bore little relation to prices in Europe or the Americas.[10] European slavers did not calculate the price they would pay for slaves in West Africa based on their value in the Americas, minus transportation costs and the risks they faced. They negotiated prices in local currencies, with the effect that price levels reflected the African market. Markets were separate and remained that way.

Export agriculture brought fundamental change. European merchants purchased peanuts in Senegal based on the price of peanuts in London or Marseilles. This direct connection to the world market had an enormous impact. The initial connection to the world market produced a boom because the "high" prices prevailing in the capitalist world were attractive to African farmers. This was true despite the fact that Africans received only a portion of the world market price. Table 6.1 shows the volume of Senegalese peanut production in the period before World War I, and the

Table 6.1 Peanut Exports, Senegal, 1890–1914

Year	Metric Tons	Value (fob Dakar)	Price per 100 Kilograms (caf Marseilles)	Price per 100 Kilograms (Local Markets)
1890	27,221	5,426,000	40.00 fr	15 fr
1891	26,391	5,479,000	25.00	15
1892	46,790	11,636,000	27.50	15
1893	59,302	11,688,000	24.00	15
1894	65,289	11,350,000	22.50	15
1895	51,600	7,675,000	19.50	12–15
1896	63,555	9,146,000	21.50	12–15
1897	48,123	8,147,000	24.50	12.5
1898	95,955	13,615,000	23.50	12.5
1899	85,543	12,119,000	24.00	12.5
1900	140,922	24,240,000	28.00	18
1901	123,483	22,117,000	30.00	24
1902	110,225	20,545,000	28.50	20
1903	148,843	34,575,000	26.50	15–20
1904	137,784	21,320,000	26.50	18–24
1905	96,175	14,851,000	28–30	20–25
1906	100,476	20,976,000	28–30	12.5–20
1907	154,000	30,721,000	28–30	15–18
1908	144,139	32,889,000	28–30	15–18
1909	224,326	43,892,000	28–30	15–18
1910	227,299	49,770,000	32.80	18–20
1911	164,907	40,943,000	31.85	18–20
1912	184,761	42,464,000	34.55	18–20
1913	242,084	59,229,000	34.50	18–24
1914	280,526	68,089,000	31.00	18–24

Source: Guiraud, *L'arachide sénégalaise*; Adam, *L'arachide*, 137–42; Fernand Batude, *L'arachide au Sénégal* (Paris, 1941); Joseph Fouquet, *La traite des arachides dans le pays de Kaolack* (Saint-Louis, 1958), 128–129; and reports in 2 G series, ANS.

commercial value of the crop. I have tried to calculate the portion of the world market price paid to producers by presenting the market price in Europe and the prices paid to African sellers in Senegal's market towns.

The contrast between the slave trade and commodity exports was dramatic, even though this brief presentation exaggerates the difference to make its point. One can allow that the prices paid for slaves in West Africa fluctuated, that the "terms of trade" varied from period to period, and that the internal market set prices for women slaves at a higher level than prices for men.[11] But the connection between markets was weak and inefficient, particularly when contrasted with the direct connection forged between markets by money in the colonial period. Taxation was not important because it forced Africans to grow cash crops, but because it accelerated the adoption of European money. My focus is on African perceptions of the prices paid for the commodities they sold. Historians have misjudged the impact of the currency and price revolution of the nineteenth century due to their interpretation of the transition from the slave trade. Hopkins framed the question in a way that emphasized continuities. In his view, slaves were simply a different kind of commodity export.[12] My interpretation focuses on the difference between slave exports and commodity exports.

During the era of the slave trade, Senegambia exported fewer slaves than any other region, despite a location close to Europe and the Caribbean that should have encouraged European slave purchases.[13] The simplest explanation is that Africans put limits on the number of slaves they sold on Atlantic markets. There was a strong local demand for slave labor throughout the region. Many slaves were retained in the region rather than being exported. In addition, slaves were sold in Saharan markets, primarily in exchange for horses. Muslims throughout the region condemned the sale of fellow Muslims, which raised the political costs of enslavement and helps explain the high proportion of slaves who were "Bambara," a code word for non-Muslim Mande speakers. More fundamentally, slaves were expensive "luxuries" that few persons were in a position to sell, not ordinary "commodities." The impact of the slave trade was nevertheless important. Politically, it increased tensions between the monarchy and Islam. Economically, it reshaped trade routes in ways that gave advantages to the Atlantic coastal region.

Before peanuts became an important export crop, Wolof producers sold surplus grain to French and desert merchants. Wolof peasants were in a good position to perceive the advantages of producing for the world market as opposed to the local market. In the 1890s, peanut exports from Kajoor and Bawol rose from about 20,000 metric tons per year to over 100,000 metric tons, while millet sales stagnated at around 1,000 metric tons.[14] Based on the prices of millet and peanuts in coastal towns, the main advantage of peanuts was a 30–50 percent higher yield in kilograms per hectare, because the prices for 100 kilograms of peanuts and the same amount of millet were about the same.[15] This comparison understates the advantage of peanuts because the prices for peanuts reflect what producers received in local markets while the millet prices are for exports from coastal ports. Based on peanut marketing, the producer price for millet was probably only 60 percent of its export value. In that case the advantage for producers was probably 2 to 1 in favor of peanuts. Millet prices were subject to severe seasonal fluctuations, with low prices in the harvest period when most producers sold their surplus, and much higher prices in the "hungry season" before the next harvest. The market for millet was small, and expanded only in bad years, as in 1903 and 1904, when drought reduced harvests and French merchants bought 3,000 to 4,000 tons, instead of 1,000.[16]

Wolof peasants were the first in West Africa to grow an annual cash crop for export. Other regions exported natural resources (gum arabic, palm oil, wild rubber), which makes peasant initiative harder to measure. The Wolof provide an important test case for the response of African peasants to the world market.[17] Peasant peanut exports expanded despite a long period when prices and terms of trade declined (1883–1899) compared to previous and subsequent periods (1860–1882, 1900–1914). This reinforces the argument that the shift from slave exports to commodity exports gave a powerful initial stimulus to export production. The stimulus was strong enough to weather fluctuations in prices. This was especially true for peasants, who compared peanuts to millet. Critics of "market" forces have not offered alternate explanations for commodity booms in colonial West Africa. They have preferred to point out that these booms failed to generate self-sustaining "autonomous development," or that they were "exceptions" when compared to other regions, where Africans resisted market production. In other words, they have changed the subject.[18]

Colonial rule did not kill the golden goose of export agriculture, but it cannot explain its success. After falling during the turmoil that accompanied the conquest, peanut production entered a new period of expansion. The major trend of this period is clear: the adoption of peanut production by peasant households. The period from 1890 to 1914 was characterized by a steady expansion of the export trade in peanuts. Peanut exports declined in 1905, the most serious drought year of this period, but expanded otherwise, even during a series of poor agricultural seasons from 1910 to 1914.[19] The growth resulted from the integration of peanuts, planted as a cash crop, into the household economies of peasant families. Wolof peasants planted peanuts in rotation with food crops in cycles designed to maximize the fertility of the soil. On good land, peanuts were grown after

two successive millet crops and then the land was left fallow in the fourth
year. On less fertile soil, peanuts were grown first, followed by millet then
a year of fallow.[20]

The strongest evidence for the positive stimulus of the world market
comes from the peasantry itself. When I did fieldwork in the Sereer
village of Bandia, one portion of the interview was devoted to the "peanut trade." With one exception,[21] all of my informants, who were born
between c. 1906 and c. 1920, judged the "peanut trade" positively. Many
of them contrasted the "colonial" period with the period after independence, saying that there had been a real economy (Wolof, *koom-koom*)
under the French. Bandia's farmers produced peanuts during the colonial period and for a few decades after independence, but they have
since abandoned peanuts for watermelons and other market-garden crops
that they sell in Dakar. Cash income from farming is supplemented by
the wages earned by young men and women who migrate to Dakar.
Bandia's elders remember peanuts as a "difficult crop," referring to its
labor demands during the harvest compared to millet and other crops.
They judged the colonial economy by what they could buy after the
harvest. Their memories cannot be dismissed as nostalgia for the past
and cynicism about the present, because they recalled in some detail
the "cheating," "theft," "usury," and "chicanery" of colonial chiefs and
merchants. The elders' positive view of the "peanut trade" also contrasted with their negative judgments of the colonial state. Wolof and
Sereer peasants were frequently the victims of middlemen, but the old
men I interviewed remembered the years when they bought cloth, goats,
and cattle with the proceeds of the harvest.

My informants single out an important aspect of peasant cash-crop
agriculture. The sale of peanuts was not simply a way to acquire European imports, but was crucial to the maintenance and reproduction of
peasant households. Some of the money earned was reinvested in the
peasant economy through the purchase of small stock and cattle. For
young dependent males, cash-crop earnings were crucial to saving money
for bride-wealth. Whether the cash from peanuts was used directly as
bride-wealth, as among the Wolof, or reinvested in cattle and stock, as
among the Sereer, peanut income became the main source of the wealth
that allowed young men to strive for social independence. Marriage was
the first step toward the respected status of household head. Cash cropping played an integral role in the reproduction of the peasant household and in the achievement of status in rural society. Colonial import
tables amply document peasant consumption of imports. In 1903, fully
a third of Senegal's imports (but much more if one excludes material

imported for large infrastructural projects) were goods bought by peasants: cloth, rice, kola nuts, perfumes, clothes, sugar, beads, jewelry, and other items.[22]

THE PEASANT HOUSEHOLD

The dominant role of peasant households in the economy was a significant historical development. The growth of the peasantry reflected the decline of slavery and the failure of "plantation" production based on wage labor. Large agricultural estates failed because peasants outperformed them. French policy did not determine the outcome, but some French decisions facilitated the trend. In 1903, Governor-General Roume issued an important decree that recognized the authority of African customary law. African systems of land tenure were given the force of law in settled areas, while the French claimed the right of eminent domain in unsettled lands.[23] This decree made it difficult for Europeans to purchase land outside urban centers after 1903. Peasants were protected from expropriation, but not freed from the customary dues they owed on the lands they cultivated. Wolof *laman* (titled landowners) and titled *sëriñ* (Muslims with landed domains) were permitted to collect dues, creating higher customary tax rates in Njambur and Kajoor, where there were overlapping claims to the land. French interpretations of customary law created important regional variations. Taxation in money and disputes over which crops could be taxed demonstrated the transformation of custom.[24]

The French recognized customary land tenure after French experiments with plantation production had failed. At the turn of the century, French merchants and administrators experimented with peanut production on plantations using wage labor. Economic experts viewed production in Africa through a Caribbean lens. Africa would produce the tropical commodities that had been produced by African labor in the West Indies. Agricultural experts planned to use botanical gardens and research stations to encourage innovations in crop plantings and to select the best strains of seed. They favored the plantation as the dominant model of labor control.[25] Although they expressed contempt for "native farming," experiments with "improved" farming techniques failed miserably. The wage rate necessary to entice labor out of the peasant economy doomed the plantations to economic failure.[26] Experiments carried out in Kajoor demonstrated that "native farming" produced a profit of 157 francs a hectare while "improved farming" produced a profit of 77 francs.[27]

Métis merchants from Saint-Louis also tried to establish estates at the turn of the century. The Devès family played the leading role. Hyacinthe Devès established a personal fiefdom in the village of N'Dioung in Bawol. In addition, the family firm, Devès and Chaumet, negotiated a concession of 1,500 hectares in Kajoor in 1899. Demba War Sall granted the land in exchange for 6,000 francs.[28] The concession included the village of N'Guick and its surrounding area, which contained a number of smaller villages. Although the goal of the merchants was the development of peanut production, they regarded the territory as a personal fiefdom. They claimed the right to collect taxes, established "rents" on land, and requisitioned the labor of their subjects as they saw fit. Colonial authorities put an end to the merchants' efforts in 1901 because the Devés estates threatened French political authority and the separation of the protectorate from the Four Communes, which was a cardinal principle of French policy. These experiments were economic failures, leaving behind many debts.

The failure of "plantation" agriculture was significant, because slavery was also in decline. The peasant household triumphed because of its flexibility and its ability to produce at a lower cost than a large estate. This flexibility came from the organization of labor within the household and the combination of food and cash-crop production that it promoted. Most households supplied the required labor from their own resources. The household had a hierarchical structure, with a clearly defined system of labor exchanges.[29]

The peasant household was a unit of production and consumption. The head of the household (*boroom-kër-ga*) was the senior male in a residential compound, living with his wife or wives, children, and other relatives who recognized his authority. The household head controlled the labor time of his dependents in ways that varied with their age, gender, and status. His control over their labor time reciprocated their dependency on him for food and access to land. The household head distributed plots of land to his wives and to dependent males after circumcision. In return he received a portion of their labor time and he was responsible for feeding the family with the food crops grown on a central plot under his control and management. The most important contributors of labor time were women and young unmarried males, called *surga* in Wolof. The defining characteristic of *surga* was the fact that they were fed by the head of the household.

The division of labor in peanut production was modeled on the gender and age roles in millet production. Males working under the supervision of the household head were responsible for the heavy work of clearing the field and preparing the ground for planting. Men also uprooted mature plants during the harvest, placing them in large piles. Women and children separated the shells from the plants. Men and women worked together on planting and weeding the fields. If there was a principle at work in the gender division of labor, it was that men performed arduous tasks, while women were responsible for repetitive, labor-intensive tasks. Some female tasks were associated with processing the crop and could be carried out near the residential compound: winnowing and pounding millet, separating the peanut shells from the plants.

Female labor was crucial to cash-crop production, even though women spent less time in the fields than men. Women's labor was carried out near the residential compound. Wives received fields from their husbands, which they cultivated with the aid of their daughters. These fields were garden plots (Wolof, *tóokër*), planted with early millet (Wolof, *sunna-si*; *Pennisetum gambiense*), manioc, vegetables, and condiments. Wives could grow peanuts as well, to earn cash income. Garden plots were located near the residential compound. Wives and daughters could be called on to go out and work on the main outlying family fields. In practice such demands were limited to labor-intensive tasks such as planting, weeding the fields, and processing the harvest. The labor demands of domestic work meant that women and daughters worked longer hours than men overall, but spent less time farming. Many female tasks, such as fetching water from wells, washing clothes, pounding millet, and cooking, were carried out in close proximity to the compound. The location of women's fields fitted in with the overall pattern of female labor. The most important contribution of women's labor to peanut farming was the labor-intensive task of separating the peanut shells from the uprooted plants.

French researchers in Murid villages, led by Jean Copans, carried out detailed studies of peasant labor in the late 1960s.[30] They quantified the percentages of labor devoted to specific tasks and assessed the contributions of various categories of dependents. These data can be compared to less detailed studies of Wolof farming in 1900. In Jean Copans' study of Murid villages, the tasks of peanut cultivation were assigned percentages of the total work time: 16 to 25 percent of the labor time was devoted to clearing and preparing the land for planting, 7 to 10 percent for planting, 30 to 40 percent for harvesting, and 45 to 70 percent for weeding and maintaining the fields under cultivation.[31] Labor exchanges within the family benefited the household head. While women's work was carried out in the company of other women, wives in a polygynous household did not aid one another in the cultivation of their individual plots. They relied on their own labor and controlled any money they earned by selling peanuts or millet. The household head worked alongside his *surga* and supervised their activities. Copans estimated that women's share of labor time was 25 to 50 percent that of the male contribution.

While Copans' study broke new ground by observing household labor in the field, his conclusions underestimate the contribution of women to cash-crop production. Jean Adam, who observed Wolof peanut farming at the turn of the century, offered a different analysis of the labor time of various tasks. More importantly, he treated the processing of the harvest as an integral part of production. He estimated that it took 25–30 days to clear a field, 3 days for planting, 30 days for weeding, 15 days for the first stage of the harvest (digging up the plants, carried out by men), and 80 days for processing the crop (carried out by women and children).[32] This gives the following percentages: 19 percent for clearing the field (male), 2 percent for planting, 20 percent for weeding, 9 percent for harvesting (male) and 50 percent for processing the crop (female). Women contributed more labor time to cash-crop production than men did, if one takes account of the time spent separating the peanut shells from the plant (the rest of the plant was saved for fodder). They also aided in weeding and planting, which suggests that women and the young children who worked under their direction contributed at least 61 percent of the total labor associated with peanut production.

The gender and age division of labor explains why young unmarried males (*surga*) were crucial to cash-crop production. Because women were frequently tied up with domestic chores, young men spent the most time in the fields working on the plots of millet and peanuts. Young men were crucial because the household head lost control over the labor of more senior males. Marriage freed men from the authority of their fathers. By the same token, young men's need for bride-wealth reinforced the authority of the household head. The only alternative was to seek a new patron outside the family compound. Males in a household were stratified by age.

The household head (*boroom-kër-ga*) was the symbol of senior male authority. He controlled the labor of his wives and children, but was responsible for feeding them and caring for them from the produce of his fields. This same authority extended over dependent males or *surga*. *Surga* owed four or five mornings of work per week to the household head. They worked from early in the morning until one or two o'clock in the afternoon, the same hours worked by slaves. *Surga* were important producers in their own right. From the head of the household they each received a field which was often planted entirely in peanuts to maximize cash income. Apart from a small sum paid to help with taxes, this income belonged to the young men. Dependent males were encouraged to work hard for themselves, to accumulate the resources needed for marriage and eventual independence. By contrast, unmarried daughters did not usually receive their own field, but worked on their mother's field and received some of its product. The expectation was that marriage would take them out of the household and provide for them. While young males were expected to earn cash so that they could help pay bride-wealth, daughters were expected to bring bride-wealth into the household at marriage.

Cultural factors related to patterns of marriage help explain why *surga* were considered crucial to peanut cultivation. Unless there were slaves in the household, *surga* labor time was crucial to feeding the family and earning cash for the household head. When a young male married, his relationship with the head of the household changed, even if he stayed within his father's compound. Married, junior males in a compound were halfway between dependency and independence. The household head had no claims over the labor of their wives, who worked for their husbands. Recognizing the "independence" created by marriage, the married couple had a choice. They could take part in the cooking rotation of the *boroom-kër-ga*'s wives, supplying the food and labor for a meal for the entire compound on certain days. Or they could form their own "eating household" within the compound. In this case, the husband was referred to as a "little" household head (*boroom-kër-gu-ndaw*). Feeding others was the concrete manifestation of household authority.[33]

Cultural patterns encouraged young men to work hard, with the ultimate goal of achieving independence. The division of the workday and the workweek provided young men with opportunities to work for themselves. These divisions predated cash-crop farming and Islam, as can be seen from an examination of Sereer "customs" with regard to the labor of young men. In Sereer households, children who had been circumcised were regarded as adults, with the dependent status of *surga*. They worked for the household head four half days a week, and were free to work for themselves on Mondays, on Thursdays, and in the afternoons.[34] Monday is a day of rest in most Sereer regions, a day when no agricultural work is permitted, a sacred day like Friday in the Muslim calendar. Millet cultivation is forbidden on Thursday, but other crops, such as peanuts, can be cultivated.[35] Giving *surga* Thursdays off encouraged them to grow peanuts. Sereer religious beliefs dictated a serious atmosphere of work in the rainy season. Drumming and other festive activities were forbidden. No one could wear red, which was a "sacred" color.[36] These taboos were enforced because it was feared that inappropriate behavior might cause the rains and crops to fail. The work ethic was not based on Islam, but on spirit religion and peasant values.

Archival sources describing slavery at the turn of the century reveal the parallels between the status of slaves and the status of *surga*. A report from Kaolack (a Sereer region) described the labor obligations of household slaves and their position in the family as follows:

> All slaves owe their labor to their masters during the week from the morning until midday, except Thursday and Monday when they work for themselves, as is also the case on other days from the afternoon to the evening. They are certainly more free than any domestic servant. . . . The master is obliged to feed and clothe them. . . . They are employed in agriculture, as weavers, and in the household they prepare the millet. They also enlist in the army and send their master half of their enlistment premium, and a part of their wages. The laborers and employees of the administration [of slave origin] follow the same practice.[37]

Another report, from a Muslim district in the same *cercle*, said that the master had to treat his slave like a relative, but not a son; he had to provide support, but was not required to be generous. The slave ate from the same food as the rest of the family, and was considered a dependent or *surga* along with the master's children. What the slave produced while laboring for the master belonged to the master, but the slave owned the product of his labors on Monday and Friday. The master was obliged to provide a plot of land for his slave's private use.[38]

The structure of the household gave considerable authority to the household head in the name of collective security, symbolized by the granaries he owned. At the same time it allowed for individual autonomy and accumulation by dependents. My informants denied that this had anything to do with recent changes (cash cropping). Household structure was related to patterns of kinship, marriage, and inheritance.[39] With variations based on whether the *surga* worked for the father or the maternal uncle, the basic pattern was common to both the Wolof and the Sereer.

Tensions were frequent between the household head and his *surga*, depending on whether the head of the household was trying to keep them in a state of dependency or helping them to marry and establish their own households. Because most *surga* were sons, the economic relations between fathers and sons were embedded in larger emotional bonds, most frequently described in terms of affection, gratitude, or disappointment. If there were many sons in the household, younger sons might feel they were being asked to postpone their independence indefinitely. If the father showed more interest in marrying additional wives than in aiding his sons, the result was the same. Young males in this position might leave the household and join another. The traditional destination of this kind of migration was the "maternal uncle" (Wolof, *nijaay*), who was regarded as a potential source of help. The maternal uncle might provide his nephew with a wife or help him establish himself.[40] Other relatives could offer a new home to the young man as well. Young men were expected to accumulate wealth in preparation for marriage. If residence in another household as a *surga* aided in that task, it was accepted. The forces that encouraged long-distance labor migrations among the Soninké led to short-distance internal migrations in Wolof society. Because the Wolof were favorably located for peanut production, young men migrated within the Wolof zone rather than leaving it.[41]

The dynamics of the peasant household help to explain both slavery and emancipation. By the early colonial period, peasant households owned the majority of slaves. Compared with the recent emphasis on "plantations," there has been less discussion of slavery in peasant societies.[42] Chayanov's discussion of the generational life cycle of peasant households provides insights into the benefits of slave ownership for peasants, even if they owned very few slaves. Chayanov argued that the productive capacity of peasant households and their income earning power were related to the ratio between total household size and the number of members in their peak years of productivity. Households with a high proportion of small children and the elderly experienced labor shortages relative to consumption needs, while households with a high proportion of young unmarried adults had an optimum balance between consumption needs and labor power, if they possessed sufficient land. The productivity and wealth of a peasant household was directly related to its age composition at any given time.[43]

Slaves could raise the labor supply to optimum levels. The peasant purchaser did not bear the costs of raising a slave to maturity, but benefited from his or her labor. Slaves born in the house were left with their parents until they could begin to work. Then they joined the *surga*. Some sources suggest that slaves worked one more day than *surga* and received less food and aid than *surga* who were sons or nephews.[44] Slaves were required to feed themselves in the afternoons and on their free days, while the *surga* ate from the family stores at all times. Even if slaves worked longer hours than *surga,* the extra work did not define their status. Slaves were permanent dependents and could not become household heads. The master took the slave's children, who became *surga* of the slave owner. The nonexistence of the slave's parental rights was at the heart of slavery.

While Chayanov's model of the peasant economy explains the advantages of slave-holding, it also predicts that the same advantages could be achieved by adding additional *surga* to the household. Peasant households absorbed migrant labor by offering migrants positions equivalent to those of *surga.* Migrants came from two sources. Young dependent males migrated within the Wolof zone, seeking opportunities to earn cash income in preparation for marriage and independence. These internal migrations coexisted with long-distance labor migrations by young males from other regions who relocated within the Wolof zone. The most favorable destinations were on the margins of the Wolof zone, where new lands were being opened up and the population was expanding. The typical Wolof internal migrant came from Njambur or Kajoor and migrated to Bawol or Saalum. Many of the early migrants were probably runaway slaves from within the Wolof kingdoms, who became migrant farmers in peasant households.

MIGRANT FARMERS

Peasant households became hosts for migrant farmers who migrated to the Wolof kingdoms to take advantage of the opportunities for cash crop production. These seasonal migrants were known as *nawetaan.* *Nawetaan* is a Wolof word that means someone who passes the rainy season.[45] *Nawetaan* supplied labor to their hosts in exchange for housing, food, and a plot of their own, which was usually devoted entirely to peanuts. The contracts that regulated relations between migrants and host families were African in their origins, and were based on principles that were widespread in the Western Sudan. The host supplied food, lodging, and a plot of land to the migrant farmer for the duration of his stay, in exchange for a proportion of his labor time. The contract was seasonal, lasting for the duration of the rainy season. While the migrants were referred to by the Wolof word *nawetaan*, the term used for the host was *njatigi*, a Mande term reflecting the origins of the majority of the migrants in the interwar period.

In Senegal the host was a Wolof or Sereer household in the peanut basin, while the migrant was usually a stranger from the east. Most migrants came from Mali, although some came from as far as Burkina Faso, and substantial numbers came from the Futa Jallon region of Guinea-Conakry, the eastern provinces of Senegal, and Guinea-Bissau. Migrants arrived a few weeks before the first rains, and departed as soon as the harvest was complete. Seasonal migration to the peanut basin began in the nineteenth century and continued until independence. But the greatest development of migrant farming occurred in the period between the two world wars, when it was heavily concentrated in the "new lands" ("terres neuves") of eastern Bawol and Saalum.

A number of factors contributed to migrant farming in the colonial era. French policies permitted many slaves to flee their masters. Some took advantage of their new mobility to become *nawetaan*.[46] The French administration noted the link between slave emancipation and seasonal migration in 1910, when "former slaves of the Sahel descended in small bands into Senegal where they have covered the lands adjacent to the new Thiès-Kayes railroad with their plantings."[47] The construction of the Dakar-Bamako railroad was the second factor that contributed to seasonal migrations. Although the link between Thiès and Kayes was not completed until 1923, major portions of the railroad were in service much earlier and facilitated migration in stages from the French Sudan to Senegal. The railroad reached Diourbel in 1909, Kaffrine in 1912, Koungheul in 1913, and Tambakounda in 1915, before World War I caused a temporary halt in construction. Many of the workers who built the railroad were villagers and former slaves from the cash-poor territories of the French Sudan, whose first acquaintance with the peanut basin was as salaried day laborers for the administration. Many broke their contracts to become migrant farmers, and they spread the word about the opportunities in Senegal when they returned home.[48]

The literature on "migrant farmers" in Senegal gives the impression that migration began just before World War I and came into its own in the interwar period.[49] This was when French officials noticed migration. The pattern in Senegal contrasted with the Gambia, where "strange" farmers pioneered the cultivation of peanuts. The first "strange" farmers were Soninke merchants seeking a replacement for their profits from the slave trade. French archival documents suggest that seasonal migration to the Wolof kingdoms began no later than the turn of the century. An administrator commenting on the difficulty of recruiting wage laborers in the *cercle* of Thiès in 1903 noted that the only people who might be available were "temporary migrants" (*gens de passage*), mainly "Socé [Wolof term for Mande], Toucouleurs and people from Firdous [the Gambia]." These groups had not come seeking wage labor, so the most likely explanation of their presence was as migrant farmers.[50] In

1910 another report from the same *cercle* repeated the complaint about the scarcity of laborers and again noted the presence of migrants, described as "Bambaras, Toucouleurs and Sarakholés [Soninke]."[51] All these groups formed part of the stream of migrant farmers known as *nawetaan*. Research on military recruitment during World War I demonstrates that migrancy was well established by 1914. "Foreigners," almost all of them *nawetaan*, were turned over to the French as substitutes for local youths. Runaway slaves from the Wolof kingdoms satisfied much of the demand for labor in the first decades of the export boom, but long-distance migrants became important in the aftermath of emancipation.

Studies of migration have shown that migrants belonged to different status groups within society. Among the Soninke, both young men from the upper strata of society and slaves became migrants.[52] What the two groups shared was the desire to earn money to improve their social status at home. Migrants traveling long distances sometimes spent the rainy season as migrant farmers and worked for wages during the rest of the year. The earnings of migrant farmers determined the minimum wage rate, which is why French plantations failed and French officials complained about the high wages and the reluctance of Africans to work, "except for themselves."[53] Migrant farmers who cultivated a hectare, relying on their own labor and cooperative work teams of young men (*santaane*), could harvest 600 kilograms to 1 metric ton of peanuts on their plots. This would yield a cash income of 80–200 francs, depending on the price and the size of the harvest.[54] This represented the earnings of five to six months' work. Since his host provided food and housing, the migrant's main expense was transportation to his host's village and back to his homeland, plus a small amount for the head tax owed to the French authorities. Wage labor was unattractive unless it paid a higher wage. The peasant economy was dominant, the wage economy marginal.

The contracts between migrant farmers and their hosts took an established form, with some variations from region to region. The host was obliged to feed the *nawetaan* for the duration of the contract, to supply him with housing, and to provide him with a plot of land for his own use. In return the *nawetaan* worked for his host. In most contracts the *nawetaan* worked for his host four days a week from just after sunrise until one or two o'clock in the afternoon.[55] The day was divided by the midday meal that was shared between the host, his family, and his clients, including the *nawetaan*. If the host furnished his *nawetaan* with seed for planting, the debt had to be repaid in kind after the harvest. The contracts between hosts and migrant farmers resembled the relations between household heads and *surga,* or masters and slaves.

Migrants escaped from dependent status at home to become migrant farmers in distant regions. Some migrants escaped an inferior status as slaves by moving from Kajoor to Bawol or Saalum. Others came to the peanut basin from cash-poor regions. The generational stratification of African households provided one incentive for migration. Almost all *nawetaan* were young unmarried males with the status of dependents in their own households. Some migrants exchanged heavier burdens at home for lighter ones abroad. For runaway slaves, migration might be the beginning of a quest for land. Household slaves wanted to escape the forms of tribute which masters attempted to impose on them. Long-distance migration typically involved movement from peripheral regions to regions more favored by proximity to railroads and ports. Whether they were slaves seeking better opportunities or young men trying to earn bride-wealth, migrants participated in the peasant economy by joining households in positions like those of the *surga.*

MONEY AND CREDIT

French merchants and administrators described the export economy as an *économie de traite,* a kind of halfway house between commercial capitalism and a barter economy. The phrase evoked the frenzied negotiations between producers and middlemen that occurred during the annual trading season. French officials portrayed the *traite* as a kind of madness that engulfed Senegal for four or five months after the harvest. For that brief period the rhythms of rural life gave way to a speculative frenzy dominated by merchants and middlemen seeking to profit from a brief opportunity to make money. Wolof peasants were also affected by the fever of the trade season, which was referred to in Wolof as the *teretu gerte,* "the peanut trade."

In the colonial period, the money economy was a seasonal phenomenon. It began with advances of credit at the beginning of the rainy season, when merchants advanced peanut seeds and millet to farmers whose stores were low. The most frenzied atmosphere occurred when merchants purchased the crop and sold their wares to farmers. Peasants with debts had to sell their crop to their creditor and deduct their debts. Officials of the colonial state hovered in the background and began collecting taxes immediately after the crops were sold. The season ended with a feverish period of speculation that determined the profitability of the year for independent merchants, who stockpiled peanuts and tried to pick the best moment to sell them. The *traite* was followed by a violent deflation as money literally disappeared from the countryside until the process began again with the arrival of the first rains in June or July.[56]

"*La traite*" also described ways of doing business that seemed unique to the African trade. French surveys emphasized the unorthodox business practices of middlemen in the peanut trade. Often they included simple dishonesty, as when merchants (French, Lebanese, and African) used faulty scales and measures to increase profit margins. In defense of these practices, they claimed that Africans tried to pass off a considerable weight of stones and dirt as peanuts in an effort to cheat merchants. Experts from the Department of Agriculture made it clear, however, that African peasants were usually the victims of these fraudulent business practices.

The whole edifice of the trade economy was based on the extensive use of credit. Credit was important on all levels, from the relations of large import-export firms based in France with the merchant firms of the colony, to the relations of rural peddlers with African peasant households. Credit was advanced on future sales throughout the year. The importance of credit was rooted in the structure of commerce and the strategies of merchants who purchased cash crops from African households. The commerce of Senegal was dominated by a small number of large import-export firms who set the price that they were willing to pay for peanuts in any given trading season. This price was expressed in the currency value of 100 kilograms of peanuts in one of the major ports (Dakar, Kaolack, Rufisque) or trading towns on the railroad (Thiès, Louga, Diourbel). Although there were minor variations in the prices paid in different markets, this price can be understood simply as the "local market" price. (See Table 6.1, column 5.)

The local market price represented a variable percentage of the price in Marseilles (or London). If one calculates the percentage from year to year, one finds typical lows of 51 percent (1897) or 53.5 percent (during parts of the trading seasons in 1907 and 1908) and a high of 80 percent in 1901. Commercial firms typically paid 60 percent of the value of peanuts on European commodity markets, allowing them to deduct their expenses and earn a profit. The large import-export firms could guarantee themselves a profit by their ability to set prices. The main potential problems for the large firms were sudden fluctuations in the value of peanuts on European commodity markets, especially late in the trading season.

Commerce was dominated by Europeans, but depended on Africans in subordinate positions. The commercial firms had their Senegalese head-

Table 6.2 European Population of Major Towns

Town	1908	1914	1916
Louga	100	67	34
Mekhé	--	34	--
Tivaouane	--	77	--
Khombole	50	49	--
Thiès	140	222	185
Bambey	26	21	--
Diourbel	28	53	86

Source: Paul E. Pheffer, "Railways and Aspects of Social Change" (Ph.D. dissertation, University of Pennsylvania, 1975), Table 18. His sources were 22 G 50, 22 G 52, ANS, and figures compiled by the railroad administration. Some of the variation in the figures is caused by the inclusion of *metis* as Europeans in the census of 1908, but not in those of 1914 and 1916.

quarters in Dakar or Rufisque, but maintained rural branch offices in the major towns located along the railroad. Until World War I, Europeans residing in Senegal for most of the year headed these branch offices. Their numbers are measured by the figures in Table 6.2, which gives the European population of major towns in three surveys from 1908 to 1916. Since administrators and railroad officials accounted for only a small portion of these residents (except in Thiès), the evidence suggests that several hundred European merchants lived off the peanut trade in the period before World War I.

Independent European merchants hoped to make a quick fortune as agents for the major trading houses in Bordeaux. They managed trading establishments in the railroad towns, where the peanut crop was bulked for export and imports were sold. Company stores bought the peanut crop directly from Africans in the immediate vicinity, usually through their African agents. They paid their clients, who were independent traders and less independent sub-traders (*traitaints* and *sous-traitants* in French documents), the price set by the large firms. Agents of European firms could earn bonuses by expanding the volume of trade at their station, but they did not control the terms of trade. Because literacy and mathematical competence were valued skills, the majority of African employees were recruited in the Four Communes. The *originaires* had privileged access to these jobs through their command of written and/or spoken French. European merchants also relied on *métis* and African sub-traders to extend their business into more remote rural villages. The number of sub-traders proliferated, but power and wealth were concentrated at the top levels of the trade network.[57]

Credit was the central mechanism through which the European firms maintained control of the export economy. The same firms that purchased the peanut crop supplied and distributed trade goods through a network of trading posts. Extensive credit was available to European merchants who worked in the interior, but Africans were allotted only the credit deemed appropriate to sub-traders. European firms justified this discrimination on economic grounds: they cited the poor credit records of African *traitants* who did not work under the close supervision of European merchants. These claims were hotly contested by the *originaires*, who viewed the credit practices as racial discrimination. European trading firms argued that Africans' poor credit records reflected their "extravagant" lifestyle and the uncontrolled credit they extended to relatives and clients. Some *originaire* traders operated substantial businesses by subcontracting directly from firms in Rufisque or Dakar, but the tendency was for Europeans to take direct control of the trade in the interior. There were a few exceptions, primarily among *originaires* with social or political ties to influential members of the merchant community. Babakar Mbodj, an *originaire* from Saint-Louis with close ties to François Carpot and the Crespin family, operated a branch office of Maurel et Prom in the Sereer provinces of the *cercle* of Thiès with an business turnover of 200,000 francs in 1910.[58] Similarly, Galandou Diouf, who was a political ally of Carpot, maintained extensive business relations in rural areas as a trader and cultivator. Such opportunities were quite rare. Most *originaire* traders had to risk their own fortunes. If business turned against them, the European commercial firms and banks refused to bail them out or extend new credit. Bankruptcies were quite common.

African merchants faced new competition from the Lebanese and Syrian traders who established themselves just before World War I. The "Lebanese" began to displace the *originaires* and then the small European traders in the interior. The Lebanese had several advantages. They had better credit records than African traders, because their position as outsiders allowed them to maintain more impersonal relations with clients. Compared to European traders, the Lebanese accepted a lower standard of living, and required fewer employees to run similar businesses. Unlike the French merchants, they learned to speak Wolof and were less dependent on African sub-traders. As a result, African traders were squeezed from above by European merchants and from below by Lebanese traders.[59] Over time, *originaire* merchants were displaced by Lebanese-Syrian merchants, who occupied the same economic niche in the trading system, and by Wolof and Tukulor shopkeepers, who manned trading stations in more isolated villages.[60] Itinerant traders, who were little more than peddlers carrying their capital (often borrowed) on their backs, extended the commercial network to the grass roots of rural society.[61]

Further down the commercial hierarchy, access to credit and the ability to extend credit became crucial. Risk and competition increased dramatically as well. Independent traders and sub-traders supplied the large commercial firms with the bulk of the peanut crop. Peasants living in villages at some distance from the railroad lines had to find ways to bring their crop to market. This could be accomplished by paying transporters who owned pack animals (camels, oxen, horses, and donkeys) a fee for transporting the crop.[62] Transporters, whether they were Mauritanians from the desert or Wolof from Ganjool, preferred to buy the peanut crop outright, offering their clients somewhat less than the going rate in the major towns. This bulking and transporting trade, while low in risk, offered slim profit margins. Independent traders and sub-traders therefore extended credit to their clients to expand business and inflate profits.

African traders (and the Lebanese-Syrians who displaced them) took the high-risk role of offering credit to African peasant households. Peanut production opened the door to commercial credit for African households. At its best, credit could function as a safety valve for poorer households or households experiencing momentary difficulties. Credit was used primarily for seed and for food during the "hungry season" that preceded the harvest. Food purchased on credit allowed consumption to be spread more evenly throughout the year. Peasants were offered "rainy season credits," which were to be paid off after the harvest. Despite the usurious rates of interest charged for these advances, they provided seed grain and food when peasant reserves were lowest. The season preceding the harvest was the most demanding period for peasants, who were fully occupied by work in the fields. Credit was an important incentive for extensive commercial production, in spite of its negative features. Like colonial currencies, credit was a crucial feature of cash cropping.

The provision of credit was also crucial for African merchants, because they could charge anywhere from 200 percent to 300 percent interest on short-term loans. Otherwise, middlemen profited only from the small margin between the bulk price of peanuts and the price they paid the producer. Middlemen who specialized in loans formed close ties with their clients, with whom they had face-to-face relations. The peasant who borrowed from a trader was obliged to sell his harvest to the same trader in order to liquidate the debt. Once such a relationship was established, it was difficult to break. On the other hand, there is little doubt that high profits were accompanied by high risks, because there were few formal means of recourse for merchants trying to collect a debt.

Competition between merchants led to the rapid extension of the trading and credit network into every nook and cranny of the peanut basin. By 1908, when Jean Adam published his study of the peanut trade, the proliferation of trading stations in the interior was well underway. Africans managed many of these smaller operations, in the one commercial sector where they had noticeable advantages. Some were working for large firms, others on their own account. They tried to maximize their purchases to benefit from the higher prices they could obtain by selling peanuts in bulk. They advanced credit to African producers, using loans to secure future purchases. While lending seed grain was routine, larger loans had to be secured with collateral. Merchant middlemen operated a number of credit rackets, including "loans for deposit" that turned the merchant's trading post into a rural pawnshop. Merchants accepted jewelry, hunting rifles, cloth, and other valuables as collateral for advances of foodstuffs and trade goods. Many merchants annually held collateral of this sort worth 15,000 or 20,000 francs. In a good year, the debts were repaid and the goods reclaimed; in a bad year the goods were lost to the merchants, who sold them by public auction.[63] Peasants who were unable to repay their debts lost their hard won savings.

The availability of high-risk credit in a peasant cash-crop economy requires further analysis. Most studies have focused on the denial of credit to Africans, particularly at the upper levels of colonial commercial systems.[64] Less attention has been paid to credit at the grass roots of the colonial economy, where private commercial firms and merchants extended credit to African producers. This form of lending was tied to the "seasonality" of money in the peasant economy. The commandant at Thiès noted this in 1904. During the trading season, 2,000,000 francs circulated in his district, but only for a short period of time. The commandant attributed this to the fact that Africans spent whatever money they earned immediately. The result was that an African "who possessed a herd of animals and slaves won't have 20 francs in cash" for most of the year.[65] Money disappeared at the end of the trading season.

Lending had its own seasons, based on the cycle of agricultural labor. Lending was particularly intense at the beginning of the rainy season, when plantings were being made and food reserves were low. Villages were visited by small traders, who offered advances of rice, sugar, kola nuts, and assorted trade goods, to be repaid by peanuts which were purchased in advance at the fixed price of 7.5 francs per 100 kilograms. Every year, thousands of sacks of rice were purchased under this system. An 18-kilogram bag of rice, with a value of 5 francs, was repaid by 100 kilograms of peanuts, with an average value of 10 to 15 francs. If lending reflected the seasonality of the money economy, it also contributed to it. When peasant producers took advantage of credit, often they were only just able to repay their debts after the harvest. Most cultivators sold their crop in one transaction and immediately spent any money remaining after paying their debts and taxes.

French administrators who observed the use and abuse of credit attributed it to African lack of foresight. Non-Muslim Sereer were condemned for drinking up their profits, which were spent on alcohol.[66] Wolof peasants were ridiculed for indulging their fantasies, spending their money on fancy clothes and other nonessential items. While all Africans were condemned for their lack of foresight, the French believed that the Wolof were particularly prone to squander future earnings on current indulgence.[67] Islam did make a difference in the economic behavior of peasant households and in borrowing patterns. Merchants profited from religiously sanctioned spending by Muslim families for the celebration of Tabaski and Korite.[68] Wolof families took on onerous debts in order to celebrate these holidays. Marriages, baptisms, circumcision ceremonies, and funerals were occasions on which peasant households were required to make extraordinary outlays. It is no surprise that the Wolof, who spent the most on such occasions, and who had the most frequent recourse to credit, also showed the most interest in extensive speculation in cash-crop agriculture.

Although the organization of trade served commercial interests, the competition to buy the harvest produced some benefits for the producer. Many of these took the form of patron-client relations between merchants and producers. It was an established practice for merchants purchasing peanuts to feed and house their customers. A daily ration was granted consisting of 300 grams of rice, 0.10 francs worth of oil, 0.10 francs worth of fish, some tobacco, and matches. The animals of the cultivator, if he had any, were also housed and fed. Gifts were a customary part of the purchase price, over and above the official price per weight. Gifts of cheap perfume, cloth, and sugar were given to the value of 0.6 francs per 100 kilograms of peanuts purchased. Such inducements were important for a merchant attempting to maintain a competitive edge and to retain his clientele from year to year.[69]

CREDIT AND THE COLONIAL STATE

One sign of the importance of credit was the intervention of the colonial state to regulate lending practices. In the period before World War I, this was one of the few examples of state intervention in the economy. The rationale was to protect the peasantry from the "usurious" interest rates charged by commercial firms. The colonial state created the *sociétés de prévoyance*, a type of rural cooperative that offered credit in the form of seed grain distributed before the planting season. The Senegalese administration pioneered the development of rural cooperatives in West Africa on models adapted from France and North Africa. The first *sociétés de prévoyance* were created in Senegal in 1907 in the *cercles* of Sine-Saloum and Bawol on the initiative of Commandants Lefilliatre and Theveniaut, and by 1914 the institution had spread throughout the colony. In 1919, decrees authorized the creation of *sociétés de prévoyance* throughout French West Africa.[70]

The *sociétés de prévoyance* were established to loan seed to cultivators. The government purchased seed in bulk, and it was then distributed to the peasantry. After the harvest, the loan was paid back with interest (25 percent), which allowed the administration to establish its own seed reserves and cover its administrative costs. Each rural subject had to pay membership dues in addition to the interest charged on loans. Compulsory membership for *indigènes* was a prominent feature of the cooperatives. The budget of the *sociétés de prévoyance* was used to finance some agricultural improvements, such as well drilling. Like other administrative tasks requiring direct contact with the rural population, the daily operation of the cooperatives was delegated to the canton chiefs. The chiefs distributed the seed grain, collected dues when the head tax was paid, and collected the repayment of the loan in grain at the harvest. The cooperatives were given paid secretaries as a check on the rudimentary accounting system used by the chiefs, but misappropriation of funds and seed stock was a constant problem. The commandant was the president of the *société de prévoyance*, but he could not supervise the distribution of grain and collection of debts.[71]

The *sociétés de prévoyance* were created to compensate for the reputed lack of foresight (*imprévoyance*) of African peasants. This was explained in cultural or racial terms: Africans lived in the present, did not plan for the future, and could not be depended upon to save enough seed stock for the next planting season. In fact, Senegalese peasants did save seed, in granaries managed by the household head, especially for the food staple, millet. The same practice was applied to peanuts, and these private grain reserves consistently supplied a substantial portion of seed. Household seed stocks proved inadequate because demands for cash led some peasants to sell seed reserves and to take loans from merchants.

European merchants and Lebanese or African sub-traders extended credit to Africans in order to tie them to the merchants and their firms. The commandant in Bawol described this practice in 1913:

> In Senegal the principal product is peanuts, a raw material that the natives cultivate to supply their cash needs and that is profitable to commerce only when purchased in large quantities. Therefore the goal of each trader is to buy as much as possible. To be sure of success he has to create a clientele to supply the product. He accomplishes this by attracting several families to his business and he tries to supply all their needs. Once confidence is established, he binds them to him through credit. Every year he buys the harvest, supplies seed grain and credit during the growing season; the account is settled at the end of the year with profits or losses. Through this system the trader enters into more intimate relations with his clients and becomes an influential and respected advisor.[72]

The combination of credit and income insecurity led to a growing problem of peasant debt. French administrators believed that once the cycle of debt began, peasants were forced to grow cash crops to liquidate their debts. The administrators feared that alienation and withdrawal from the market might result from this process.

The second justification for the creation of the *sociétés de prévoyance* was the "usurious" interest rate charged on advances of seed grain by private commercial firms. Since the peasants' lack of foresight prevented them from escaping the debt trap, the administration intervened to supply cheaper credit. On the eve of the creation of the first cooperative in Sine-Saloum, Commandant Lefilliatre reported that private firms charged 100 percent interest on loans of seed grain.[73] The *sociétés de prévoyance* would lower the cost of these transactions for the peasantry. The administration offered seed grain at fixed rates of interest well below those offered by private firms. The cooperatives expressed the administration's vision of itself as the liberator of the peasantry from exploitation.

There is evidence that commercial interests opposed the new institutions. The commandant at Thiès reported in 1909 on opposition to the *société de prévoyance* in his *cercle*:

Such an institution will encounter determined adversaries in commerce. In effect, by lending grains to the natives at the time of planting the commercial firms assure themselves first a substantial profit on the loan and secondly the allegiance of the borrowers, who are morally obliged to sell their harvest to those who lent them seed grain. [74]

In 1912 an inspector of native affairs, Nebout, was sent to Bawol to investigate charges of abuse in the management of the *société de prévoyance*. The abuses included overcollection of dues, and reports that wells had been closed to pressure residents to repay their debts. The complaints were directed at Commandant Theveniaut and the canton chiefs under his command. Nebout discovered that M. Barthes, the president of the Chamber of Commerce of Rufisque and a major trader at Diourbel, had hired Mody Mbaye, a well-known *originaire* activist, to solicit complaints against the *société de prévoyance*. Nebout concluded that the complaints were exaggerated and reflected the hostility of commercial interests to the cooperative. He used his report to express the administration's view of commercial exploitation:

I will add that several chiefs and notables asked that the administration intervene to protect them against commerce, which sells them millet and peanuts at ruinous prices. Such practices speak for themselves. They would greatly surprise the President of the Chamber of Commerce of Rufisque, the self-proclaimed champion of the native against an aggressive and rapacious administration. In reality, you only have to understand the enormous profits that commerce reaps from the *imprévoyance* of the Wolof to understand the reasons for the attacks on the *sociétés de prévoyance*. . . . The poverty that so moves the President of the Chamber is caused in part by the usury practiced by commerce; powerful *sociétés de prévoyance* will destroy this usury and the profits based on it. But by bringing prosperity to the country they will create economic activity that will benefit commerce.[75]

Nebout's comments reflected the anti-mercantile bias of the colonial administration, which attempted to shield African peasants from the worst abuses of the commercial economy.

Murid leaders opposed the cooperatives for different reasons. Shaykh Anta Mbacké allied himself with French merchants who opposed the cooperatives. Murids opposed the obligatory membership fees. Murid communities had their own grain reserves and seed stocks and almost never borrowed seed from the cooperatives. They therefore resented the membership fees and the additional power granted to the canton chiefs.[76] Murid informants had little good to say about the cooperatives, for the same reasons. They were "things of the state"[77] (*afeeru nguur*), like taxes and the obligation to give soldiers to the French during the war.

The farmers I interviewed in Bandia expressed similar attitudes. The canton chiefs "cheated" the farmers when they weighed their grains.[78] Having anything to do with the cooperatives meant dealing with Wolof chiefs, which brought its own dangers. The taxes and membership fees collected by the chiefs were "small," perhaps amounting to 30 francs for an average household. But the chief might take a cow with a value of more than 100 francs as his "personal gift" (*Mu lajj nag ci boppam*).[79] My informants disagreed over the interest rates on the "rainy season credits" (*lebalu-nawet* or *lebalu gerte*, literally, "rainy-season loans" or "peanut loans") advanced by merchants. One farmer told me he borrowed to buy millet only when he ran out and that the interest rates were low. He then explained that he took his credit from a French or *métis* merchant named "Paul" and that higher rates were charged by "Arabs" (Wolof, *naar*).[80] Another informant described an interest rate of 500 percent. When he talked about the loans, he imitated the way a "humble" farmer would approach a French merchant with downcast eyes and a subdued, polite voice.[81] The differing testimonies about interest rates may describe the practices of different merchants. Or they may result from confusion created by disguising the interest rate on loans. Crops sold in advance were purchased at prices well below their full market value.

In the opinion of my informants, the fact that the cooperatives were managed by the colonial state, or more precisely its Wolof agents, made them suspect. But the colonial cooperatives were better than the cooperatives after independence, when the state marketed the peanut crop and fixed the price paid to farmers at well below market value.[82] Peasant comments did not directly echo the anti-mercantile arguments of the colonial administration. "French" merchants were remembered with some fondness, while "Arabs" were criticized for squeezing every centime they could get out of African farmers.

CONCLUSION

The analysis in this chapter has focused on the interaction between the peasant household and the colonial commercial system. As cash cropping was integrated into the microeconomy of the household, it altered but did not overturn the hierarchies of age and gender within the household. Its most dramatic impact was to accelerate the process of household formation. Young men devoted almost all their free time to peanut production, earning cash that allowed them to marry and leave their father's households earlier than in the past. Despite a gradual inflation in bride-wealth payments, increasingly paid in cash by Wolof peasants, these social changes encouraged the formation of new villages and major migrations, leading to a substantial redistribution of Wolof populations, as migrating households sought new land in Bawol and Saalum. Railroad construction contributed to this process.

Peasant households employed migrant farmers, who accepted positions in households analogous to those of unmarried sons and other dependents. Household heads who saw their sons marry and depart at a younger age could maintain household income and production by engaging migrant labor. Migrant farmers had diverse origins. Many were long-distance migrants from regions marginalized by the cash-crop economy, including slaves and free persons. These long-distance streams of migration caught the attention of French officials. In this chapter I have argued that slaves from within the Wolof region took advantage of the same opportunities. This seems the most likely explanation for the rapid decline of slavery in Kajoor and Bawol, where the slave populations seem to have evaporated without leaving a trace in the colonial archives. If slaves first became migrant farmers and then joined peasant migrations to the "new lands" of Bawol and Saalum, they would have been absorbed into new peasant villages without calling attention to themselves.

The main threat to peasant accumulation and peasant prosperity came from the intense competition among merchant groups to maximize profits. Large European import-export firms dominated the commercial sector due to their ability to fix the price paid for peanuts in the major towns and ports of Senegal. They stayed above the fray of competition that characterized the bottom of the commercial hierarchy, where independent French, "Arab," and African merchants employed a host of petty traders working at the village level. Small merchants and traders extended credit to peasant households, charging usurious rates of interest in return for advancing seed stock, imported rice, and other goods. Peasants who accepted "rainy-season credit" had to pay off their loans by selling their peanuts at a fraction of market value.

The proliferation of credit and peasant debt alarmed French officials, but their efforts to intervene and supply cheaper loans of seed stock through cooperatives run by the colonial state created new problems. The colonial chiefs who managed the cooperatives saw them as an opportunity to enrich themselves at the expense of peasants. The cooperatives were created in a period when French officials were cutting the salaries of canton chiefs and waging war on more traditional forms of aristocratic "corruption." As a result, many peasants have bitter memories of being cheated by the cooperatives that had been created to save them from exploitation by merchants.

NOTES

1. See the discussion in Carrère and Holle, *De la Sénégambie*, 63–65, with contrasting descriptions of *ceddo* and *baadoolo*.

2. The colonial studies of African agriculture were uneven in quality, but there are some good studies of the peanut basin: Jean Adam, *L'arachide: Culture, produits, commerce, amélioration de la production*, (Paris, 1908); Joseph Fouquet, *La traite des arachides dans le pays de Kaolack* (Saint-Louis, 1958); Fernand Batude, *L'arachide au Sénégal* (Paris, 1941); and Philippe David, *Les navétanes: Histoire des migrants saisonniers de L'arachide en Sénégambie des origines à nos jours* (Dakar-Abidjan, 1980).

3. Frederick Cooper, "Africa and the World Economy," in *Confronting Historical Paradigms: Peasants, Labor and the Capitalist World System in Africa and Latin America*, eds. Frederick Cooper, Allen F. Isaacman, Florencia E Mallon, William Roseberry, and Steve J. Stern (Madison, Wis., 1993), 84–186.

4. Mohamed Mbodj, "Sénégal et dépendence: Le Sine-Saloum et L'arachide, 1887–1940," in *Sociétés Paysannes du Tiers-Monde*, ed. C. Coquery-Vidrovitch (Lille, 1980), 139–54.

5. H. Myint, "The 'Classical Theory' of International Trade and the Underdeveloped Countries," *The Economic Journal* 68 (1958): 317–37.

6. Cooper, "Africa and the World Economy," 90–92.

7. For an excellent survey of recent trends, see Allen Isaacman, "Peasants and Rural Social Protest in Africa," *African Studies Review* 33, no. 2 (1990): 1–59.

8. Anthony G. Hopkins, "The Currency Revolution in South-West Nigeria in the Late Nineteenth Century," *Journal of the Historical Society of Nigeria* 3 (1966): 471–83. For a recent discussion, see Jane I. Guyer, "Introduction: The Currency Interface and its Dynamics," in *Money Matters: Instability, Values and Social Payments in the Modern History of West African Communities,* ed. Jane I. Guyer (Portsmouth, N.H.,1995), 1–33.

9. For comparisons of slave prices in West Africa and the Americas in the nineteenth century, see David Eltis, *Economic Growth and the Ending of the Transatlantic Slave Trade* (New York, 1987), 263. American prices were higher by a factor of 4 to 1 or even 10 to 1 from 1815 to 1845 in Cuba and Brazil.

10. For a more detailed discussion, see Searing, *West African Slavery*, 63–71, 79–88.

11. The price paid by Europeans on the Atlantic coast was generally higher than in internal markets. See Paul E. Lovejoy and David Richardson, "Competing Markets for Male and Female Slaves: Prices in the Interior of West Africa," *International Journal of African Historical Studies* 28 (1995): 261–93.

12. For a recent discussion of the transition, see Law, ed., *From the Slave Trade to "Legitimate" Commerce*.

13. David Eltis, *The Rise of African Slavery in the Americas* (Cambridge, 2000), 164–92.

14. Courtet, *Étude sur le Sénégal*, 20–21, 48–49.

15. For yields per hectare, see Adam, *L'arachide*, 65–66; and Sarr, *Louga et sa région*, 70–71.

16. Marcel Olivier, *Le Sénégal* (Paris, 1907), 315.

17. Extractive industries like palm oil processing involved important adjustments, but the high demand for female labor in processing oil may have given slave owners an advantage. See Bay, *Wives of the Leopard*, 192–98; and several essays in Law, ed., *From Slave Trade to "Legitimate" Commerce*.

18. This applies to Cooper, "Africa and the World Economy," for example.

19. See Andrew F. Clark, *From Frontier to Backwater: Economy and Society in the Upper Senegal Valley (West Africa), 1850–1920* (Lanham, Md., 1999), 173–78, 204–10, for difficulties in other regions.

20. Adam, *L'arachide*, 53–57. Adam's observations describe peanut cultivation at the turn of the century.

21. The exception was Malik Pouye, the oldest man in the village. Most of his angry comments were based on what happened to the cooperatives after independence. Interview, Malik Pouye and others, Bandia, July 19, 1995.

22. Oliver, *Le Sénégal*, Table of Imported Merchandise, 1894–1904.

23. Pierre Meunier, *Organisation et fonctionnement de la justice indigène en Afrique Occidentale Française* (Paris, 1914), gives the decree of 1903 in an appendix.

24. On this theme, see Berry, *No Condition is Permanent*.

25. H.C. Sampson and E.M. Crowther argued that the Caribbean model dominated British agricultural policy in West Africa until the 1930s, when officials from India introduced a more "peasantist" perspective: *The West Africa Commission 1938–39: Technical Reports* (London, 1943). For Senegal, the agricultural experiments discussed by Georges Hardy, *La mise en valeur du Sénégal de 1815 à 1854* (Paris, 1921), show the influence of the Caribbean model, as do the efforts at improvement discussed by Adam, in *L'arachide*.

26. Jean Adam, *L'arachide*, 151–65.

27. Ibid., 154–55.

28. 2 D 14–3, Cercle de Cayor, Corres. 1901, Rapport de tournée de Vienne, June 25, 1901.

29. This portrait of the household portrays the norm during the early colonial era.

30. Jean Copans, *Les Marabouts de L'arachide: La confrérie mouride et les paysans du Sénégal* (Paris, 1980); and Jean Copans, Phillipe Couty, Jean Roch, and Guy Rocheteau, *Maintenance sociale et changement économique au Sénégal: Doctrine économique et pratique du travail chez les Mourides* (Paris, 1972).

31. Copans, *Les marabouts de L'arachide*, 128–39.

32. Adam, *L'arachide*, 53–65.

33. For a good discussion of Wolof households, based on fieldwork, see Venema, *Wolof of Saloum*, 103–23.

34. L. Aujas, "Les Sérères du Sénégal: Moeurs et coutumes de doit privé," *Bulletin du Comité des Études Historiques et Scientifiques sur l'Afrique Occidentale Française* 14 (1931): 307.

35. Field notes, Bandia, July 14, 1995. Based on tour of fields and discussion with various farmers about work schedules.

36. Ibid.

37. K 18 (13), Cercle de Kaolack: Captivité, 1904.

38. 1 G 330, Chemise 5, Rapport sur les Coutumes: Sine-Saloum, 1907.

39. Interview, Ibrahima Ciss, July 16, 1995.

40. For the relationship between residence and life cycle and the maternal uncle, see Irvine, "Caste and Communication," 244–61.

41. For the Soninke, see Manchuelle, *Willing Migrants*.

42. One exception is the work of Polly Hill, "From Slavery to Freedom: The Case of Farm-Slavery in Nigerian Hausaland," *Comparative Studies in Society and History* 18 (1976): 395–426.

43. A.V. Chayanov, *The Theory of Peasant Economy,* eds. Daniel Thorner et al. (Homewood, Ill., 1966).

44. Other sources say that slaves and *surga* worked the same hours.

45. *Nawet-bi* is the Wolof word for the rainy season. The French "navétane" is borrowed from the Wolof. David, *Les navétanes*, 166–67.

46. Klein and Roberts, "The Banamba Slave Exodus of 1905," 375–94, for one well-documented incident.

47. 2 G 10–8, Rapport d'ensemble de l'AOF, 1910. See the discussion in David, *Les navétanes*, 122–23, 146–48.

48. On Sudanese railway workers, see 2 G 8-10, Rapport, premier trimestre 1908; and Pheffer, "Railroads and Aspects of Social Change in Senegal."

49. On the Gambia, see George Brooks, "Peanuts and Colonialism: Consequences of the Commercialization of Peanuts in West Africa, 1830–1870," *Journal of African History*, 16 (1975): 29–54; and Ken Swindell, "SeraWoolies, Tillibunkas and Strange Farmers: The Development of Migrant Groundnut Farming along the Gambia River, 1848–1895," *Journal of African History* 21 (1980): 93–104.

50. 1 G 296 (6), Monographie, Cercle de Thiès, 1903.

51. 1 G 337, Monographie: Thiès, 1910, p. 36.

52. See Manchuelle, *Willing Migrants*, 53–57, for specific comments on Soninke *nawetaan*.

53. 1 G 337, Monographie: Thiès, 1910, p. 36.

54. For estimates of *nawetaan* production, see David, *Les navétanes*, 24–26, 197–205; Manchuelle, *Willing Migrants*, 58.

55. In some regions, five half days of labor was the norm. In the 1930s and 1940s, three days became more common as contracts were revised in favor of the migrant farmers.

56. For the economy at various points in time, see Adam, *L'arachide*; Fouquet, *La traite des arachides*; Batude, *L'arachide au Senegal*; and Xavier Guiraud, *L'arachide sénégalaise: Monographie d'economie coloniale* (Paris, 1937). For interpretations, see Mbodj, "Sénégal et dépendence: Le Sine-Saloum et L'arachide, 1887–1940," 139–54; Sarr, *Louga et sa région*.

57. General descriptions of the trade system are found in Marcel Capet, *Traité d'économie coloniale. Les économies d'AOF* (Paris, 1958), 121–35; Guiraud, *L'arachide sénégalaise*; Jean and René Charbonneau, *Marchés et marchands d'Afrique noire* (Paris, 1961); and Fouquet, *La traite des arachides.*

58. For Babacar Mbodj, see 2 D 13-7, Cercle de Thiès, Corres. 1910; Oct. 1910 and 2 D 13-20, Cercle de Thiès, Chemise 11: Affaire Babakar Mbodj-Abdel Kader, August 3, 1912.

59. For a portrait of the *originaire* merchant, see Ousman Soce, *Karim: Roman sénégalais suivi de contes et légendes d'Afrique noire* (Paris, 3rd ed. 1935). This novel examines the dilemma of a young man who goes into debt because he tries to live as a "samba lingeer," an aristocrat, during his courtship of a young woman.

60. For the ethnic identity of African traders in the *cercle* of Thiès in 1910, see 1 G 337, Monographie, p. 36.

61. Adam, *L'arachide*, 106–07.

62. Ibid., 105-7, for data on the amount each animal carried, with photographs of camel caravans bringing peanuts to market.

63. Ibid., 104–6.

64. Guyer, "Introduction," 12, reflects this view: restrictions on credit for African businessmen and the paucity of credit instruments. For a discussion that parallels mine, focusing on the "informal" sector among the Yoruba, see Toyin Falola, "Money and Informal Credit Institutions in Colonial Western Nigeria," in *Money Matters: Instability, Values and Social Payments in the Modern History of West-African Communities*, ed. Jane I. Guyer (Portsmouth, N.H., 1995), 162–87, especially 172, which discusses seasonal loans secured by the coming harvest.

65. 1 G 296, Pièce 6, Monographie: Cercle de Thiès, 1904, p. 21.

66. 1 G 296, Pièce 6, Monographie: Cercle de Thiès, pp. 21–22.

67. Adam, *L'arachide*, 106–9.

68. *Tabaski* is the Wolof term for the Muslim ritual of sacrifice (*id al kabir*); *Korite* is the Wolof term for the feast marking the end of the month of fasting (Ramadan).

69. Adam, *L'arachide*, 109–10.

70. The *sociétés* de prévoyance are discussed in Guiraud, *L'arachide sénégalais*; Margaret Coumboulives, *L'organisation coopérative au Sénégal* (Paris, 1967); and Abdoulaye Sow, "Les sociétés indigènes de prévoyance au Sénégal 1909–1936," mémoire de maîtrise, Université de Dakar, 1977. For a recent analysis, see Robert L. Tignor, "Senegal's Cooperative Experience, 1907–1960," in *The Political Economy of Risk and Choice in Senegal*, eds. John Waterbury and Mark Gersovitz, (London, 1987), 90–122.

71. 13 G 294 (11), Cercle de Baol, Inspection des affaires administrative: Rapport no. 34, Inspecteur Nebout, April 7–8, 1912.

72. 4 D 55 (1), Recrutement: 50,000, Lieutenant Gouverneur Antonetti à Gouverneur General, quoting Commandant de cercle de Baol, July 10, 1913.

73. Guiraud, *L'arachide sénégalaise*, 53.

74. 2 D 13–6, Cercle de Thiès, Corres. 1909, Commandant à Lieutenant Gouverneur, Feb. 23, 1909.

75. 13 G 294 (11), Cercle de Baol, Inspection des affaires administratives: Rapport no. 34, Inspecteur Nebout, April 7–8, 1912.

76. On Shaykh Anta's opposition, see 2 G 12-60, Cercle de Diourbel, Rapport, March 1912.

77. Interview, Serigne Bassirou Anta Niang Mbacké, July 25, 1995.

78. Interview, Samba Seck, July 17, 1995.

79. Interview, Ablaye Faye, July 18, 1995.

80. Interview, Samba Seck, July 17, 1995.

81. Interview, Ibrahima Cisse, July 16, 1995.

82. These were common policies in West Africa. For a general analysis of the anti-farmer bias of many governments in West Africa, see Robert Bates, *Essays on the Political Economy of Rural Africa* (Cambridge, 1983).

Figure 7.1 Maam Cerno Ibrahim Mbacké (Ibra Fati). (Courtesy of the National Archives of Senegal. Reprinted with permission.)

CIVILIZING MISSIONS AND THE PEASANTRY: MURID ISLAM AND THE COLONIAL STATE

French colonial officials characterized their mission in West Africa as an effort to liberate the peasantry from the oppression of aristocratics and unscrupulous Muslim leaders, whose wealth and power was a reflection of their parasitic exploitation of the peasantry. While the French could never entirely dispense with the services of aristocratic chiefs, vigilance against corruption and extortion was a watchword of administrative policy. Because the French colonial state supervised colonial chiefs, Muslim leaders represented the greatest threat to peasant autonomy and prosperity after 1900, in the eyes of colonial officials. For many French officials, Murid Islam was the most important example of this new threat. French repression had prevented Amadu Bamba from realizing the political ambitions that the French believed were at the core of his mission. After 1903, the French turned their focus to the new threat created by Murid exploitation of the peasantry.

French suspicions of the Murid order persisted even after it was clear that Murid districts were playing a growing role in the colonial export economy. Governor-General Ponty, who replaced Roume, ordered a general program of surveillance of Muslim leaders in French West Africa. In January 1912, he wrote at length about his suspicions of the Murid order. He described the sect as a "deviation" which, if the French did not take care, would lead to the "creation of a sort of politico-religious association where religion only serves as a pretext for the exploitation

Figure 7.2 Shaykh Ibra Fall, with disciples in Thiès. (Courtesy of the National Archives of Senegal. Reprinted with permission.)

of the ignorant masses." He argued that the French could not remain indifferent to a movement which affected "in the same degree our political, administrative, social and economic action" and that the further development of the order would constitute a threat to the future economic development of Senegal.[1] French hostility to the Murid order was based on the perception that it constituted a state within a state, based on the hierarchies of authority that existed within the order. In addition, French officials believed that the accumulation of wealth within the order was a direct result of the exploitation of Murid disciples by their spiritual masters.

Colonial interpretations of Murid Islam have shaped subsequent debates about the order, which have focused on the themes of accumulation and exploitation and the links between the Murid order and the peanut export economy. This chapter begins with an analysis and critique of the existing literature on the Murid order, focusing on peanut cultivation, education, and work. I propose an alternate interpretation of the economic significance of the Murid order, which draws upon previous research but reformulates the questions. My point of departure is the role of the Murid order in the creation and settlement of new lands and villages, a theme that appears in both colonial and postcolonial studies of the order. I argue that in the historical context of the early colonial period, the Murid order offered concrete advantages to the peasants and slaves who migrated to the new settlements. French hostility to the order echoed the protests of established Wolof elites, who lost control over migrants. It also echoed the hostility of French merchants, who saw the self-sufficiency of Murid villages as a detriment to French commerce.

My interpretation of Murid Islam derives from the way I have situated the order in relation to Wolof society and history. It makes little sense to decry Murid exploitation if, in fact, conditions in Murid villages were more favorable to peasants than those in more traditional Wolof districts. For similar reasons I have included an analysis of the economic impact of the French colonial state in rural Bawol, the heartland of the Murid order. My purpose is to facilitate a direct comparison between the "civilizing mission" of French colonialism and Sufi Islam in the Wolof countryside between 1900 and 1914.

THE MURID ORDER AND THE PEASANT ECONOMY

The relationship between the Murid order and the cash-crop economy is the most researched topic in modern Wolof history. The literature that has developed since independence, in both English and French, builds upon French colonial sources and studies, which were already significant.[2] There is remarkable consensus among researchers about the main outlines of the story. In a nutshell, the Murid order is interpreted as an "adaptation" to the demands of colonialism, in which the cultivation of peanuts plays a prominent role. This "adaptation" was preceded by the "crisis" created by the French conquest. Amadu Bamba and his new order provided a path that allowed the Wolof (or at least a significant number of the Wolof) to weather this crisis by directing displaced social groups to cultivate peanuts under the guidance of Murid leaders.

Cruise O'Brien's discussion of the origins of the Murid order is a reformulation of Paul Marty's master narrative of Wolof history, in which marabouts replace the aristocracy after the French conquest. For Cruise O'Brien, the conquest provoked a "crisis" that traditional forms of social dependency could not survive.[3] The conquest led to a rapid decline in the legitimacy of chiefs appointed by the French as the successors of the old regime. They became mere salaried dependents of the French administration.[4] The crisis was extremely intense. Cruise O'Brien says Wolof society was "shattered by French conquest" and therefore had to rapidly "reconstitute" itself around religious leaders.[5] As proof of the intensity of the crisis, Cruise O'Brien emphasizes the fact that the Murid order grew from nothing to a movement with 70,000 members by 1912.[6] Socially, Cruise O'Brien emphasizes the special attraction of the Murid order for the more "traditional" strata of Wolof society. He refers to the *ceddo*, who were "forced to seek a living as peasant farmers," and to aristocratic warriors who were "forced to surrender arms in favor of the tools of a peasant farmer."[7] He quotes a passage from Marty that links these social groups with "slaves":

> Amadu Bamba's clientele is recruited from among the ex-*tyéddo* [*ceddo*], or among the slaves of Kayor and Baol who upon emancipation hastened to place themselves under the yoke again by offering themselves the luxury of a religious sovereign.[8]

These groups, disoriented by the collapse of the social hierarchies that had ordered their lives, flocked to the Murid order. Amadu Bamba's teachings, distilled by Cruise O'Brien into the command to "Go and work," answered a social need. Murid disciples threw themselves into the work of growing peanuts, which answered their needs and enriched their leaders.[9]

French researchers who surveyed Murid villages in the 1960s offered a nearly identical interpretation, based on Marty and Cruise O'Brien's work. They argued that the Murid order emerged from a "crisis" created by the colonial conquest, the imposition of taxes, and the cash economy.[10] They believed the Murid order was an "original" social form created in response to the commercialization of peanuts. It was subordinate to and dependent upon the "money economy." The French researchers' formulation was more abstract than Cruise O'Brien's. It placed more stress on "commercialization" and "money," both imposed by the French. The French researchers argued that the Murid order was inherently "conservative," since it preserved aspects of the old social order in a new form. It was "pre-capitalist," because the money economy was kept at a distance as well as internalized. Wage labor (in their view essential to capitalism) did not emerge, so the Murid order produced a dependent, peasant economy. The teachings of the founder mediated the adaptation of the Wolof to colonial rule. What distinguished the work of Copans and his research team was their attempt to describe and quantify Murid labor practices at the level of the household and the village. This effort was inspired by the association between the Murid order and "work" and by Marty's argument that the Murid leaders lived off the exploitation of their disciples. The conclusions reached from an analysis of the fieldwork seemed to contradict the premise of the study. Murids did not seem to work longer or harder than other peasants (although no systematic comparisons were made), and they donated less labor and money than expected to leaders of the order.

Cruise O'Brien and Copans de-emphasize one important theme of Marty's study. Marty's study of Islam in Senegal was comparative. His argument that the more "traditional" groups in Wolof society (aristocrats, *ceddo*, and slaves) flocked to the Murid order was grounded in a comparison with the Tijani order, which dominated the older Muslim provinces (Njambur and Kajoor). Marty saw the Tijani order, led by Malik Sy, as more "orthodox" than the Murid order. It was attractive to the sophisticated, urbanized, and educated Wolof populations of the coastal cities and to the long-standing Muslim populations of Kajoor. These groups, by implication, did not need Amadu Bamba to guide them into the "modern" world of colonialism, cash crops, and money.[11]

My critique of the shared presumptions of Marty, Cruise O'Brien, and Copans focuses on three interrelated themes. The first is the connection between the Murid order and peanut cultivation. The second is the failure to distinguish between the characteristics of the peasant economy and the Murid order. The third relates to misunderstandings about the nature of dependency or "exploitation" within the Murid order, linked to confusion about the relationship between work and education. I compare developments within the Murid order to developments in Wolof society as a whole, because that is the only way to distinguish what is specifically Murid from the larger context in which Murid history unfolded.

The notion of a sudden, shattering "crisis" in Wolof society brought on by the colonial conquest and the death of Lat Joor in 1886 is a amalgamation of French archival reports and dynastic traditions that telescopes decades of social change into a single event.[12] There is no evidence for the argument that conflicts between the Murid order and the Wolof old regime arose because large segments of Wolof society were at a loss as to how to respond to "modernity," cash cropping, or the money economy. Extensive cash cropping began in Kajoor in the 1860s. By the 1880s it had been integrated into the economy of the old regime, and was accepted by the aristocracy and the *ceddo*. The idea that the Wolof needed a charismatic Muslim leader to get them to accept cash crops and money is based on ahistorical stereotypes about African resistance to economic change.

There is no basis for the idea that there was a special connection between the Murid order and peanut cultivation. The French did not really make the connection until 1907, when the railroad approached Diourbel. By that time, the Wolof districts near the Senegal River and the ports of Cap Vert had been exporting peanuts for over fifty years. The Saint-Louis–Dakar railroad, completed in 1886, had been in operation for over twenty years. Wolof, of all religious affiliations, grew peanuts for export. If one examines the triangle of land settled by the Murids in Kajoor and Bawol between 1883 and 1912, defined by the holy towns of Darou-Salam, Touba, and Darou-Mousty, it is clear that none of them were situated with reference to the grid created by the railroad. French colonial sources and subsequent scholarship misinterpreted this process of settlement by linking it to French railroad construction and peanut cultivation.[13] If Amadu Bamba had wanted to be near the railroad he would not have left Kajoor in 1883 and settled in the interior of Bawol. The Dakar-Kayes railroad did not reach Diourbel until 1909, long after the foundation of the major Murid towns (Darou-Salam, c. 1885, Touba c. 1887). Diourbel was not in the core Murid settlement zone, but became an important Murid center after the founder was sent there under house arrest in 1912. The "Murid" colonization of "new lands" near the railroad in Bawol and Saalum was a later development and was carried out by minor figures in the order, not by Amadu Bamba and his inner circle of disciples.[14] The same is true of the association between the Murid order and peanut cultivation. Murid informants always spoke of "millet and peanuts" (*dugub ak gerte*) and placed most emphasis on millet.

Although Islam contributed to the degree to which Wolof peasants embraced the cash-crop economy (by comparison with non-Muslim Sereer), Islam was not the only factor. Wolof-speaking merchants from Saint-Louis and other coastal towns were crucial agents in the spread of peanut cultivation and colonial currencies. Even the difference be-

tween the Wolof and the Sereer was one of degree, not between growing peanuts and not growing peanuts. Wolof social transactions became
monetized more rapidly. The best example is bride-wealth payments.
Colonial sources indicate that many Wolof paid bride-wealth in cash by
the turn of the century, while the Sereer still utilized cattle and other
traditional measures of wealth.[15] A more telling point is that the Sereer
cultivated cash crops, without experiencing social disorientation and
without abandoning their local religion centered on the village shrine.
What distinguished the Murids from other Muslims was not their focus
on peanuts, but the mysticism of the founder, the Murid's hostility to
the monarchy, and their location on the periphery of established centers
of power.

Another problem is the tendency of researchers to confuse aspects of
the peasant household economy with the social organization of the Murid
order. This is especially clear in the fieldwork carried out by Copans
and his associates. They describe in detail the labor contributions of
household members (household heads, wives, daughters, *surga*,
nawetaan) in the region where they carried out their fieldwork. They
also describe the voluntary labor groups formed by young men for
peanut cultivation (*santaane*). Finally, they try to estimate the labor time
donated to the leaders of the order and the size of gifts and donations
in cash. The problem is that only the donations of labor and cash to
marabouts distinguish Murid practices from those of other Wolof households. Since no comparisons are made, it is difficult to draw specific
conclusions about the Murids from Copans' data. Yet Copans' analysis
examines the "Murid" social order and Islam. Most of the labor rou-
tines observed also apply to non-Muslim Sereer, if one takes into account the variations produced by matrilineal and patrilineal kinship
(nephews working for maternal uncles instead of sons for fathers).
Copans' detailed fieldwork tells us much about Wolof peasant society
in the 1960s, but little about the Murid order.

Most studies of the Murids simply explore Marty's argument that
Murid disciples chose a new form of bondage to the leaders of the order.
Few new questions emerge from this method. In Cruise O'Brien, "exploitation" mutates into the workings of a patron-client network, founded
by a mysterious saint about whom little can be known, but run by
"bosses" like Shaykh Ibra Fall, who reveal the "social" meaning of the
movement. Cruise O'Brien emphasizes the most "colorful" traits of Ibra
Fall, his "brightly colored robe," "hair worn in long tresses," in short,
his *ceddo* identity.[16] Ibra Fall brought behavior like that of a "pagan
slave" into the Murid order.[17] The famous work groups of the Murid

order, the *daara* of unmarried young men, are presented as Ibra Fall's invention, substituting agricultural labor for military service.[18] Cruise O'Brien makes Ibra Fall central to his interpretation of the Murid order and opts for the most "colorful" Ibra Fall possible, a figure from Wolof folklore.[19] In an advance on Marty, Cruise O'Brien argues that the settlement of new lands benefited Murid disciples in the long run, as they gained control over land after an apprenticeship of service. Copans assumed the social "dependency" of Murid disciples in his study, although he had difficulty quantifying the significance of their "donations" in the 1960s. For the past, he assumed that a more demanding period of *daara* labor preceded the formation of the peasant societies he observed.[20]

Cruise O'Brien and Copans agree that education was "unimportant" to the Murid order. Copans, who relies on Cruise O'Brien for the centrality given to Ibra Fall, takes the disassociation between work and education in traditions about Ibra Fall as the literal truth for the order as a whole. He writes:

> The *daara* is therefore a Murid invention. It is a community of bachelors, called *tak-der,* who work under the direction of a marabout, or, more often, his representative, the *diawrigne* [Wolof, *jawriñ*], and devote themselves entirely to agriculture. The conditions of life and work in the *daara* are such that study of the Quran is a pious wish more than a reality. There must be no confusion between the *daara* and the Quranic school [also *daara* in Wolof]. . . . There were no *daara* [here, presumably, Quranic schools] in our zone of study.[21]

This passage sums up the received wisdom on work and education in the Murid order. Based on the cultural values of its *ceddo* adherents, the Murid order developed unique attitudes toward work and education. Disciples worked for their marabouts, but did not study. Frequently, they did not fast or pray, following the example of Ibra Fall. Work teams emerged, which the Murids called *daara*. Copans warns us not to confuse this institution with the Quranic school (*daara* in Wolof) and assures us that no true Quranic schools existed. Despite Copans' arguments to the contrary, the Murid work *daara* developed from patterns common to all Wolof Quranic schools.

Murid sources reveal attitudes toward education quite different from those ascribed to the order, but still distinct from those of other Sufi orders. Instead of offering a single form of education, Amadu Bamba based his decisions on the character of those who submitted to his authority. For some disciples, this meant training in the religious sciences, but for the majority it meant an education based on work, moral discipline, and obedience to the religious authorities within the order.[22] This attitude was expressed in the letter of instructions Amadu Bamba left with his disciples after his second arrest and exile in 1903. He directed his disciples to the most suitable teacher, given their own dispositions. Those who wished to work without studying were told to go to Shaykh Anta. Contemporaries saw Shaykh Anta as someone primarily interested in the affairs of this world. He corresponded with the French, had relations with *originaire* politicians in Saint-Louis, and controlled business interests in colonial towns. One of his Murid praise epithets, *boroom dërëm ak ngërëm* ("master of money and thanks"), indicates that his success was measured in things of "this world" (*zahir*). Disciples with similar characters were directed to him. Maam Cerno, on the other hand, was named as the teacher for those who wished to study or to combine work with study. The Murid order recognized the validity of these separate "ways." Each disciple would find his teacher and path in the order.

In the spectrum of Murid "ways," Ibra Fall represented one extreme, rather than the norm. He devoted his energies to hard physical labor and the affairs of this world. Ibra Fall was himself literate, as are many of his followers.[23] However, in contemporary Senegal, the popular image of Ibra Fall is based on the notion that he worked instead of studying or praying. Converted *géwél* who sing his praises use his life story to illustrate the idea that work can be better than study.[24] This does not mean that all Murids should follow his example, but it illustrates the meaning of the *lamp Faal*, the "way" of Ibra Fall. The plurality of paths meant that all disciples could find a place that suited their intellectual capacities and needs. Murid disciples comment on this philosophy of education by saying that "not everyone can become a master of knowledge" (Wolof, *boroom xam-xam*). It would be a mistake to organize the order on the principle of scholarship. Murids take pleasure in stories that illustrate the "shocking" paradoxes produced by tailoring a disciple's education to a divination of his character. Disciples who saw themselves as "learned" scholars were ordered to work in the fields, while "Sereer converts" were sometimes sent to the most learned scholars for a formal education.[25]

The Murid order placed great emphasis on institutions of formal education. Marty's description of the order in 1915 gives an important snapshot of the movement. Touba was the most important center of education. Marty described the *zawiya* there as a "miniscule" university where fifty students from ten to twenty-five years of age studied "the-

ology, Quranic exegesis, law, grammar, logic, rhetoric and prosody."
The main teachers at the school were two of the founder's sons
(Mamadou Moustapha and Mohamed Fadel) and his youngest brother,
Massamba. The school was visited from time to time by Shaykh Mbacké
Bousso, Amadu Bamba's brother-in-aw, described by Marty as a *docteur
ès lettres islamiques*. Even though the founder was under house arrest
in Diourbel and could not visit the school, Marty believed that he over-
saw every detail of its organization.[26] Murid sources emphasize the same
general points but give an expanded portrait of the faculty at the school.
Shaykh Abdu Rahman Lô, who came from a prestigious family in
Njambur, taught the recitation of the Quran for many years.[27]

In addition to the school at Touba, each major Murid settlement had
its own schools. Shaykh Mbacké Bousso, who came from one of the
most famous scholarly families in Kajoor, taught 60 students in Darou-
Salam.[28] In Gaouane, which was the residence of Shaykh Anta, 50 students were receiving a formal education.[29] In Mbacké-Kajoor, which
was still the main Murid settlement in Kajoor in 1915, 30 students were
studying under the direction of three "professors" (Marty's term) chosen by Maam Cerno.[30] Finally, in Keur Ibra Fall, just outside of Thiès,
75 students were studying under three professors selected by Ibra Fall.[31]
Marty's census distinguished carefully between these students, who were
receiving a formal, academic education, and the mass of Murid disciples. His survey suggested that there were at least 265 students in
Murid schools directed by the inner circle of the order in 1915. The
same tradition of education persists to the present in major Murid towns,
on an expanded scale.[32]

Murid attitudes toward education and work can be illuminated by comparisons with the practice of other Sufi orders. Al Hajj Malik Sy represented the Tijani order in the Wolof states. He established his residence at
Tivaouane, in the heart of Kajoor, in 1902.[33] In 1910, the French commandant described Malik Sy's school as "having 30 adult *taalibe* and 20 children." They came to receive an Islamic education that was reputed to be
the best in Senegal. In addition to running his school, writing short devo-
tional works, and collecting charitable donations that he distributed to the
poor, Malik Sy "cultivated vast fields of peanuts that gave him an annual
income of 4000 francs."[34] Marty's discussion of the Tijani *zawiya* in
Tivaouane is more complete. He describes a series of schools with 140
students; 20 were pursuing advanced studies, while the rest were children
taught by four or five professors under the guidance of Malik Sy. Although
his income was substantial by Wolof standards, Malik Sy was essentially a
scholar and a teacher. His income came from the labor of his family and
his students, not from the donations of a vast network of disciples. By

comparison, in the same time period Shaykh Ibra Fall gave Amadu Bamba 50,000 francs a year from contributions collected from over 1,000 disciples, including 100 students.[35] Malik Sy's prestige and moral authority was undeniable, but it was based on his authority as a scholar and teacher. He did not seek direct authority over disciples affiliated to his branch of the Tijani order. There was no Tijani community comparable to the Murid community.

At the other end of the spectrum, Bou Kounta's branch of the Qadiri order came much closer to the emphasis on work that Copans attributed to the Murid order and that Cruise O'Brien saw as the essence of Shaykh Ibra Fall's role in defining the Murid way. French experts on Islam described Bou Kounta as "uneducated" and virtually illiterate, despite the prestige attached to the Kounta name. There was no real school at his *zawiya*, which called for this comment:

> These facts are exceptional in the Lower Senegal where black marabouts feel obliged as a matter of honor, conscience and religious duty to teach their students at least the letters of the Arabic alphabet, some ritual prayers and suras of the Quran. But Bou Kounta has Moorish blood in his veins. In his view, the black is always a slave; by divine inspiration or by terrestrial experience he will lead him to paradise by the certain path of material work and passive obedience.[36]

The social base of Bou Kounta's movement bore an uncanny resemblance to Cruise O'Brien's and Copans' portrait of the Murid order as a *ceddo*-dominated movement emerging from the crisis of the conquest in 1886. According to Marty, Bou Kounta gave military support to the French in 1886.

> When calm was restored, he welcomed a large number of former royal slaves and settled them in villages where they could live in peace and habituate themselves to the new regime.[37]

Bou Kounta's connection with the court was important. The Sall family of Kajoor affiliated itself with the Qadiri order, rather than with the Tijani or the Murids.[38]

Scholarship on the Murids is unbalanced, because of its obsessive emphasis on peanuts and work. It tends to reach unwarranted conclusions, because it fails to compare the Murid order to anything else. It is important to reexamine the reasons why the order was able to attract so many disciples to the new towns and villages that were founded between 1883 and 1912. In place of the emphasis on peanuts, I will examine the role of the

Murids as the creators of new villages and towns on previously uncultivated lands. This theme will be explored through the career of Maam Cerno
Ibrahim, one of the founder's younger brothers. He played a key role as
his "brother's keeper" during the years of Amadu Bamba's exile in Gabon
(1895–1902) and then as the founder of many new villages in Kajoor in
the period 1903–1912. Then I reexamine the association between the Murid order and the accumulation of wealth, in an attempt to refocus our
understanding of the link between Murid Islam and economic and social
change in Wolof society. For disciples, the Murid path led to emancipation,
not to dependency.

SETTLEMENT AND ACCUMULATION IN THE MURID
ORDER: MAAM CERNO AND IBRA FALL

Darou-Mousty is the largest Murid town in Kajoor. It was founded
by Maam Cerno in the period from 1903 to 1912. Maam Cerno Ibrahim
Mbacké is one of the great figures of Murid Islam, along with the
founder, Shaykh Ibra Fall, and (especially for women in the order) Maam
Jaara Buso, Amadu Bamba's mother. Maam Cerno is remembered as
the founder of over twenty settlements in Kajoor, which were created
by opening new land to agricultural settlement. In conversation he was
referred to as *boroom-Daaru*, the "owner" or "master" of Darou-Mousty,
just as Amadu Bamba is referred to as Sëriñ Tuuba, the marabout of
Touba. The association between Murid leaders and the towns and villages they founded points to one of the most important achievements of
the order, which created a whole series of new towns and villages in
Bawol and Kajoor. Today the most important and sacred villages are
those connected with the life of the founder and his disciples: Darou-
Salam and Touba in Bawol, Darou-Mousty and Darou-Marnane in
Kajoor.

The founding of new agricultural settlements grew out of the core
beliefs of the Murid "path." During my interview with Sëriñ Bassirou,
he interrupted the flow of questions at one point and asked me if I
wanted to learn about Murid beliefs. He began by reminding me that
the Murids were Muslim and that their path (*yoonu Murit*)[39] was something added to the five pillars of Islam, which he recited for my benefit. Amadu Bamba added the Murid path (*yoonu Murit*), which Sëriñ
Bassirou summarized: (1) "Peace with God" (*jàm Yalla*, i.e., following
Islam); (2) "Don't harm anyone, raise them" (*do toñ kenn, yéegal ko*);
(3) "Work, work until you are tired, work until you sweat" (*liggéey,
sonn, ñaq*); (4) "Don't ask anyone for anything, give something" (*do
lajj kenn dara, jox ko*).[40] The Murid settlements were created by hard

work on unclaimed wilderness (*àll bi*).[41] The Murids asked for no help and depended on no one. Amadu Bamba and his followers searched for unoccupied land. Sites for settlement were chosen by a process of "divination" (*gisaane*), which looked for mystical signs. The key phrase used to describe the work that followed was "cutting down trees" (*gor garab*) and "clearing the wilderness" (*gor àll ba*).[42] The new settlements formed an integral part of the vision of the founder.

In the period from 1903 to 1912, Maam Cerno founded a series of new Murid settlements in Kajoor. French archival sources suggested that Ibra Fati left Bawol for Kajoor after the arrest of his brother because of disagreements with Shaykh Anta and the chiefs of Bawol.[43] In Darou-Mousty, where Maam Cerno's branch of the Murid order has its center, the emphasis is strikingly different. When I asked why Maam Cerno decided to leave Bawol for Kajoor in 1903, I was told that Maam Cerno "never decided anything on his own." He moved to Kajoor on the orders of Amadu Bamba. The reason was the recent death of Sëriñ Mbacké Ibra, who had been the leader of the community at Mbacké-Kajoor. Maam Cerno was chosen to succeed Ibra because of Cerno's close relations with the deceased, who had been like a father to him in his youth. Maam Cerno, who was born in Saalum around 1863, grew up in Mbacké-Kajoor.[44] However, my informants did confirm that Maam Cerno had serious conflicts with the Wolof chiefs in Bawol. He made sure that the new settlements were located in Kajoor and therefore under the jurisdiction of Tivaouane and the chief of Guet province.[45]

Maam Cerno's authority derived from his close relationship with his half-brother, Amadu Bamba. Maam Cerno was born within days of the death of Amadu Bamba's mother in Saalum. Their father decided to entrust the education of Maam Cerno to his older brother.[46] Amadu Bamba supervised Maam Cerno's education from the age of seven to the age of thirteen.[47] The relationship between Amadu Bamba and Maam Cerno was compared to the relationship between Musa (Moses) and Harun (Aaron) in the Quran. M'Baye Guèye Sylla recited the passage from the Quran where Moses prayed for God's help in choosing someone from his family to aid him in his mission.[48] He then described how Amadu Bamba chose this passage from the Quran when practicing *listixaar* (from Arabic, *istikhara*), a form of divination using the Quran. The literary source for the comparison with Moses and Aaron is a book-length Wolof poem on the life of Maam Cerno by Moussa Ka, which describes these events.

Fekkoon na Séex Bamba di ñaan buur Yàlla
Jàmbaar ju askanoo ci Mbacké-ballo.

At that time Shaykh Bamba prayed to Lord God
For a courageous hero from the Mbacké patrilineage.[49]

Praising Maam Cerno as a "hero" from the Mbacké family elevates Maam
Cerno above Shaykh Ibra Fall in the history of the Murid path.[50] While
Shaykh Ibra Fall was the first disciple from outside the family to convert,
the followers of Maam Cerno emphasize Cerno's status as the first true
disciple within the family.

The importance of Maam Cerno was underscored by his key role in the
early history of the order. When Amadu Bamba's father died, he renounced
the property he could have inherited and said "Maam Cerno alone suffices
for my share."[51] They traveled together for a time to perfect their education
by visiting famous scholars. When they returned to Mbacké-Kajoor to pre-
pare for their departure for Bawol, Amadu Bamba announced that he would
no longer teach and that Maam Cerno would take over his role. Maam
Cerno was entrusted with clearing land at Touba after Amadu Bamba had
a vision of where to found the village.[52] Most importantly, Amadu Bamba
entrusted his family to Maam Cerno when Bamba was exiled to Gabon in
1895. As his "brother's keeper," Maam Cerno personally educated Amadu
Bamba's sons.[53] In the difficult years of the founder's exile, Maam Cerno
led the community in Bawol. In defining Maam Cerno's identity within the
Murid order, he was described as combining learning with work, based on
the role assigned to him when the founder was exiled for a second time in
1903.

Maam Cerno's role in creating new settlements in Kajoor was recognized by the French, even though they feared the consequences. In 1919
the new commandant at Tivaouane was warned to "keep a close watch
on him so he knows he will be arrested at the least sign of trouble."
But the same report noted that he had "never created any difficulties"
and concluded: "The region of Darou-Mousty (South-East Kajoor),
which resembled a desert in the past, has become in the past few years
the most fertile and populous region of the *cercle* because of him."[54]
The settlement of new lands by the Murid order explains its impact on
Wolof society.

Maam Cerno worked closely with the Sall family in Kajoor. While
Demba War Sall had resisted the growth of the Murid order, after his
death in 1902 his successors welcomed it. This reflected a reversal in
power between the monarchy and Islam. My informants described a
close "friendship" between Macodou Sall, the chief of Guet province,
and Maam Cerno. Although I was aware that Maam Cerno advocated
correct relations with the French administration, finding out about his
friendship with the Sall family was one of the surprises of my field-

work in Darou-Mousty. Macodou Sall and his brothers granted (*lewal*) the 160-square kilometer concession of land that forms the rural domain of Darou-Mousty.[55] One of Maam Cerno's sons described the friendship with Macodou as a "friendship of one nose (or breath)" (*xaritoo bena bakken*). Macodou Sall petitioned the commandant at Tivaouane for the equipment needed to dig the first well for his "friend."[56] Sëriñ Bassirou also provided an interesting explanation of Wolof perceptions of the relationship between the French and the Sall family. "Demba War formed an alliance with the French and granted them the railroad. The French trusted Demba War and his family. . . . Whatever they said, the French agreed."[57] The French were the "yes men" for the Sall family, rather than the other way around.

The major difficulty in the first years was conflict with Fulbe over land. The conflicts derived from the opposition between farming and pastoralism (*bey ak samm*), but they were fueled by the support given to the Fulbe by Mbakhane Diop, the chief of East Bawol. What ensued was a small-scale war in which at least three Murid disciples were killed. The Fulbe were armed with guns, arrows, and swords, while Maam Cerno had few weapons. Once again the Sall family intervened to help. Maam Cerno went with Macodou Sall to Tivaouane to see the commandant. He wanted guns and ammunition. The commandant, after admiring several horses in Maam Cerno's company, agreed to give Maam Cerno a case of ammunition and a number of rifles in exchange for four horses.[58] Although such transactions were "illegal," French sources confirm cases where commandants were disciplined for receiving gifts and bribes from the populations they administered.[59] In Moussa Ka's biography, Maam Cerno is depicted as habitually carrying two pistols in his robe and a double-barreled gun, as protection against the threat of Fulbe attacks and wild animals. He is described as a "hero" (*jàmbaar*) who "felt no fear."[60]

Teams of disciples made up of young unmarried men were assigned the work of creating new settlements. Maam Cerno commanded a work group of 220 disciples recruited in Darou-Marnane and Mbacké-Kajoor when they broke the ground for the cluster of settlements that surround Darou-Mousty. They arrived with tools and supplies and planted crops of millet and peanuts after laying out the location of the mosque. When a settlement became established, women arrived and village life began. In my informants' narratives, the arrival of women meant that the work teams of young men would move on to found a new settlement. In this way the 160-square kilometer concession was gradually settled.[61]

When asked about the economic importance of Maam Cerno's activities in Kajoor, Murid informants referred less often to peanuts than to

bursting granaries of millet. Shortly after Amadu Bamba was allowed
to settle in Diourbel in 1912, Maam Cerno sent him a "gift" of seventy-
eight granaries of millet (*sàq mi*). Maam Cerno had three large grain
stores (*dàgga ji*) at Darou-Mousty. The gift was loaded onto a hundred
donkeys that carried the millet to Diourbel.[62] I was assured that even
today, with tractors and modern equipment, there was almost no one in
Senegal who could produce as much grain. Food stores were freely
opened for visitors who came to the settlements. During the famine of
1914, many people came to Darou-Mousty for three months or more
just to be fed.[63] Informants also recalled that the French administration
had twice turned to Maam Cerno for loans of seed and grain. During
the depression of the 1930s, the French borrowed peanut seed when
there was a commercial shortage, and during World War II, food was
borrowed to feed prisoners of war held in Dakar.[64]

While Murid informants willingly discussed religious authority in the
order, it was more difficult to obtain information about the social origins
of the disciples who left their homes to join the new community. I finally
decided to pose the question directly, historian to historian, by referring to
the repeated complaints (preserved in the archives) that runaway slaves,
children, and wives had joined the order. I described some of the complaints filed against the Murids by Wolof chiefs. One of the questions that
I posed to Bassirou Anta Niang Mbacké referred to archival sources that
depicted the Murid order as a haven for runaway slaves. I summarized in
Wolof the letters and reports written by Demba War Sall and his allies in
1901 and 1902 that said that children, slaves, and girls were fleeing their
homes in Kajoor to become *taalibe*, often against the will of their masters
and families. My informant began his answer by stressing that, in the teachings of Amadu Bamba, faith in God was the only measure of a human
being. If someone came to become a disciple, Murids did not ask "how
much money someone had, what they looked like" or inquire into their
family origins by asking about their father's name or their mother's name.
People came and pledged themselves to the order and that was all that
mattered. Mbacké dismissed the charges against the Murids as the "groan-
ing" of the canton chiefs. But he did not rule out the possibility that there
was some truth behind their complaints.

> What God causes human beings to do, the Europeans could find out
> about, because God can create conditions that cause human beings to
> want something, to seek something.[65]

But he denied that the Murids had ever encouraged a single child, slave, or
women to come to them. Those who came to the Murid settlements did so

of their own accord (*ci boppam*). He also said that all young people who came were advised to return to their families, but he admitted that many of them refused (*lànk*) and stayed anyway. The people who came were God's people. They were motivated by their search for God, and by the absence of God in the homes they left behind.[66]

The crucial distinction was between what people did on their own, as opposed to what they did on the order (*ndigal*) of the Murids. There is little doubt that the social teachings of Amadu Bamba had radical implications for Wolof society. In *Blessings of the Eternal,* these teachings are presented as part of a discussion of education. Amadu Bamba judged the Wolof of his generation harshly. He emphasized the superficiality of Islam and ignorance as the source of most problems. The people of Bawol had a reputation for "laziness" which went along with the pride and vanity common to all humanity. He therefore ordered that their first duty, after their religious obligations, was to "work in the fields." After they had learned to work together in the fields they also learned that "there was complete equality between human beings, and that the only distinctions worth honoring were virtues and the ability to accomplish things."[67] Distinctions of piety and submission to God were the only distinctions worth making. This was interpreted as an attack on distinctions of aristocracy, caste, and slavery.

Although Murid teachings stressed the equality of believers, they did not attack the institution of slavery directly. One anecdote in *Blessings of the Eternal* showed how the shaykh's admonition to the Murids to respect others' property was applied to the case of a slave who belonged to several owners, a situation not uncommon under Islamic rules of inheritance:

A slave who belonged to several owners, one of whom was a disciple of the Shaykh, joined the latter without informing his other masters. When the Shaykh learned of the presence of this slave, he told the Murids: "Tell him to return to his masters and do not accept in your ranks anyone in these conditions. Determine the value of his work while he was here and pay it to his owners."[68]

The only other teaching on the issue of slavery was the shaykh's order to his disciples to free any slaves taken in the war of Amadu Séexu in 1875. This stemmed from a legal ruling that the war had been a conflict between Muslims, and that no prisoners could be enslaved. Because this ruling challenged the court and the official judges of Kajoor, it gave force to the refusal to recognize the enslavement of any Muslim.

The Murid teachings on slavery were ambiguous. Amadu Bamba condemned the enslavement of Muslims under any pretext and he rejected jihad of the sword for his followers. This severely constricted the possibilities of acquiring new slaves. Within the order, the equality of all Murids before God was stressed. Obedience to a shaykh by a disciple was the only social-spiritual hierarchy sanctioned. On the other hand, Amadu Bamba warned his followers against taking the legitimate property of another person. In his teachings about jihad, Amadu Bamba criticized Màbba for allowing slave owners to enlist their slaves in the war, but he also said that God had aided Màbba because of the "labor" of those same slaves, who sought freedom through Islam.[69] The actions of runaway slaves who fled households where Islam was absent could be interpreted as *hijra*, a flight from unbelief that transformed slavery into freedom.[70]

Murid informants stressed the religious motivations of the *taalibe*, who came to Darou-Mousty and other Murid towns on their own initiative. During the early days of the order, many young men volunteered to work in the *daara*. The apprentices considered themselves pioneers, bringing settled agriculture to the wilderness, and apprentices in Islam, whose labors would eventually bring them material and spiritual rewards in this life and redemption in the hereafter.

French archival sources, reflecting hostile complaints made by communities that were losing people, suggest that recruitment of youth for the *daara* was a specialized activity, carried out by special emissaries of the Murid leaders. A French report of 1914 described the recruitment of youth in Kajoor:

> To recruit new adepts who will work and beg for them, the great marabouts of Bawol, Shaykh Anta, Amadu Bamba, Shaykh Thioro, Balla Mbacké, proceed in two ways. Some of them send their most devoted *taalibe* to a village or town where they establish themselves to teach the children. I have seen children who have come from Mboul, Mbakel, from Guet, and from North and South Njambur, and even from the *cercle* of Dagana, in their schools. At the end of one year, or two at the most, these emissaries declare that the students have had enough instruction through their agency. To complete their education they send them in groups of eight or ten to join with the great marabout, or they all leave together one day to place themselves under his authority.[71]

The "students" then joined a *daara*, where they would work for their new masters. Many of these children were seduced by the thought that they would become marabouts themselves one day. All of them believed their labors would be rewarded with a place in paradise.

> Other marabouts simply send their *taalibe* around the country to attract new recruits who are lured by the same promises into following and serving them. I have received numerous complaints from heads of families who are thus deprived of their children at the very moment when they are capable of work and can be of service to them.[72]

Recruitment practices changed over time, but there were persistent features. Recruits were sought in older, settled regions, primarily in Kajoor. The recruits were then sent to the Murid frontier zone in Bawol. The most likely recruits were young people of all classes. They exchanged a familial apprenticeship as dependent *surga* for a religious apprenticeship as *taalibe*. Recruits from poor families, from regions suffering bad harvests, and from oppressed social groups like slaves probably formed a majority of the new disciples, although it is not possible to make any exact estimates. Because *taalibe* status compared favorably to *surga* status, youth from free families formed a substantial portion of the migrants and their numbers increased over time as the population of slaves declined.

Court records from regions losing people to the Murid community document efforts to stop these migrations. A "native" tribunal in Njambur condemned four Murids for a series of vague and bizarre crimes. These included causing trouble in the village, refusing to obey the orders of the village chief, dumping garbage in the mosque, and threatening to beat the village chief. However, the most serious charge "was forcing women to leave their husbands to come with them." No defense was recorded, except the explanation that whatever they did was caused "by religious madness" and "the grandeur of Amadu Bamba." The accused repeated over and over again that they recognized no authority except that of Amadu Bamba. According to the court records, they also said Amadu Bamba "was the only God."[73] This portrait of Murids through the eyes of their enemies has to be taken skeptically, but it reveals some of the tensions and conflicts caused by Murid efforts to attract immigrants to the new settlements. Muslims hostile to the Murids dominated the courts in Njambur.

Njambur province had a long history of hostility to the Murids, dating back to the 1880s and 1890s when Murids had been persecuted and expelled from the region. The effects were still evident in Marty's census of the order in 1915. There were only 450 Murids in Njambur, while there were 28,000 in the *cercle* de Cayor (Tivaouane) and 32,000 in the *cercle* de Baol (Diourbel).[74] Since Njambur was the homeland of many Murid migrants, this raises questions about the reasons for their emigration. Most scholars have not examined the "push" factors in the homelands of migrants, beyond the escape from slave status. They argue that the Murids were unemployed *ceddo* or runaway slaves, and they attribute the culture of obedience and "dependency" to the slave origins of many of the disciples. However, an examination of Wolof land tenure suggests other dimensions of the emigration out of Kajoor and Njambur to the newly settled Murid lands.

In Njambur, *sëriñu-làmb* controlled much of the land and they used their influence with the colonial administration to formalize their claims. By 1907, the most influential family was that of the Cissé. Samba Khary Cissé became chief of southern Njambur in 1907.[75] The Cissé were considered one of the most ancient Muslim families in the province, associated with the founding of Louga.[76] In 1910, the French sponsored Samba Khary Cissé's pilgrimage to Mecca and provided financial aid for him. They hoped that the prestige he gained would help him combat Murid inroads in his province.[77] Pro-French families from the old Muslim party played the anti-Murid card for all it was worth. In 1911, Al Hajj Samba Khary's brother, Goumbo Cissé, was named assessor to the court in northern Njambur.[78] The power of the Cissé family was used to consolidate its title to land. In the period after independence, the Cissé family held 562,489 hectares of land in Louga and its outskirts.[79] Colonial studies of customary law and land tenure found that the highest rents were paid in parts of Kajoor and Njambur, where ancient land grants to aristocrats and marabouts had been preserved. The titleholders collected *assaka* as a tax, along with other rents. If Muslims wanted to pay *assaka* to their spiritual guide to express their religious affiliation, they had to pay twice.[80]

Free emigrants from Njambur or Kajoor would pay fewer taxes in the new Murid settlements than in their homeland. The French colonial officials never drew the connection between "oppressive" conditions in the old Wolof provinces and migration to the newly settled Murid communities. In Njambur, *sërinu-làmb* treated Wolof peasants as mere "tenants." This inherited authority was resented because it represented power rather than religious authority. The appeal of the new Sufi orders, whether Tijani or Murid, was rooted in the voluntary link between disciple and spiritual guide. Such bonds differed from the old claims of inherited subordination and dependency. The French officials were unable to perceive this contrast because they accepted without question

Marty's thesis that the Murid order was a new form of servitude. Officials compiling summaries of customary law in the 1930s argued that anyone who sought land in Murid settlements first had to become a disciple, which they interpreted as accepting a state of "absolute dependence," like medieval serfdom. "Like the serf, the Talibé depends upon a powerful clerical seigneur, to whom he owes one hundred percent of his work."[81]

Colonial interpreters of the Murid order misread the motivations of disciples who migrated. They stereotyped the Murids as slaves and backward-looking *ceddo* who sought out a new form of servitude, offering their labor to new masters in exchange for the promise of paradise. But migrants left behind situations they found oppressive. In their own eyes, they chose a path that brought them closer to God and provided for worldly success. In a peasant society, worldly excess meant shelter, food, and land, but the Murid path also provided a community of mosques, schools, and shops, a Wolof version of modernity.

Colonial misinterpretations of migration and labor were reinforced by colonial hostility to the accumulation of wealth in the Murid order. French commentators affected a tone of paternalistic concern to voice their opinion that Murid disciples were being fleeced of their worldly wealth by unscrupulous "charlatans" who profited from the saintly charisma of the founder. For Marty, the best example of the charlatans was Shaykh Ibra Fall, whom he described as the "Minister of economic affairs." Ibra Fall "owned homes in Saint-Louis and Dakar and concessions in Thiès, Diourbel, Ndande and Kébemer. He has created houses of commerce in several towns and has them managed by his disciples and his wives."[82] In addition, Ibra Fall had extensive fields that were cultivated by his disciples and he had created an orchard of fruit trees which included "mangos, bananas, goyavas, papayas, lemons, and oranges which he obtained from the botanical garden in Saint-Louis."[83] The quarter where he lived in Thiès contained a mosque, schools, and shops run by his disciples.

Murid leaders did not simply rely on the gifts they received, but were actively engaged in commerce and agriculture. Ibra Fall symbolized the qualities of this group of Wolof merchants and businessmen, who invested part of their capital in commercial ventures and urban property.[84] In 1913 an administrative report on Shaykh Ibra Fall noted that he was a "proprietor thirteen times over." His revenues from agriculture were estimated to be at least 50,000 francs a year, but that figure represented only a fraction of his income because it did not include the donations he received from his disciples.[85] The donations were substantial: in 1909 the commandant at

Thiès reported that Ibra Fall had received 35,000 francs from five marabouts in the *cercle*.[86] His revenues were sufficient to allow Ibra Fall to give over 50,000 francs as his annual gift to Amadu Bamba in 1913. This equaled the salary of the governor-general of French West Africa. The social basis for this wealth was the labor and donations of Shaykh Ibra Fall's 1,000 disciples. Like other marabouts of similar standing, Ibra Fall maintained an aristocratic lifestyle to match his social status. In 1913 he had five wives; four of them were *garmi* princesses, and the fifth was the widow of Demba War Sall. Only French intervention prevented Ibra Fall from marrying into the family of the Bour Saloum in 1916.[87]

The ostentatious display of wealth was a sign of social standing and success. This was true even of Amadu Bamba, who was known for his personal indifference to wealth and material comforts. When the French visited the compound that had been prepared for him by Maam Cerno in 1903, they said it was instantly recognizable as that of a major Wolof notable. It covered 100 square meters, and consisted of a series of enclosed courtyards with a residence "larger and more comfortable than that of the great chiefs of the Fleuve [Fuuta]." There was a large library and a mosque, and the inner courtyard was filled with hundreds of chests that contained money, cloth, and other gifts.[88] The personal fortunes of the Murid leaders were impressive, but much of their wealth was reinvested in the community. Unlike the resources accumulated by the administration or by commerce, the "capital" accumulated by the Murid order remained within rural society, whether it was invested in agricultural expansion or in commercial ventures.

French criticisms focused on the cash contributions of the *taalibe*. Since the French admitted these to be voluntary, they denounced the superstition and ignorance that perpetuated the exploitation of the peasantry. The individual *taalibe* made his donations to his personal marabout, the *sëriñ* to whom he had said the *njebbel* or oath of submission.[89] Only freely given gifts (Wolof, *addiya*) had spiritual merit. Most marabouts were local leaders with a limited following, but they were linked to the order through their own shaykh. A marabout was expected to keep some of the income he collected for his personal use, and to use some as charity or aid within his community. Each marabout made his own payment to his shaykh, roughly in proportion to the marabout's stature and the number of his followers. Substantial sums were collected and passed on through the interlocking ties of religious affiliation until they reached the apex of the brotherhood. The wealth of Amadu Bamba, Shaykh Anta, Maam Cerno, and Shaykh Ibra Fall reflected the cumulative ties, direct and indirect, linking shaykh, *sëriñ*, and *taalibe*.[90]

The most important investment was in the new towns themselves. When I was in Darou-Mousty, I was told by one disciple that when the town was founded Maam Cerno told the settlers to be "patient," but that one day they would "have everything here that they had in Saint-Louis."[91] Murid settlements were "modern." The houses were constructed of cement and laid out along wide streets. Over time they were provided with modern bore wells, connected to the electrical grid, and provided with bakeries and other symbols of urban life. This infrastructure was provided to Darou-Mousty from the savings that Maam Cerno accumulated from the donations of his disciples.

The order mobilized resources and set in motion a process of accumulation by settling new lands.[92] Such colonization required the mobilization of manpower, capital, and political influence. The Murids overcame the hostility of the French by working with Wolof chiefs wherever they could. When land was taken from Fulbe pastoralists, the Murids had to muster superior power. The settlers who arrived in new zones had to be provided with the essential tools, food, and supplies to survive the difficult initial period. Volunteers had to be recruited and organized. The social prestige of the marabout was essential in gaining the allegiance of the young men who became *tak-der* and accepted a life of hard work and sacrifice. The role of the *tak-der* recalled the traditional activities of young men in age-grade groups, although the age-grade institution was transformed into an Islamic rite of passage. After a number of years, the pioneers gained title to land as the settlement became a Murid village.[93] Murid patronage provided employment for *taalibe* in commercial ventures and other business activities. *Taalibe* could serve as employees, or obtain from their marabout loan capital that allowed them to open small businesses. Most of these were in the so-called "informal sector," or served the needs of the Murid community. Profits were shared between the *sërin* and his *taalibe*. Through such arrangements, Murid merchants made inroads in urban as well as rural markets.

French officials believed that Murid disciples obeyed orders from canton chiefs only when they were told to by the Murid order. Although this power was seldom exercised and led to few overt cases of resistance, the primary allegiance of Murid disciples to their marabouts was perceived as a threat to colonial domination.[94] The problem was compounded by the inability of the administration to control the marabouts except through measures of repression. The French had relatively poor information on the activities of the marabouts, who remained outside colonial intelligence networks.

French commercial interests complained about "unfair competition" from Murid businessmen and viewed the Murid community as a closed market, providing less business than other regions with equal incomes. The complaints reflected the success of the Murids in controlling the circulation of wealth within the Murid community.[95] Murid towns borrowed less than other communities. Murid peasants did not turn to merchants for "rainy season" credits as often as other peasants, because they could borrow within their community. The lack of commerce about which French merchants complained reflects the emphasis placed on self-sufficiency by Murid informants. Maam Cerno raised "everything himself." He had disciples who raised "pigeons, goats, sheep, ostriches, donkeys." "He never had to buy anything. He slaughtered a sheep every day. He lived eighty years and he had the reputation of someone who never had to buy anything."[96]

THE ADMINISTRATION AS AN ECONOMIC SYSTEM

A final question needs to be considered: What did the French administration contribute to the peasant economy, beyond colonial "peace," railroads, and rural cooperatives supplying seed? The administration's first goal was to collect taxes. These taxes paid for the rural bureaucracy and allowed the French to send substantial sums to Saint-Louis. From a peasant point of view, the "salary men" on the government payroll (and they were all men) were very well paid. The peasants in a rural district paid the salaries of half a dozen French "bureaucrats" and several dozen African "bureaucrats," inferior in status but still well paid. The rest of the peasants' taxes were sucked into the bureaucracy in Saint-Louis, where most was spent in cities and towns. The federal bureaucracy in Dakar helped subsidize a few schools, but the educational effort was feeble and elitist. Private Muslim schools taught ten times the number of students enrolled in French schools. The colonial state expressed the power of the cities over the rural areas.

The colonial administration was linked to the export economy. The head tax was the only source of revenue for the local budget. Through the head tax, the administrative cycle was closely tied to the agricultural cycle. The head tax was a fixed sum paid by every rural resident in the protectorate who was an *indigène* ("native") by status. The head tax was raised and lowered in accordance with French assessments of rural income.[97] The canton chiefs collected the tax, using the village chiefs as intermediaries with household heads. The canton chiefs also established the census figures, which were used to predict tax yields. In the period from 1890 to 1914, the head tax rose from 2 to 5 francs per person on average. The tax was collected after the harvest during the commercial season. The head tax had to be collected then or it risked being lost altogether. Tax collection was carried out entirely by the canton chiefs and their retainers. The French monitored taxation through a simple system of accounting based on numbered tickets. One half of the ticket was kept by the taxpayer as proof of payment. The canton chiefs returned the other half with the tax receipts, which were turned over to the commandant.[98]

The head tax was a tax on rural cash income earned from peanuts. Some idea of the system can be provided by an analysis of statistics from the *cercle* of Bawol, a major peanut-producing region. In 1911, the population of Bawol was 180,352 according to the census figures of the canton chiefs, 90,608 in West Bawol, and 89,744 in East Bawol. The estimate for the head tax in 1911 was 815,000 francs, 777,854 of which had been collected by the canton chiefs by January 1911. The rest of the tax was in arrears. The taxes collected represented a per capita yield of 4.5 francs: the *impôt personnel* was fixed at 5 francs, but small children were exempted from the tax.[99]

The head tax was paid with income earned during the trading season of 1910–1911: 13,200 metric tons of peanuts had been commercialized at Diourbel, 19,520 metric tons at Bambey, and 12,120 tons at Khombole. The total sales at the three *escales* (trading towns) of the *cercle* were 44,840 metric tons. On the assumption that this was all sold at the average 1911 price of 275 francs a ton, which was considered an exceptionally good price, this yielded an income of 12,331,000 francs for the *cercle* or a per capita income of 68.37 francs. The head tax represented 6.6 percent of cash earnings in 1911. This underestimates the size of the head tax, because most peasants were paid less than the full price offered in the *escales*. Most peasants also had to repay debts to commercial firms for advances in seed and goods received on credit. If the exceptionally high prices paid in 1911 are factored out, the head tax represented about 10 percent of gross cash income.[100]

Taxes in cash were supplemented by taxes in kind, in the form of labor services *(prestations)*. By 1911, *prestations* were synonymous with work on public roads. Villagers were recruited during the dry season, when the harvests were in. Canton chiefs recruited laborers and organized road gangs that cleared and maintained the roads in their canton. Each rural subject was liable to four days of labor, or could obtain exemption by a cash payment. During labor service, food was provided by the administration. Forced labor of this kind provided the colony with a rudimentary road system.[101]

Prison labor was used in a similar but more restricted fashion. Prisoners cleaned and maintained the French Residency and its garden, and prison work gangs carried out public service work in colonial towns. Most of the prisoners were peasants serving short sentences under the "native code," often for failure to obey orders promptly and respectfully. The testimony of a chief, interpreter, or guard was enough to send a troublemaker to jail on the orders of the commandant.[102] The labor provided by prisoners more than compensated for the minimal costs of feeding and housing them.

Bawol conformed to the ideals laid down in the "native" policy of Governors-General Roume and Ponty. There were no "great chiefs": the last superior and province chiefs had been dismissed before Bawol was separated from the *cercle* of Thiès in 1907. In 1911 there were twelve more or less equal cantons in Bawol. Ten canton chiefs collected the head tax. Each chief had an average of 15,000 subjects under his jurisdiction, although two chiefs commanded two cantons each and a correspondingly larger population. Even a casual comparison of the salaries of the chiefs and the amount of tax revenue that passed through their hands suggests why it was difficult for the French to eliminate "corruption."

The largest single item in the district budget was the salaries paid to the European and African staff. Approximately 12.5 percent of the total tax receipts and 25 percent of the local budget[103] went for salaries. The seven Europeans on the staff included four administrators and three police commissioners, with annual salaries ranging from 15,000 to 3,000 francs, making a total of 42,000 francs. The African "salary men" included one clerk, two interpreters, five schoolteachers, and twenty-two police guards of various ranks. Their combined annual salaries were 31,300 francs for thirty individuals. Eleven canton chiefs were paid a total of 29,600 francs for annual salaries ranging from 2,400 to 5,000 francs. The "salary men" as a whole were paid 102,900 francs. Apart from the five schoolteachers, they were all occupied with administration and policing.[104]

The "salary men" represented a new salaried class of civil servants working for the government. Their privileged position is clear when their income is compared to that of peasants. If the production and income figures calculated previously for the *cercle* of Bawol in 1911 are translated into income on the basis of households of five active members, peasant income can be estimated at 345 francs per household.[105] Europeans earned 3,000 to 15,000 francs a year, canton chiefs earned 2,400 to 5,000 francs, schoolteachers earned 1,500 to 2,400 francs, interpreters and clerks earned

Table 7.1 Canton Chiefs and Tax Collection, Bawol 1911

Canton Chief	Canton	Salary	Taxes Paid
Salmon Fall	Mbayar	3600	86,555
Vende Dieng	Diète-Galao	2400	50,551
Mandikou Diaye	Tidiar	2400	38,900
Latsoukabé Fall	Dadène	3600	43,912
Amady Demba	Lô	2400	63,046
Alioune Sylla	Ngoye	2400	59,972
Salla Dior	Diack	5000	70,918
Salla Dior	Fandène	--	49,648
Niokhor Mbore	Gueoul	2400	62,028
Coumba Arène Fall	Pegue	2400	55,342
Coumba Arène Fall	Dondole	--	60,852
Mbaye Kama	Thièpe	2400	63,396

Source: Archives Nationales du Sénégal, 2 D 7-3, Corres. 1911, Commandant Theveniault à Lieutenant Gouverneur, April 27, 1911.

1,000 to 2,000 francs, and police guards earned 800 francs. The advantage of a salary was great, because the families of many "salary men" grew peanuts as well. "Salary men's" incomes were protected from bad weather and other misfortunes.[106]

Chiefs and teachers were the best paid. Chiefs made substantially more than teachers, but they had higher expenses. This disadvantage was offset by the potential to acquire "unofficial" income. The high pay of teachers made teaching a prestigious profession. A substantial number of French-educated sons of chiefs who could not obtain appointments in the administration chose to become teachers.[107] Interpreters were at a relative disadvantage in the ranks of "salary men" and had few possibilities for advancement. As a result, interpreters often sought employment as chiefs at the end of their careers, a situation that led to periodic conflict with canton chiefs. The easiest way for an interpreter to gain an appointment as a chief was to engineer the downfall of a chief by feeding information (true or false) to the French commandant. Demand for the best positions in the administration far exceeded the number of available posts. There was intense competition among families and individuals for administrative appointments. The French-controlled bureaucracy was an important source of wealth and patronage.[108]

Much of the hard-earned cash collected from peasants was sent to Saint-Louis. The administration spent little money in the rural areas. Investment was either self-financed (as with the *sociétés de prévoyance*) or achieved through the recruitment of forced labor. The shoestring budgets of rural districts allowed substantial revenue transfers to the central government. One reason for these transfers was the low rate of taxation in the Four Communes, where politicians had to approve taxes. Until 1912, virtually no direct taxes were paid in the Four Communes. Even after 1912, when a personal tax was passed after Governor-General Ponty threatened to dissolve the Conseil Général, there was still a wide discrepancy in the rate of taxation. In 1912 the five *cercles* of the peanut basin (Louga, Tivaouane, Thiès, Bawol, and Sine-Saloum) paid a 5-franc head tax, so that a family of six active members paid 30 francs. In the Four Communes, the same family would have paid only 5 francs, since only heads of families or single employed adults paid the 5-franc tax.[109]

French officials sometimes provided candid assessments of the exploitation of the countryside by the cities. The most revealing comments were written to expose the inequalities of taxation that French officials blamed on *originaire* politicians from the Four Communes. The population of the protectorate was over a million, while the population of the Four Communes and the other territories of direct administration was about 60,000. The rural areas paid the entire cost of the central administration in Saint-Louis, plus the cost of the telegraph system, and they subsidized the Four Communes. On the other hand, per capita expenditure for education and all other social services was much lower in rural areas than elsewhere. Governor-General Clozel analyzed this situation for the budget year 1916, but his comments apply to the entire prewar era. If anything, they understate the financial exploitation of the protectorate by the urban areas.

> The total revenues anticipated in the protectorate areas for 1916 come to 6,404,545 francs, of which 4,949,400 or five million in round figures come from direct taxes. Of this latter sum 4,720,000 are generated by the head tax paid by *indigènes*. Now, of this above total, what fraction will be used to cover the expenses of the protectorate? A very minimal fraction, and in any case completely out of propor-

tion with the sacrifices demanded of the population. Remember that the expenditure for postal and telegraph service, for public health, for public works, for education, etc., is spent almost entirely in the territories of direct administration [the Four Communes and the colonial towns] and for their benefit.[110]

Few statements express as succinctly the subordinate position of the rural areas in the colonial system.

Clozel's comments cast a different light on the French *mission civilisatrice* than the ideological vision of "native policy." The "sacrifices" of the rural population financed privileged urban centers and their European elites. A substantial portion of the revenues collected by the colony simply financed the costs of the colonial administration and the amenities of European life. The domination and exploitation of the countryside by the colonial cities and towns was one of the major innovations of the political system created by colonial rule. One of the major functions of the rural administration was to engineer the transfer of income from the rural areas to the urban centers. Not surprisingly, the ideology of the colonial administration obscured this process.

French schools should have been the showpiece of the civilizing mission. Expenditures for the French school system were an investment with potential benefits for the local population. Schools trained Africans for administrative or commercial employment. Each *cercle* maintained a number of schools, but the number of students was extremely small. This can be seen in statistics from Bawol in 1903–1904 and in 1911. In 1903 when Bawol was part of the *cercle* of Thiès, there were four schools and 66 students in the *cercle*, including 22 in the Sereer provinces, which remained part of the *cercle* of Thiès after 1907. There were 176,839 inhabitants in Bawol when the first complete census was taken in 1908.[111] In 1911, when the population of Bawol was 180,352, there were 124 students taught by five African teachers from the Four Communes. In 1910, 31 students were granted the *certificat de primaire* in Bawol. Of these the administration noted that 10 were continuing their studies in Dakar or Saint-Louis, 2 were continuing their studies in Arabic schools, 7 had obtained employment in commerce, 6 were variously employed, and 6 had returned to their families.[112] The French effort was minimal. In Bawol, private Muslim schools taught between 800 and 1,000 students.[113]

In practice, the French school system was targeted at elite families. A comment on the schools of Bawol in 1903 described the general situation in rural Senegal:

Most of the students are sons of chiefs or former chiefs who intend to give their children an elementary education before soliciting their admission to the School for Sons of Chiefs, now part of the *Ecole Normale* at Saint-Louis. The rest are children of notables from the diverse provinces of the *cercle*.[114]

The elitism of rural schools contradicted the official policy described by Governor-General Ponty in 1909. According to Ponty, "Education should be above all extensive; its first objective is not to assimilate but to give the greatest number of students and young people exposure to French civilization."[115] But the funds for such a program did not exist. Rural schools became primary schools for *originaires* and rural notables seeking access to a second tier of overtly elitist schools in the urban centers. Georges Hardy, who managed the Education Department in French West Africa, described the role of these schools. Hardy referred particularly to the medersas, which were intended for rural elites:

> The medersas train official interpreters, judges, and secretaries for native tribunals, in a word the auxiliaries of our administration and justice. This collaboration in the administration and judicial spheres presupposes that our medersas do not recruit by hazard, but are populated by a social elite.[116]

Budgetary restraints meant that rural schools were reserved for a special clientele of *originaires* and rural notables. The schools trained the auxiliaries needed by the administration and commerce in such a way as to reinforce existing social inequalities.

CONCLUSION

Cash-crop agriculture transformed the Wolof landscape between 1890 and 1914. Most of the changes were connected to the new possibilities of social advancement and mobility that came with peanut cultivation. The cash earnings of young men often allowed them to accumulate the capital required for marriage more rapidly than in the past. The formation of new households was accelerated, leading to the breakup of larger households and villages, as new satellite settlements were founded. Over time, the same process led to migration within the Wolof zone and the creation of new farming frontiers in Bawol and Saalum.[117] While the size of the average farming village declined as migrants dispersed in the countryside, old and new towns along the railroad grew rapidly, providing additional opportunities for migration and resettlement.

Murid migrations were a variation on a larger theme. Slaves from inside and outside the Wolof zone were among the first to take advantage of the new opportunities. The migrations of runaway slaves gradually merged into the larger movements of migration that created new villages and zones of settlement. Young people led these migrations. They believed that a fresh start in a new village as a migrant or *taalibe* would lead to more rapid social advancement than staying at home. Cash cropping did not free all slaves or cause all young dependents to leave their households. But the cash-crop economy made it much easier for slaves to transform flight into migration and for ambitious or discontented youth to relocate. Cash cropping facilitated social change by providing opportunities for those eager to change their social status. The goal was to exchange dependency for independence.

Specific peasant and slave migrations illustrate these themes. For the Murids, various sources name slaves, young people just beginning to work, and young women (many of them slaves) as the core groups involved. Religious scholars and students from various regions also migrated to join the order. French sources depict these migrants as "dupes," tricked by promises of paradise into a lifetime of enforced servitude. Murid sources emphasize work as well, but give it meaning. Living by the sweat of your brow as a farmer and serving a religious guide are marks of honor in the Murid community. The goal of the *taalibe* was to become part of a community, as a peasant and as a Muslim. The Murid villages and towns were modern, symbolized by the wide lanes between cement houses laid out on a grid aligned with Mecca. Since the 1930s, this modern image has been enhanced by efforts to construct monumental mosques in each major settlement. From a very early date, the Murid order also ensured the accumulation of new wealth in the Wolof countryside. This occurred against the odds in a colonial economy biased toward urban investment.

Murid villages and towns, like the migrations that created them, embody some of the social transformations of the period. In that sense they are a microcosm of the larger changes taking place in the peasantry as a whole. While the dynamic interaction between the microeconomy of the household and commerce can explain some aspects of the peasant economy, the Murid settlements were created by the collective action of new communities. They included powerful and wealthy leaders, seen by the French as exploiters of the peasantry. I emphasize the role played by the Murid leadership in organizing and financing the migration of peasants and slaves to new towns and villages. The difficulties that had to be overcome in creating these new settlements and the farming frontiers they opened were beyond the capacity of individual migrants or migrating households. Collective initiatives contributed to the transformation of rural society.

Most historians have emphasized the negative trends foreshadowed in the cash-crop economy. There are strong arguments in favor of such views, but I will not repeat them here. Instead I have chosen to emphasize the social transformations that occurred during the first long export boom. I have followed the clues that I found in interviews and other sources that seemed attuned to the peasantry, to the *beykat* who emerged from the period with a new sense of dignity. The Muslim peasantry that is depicted in sources dealing with Wolof society from the 1930s onward emerged out of the population of *baadoolo* and slaves who witnessed the conquest.

NOTES

1. 17 G 39 (7), Politique indigène, Instructions au Gouverneur Général p.i., Jan. 12, 1912. Ponty echoes French merchants' fears of "unfair competition" from the Murids.

2. See the work of Paul Marty, *Etudes sur l'Islam au Sénégal*.

3. Cruise O' Brien, *The Mourides of Senegal*, 13–14.

4. Ibid., 32–34.

5. Ibid., 57.

6. Ibid., 15. He takes this figure from Marty, *Etudes sur l'Islam au Sénégal*, vol. 1, 280.

7. Cruise O'Brien, *The Mourides of Senegal*, 35, 14.

8. Marty, *Etudes sur l'Islam au Sénégal*, vol. 1, 206, as quoted by Cruise O'Brien, *The Mourides of Senegal*, 56.

9. For work and peanuts, see Cruise O'Brien, *The Mourides of Senegal*, 34 and 57.

10. Two works are particularly important: Copans, *Les marabouts de l'arachide*; and Copans, Couty, Roch, and Rocheteau, *Maintenance sociale et changement économique*. For the "crisis," see Copans, *Les marabouts de l'arachide*, 77; and Copans et al., *aintenance sociale et changement économique*, 22.

11. Marty, *Etudes sur l'Islam au Sénégal*, vol. 1, 202–3. See also Pelissier, *Les paysans du Sénégal*, 118–19, for a similar contrast between the social base of the Tijani and Murid order.

12. In Cruise O'Brien, *The Mourides of Senegal*, for the first time.

13. This interpretation begins with Marty, but is picked up by most other scholars. It is enshrined in the title of Jean Copans' book, *Les marabouts de l'arachide*.

14. Archival reports on this phenomenon date from 1910 onward. See 2 D 8-2, Cercle de Sine-Saloum, Corres. 1912, Commandant de cercle à Lieutenant Gouverneur, Jan. 7, 1912; 1 G 337, Monographie: Cercle de Thiès, p. 43; 2 D 7-3, Cercle de Baol, Corres. 1910, Commandant à Lieutenant Gouverneur, n.d.; 2 D 13-8, Cercle de Thiès, Corres. 1915, Lieutenant Gouverneur à Commandant, July 7, 1915.

15. L. Geismar, *Recueil des coutumes civiles des races du Sénégal* (Saint-Louis, 1933), 60–61, for the comparison between Wolof and Sereer bride-wealth payments.

16. Cruise O'Brien, *Saints and Politicians*, 43.

17. Ibid., 44 and 45.

18. Ibid., 46.

19. For his image, he takes the colorful figure from contemporary Senegalese art rather than the drably dressed man in the one surviving photograph.

20. Copans, *Les marabouts de l'arachide*, 87–88.

21. Ibid., 87.

22. Mbacké, "Les bienfaits (1)," 596–97.

23. The most detailed colonial report on Ibra Fall is his Fiche de renseignements: 13 G 68, Pièce 12. Researchers have to distinguish between "real Bay Fall" and urban hustlers who use his image and name to beg in Dakar and other cities.

24. For example, the audiocassettes of Bouchera Samb and Modou Mamoun Ammar.

25. Field notes, Darou-Mousty, July 1995, based on conversations with Ibou Saar and Cheikh Njaay. Ibou Saar was repeating what he had heard another "popular preacher" (Dame Njaay) say.

26. Marty, *Etudes sur l'Islam au Sénégal*, vol. 1, 235–36.

27. Mbacké, "Les bienfaits (1)," 621.

28. Marty, *Etudes sur l'Islam au Sénégal*, vol. 1, 237.

29. Ibid., 239.

30. Ibid., 253.

31. Ibid., 247.

32. I visited the school (*daara*) of Serigne Bassirou Anta Niang Mbacké in Darou-Mousty in July, 1995. His students lived with him and helped him cultivate his fields, in exchange for an academic education.

33. On his life, see Marty, *Etudes sur l'Islam au Sénégal*, vol. 1, 175.

34. 2 D 14-5, Cercle de Tivaouane, Corres., 1910, rapport de Coppet, Oct., 1910.

35. 13 G 68, Fiche de renseignements: Ibra Fall.

36. 13 G 67, Pièce 250, Chemise: Bou Kounta, June 11, 1915, p. 14.

37. Ibid., p. 25.

38. Interview, Serigne Bassirou Anta Niang Mbacké, Darou-Mousty, July 25, 1995.

39. In Wolof the order is referred to as "the Murid path," a literal translation of *tariqa* (Arabic). This phrase evokes a set of teachings, not an organization, as is suggested by "brotherhood."

40. Ibid. Interview, Serigne Bassirou Anta Niang Mbacké, Darou-Mousty, July 25, 1995.

41. The land was unclaimed by agriculturists. There were conflicts with pastoral Fulbe, which are discussed below.

42. Interview, Serigne Bassirou Anta Niang Mbacké, July 25, 1995; interview, Serigne M'Baye Guèye Sylla, July 28, 1995.

43. 2 D 14-4, Cercle de Cayor, Corres. 1903, Commandant Allys à Lieutenant Gouverneur, July 6, 1903.

44. Interview, Serigne Bassirou Anta Niang Mbacké, July 25, 1995.

45. Serigne M'Baye Guèye Sylla, July 28, 1995.

46. M'Baye Ngirane, *Waxtaan ci Sëriñ Tuuba.*

47. Interview, M'Baye Guèye Sylla.

48. Ibid. He identified this as the Khassas sura.

49. Quoted by M'Baye Guèye Sylla. A copy of the manuscript by Moussa Ka is in my possession. The manuscript is hereafter referred to as Ka, "Biograhpy."

50. This point was made explicitly by M'Baye Guèye Sylla, who mentioned Ibra Fall, but it was implicit in other interviews.

51. *Maam Cerno rekk doy na ma.* This is based on a passage from Ka, "Biography." Interview, M'Baye Guèye Sylla.

52. Interview, M'Baye Guèye Sylla.

53. Interview, Serigne Bassirou Anta Niang Mbacké, July 25; interview, M'Baye Guèye Sylla. See also Mbacké, "Les bienfaits (1)"

54. 2 D 14-13, Cercle de Tivaouane, Passation de service, May 5, 1919.

55. Interview, M'Baye Guèye Sylla; Ka, "Biography."

56. Interview, Serigne Bassirou Anta Niang Mbacké, July 25, 1995.

57. Ibid.

58. Interview, M'Baye Guèye Sylla.

59. See, for example, 13 G 294, Baol, Inspection de Theveniaut, June 11, 1912. Theveniaut was charged with receiving four horses from Shaykh Anta Mbacké in exchange for a price well below their value. Shaykh Anta had thrown a party for French administrators and their wives in Diourbel, at a cost of over 300 francs.

60. Ka, "Biography."

61. Interview, M'Baye Guèye Sylla.

62. Ka, "Biography." Interview, M'Baye Guèye Sylla.

63. Interview, M'Baye Guèye Sylla.

64. Interview, Serigne Bassirou Anta Niang Mbacké, July 25, 1995.

65. Ibid.

66. Ibid.

67. Mbacké, "Les bienfaits (1)," 597.

68. Ibid., 570.

69. Interview, Serigne Bassirou Anta Niang Mbacké, July 29, 1995. The criticism of bringing slaves into war alludes to Tijani practice, based on the teachings of Al Hajj Umar, who permitted bringing slaves into war if the slaves were willing. See Allan G.B. Fisher and Humphrey J. Fisher, *Slavery and Muslim Society in Africa* (New York, 1971), 48. See also John Ralph Willis, "Jihad and the Ideology of Enslavement," in *Slaves and Slavery in Muslim Africa*, ed. John Ralph Willis (London, 1985), vol. 1, 16–26.

70. Willis, "Jihad and the Ideology of Enslavement," 21–22.

71. 2 D 14-6, Cercle de Tivaouane, Corres. 1914, Rapport du tournée dans le M'Baouar, March 3 to April 3, 1914, Adjoint Carrera.

72. Ibid.

73. 2 D 9-21, Cercle de Louga, Justice indigène: 1912, Diambour septentrional, May 20, 1912.

74. Marty, *Études sur l'Islam au Sénégal,* vol. 1, 304.

75. 13 G 71, Pièce 63, Rapport sur les chefs indigènes, Lieutenant Gouverneur Camille Guy, 1907; and 2 D 9-13, Cercle de Louga, Correspondance, March 24, 1907.

76. Sarr, *Louga et sa région*, 29, 50. The Cissé are from the group called *xollbit* in Wolof: marabouts of Mande origins, with a long history in the region.

77. 2 D 9-7, Cercle de Louga, Corres., 1910, Commandant à Lieutenant Gouverneur, Sep. 7, 1910.

78. 2 D 9-16, Pièce 8, Cercle de Louga, Dossier: Personnel, Justice indigène, March 29, 1911.

79. Sarr, *Louga et sa région*, 50.

80. *Assaka* is Wolof for *zakat*, the Muslim alms for the poor. In most regions, Muslims paid *assaka* to their spiritual guide. In Njambur, *assaka* had become a rent on the land. See Geismar, *Recueil des coutumes civiles*, 141–43; and M. Campistron, "Coutume Ouolof du Cayor (Cercle de Thiès)," in *Coutumiers juridiques de l'Afrique Occidentale Française, Volume 1, Sénégal* (Paris, 1939), 136–37.

81. J. C. Fayet, "Coutume des Ouolof musulmans (Cercle du Baol)," in *Coutumiers juridiques de l'Afrique Occidentale Française, Volume 1, Sénégal* (Paris, 1939), 176–77.

82. Marty, *Études sur l'Islam au Sénégal,* vol. 1, 246.

83. Ibid., 247.

84. For Murid economic activities, see 13 G 67, Mémoire: Islam dans le domaine économique; and in Marty, *Etudes sur l'Islam au Sénégal*.

85. 13 G 68 (12), Fiche de renseignement: Cheikh Ibra Fall.

86. 2 D 13-6, Cercle de Cayor, Corres. 1909, Commandant Dolisie à Lieutenant Gouverneur, July 5, 1909.

87. On Shaykh Ibra Fall's wives, see 13 G 68 (12), Fiche de renseignement: Cheikh Ibra Fall. On his negotiations with a Guelowar princess, see 13 G 72 (159), Commandant de cercle de Sine-Saloum à Lieutenant Gouverneur, Nov. 10, 1916.

88. 2 D 13-14, Cercle de Thiès, Rapport de tournée de Prempain, August 14–20, 1903. The report also describes Shaykh Anta's opulent residence.

89. Cruise O'Brien, *The Mourides of Senegal*, 83–100, discusses the role of submission.

90. Ibid., 101–21.

91. Field notes, July 1995. The disciple in question, named Diouf, was described as the *jawriñ* or *bëkk-néeg* (house steward) of Moustapha Apsa Mbacké. He cared for the public dormitories of the house where I was staying, among other duties.

92. Murid settlement of new lands was noted periodically, usually with alarm, by the administration: 2 D 8-2, Cercle de Sine-Saloum, Corres. 1912, Commandant de cercle à Lieutenant Gouverneur, Jan. 7, 1912; 1 G 337, Monographie: Cercle de Thiès, p. 43; 2 D 7-3, Cercle de Baol, Corres. 1910, Commandant de cercle à Lieutenant Gouverneur, n. d.; 2 D 13-8, Cercle de Thiès, Corres. 1915, Lieutenant Gouverneur à Commandant de cercle, July 7, 1915.

93. On migrations see E. N'Doye, "Migration des pionniers Mourides wolof vers les terres neuves: Role de l'économique et du religieux," in *Modern Migrations in Western Africa*, ed. Samir Amin (Oxford, 1974.); and Cruise O'Brien, *The Mourides of*

Senegal, 58–78. On the *terres neuves,* see G. Rocheteau, *Système mouride et rapports sociaux traditionnels: Le travail collectif dans une communauté pionnière du Ferlo Occidentale* (Dakar, 1969); and Rocheteau, "Pionniers Mourides: Colonisation des terres neuves et transformation d'une économie paysanne," *Cahiers ORSTROM,* série sciences humaines, 12, no. 1, (1975): 19–53.

94. On Murid attitudes, see 2 G 3-35, Baol: Rapport politique, Oct. 1903; 1 G 337, Monographie: Cercle de Thiès 1910, p. 43; 2 G 11-42, Baol: Rapports mensuels d'ensemble; 2 D 9-21, Cercle de Louga, Justice indigène 1912, Diambour septentrional, May 20, 1912.

95. 17 G 39 (7), Politique indigène, Instructions de Ponty à Gouverneur Général p.i., Jan. 12, 1912. On Murid organization of commerce, see 13 G 67, Mémoire: Islam dans le domaine économique, p. 23; 13 G 69 (38), Fiche de renseignement: Cheikh Anta Mbacke; and Paul Marty's comments on Shakh Ibra Fall, the "economic minister" of the Murids, in *Etudes sur l'Islam au Sénégal,* vol. 1, 246.

96. Interview, M'Baye Guéye Sylla, Darou-Mousty, July 28, 1995.

97. The head tax was lowered in bad years.

98. On the head tax and its collection, see 2 G series. Some dossiers in the 2 D series (archives des cercles) give detailed information on the collection of the head tax.

99. For statistics on Bawol, see 2 G 11-42, Cercle de Baol, Rapports mensuels d'ensemble.

100. These figures give a general idea of income based on available data. My calculations assume that peanuts were the sole source of peasant cash income and that all of Bawol's production was commercialized locally.

101. Records of *prestation* (*corvée,* or forced labor) service occur in the 2 G series periodic reports.

102. The reports in the 2 G series contain sections on prisons, listing prisoners, reasons for arrest, and lengths of sentences.

103. This figure is based on 4 E 10, Conseil Général, which contains a series of analyses of Senegal's budget, prepared in anticipation of the reform of the Conseil Général. The most detailed report is 4 E 10 (40), "Rapport sur l'organisation administrative et financière du Senegal," by Governor-General Clozel, June 10, 1916. Similar documents are filed in 4 E 7 to 4 E 9, prepared from 1904 to 1914: e.g., 4 E 8 (65–66), Conseil Général, Session Feb. 17–22, 1912, Lieutenant Gouverneur à Gouverneur Général, which presents the new tax amounts voted that year.

104. Data from 2 G 11-42, Cercle de Baol, Rapports mensuels d'ensemble.

105. Small children were not counted in the census data created for the tax rolls.

106. Canton chiefs were major agricultural producers, although no administrative records cover this. Records on chiefs who were in debt and financial statements after the death of chiefs show they relied on income from peanuts to make major purchases and pay off debts. See 2 D 7-10, Cercle de Baol, Corres. 1911, Chemise 7: Succession de Salmon Fall.

107. Georges Hardy, *Une conquete morale: L'enseignement en AOF* (Paris, 1917), 155.

108. 13 G 70 contains applications for appointment.

109. 4 E 8 (65 and 66), Conseil Général, Session Feb. 17–22, 1912, Lieutenant Gouverneur à Gouverneur Général, March 23, 1912.

110. 4 E 10 (40), Conseil Général, Rapport sur l'organisation administrative et financière du Sénégal, Gouverneur Général Clozel à Ministre des Colonies.

111. Pheffer, "Railroads and Aspects of Social Change," 525, Table 19.

112. 2 G 11-42, Baol, Rapports mensuels d'ensemble.

113. See 1 G 296 (7), Monographie: Cercle de Thiès 1903–1904, pp. 14–18; and 2 G 11-42, Baol, Rapports mensuels d'ensemble.

114. 1 G 296 (7), Monographie: Cercle de Thiès 1903–1904.

115. J 19 (100), Rapport: Organisation de l'enseignement au Sénégal, 1909, pp. 3–5.

116. Hardy, *Une conquete morale*, 111–12.

117. These trends are emphasized by Paul Pelissier, in *Les paysans du Sénégal*.

CONCLUSION

If I had to pick a date marking the end of monarchy and slavery, and the triumph of Islam and emancipation, the date would be 1904. A balance sheet of losses and gains on these issues shows their intertwined histories.

Words and drums of praise for the monarchy come to a symbolic end in 1902, with the death of Demba War Sall. He was the last important figure of the old regime, a historic persona in both epic poems and French archives. His sons and nephews would inherit a portion of his power, but none of his fame. Ironically, Demba War Sall, a royal slave, was the most vocal defender of the slave trade and slavery in Wolof society. Demba War was also one of the most determined enemies of the Murid order. Demba War was one of the advocates of Amadu Bamba's arrest (or worse) in 1895, and from 1900 until his death he denounced the Murid settlements as havens for runaway slaves, kidnapped children, and other undesirables. On the other hand, Demba War was a loyal ally of the French and a friend of merchants and politicians from Saint-Louis. Colonial chiefs fought rearguard actions, but could not impose their agenda on the crucial issues of slavery and migration.

The conquest was a turning point for the monarchy. The Wolof sources that have informed my interpretation of the conquest explain the rapid decline of the monarchy. The bard's narrative presents Lat Joor as the last *ceddo* king, who died for honor, and Demba War as a patriot defending the traditions of Kajoor. When the bard's narrative is read alongside information from the Muslim party in Kajoor and the Murid order, it becomes clear that the monarchy had little legitimacy despite its firm grasp on power. Marty and Cruise O'Brien exaggerated Lat Joor's Muslim credentials, linking him erroneously to Amadu Bamba and the Murid order. Most Muslims detested the monarchy and welcomed the restraints placed upon aristocratic power by the conquest.

The decline of aristocratic power after 1886 was the last chapter in a long, bitter struggle between monarchy and Islam that continued after the conquest. The first new activity in this war was the persecution of the Murid order from 1888 onward by the Wolof chiefs who ruled Kajoor for the French. But the conquest sapped the power of the aristocracy. After 1886 they could not make war, or pillage, or use force against their enemies. The flight of slaves and the rapid transformation of the remaining slaves into clients further undermined aristocratic wealth and power. Despite Demba War Sall's efforts, the slave trade ended within a decade, and slavery was a shadow of its former self when the French completed their survey in 1904. The Colonial chiefs lacked the power to stop slaves from leaving their masters or peasants from migrating. French attitudes contributed to this outcome by keeping Wolof chiefs on a short leash. Demba War's attacks on Amadu Bamba and the Murid order reflect a new colonial strategy in the old war between monarchy and Islam. Demba War tried to stop one current of migration out of Kajoor by striking at its cause, the Murid order, which attracted both runaway slaves and peasants. Claiming that Amadu Bamba was preparing holy war, Demba War and his allies in Njambur tried to use the French as their agents against the Murids. This ploy succeeded in rousing the French to action, but had unexpected results. Amadu Bamba's exile in 1895 and return to Senegal in 1902, only to be denounced and exiled once again in 1903 and to return again in 1907, is a parable about the decline of monarchy. Each time Amadu Bamba returned he was stronger, and by 1907 his accusers were either dead or disgraced. Mbakhane Diop, his enemy in 1903, would later become his disciple and client. By 1904, there were no Wolof chiefs in Kajoor or Bawol who could credibly claim to represent the monarchy.

In this book I have argued for an early decline of slavery. The export economy declined sharply after the conquest, which I interpret as a sign that many slaves fled in this period of instability. During the period of indirect rule that followed, French records are sparse, but I assume that slaves continued to flee, which reduced the impact of slave imports between 1883 and 1895. After 1895 there was only a small clandestine slave trade, insufficient to maintain slave populations. Most runaways escaped slavery by becoming peasants in stages, first as migrants in peasant households, and then as peasant farmers in nearby regions where land was available. The main directions of movement were south and east, from Njambur and central Kajoor to Bawol and Saalum. The general direction followed paths that predated colonialism, Murid Islam, and the railroad. These migrant streams all developed rapidly with the development of peanut exports. For a runaway slave, the main requirements for success after initial flight were some savings, some distance from the point of departure, and fluency in Wolof sufficient to negotiate a position as a migrant farmer. Some runaways became Murids. The Murid order offered food, shelter, and the promise of land and marriage in the near future. Other slaves joined migrants seeking land in Bawol and Saalum, in regions eager to attract settlers.

These movements were well under way by 1904, when the French counted slaves. Rather than disputing the general findings of the census, I see the census as confirming the decline of slavery. By 1912, the Murid order had attracted a following of 70,000. Many were immigrants, who had left homelands elsewhere to settle in new Murid villages and towns. If only one-third of the 50,000 migrants were former slaves (no more than in the population as a whole in 1880), then by itself the Murid order accounts for about 16,000 runaway slaves. Many more would have to be added to that number to account for slaves resettling in non-Murid villages in Bawol and Saalum. Sereer regions in western Bawol, which were historically hostile to slavery, absorbed many migrants and runaway slaves in the same period.

By 1904, two Muslim leaders had come to symbolize the Muslim triumph over the monarchy. Al-Hajj Malik Sy, in Tivaouane, was the successor to the Muslim party in Kajoor. Kajoor's Muslims might have paraphrased what the French had said about letting Màbba accomplish part of his mission, the destruction of the *ceddo*, applying the same wisdom to French colonial rule. This was the essence of Malik Sy's famous justification of obedience to the French authorities: the French had ended the warfare and enslavement that characterized the old regime. The alliance between the French and the aristocracy was fatal to both in the long run. As servants of French power, Wolof aristocrats became the enforcers of the colonial regime. As the aristocrats' legitimacy declined, the French colonial state lost legitimacy as well. Muslims benefited most from the slow death of aristocratic power.

In contemporary Senegal, Malik Sy's friendly relations with the French would fit less easily with postcolonial attitudes than Amadu Bamba's conflicts with the colonial regime. I have focused on the Murids because of their conflicts with the monarchy and colonial chiefs and their ties to the history of slave emancipation. Those conflicts emerged directly from the creation of new Murid settlements, which attracted migrants from settled Wolof regions. Nevertheless, the attitude of Malik Sy was more typical. His branch of the Tijani order defined Islam for the majority of Wolof

Muslims in the period studied. His order won the adhesion of many established Muslim families and gained an important following in the Four Communes. Although Malik Sy was not directly involved in conflicts with colonial chiefs, his view of history expressed criticism of the monarchy and the old regime. Colonial rule was welcomed because it had ended the warfare and enslavement that typified the old order in the eyes of Muslims.

By contrast, the urban "Senegalese" party had not yet won the political battles that would give it a prominent historical role in the period from 1914 to 1945. The election of François Carpot, the first *métis* deputy, in 1902, symbolized the beginnings of this process. Carpot, a lawyer, was a politician rather than a merchant, and his political rise paralleled the decline of merchant-politicians like Justin Devès. The election of Galandou Diouf as the representative of Rufisque in 1907 was the first concrete victory for African *originaires*, who would play a crucial role after 1914. In this book I have followed the activities of *originaire* activists in the protectorate. Mody Mbaye, who worked with Carpot and Diouf, symbolizes the aspirations of this group, who campaigned against "native feudalism" and pressured the French to adopt policies of direct rule that would favor urban Africans from the Four Communes. The racially conscious, "French," and modernist politics of the *originaires* had not yet won a decisive victory over policies designed to protect the declining fortunes of African merchants.

This last point simply reinforces the argument that the conflict between the monarchy and Islam, with its roots in the nineteenth century, was the dominant force for change in the period between 1860 and 1914. The triumph of Islam and the decline of slavery reflected the Muslim view that God alone was king in the aftermath of the colonial conquest.

BIBLIOGRAPHY

ARCHIVAL SOURCES CITED.
ARCHIVES NATIONALES DU SENEGAL (ANS).

Archives of the Government General: Dakar[1]
E Series: Legislative Councils

4 E 6, Conseil Général, 1903–1907. Session 1904. Projet Roume.
4 E 7, Conseil Général, 1908.
4 E 8, Conseil Général. Session Feb. 1912.
4 E 9, Conseil Général. Session 1913.
4 E 10, Conseil Général. Rapport sur l'organisation administrative et financière du Sénégal, Clozel, June 10, 1916. Projet Clozel, 1916.

1 G Series: Monographs, Studies

1 G 296, Monographie: Cercle de Thiès, 1903–1904.
1 G 330, Chemise 5, Rapport sur les coutumes, Sine-Saloum, 1907.
1 G 333, Monographie: Thiès, 1910.
1 G 337, Monographie: Thiès.

2 G Series: Periodic Reports

2 G 2-32, Rapport mensuel, Cercle de Thiès, July 1902.
2 G 2-34, Rapport mensuel, Baol Oriental, 1902.
2 G 2-35, Rapport politique, Baol, 1902–1903.
2 G 3-35, Rapport politique, Diourbel, Sep. 1903, Dec. 1903.

---

1. This designation describes files in the French West Africa (AOF) archive. They are divided by series, represented by combinations of letters and numbers.There are two subdivisions, one before World War I, with simple combinations of letters and numbers (13 G 79), and the other after World War I, with more complex combinations (13 G 6-17). I have listed important documents or file subdivisions (*chemises*) when documents are cited more than once.

2 G 8-10, Rapport, 1908.

2 G 11-42, Baol: Rapports mensuels d'ensemble, 1911.

13 G Series: Senegal, Political Affairs

13 G 12-17, Dossier: Mourides 1912–1932. Chemise, Amadou Bamba, 1912. Chemise, Décoration, 1918–1919.

13 G 43, Correspondance.

13 G 44, Correspondance.

13 G 50, Chefs indigènes.

13 G 51, Chefs indigènes.

13 G 57, Cayor, Correspondance avec les chefs indigènes, 1861.

13 G 67, Mémoire: Islam dans le domaine économique. Chemise, Bou Kounta, June 1915.

13 G 68, Fiches de renseignements sur les marabouts.

13 G 69, Fiches sur marabouts, Baol.

13 G 70, Politique indigéne.

13 G 71, Politique indigène. Rapport sur les chefs indigènes, Camille Guy, 1907.

13 G 72, Politique indigène, 1912–1914. Instructions générales sur le recrutement des troupes noires, 1912.

13 G 75, Politique indigène, 1916.

13 G 76, Politique indigène. Rapports, 1905–1909. Dossier Salmon Fall, 1905.

13 G 77, Dossier Mody Mbaye.

13 G 78, Politique indigène.

13 G 79, Politique indigène.

13 G 257, Cayor, Correspondance, 1861–1866.

13 G 258, Cayor, Correspondance, 1870–1874.

13 G 259, Cayor.

13 G 260, Cayor.

13 G 264, Cayor.

13 G 265, Cayor.

13 G 294, Baol.

13 G 295, Djolloff: Agitation des Peulhs, 1905.

13 G 296, Affaire Chautemps, 1904.

13 G 297, Affaire Chautemps, 1904.

13 G 304, Gorée: Correspondance, 1862–1864.

17 G Series: Political Affairs, French West Africa

17 G 39, Politique indigène, AOF, 1912–1917.

17 G 47-17, Quatre communes: État juridique, rapport, Ponty, 1913.

18 G Series: Administrative Affairs

18 G 62-17, Commandement indigène, 1917.

18 G 78-17, Collectivité Lebou de Dakar.

19 G Series: Islamic Affairs

19 G 1, Affaires musulmanes. Mesures prises en raison de l'état de guerre, 1914.

20 G Series: Elections

20 G 12, Elections législatives, 1902.

20 G 17, Elections. Rapport de l'Inspecteur Verrier, 1905.
20 G 18, Elections: Conseil Général, 1909.

J Series: Education
J 7, Rapport sur le Collège des fils de chefs, 1892.
J 19, Rapport: Organisation de l'enseignment au Sénégal, 1909.

K Series: Slavery
K 11, Esclavage.
K 12, Esclavage.
K 13, Esclavage.
K 15, Captivité et esclavage, 1900–1903.
K 16, Enquête sur la captivité, 1903–1905.
K 17, Rapport sur la captivité de M. Poulet, 1905.
K 18, Rapports sur l'esclavage au Sénégal.

Archives des Cercles: Saint-Louis[2]

2 D 7-1, Baol, Correspondance, 1888–1892.
2 D 7-2, Cercle de Baol, Correspondance, 1893–1895.
2 D 7-3, Cercle de Baol, Correspondance, 1911.
2 D 7-6, Cercle de Baol, Rapports, 1891–1911. Chemise 3, Enquête sur l'autorité de la justice . . . chez les indigènes du Cercle du Baol (Tribu des Sérères), Leon Dupuy, April 1911.
2 D 7-7, Baol, Rapports, tournées, 1898.
2 D 7-10, Baol, Rapports, dossiers, 1899–1913. Chemise 7, Succession de Salmon Fall. Chemise 8, Affaire Mar Codé Fall. Chemise 9, Affaire Alioune Sylla, 1914–1916.
2 D 8-2, Cercle de Sine-Saloum, Correspondance, 1912.
2 D 8-15, Cercle de Sine-Saloum, Correspondance. Chemise 3. Chemise 8, Saer Gueye.
2 D 9-4, Cercle de Louga, Correspondance, 1889–1898.
2 D 9-5, Cercle de Louga, Correspondance, 1899–1901, Enquête sur l'émigration, Georges Poulet, 1899.
2 D 9-6, Cercle de Louga, Correspondance.
2 D 9-7, Cercle de Louga, Correspondance, 1907–1910.
2 D 9-8, Cercle de Louga, Correspondance, affaires diverses.
2 D 9-13, Cercle de Louga, Rapports, tournées, missions, 1891–1907.
2 D 9-16, Cercle de Louga, Correspondance. Dossier: Personnel, Justice indigène, 1911.
2 D 9-19, Cercle de Louga, Correspondance, 1915. Plaintes et réclamations, 1910.
2 D 9-20, Cercle de Louga. Chemise 10 bis, Amadou Bamba, 1908. Chemise 11, Incidents de frontière, Guett-Djollof. Chemise 12, Affaire Grandry. Chemise 13, Peulhs, 1918.
2 D 9-21, Cercle de Louga, Justice indigène, 1912.

---

2. These dossiers contain correspondence between the lieutenant governor and the commandants in the protectorate. Many of these files have recently been reclassified, but I use the numbers in use when I did my research.

2 D 13-3, Cercle de Cayor, Correspondance, 1898.

2 D 13-4, Correspondance, 1901–1902

2 D 13-5, Cercle de Dakar-Thiès, Correspondance, 1903.

2 D 13-6, Cercle de Cayor, Correspondance, 1909.

2 D 13-7, Cercle de Thiès, Correspondance, 1910–1914.

2 D 13-8, Cercle de Thiès, Correspondance, 1915–1917.

2 D 13-14, Cercle de Thiès, Rapports, tournées, missions. Rapport Sidi Mohammed, 1893. Rapport de tournée de Prempain, August 14–20, 1903.

2 D 13-20, Cercle de Thiès, Correspondance, dossiers, 1912–1918. Chemise 11, Affaire Babacar Mbodj-Abdel Kader, 1912.

2 D 14-2, Cercle de Cayor, Correspondance.

2 D 14-3, Cercle de Cayor, Correspondance, 1901–1902

2 D 14-4, Cercle de Cayor, Correspondance, 1903–1905.

2 D 14-5, Cercle de Tivaouane, Correspondance, 1909–1911.

2 D 14-6, Cercle de Tivaouane, Correspondance, 1912–1914. Rapport du tournée dans le M-Baouar.

2 D 14-11, Cercle de Tivaouane. Chemise, Réorganisation de 1909. Chemise, Réorganisation, 1911–1912. Chemise, Incidents de frontière, 1913.

2 D 14-13, Cercle de Tivaouane.

INTERVIEWS, RECORDINGS, MANUSCRIPTS.

Audiocassettes, CDs Cited in Text

Ammar, Modou Mamoun. *Waxtaan ci yoonu geej.* Audiocassette.

Lo, Cheikh. *Né la Thiass.* World Circuit, 1996. CD.

Mbaye, Ngirane. *Waxtaan ci Sëriñ Tuuba.* Audiocassette.

Samb, Bouchera. *Waxtaan ci mbir tuuki Sëriñ Tuuba yonnu geej.* Tape 1, side 1.

Samb, Bouchera. *Waxtaan ci mbir tuuki Maam Cerno ak seex Ibra Faal.* Audiocassette.

Interviews, Field Notes

Dieng, Pathé (Serigne). At Darou-Marnane, July 26, 1995.

Gueye, Mor. Dakar, in the Tileen Market, July 20, 1995.

Mbacké, Bassirou Anta Niang (Serigne). At Darou-Mousty (Kajoor), July 25 and July 29, 1995.

Moussa Ka, "Biography of Maam Ceron," Wolof Poem. Manuscript.

Sylla, M'Baye Guéye (Serigne). At Darou-Mousty, July 28, 1995.

Field notes, Darou-Mousty, July 1995.

Collective interview, Bandia elders: Farba Cisse, principal informant, March 28, 1989.

Cisse, Ibrahima. At Bandia (Bawol), July 16, 1995.

Faye, Ablaye (Latir). At Bandia , July 18, 1995.

Loem, Nguere, and Seck, Moussa. At Bandia, July 15, 1995.

N'Dione, Babacar (Serigne). At Bandia, July 14, 1995.

Ndione, Babacar; Pouye, Malik; Sène, Ibrahima; Sène, Ousmane. At Bandia, July 19, 1995.
Seck, Samba. At Bandia, July 17, 1995.
Field notes, Bandia, July 1995.

PUBLISHED SOURCES

Newspapers, Official Publications

Annuaire du Ministère des Colonies, 1904.
Atlas National du Sénégal (Paris, 1977.)
La Démocratie du Sénégal, 1914, 1915.
La Dépêche de Toulouse, May 18, 1904.
Journal Officiel du Sénégal, 1892, 1894.
Moniteur du Sénégal et Dépendances, 1856, 1857.
Le Petit Sénégalais, Oct. 14, 1886; April 7, 1918.
Le Réveil du Sénégal, Oct. 10, 1886; Nov. 14, 1886.

Books, Articles, and Dissertations

Abdallah, Dedoud ould. "Guerre sainte ou sédition blamable? *Nasiha* de shaikh Sa'd Bu contre le *jihad* de son frère Ma al-Ainin," in *Le temps des marabouts: Itinéraires et stratégies islamiques en Afrique Occidentale Française v. 1880-1960,* ed. David Robinson and Jean-Louis Triaud, 119-53. Paris, 1997.
Adam, Jean. *L'arachide: Culture, produits, commerce, amelioration de la production.* Paris, 1908.
Andrew, C.M. *Theophile Delcassé and the Making of the Entente Cordiale.* London, 1968.
Andrew, C.M. and A.S. Kanya-Forstner. "The French 'Colonial Party': Its Composition, Aims and Influence, 1885–1914." *Historical Journal* 14 (1971): 99–128.
———. "The *Groupe Colonial* in the French Chamber of Deputies, 1892–1932." *Historical Journal*, 17 (1974): 837–66.
Andrew, C.M., P. Grupp, and A.S. Kanya-Forstner. "Le mouvement colonial français et ses principales personalités." *Révue Française d'Histoire d'Outre-Mer* 62 (1975): 640–73.
Ane, Mouhamed Moustapha. *La vie de Cheikh Ahmadou Bamba.* Translated by Amar Samb. Dakar, n. d.
Angrand, Armand Pierre. *Les Lebous de la presqu'île de Cap Vert.* Dakar, 1950.
Atanda, J.A. *The New Oyo Empire: Indirect Rule and Change in Western Nigeria 1894–1934.* New York, 1973.
Aujas, L. "Les Sèréres du Sénégal: Moeurs et coutumes de droit privé." *Bulletin du Comité des Études Historiques et Scientifiques sur l'Afrique Occidentale Française* 14 (1931): 293–333.
Ba, Abdou Bouri. "Essai sur L'histoire du Saloum et du Rip." *Bulletin de l'Institut Fondamental de l'Afrique Noire* 38, B (1976): 845–47.
Ba, Oumar, ed. *La pénétration française au Cayor.* Paris, 1976.
———, ed. *Ahmadou Bamba face aux autorités coloniales.* Dakar and Paris, 1982.

Ba, Ousmane Tamsir. "Essai historique sur le Rip." *Bulletin L'Institut Fondamental de L'Afrique Noire* 19, B (1957): 564–91.

Balandier, Georges, and Paul Mercier. *Les pêcheurs Lebou: Particularisme et évolution.* Saint-Louis, 1952.

Balesi, Charles. *From Adversaries to Comrades-in-Arms: West Africa and the French Military, 1885–1918.* Waltham, Mass., 1979.

Barry, Boubacar. *Le Royaume du Waalo: Le Sénégal avant la conquête.* Paris, 1972.

———. *Senegambia and the Atlantic Slave Trade.* Cambridge, 1998.

Bates, Robert. *Essays on the Political Economy of Rural Africa.* Cambridge, 1983.

Batude, Fernand. *L'arachide au Senegal.* Paris, 1941.

Bay, Edna G. *Wives of the Leopard: Gender, Politics, and Culture in the Kingdom of Dahomey.* Charlottesville, Va., 1998.

Berry, Sara. *No Condition Is Permanent: The Social Consequences of Agrarian Change in Sub-Saharan Africa.* Madison, Wis., 1993.

Boilat, David, *Esquisses sénégalaises.* Paris, 1853.

Bouche, Denise. *L'enseignment dans les territoires français de l'Afrique Occidentale.* 2 vols. Paris, 1974.

Bousbina, Said. "Al-Hajj Malik Sy: Sa chaîne spirituelle dans la Tijaniyya et sa position à l'égard de la présence française au Sénégal." In *Le temps des marabouts: Itinéraires et stratégies islamiques en Afrique Occidentale Francçaise v. 1880–1960*, eds. David Robinson and Jean-Louis Triaud, 181-98. Paris, 1999.

Brenner, Louis. *West African Sufi: The Religious Heritage and Spiritual Search of Cerno Bokar Saalif Taal.* Berkeley, Calif., 1984.

Brett-Smith, Sarah C. *The Making of Bamana Sculpture: Creativity and Gender.* Cambridge, 1994.

Brooks, George. "Peanuts and Colonialism: Consequences of the Commercialization of Peanuts in West Africa, 1830–1870." *Journal of African History* 16 (1975): 29–54.

Camara, Camille. *Saint Louis du Sénégal: Evolution d'une ville en milieu africain.* Dakar, 1968.

Campistron, M. "Coutume Ouolof du Cayor (Cercle de Thiès)." in *Coutumiers juridiques de l'Afrique Occidentale Française: Volume I, Sénégal*, 119–46. Paris, 1939.

Capet, Marcel. *Traité d'économie coloniale. Les économies d'AOF.* Paris, 1958.

Carrère, Frédéric, and Paul Holle. *De la Sénégambie française.* Paris, 1855.

Charbonneau, Jean, and René Charbonneau. *Marchés et marchands d'Afrique noire.* Paris, 1961.

Charles, Eunice A. *Precolonial Senegal: The Jolof Kingdom, 1800–1890.* Boston, 1971.

Chayanov, A.V. *The Theory of Peasant Economy.* Ed. Daniel Thorner et. al. Homewood, Ill., 1966.

Clark, Andrew F. *From Frontier to Backwater: Economy and Society in the Upper Senegal Valley (West Africa), 1850–1920.* Lanham, Md., 1999.

Colvin, Lucie G. "Kayor and Its Diplomatic Relations with Saint Louis du Sénégal, 1763–1861." Ph.D. dissertation, Columbia University, 1972.

———. "Islam and the State of Kajoor: A Case of Successful Resistance to Jihad." *Journal of African History* 15, no. 4 (1974): 587–606.

Comaroff, Jean. *Body of Power, Spirit of Resistance: The Culture and History of a South African People.* Chicago, 1985.

Conklin, Alice L. *A Mission to Civilize: The Republican Idea of Empire in France and West Africa, 1895–1930.* Stanford, Calif., 1997.

Conrad, David C. *A State of Intrigue: The Epic of Bamana Segu according to Tayiru Banbera.* Oxford, 1990.

Cooper, Frederick. "Africa and the World Economy." in *Confronting Historical Paradigms: Peasants, Labor, and the Capitalist World System in Africa and Latin America,* eds. Frederick Cooper, Allen F. Isaacman, Florencia E. Mallon, William Roseberry, and Steve J. Stern, 84–186. Madison, Wis., 1993.

Copans, Jean. *Les marabouts de l'arachide: La confrérie mouride et les paysans du Sénégal.* Paris, 1980.

Copans, Jean, Phillipe Couty, Jean Roch, and Guy Rocheteau. *Maintenance sociale et changement économique au Sénégal: Doctrine économique et pratique du travail chez les Mourides.* Paris, 1972.

Coquery-Vidrovitch, Catherine. "De la traite des esclaves à l'exportation de palme et des palmistes au Dahomey." in *The Development of Indigenous Trade and Markets in West Africa,* ed. Claude Meillassoux, London, 1971. 107–23

Coulon, Christian. *Le marabout et le prince: Islam et pouvoir au Sénégal.* Paris, 1981.

Coumboulives, Margaret. *L'organisation coopérative au Sénégal.* Paris, 1967.

Courtet, M. *Étude sur le Sénégal.* Paris, 1903.

Cruise O'Brien, Donal B. *The Mourides of Senegal: The Political and Economic Organization of an Islamic Brotherhood.* Oxford, 1971.

———. *Saints and Politicians. Essays in the Organization of a Senegalese Peasant Society.* Cambridge, 1975.

Cruise O'Brien, Rita. *White Society in Black Africa: The French in Senegal.* London, 1972.

David, Philippe. *Les navétanes: Histoire des migrants saisonniers de l'arachide en Sénégambie des origines à nos jours.* Dakar-Abidjan, 1980.

Debien, G., ed. "Journal du Docteur Corre en pays sérère (Décembre 1876–Janvier 1877)." *Bulletin de l'Institut Fondamental de l'Afrique Noire,* 26, B (1964): 532–600.

Delafosse, Maurice. *Haut-Sénégal-Niger.* 3 volumes. Paris, 1912.

Diallo, Mamadou. "Galandou Diouf." Mémoire de maîtrise, Université de Dakar, 1972.

Dieng, Bassirou, ed. *L'épopée du Kajoor.* Dakar, 1993.

Diop, Abdoulaye Bara. *La société Wolof: Les sytemes d'inégalité et de domination.* Paris, 1981.

Diop, Amadou Bamba. "Lat Dior et le problème musulman," *Bulletin de l'Institut Fondamental de l'Afrique Noire,* B, 28 (1966): 493–539.

Diop, Aram, Oumar Ben Khatab Dia, and Jean-Claude Galdin. *Jukib Tanneefu Baat-Yu-Sax/Recueil de Textes Choisis.* Dakar, Centre de linguistique appliquée de Dakar, 1975.

Diouf, Mamadou. *Le Kajoor au XIXe siecle: Pouvoir ceddo et conquête coloniale.* Paris, 1990.

Duguay-Clédor, Amadou. *La Bataille de Guîlé.* Ed. Mbaye Gueye, Dakar, 1985.

Dumont, Fernand. *La pensée religieuse d'Amadou Bamba: Fondateur du Mouridisme sénégalais* Dakar, 1975.

Echenberg, Myron. *Colonial Conscripts: The "Tirailleurs Sénégalais" in French West Africa, 1857–1960.* Portsmouth, N.H.,1991.

Eltis, David. *Economic Growth and the Ending of the Transatlantic Slave Trade.* New York, 1987.

———. *The Rise of African Slavery in the Americas.* Cambridge, 2000.

Faidherbe, Louis. "Notice historique sur le Cayor." *Bulletin de la Société de Géographie de Paris,* series 7, vol. 4 (1883): 527–64.

Fal, Arame, Rosine Santos, and Jean Léonce Doneux. *Dictionnaire wolof-français.* Paris, 1990.

Fall, Tanor Latsoukabé. "Recueil sur la vie des Damel." *Bulletin de l'Institut Fondamental de l'Afrique Noire,* B, 36 (1974): 93–145.

Falola, Toyin. "Money and Informal Credit Institutions in Colonial Western Nigeria." In *Money Matters: Instability, Values and Social Payments in the Modern History of West African Communities,* ed. Jane I. Guyer, 169–87. Portsmouth, N.H., 1995.

Fayet, J.C. "Coutume des Ouolof musulmans (Cercle du Baol)." in *Coutumiers juridiques de l'Afrique Occidentale Française: Volume 1, Sénégal,* 147–93. Paris, 1939.

Fields, Karen E. *Revival and Rebellion in Colonial Central Africa.* Princeton, N.J., 1985.

Fisher, Allan G.B. and Humphrey J. Fisher, *Slavery and Muslim Society in Africa.* New York, 1971.

Foner, Eric. *Nothing but Freedom: Emancipation and Its Legacy.* Baton Rouge, 1983.

Fouquet, Joseph. *La traite des arachides dans le pays de Kaolack.* (Saint-Louis, 1958).

Freeman-Grenville, G.S.P. *The Muslim and Christian Calendar: Being Tables for the Conversion of Muslim and Christian Dates from Hijra to the Year A.D. 2000.* London, 1963.

Gamble, David P. *The Wolof of Senegambia.* London, 1957.

Ganier, Germaine. "Lat Dior et le chemin de fer de l'arachide." *Bulletin de l'Institut Fondamental de l'Afrique Noire* 27, B (1965): 223–81.

Gastellu, Jean-Marc. *L'égalitarisme économique des Serer du Sénégal.* Paris, 1981.

Geismar, L. *Recueil des coutumes civiles des races du Sénégal.* Saint-Louis, 1933.

Gerresch, Claudine. "Le livre de metrique 'Mubayyin al-Iskal' du Cadi Madiakhate Kala: Introduction historique, texte arabe, traduction et glossaire." *Bulletin de l'Institut Fondamental de l'Afrique Noire* 36, B, no. 4 (1974): 714–68.

Godinho, Victorino. *L'économie de l'empire portugais au XVe et XVIe siécles.* Paris, 1969.

Gueye, Mbaye. "L'Affaire Chautemps et la suppression de l'esclavage de case au Sénégal." *Bulletin de l'Institut Fondamental de l'Afrique Noire.* 27, B, nos. 3–4 (1965): 543–59.

Gueye, Mbaye, and A. Adu Boahen. "African Initiatives and Resistance in West Africa." In *UNESCO General History of Africa,* Vol. 7, New York, 1985.

Guiraud, Xavier. *L'arachide sénégalaise: Monographie d'économie coloniale.* Paris, 1937.

Guyer, Jane I. "Introduction: The Currency Interface and Its Dynamics," in *Money Matters: Instability, Values and Social Payments in the Modern History of West African Communities*, ed. Jane I. Guyer, 1–33. Portsmouth, N.H., 1995.

Hanson, John H. *Migration, Jihad, and Muslim Authority in West Africa: The Futanke Colonies in Karta*. Bloomington, Ind., 1996.

Hardy, Georges. *Une conquête morale: L'enseignement en AOF*. Paris, 1917.

———. *La mise en valeur du Sénégal de 1815 à 1854*. Paris, 1921.

Harms, Robert. "Sustaining the System: Trading Towns along the Middle Zaire." In *Women and Slavery in Africa*, eds. Claire C. Robertson and Martin A. Klein, 95–110. Madison, Wis., 1983.

Harries, Patrick. *Work, Culture and Identity: Migrant Laborers in Mozambique and South Africa, c. 1860–1910*. Portsmouth, N.H., 1994.

Hill, Polly. *The Migrant Cocoa Farmers of Southern Ghana: A Study in Rural Capitalism*. Cambridge, 1963.

———. "From Slavery to Freedom: The Case of Farm-Slavery in Nigerian Hausaland," *Comparative Studies in Society and History* 18 (1976): 395–426.

Hogendorn, Jan S. *Nigerian Groundnut Exports: Origins and Early Development*. Zaria, 1978.

Holt, Thomas C. *The Problem of Freedom: Race, Labor, and Politics in Jamaica and Britain, 1832–1938*. Baltimore, 1992.

Hopkins, Anthony G. "The Currency Revolution in South-West Nigeria in the Late Nineteenth Century." *Journal of the Historical Society of Nigeria* 3 (1966): 471–83.

———. "Economic Imperialism in West Africa: Lagos, 1880–92." *Economic History Review* 21 (1968): 580–606.

———. *An Economic History of West Africa*. New York, 1973.

Irvine, Judith T. "Caste and Communication in a Wolof Village." Ph.D. dissertation, University of Pennsylvania, 1973.

Isaacman, Allen. "Peasants and Rural Social Protest in Africa." *African Studies Review* 33, no. 2 (1990): 1–59.

Johnson, G. Wesley. *The Emergence of Black Politics in Senegal: The Struggle for Power in the Four Communes, 1900–1920*. Stanford, Calif., 1971.

Johnson, John William. *The Epic of Son-Jara: A West African Tradition*. Bloomington, Ind., 1986.

July, Robert. *The Origins of Modern African Thought*. New York, 1968.

Kanya-Forstner, A.S. *The Conquest of the Western Sudan: A Study in French Military Imperialism*. Cambridge, 1969.

Klein, Martin A. *Islam and Imperialism in Senegal: Sine-Saloum, 1847–1914*. Stanford, 1968.

———. "Social and Economic Factors in the Muslim Revolution in Senegambia." *Journal of African History* 13 (1972): 419–41.

———. "Women and Slavery in the Western Sudan." In *Women and Slavery in Africa*, eds. Claire C. Robertson and Martin A. Klein, Madison, Wis., 1983.

———. "Slavery and Emancipation in French West Africa." In *Breaking the Chains: Slavery, Bondage, and Emancipation in Modern Africa and Asia*, ed. Martin A. Klein, 171–96. Madison, Wis., 1993.

———. *Slavery and Colonial Rule in French West Africa*. Cambridge, 1998.

Klein, Martin A., and Richard Roberts. "The Banamba Slave Exodus of 1905 and the Decline of Slavery in the Western Sudan." *Journal of African History* 21 (1980): 375–94.

Kopytoff, Igor. "The Cultural Context of African Abolition." In *The End of Slavery in Africa*, eds. Suzanne Miers and Richard Roberts, 485–503. Madison, Wis., 1988.

Laborde, Cécile. *La confrérie layenne et les Lébou du Sénégal. Islam et culture traditionnelle en Afrique.* Bordeaux, 1995.

Landau, Paul S. *The Realm of the Word: Language, Gender and Christianity in a Southern African Kingdom.* Portsmouth, 1995.

Law, Robin, ed. *From Slave Trade to 'Legitimate' Commerce: The Commercial Tranistion in Nineteenth Century West Africa.* Cambridge, 1995.

Legier, Henri Jacques. "Institutions municipales et politique coloniale: Les Communes du Sénégal," *Revue Française d'Histoire d'Outre-Mer* 55 (1968): 414–64.

Lenz, Oskar. *Timbuktu: Reise durch Marokko, die Sahara und den Sudan.* 2 vols. Leipzig, 1884.

Leymarie, Isabelle. "The Role and Functions of the Griots among the Wolof of Senegal." Ph.D. dissertation, Columbia University, 1979.

Lovejoy, Paul E. "Plantations in the Economy of the Sokoto Caliphate." *Journal of African History*, 19 (1978): 341–68.

Lovejoy Paul E., and Hogendorn, Jan S. "The Reform of Slavery in Colonial Northern Nigeria." In *The End of Slavery in Africa*, eds. Suzanne Miers and Richard Roberts, 391–414. Madison, Wis., 1988.

———. "Revolutionary Mahdism and Resistance to Colonial Rule in the Sokoto Caliphate." *Journal of African History* 31 (1990): 217–44.

———. *Slow Death for Slavery: The Course of Abolition in Northern Nigeria, 1897–1936.* Cambridge, 1993.

Lovejoy, Paul E., and A. S. Kanya-Forstner. *Slavery and Its Abolition in French West Africa: The Official Reports of G. Poulet, E. Roume, and G. Deherme.* Madison, Wis., 1994.

Lovejoy, Paul E. and David Richardson. "Competing Markets for Male and Female Slaves: Prices in the Interior of West Africa, 1780–1850." *International Journal of African Historical Studies* 28 (1995): 261–93.

Lunn, Joe. "Memoirs of the Maelstrom: A Senegalese Oral History of the First World War." Ph.D. dissertation, University of Wisconsin-Madison, 1993.

———. *Memoirs of the Maelstrom: A Senegalese Oral History of the First World War.* Portsmouth, N.H., 1999.

———. "'Les Races Guerrières': Racial Preconceptions in the French Military about West African Soldiers during the First World War." *Journal of Contemporary History* 34, no. 4 (1999): 517–36.

Malik ibn Anas. *Al-Muwatta of Imam Malik ibn Anas: The First Formulation of Islamic Law.* Translated by Aisha Addurrahman Bewley. London, 1989.

Manchuelle, François. "Métis et colons: La famille Devès et l'émergence politique des Africains au Sénégal, 1881–1897." *Cahiers d' Études Africaines* 24 (1984): 477–504.

———. *Willing Migrants: Soninke Labor Diasporas, 1848–1960.* Athens, Ohio, 1997.

Mangin, Charles. *La Force Noire.* Paris, 1910.

Marcoccio, Katherine R. "Identity Conflict and Ceremonial Events in a Sereer Community of Saalum, Senegal." Ph.d. dissertation: Brandeis University, 1987.

Marty, Paul. *Etudes sur l'Islam au Sénégal.* 2 vols. Paris, 1917.

Mbacké, Serigne Bachir. "Les bienfaits de l'Eternel ou la biographie de Cheikh Ahmadou Bamba Mback" (translated by Khadim Mbacké) (1). *Bulletin de l'Institut Fondamental de l'Afrique Noire,* 42, B (1980): 554–631.

———. "Les bienfaits de l'Eternel ou la biographie de Cheikh Ahmadou Bamba Mbacké" (translated by Khadim Mbacké) (2). *Bulletin de l'Institut Fondamental de l'Afrique Noire* 43, B (1981): 47–108.

———. "Les bienfaits de l'Eternel ou la biographie de Cheikh Ahmadou Bamba Mbacké" (translated by Khadim Mbacké) (3). *Bulletin de l'Institut Fondamental de l'Afrique Noire,* 45, B (1983): 117–96.

Mbodj, Mohamed. "Un exemple d'économie coloniale. Le Sine-Saloum (Sénégal) de 1887 à 1940: Cultures arachidières et mutations sociales." Thése de troisième cycle, Université Paris VII, 1977–1978).

———. "Sénégal et dépendence: Le Sine-Saloum et l'arachide, 1887–1940." In *Sociétés paysannes du Tiers-Monde,* ed. C. Coquery-Vidrovitch, 139–54. Lille, 1980.

———. "The Abolition of Slavery in Senegal, 1820–1890: Crisis or the Rise of a New Entrepreneurial Class." in *Slavery, Bondage, and Emancipation in Modern Africa and Asia,* ed. Martin Klein, 197–211. Madison, Wis., 1993.

McNaughton, Patrick. *The Mande Blacksmiths: Knowledge, Power and Art in West Africa.* Bloomington, Ind., 1988.

Meillassoux, Claude. "Female Slavery." In *Women and Slavery in Africa* ed. Claire C. Robertson and Martin A. Klein, 49–68. Madison, Wis., 1983.

Meunier, Pierre. *Organisation et fonctionnement de la justice indigène en Afrique Occidentale Française.* Paris, 1914.

Miers, Suzanne, and Richard Roberts, eds. *The End of Slavery in Africa.* Madison, Wis., 1988.

Mintz, Sidney W. *Caribbean Transformations.* New York, 1974.

Moitt, Bernard. "Peanut Production and Social Change in the Dakar Hinterland: Kajoor and Bawol, 1840–1940." Ph.D. dissertation, University of Toronto, 1985.

———. "Slavery and Emancipation in Senegal's Peanut Basin: The Nineteenth and Twentieth Centuries." *International Journal of African Historical Studies* 22 (1989): 27–50.

Monteil, Vincent. "Le Dyolof et Al-Bouri Ndiaye." in Vincent Monteil, *Esquisses sénégalaises.* Dakar, 1966.

———. "Lat Dior, Damel du Cayor, et l'islamisation des Wolofs au XIXe siècle." In Vincent Monteil *Esquisses sénégalaises.* Dakar, 1966.

Moodie, T. Dunbar, with Vivienne Ndatshe. *Going for Gold: Men, Mines, and Migration.* Berkeley, Calif., 1994.

Munson, Henry, Jr. *Religion and Power in Morocco.* New Haven, Conn. 1993.

Myint, H. "The 'Classical Theory' of International Trade and the Underdeveloped Countries." *The Economic Journal* 68 (1958): 317–37.

N'Doye, E. "Migration des pionners Mourides wolof vers les terres neuves: Role de l'économique et du religieux." In *Modern Migrations in Western Africa,* ed. Samir Amin. Oxford, 1974.

Newbury, Colin. "The Formation of the Government General of French West Africa."
    Journal of African History 1 no. 1 (1960): 111–28.
————. "The Government General and Political Change in French West Africa." *St.
    Anthony's Papers*, No. 10, *African Affairs*, no. 1, London, 1961.
Nora, Pierre, ed. *Realms of Memory: Rethinking the French Past. Volume I: Conflicts
    and Divisions.* New York, 1996.
Okonjo, I.M. *British Administration in Nigeria, 1900–1950: A Nigerian View.* New
    York, 1974.
Olivier, Marcel. *Le Sénégal.* Paris, 1907.
Park, Mungo. *Travels in the Interior Districts of Africa in the Years 1795, 1796, and
    1797.* London, 1799.
Peel, J.D.Y. *Aladura: A Religious Movement among the Yoruba.* London, 1968.
Pelissier, Paul. *Les paysans du Sénégal.* Saint Yrieix, France, 1965.
Persell, Stuart Michael. *The French Colonial Lobby 1889–1938.* Stanford, Calif., 1983.
Pheffer, Paul E. "Railroads and Aspects of Social Change in Senegal." Ph.D. disserta-
    tion, University of Pennsylvania, 1975.
Ranger, Terence. "The Invention of Tradition in Colonial Africa." In *The Invention
    of Tradition*, eds. Eric Hobsbawn and Terence Ranger, 211–62. Cambridge,
    1983.
————. *Peasant Consciousness and Guerrilla War in Zimbabwe: A Comparative Study.*
    Berkeley, Calif., 1985.
Ransom, Roger L., and Richard Sutch. *One Kind of Freedom: The Economic Conse-
    quences of Emancipation.* Cambridge, 1977.
Ray, Benjamin C. *African Religions: Symbol, Ritual and Community.* Upper Saddle
    River, N.J. 2nd edition, 2000.
Renault, François. "L'abolition de l'esclavage au Sénégal: L'attitude de l'administration
    française (1848–1905)." *Revue Française d'Histoire d'Outre-Mer* 58, no. 210
    (1971): 5–80.
Richardson, David. "Slave Exports from West and West-Central Africa 1700–1800:
    New Estimates of Volume and Distribution," *Journal of African History*, 30
    (1989): 1–22.
Roberts, Richard. "Production and Reproduction of Warrior States: Segu Bambara and
    Segu Tokolor c. 1712–1890." *International Journal of African Historical Stud-
    ies* 13, no. 3 (1980): 389–419.
————. *Warriors, Merchants, and Slaves: The State and the Economy in the Middle
    Niger Valley, 1700–1914.* Stanford, Calif., 1987.
————. "The End of Slavery in the French Soudan, 1905–14." In *The End of Slavery
    in Africa*, eds. Suzanne Miers and Richard Roberts, 282–307. Madison, Wis.,
    1988.
Robinson, David. *Chiefs and Clerics: Abdul Bokar Kan and Futa Toro, 1853–1891.*
    Oxford, 1975.
————. *The Holy War of Umar Tal: The Western Sudan in the Mid-Nineteenth Cen-
    tury.* Oxford, 1985.
————. "French 'Islamic' Policy and Practice in Late Nineteenth Century Senegal."
    Journal of African History 29 (1988): 415:35.
————. "Beyond Resistance and Collaboration: Amadu Bamba and the Murids of
    Senegal." *Journal of Religion in Africa.* 21, no. 22 (1991): 149–71.

————. "Ethnography and Customary Law in Senegal. *Cahiers d'Études Africaines* 32, no. 2 (1992): 221–37.

————. "An Emerging Pattern of Cooperation between Colonial Authorities and Muslim Societies in Senegal and Mauritania," in *Le temps des marabouts*: Itineraires et stratégies islamiques en Afrique Occidentale Française v. 1880–1960, eds. David Robinson and Jean-Louis Triaud, 155-80. Paris, 1997.

————. "The Murids: Surveillance and Collaboration." *Journal of African History* 40 (1999): 193–213.

Rocheteau, G. *Système mouride et rapports sociaux traditionnels: Le travail collectif dans une communauté pionnière du Ferlo Occidentale.* Dakar, 1969.

————. "Pionniers Mourides: Colonisation des terres neuves et transformation d'une économie paysanne." *Cahiers ORSTROM*, serie sciences humaines, 12, no. 1 (1975): 19–53.

Rousseau, R. "Le Sénégal d'autrefois. Étude sur le Oualo, Cahiers de Yoro Dyâo." *Bulletin du Comité d'Études Historiques et Scientifiques sur l'Afrique Occidentale Française* 12 (1929): 133–211.

————. "Le Sénégal d'autrefois. Étude sur le Toube. Papiers de Rawane Boy" *Bulletin du Comité d'Études Historiques et Scientifiques sur l'Afrique Occidentale Française* 14 (1931): 1–31.

————. "Le Senegal d'autrefois. Étude sur le Cayor. Cahiers de Yoro Dyâo." *Bulletin du Comité d'Études Historiques et Scientifiques sur l'Afrique Occidentale Française* 16 (1933): 237–98.

Sabatié, A. *Le Sénégal: Sa conquête et son organisation (1364–1925).* Saint-Louis du Sénégal, 1925.

Saint-Martin, Yves. *Une source de l'histoire coloniale du Sénégal: Les rapports de situation politique (1871–1891).* Dakar, 1966.

Samb, Amar. *Essai sur la contribution du Sénégal à la littérature d'expression arabe.* Dakar, 1972.

————. "Jaaraama: Un poème wolof de Moussa Ka." *Bulletin de l'Institut Fondamental de l'Afrique Noire* 36, B (1974): 592–612.

Sampson, H.C. and E.M. Crowther, *The West Africa Commission 1938–39: Technical Reports.* London. 1943.

Sarr, El Hadji Malik. *Ñaa koon, laa koon, faa koon ou les Lebou parlent d'eux-mêmes.* Dakar, 1980.

Sarr, Moustapha. *Louga et sa région: Essai d'intégration des rapports ville-campagne dans la problématique du développement.* Dakar, 1973.

Schimmel, Annemarie. *And Muhammad Is His Messenger: The Veneration of the Prophet in Islamic Piety.* Chapel Hill, N.C., 1985.

Schoelcher, Victor. *L'esclavage au Sénégal en 1880.* Paris, 1880.

Scott, Rebecca J. *Slave Emancipation in Cuba: The Transition to Free Labor, 1860–1899.* Princeton, N.J., 1985.

Searing, James F. "Accommodation and Resistance: Chiefs, Muslim Leaders and Politicians in Colonial Senegal, 1890–1934." Ph.D. dissertation, Princeton University, 1985.

————. "Aristocrats, Slaves and Peasants: Power and Dependency in the Wolof States, 1700–1850." *International Journal of African Historical Studies* 21 (1988): 475–503.

————. *West African Slavery and Atlantic Commerce: The Senegal River Valley, 1700–1860.* Cambridge, 1993.

Siga, Niang Fatou Niang. *Reflets de modes et traditions Saint-Louisiennes.* Dakar, 1990.

Silla, Ousmane. "Persistance des castes dans la société wolof contemporaine." *Bulletin de l'Institut Fondamental de l'Afrique Noire,* B, 28 (1966): 731–70.

Socé, Ousmane. *Karim: Roman sénégalais suivi de contes et légendes d'Afrique noire.* Paris, 3rd ed., 1966.

Sow, Abdoulaye. "Les sociétés indigènes de prévoyance au Sénégal, 1909–1936." Mémoire de maîtrise, Université de Dakar, 1977.

Strobel, Margaret. "Slavery and Reproductive Labor in Mombasa." In *Women and Slavery in Africa,* eds. Claire C. Robertson and Martin A. Klein, 111–29. Madison, Wis., 1983.

Swindell, Ken. "SeraWoolies, Tillabunkas and Strange Farmers: The Development of Migrant Groundnut Farming along the Gambia River, 1848–1895." *Journal of African History* 21 (1980): 93–104.

Sy, Cheikh Tidiane, *La confrérie sénégalaise des Mourides.* Paris, 1969.

Sylla, Assane. *La philosophie morale des Wolof.* Dakar, 1978.

Tamari, Tal. "The Development of Caste Systems in West Africa." *Journal of African History* 32 (1991): 221–50.

Tignor, Robert. "Senegal's Cooperative Experience, 1907–1960." In *The Political Economy of Risk and Choice in Senegal,* eds. John Waterbury and Mark Gersovitz, 90–122. London, 1987.

Vail, Leroy, and Landeg White. *Power and the Praise Poem: Southern African Voices in History.* Charlottesville, Va., 1991.

Venema, L.B. *The Wolof of Saloum: Social Structure and Rural Development in Senegal.* Wageningen, The Netherlands, 1978.

Villalón, Leonardo A. *Islamic Society and State Power in Senegal: Disciples and Citizens in Fatick.* Cambridge, 1995.

Vogel, Susan M. *Baule: African Art, Western Eyes.* New Haven, Conn. 1997.

Waterbury, John, and Mark Gersovitz. *The Political Economy of Risk and Choice in Senegal.* London, 1987.

Webb, James L.A. "The Trade in Gum Arabic: Prelude to the French Conquest in Senegal." *Journal of African History* 26 (1985): 149–68.

————. *Desert Frontier: Ecological and Economic Change along the Western Sahel, 1600–1850.* Madison, Wis., 1995.

Willis, John Ralph. "Jihad and the Ideology of Enslavement." In *Slaves and Slavery in Muslim Africa,* ed. John Ralph Willis, vol. I, 16–26. London, 1985.

Witherell, Julian Wood. "The Response of the Peoples of Cayor to French Penetration, 1850–1900." Ph.D. dissertation, University of Wisconsin-Madison, 1964.

INDEX

About the Author

JAMES F. SEARING is Associate Professor at the University of Illinois at
Chicago, where he teaches African history. His current research focuses on
the Sereer and religious conversion in colonial Senegal.